THE PRINCE OF TENNIS
VOL. 1
The SHONEN JUMP Graphic Novel Edition

STORY AND ART BY
TAKESHI KONOMI

English Adaptation/Gerard Jones
Translation/Joe Yamazaki
Touch-up & Lettering/James Hudnall
Graphics & Cover Design/Sean Lee
Editor/Urian Brown

Associate Managing Editor/Albert Totten
Managing Editor/Annette Roman
Production Manager/Noboru Watanabe
Executive Vice President/Editor in Chief/Hyoe Narita
Sr. Director of Licensing and Acquisitions/Rika Inouye
VP of Marketing/Liza Coppola
VP of Strategic Development/Yumi Hoashi
Publisher/Seiji Horibuchi

THE PRINCE OF TENNIS LOGO is a trademark of VIZ, LLC

PARENTAL ADVISORY
THE PRINCE OF TENNIS is rated "A" for all ages. It is recommended for any age group.

Printed in the U.S.A.

Published by VIZ, LLC
P.O. Box 77064
San Francisco, CA 94107

SHONEN JUMP Graphic Novel Edition
10 9 8 7 6 5 4 3 2 1
First printing, April 2004

www.viz.com

THE WORLD'S
MOST POPULAR MANGA

SHONEN JUMP
GRAPHIC NOVEL
www.shonenjump.com

許斐　　剛

I always liked being out-
doors, so I played all kinds
of sports.
My parents influenced me
to play tennis from a young
age. I joined my junior high
and high school team, and
during college, there was a
time I earned money as a
tennis instructor. Now I'm
writing a comic about tennis, which has always been
a part of my life. To those
who read it, I hope you fall
in love with tennis!

Konomi

About Takeshi Konomi

Takeshi Konomi exploded onto the manga scene with the
incredible manga The Prince of Tennis. His refined art style
and sleek character designs proved popular with **Weekly
Shonen Jump** readers and The Prince of Tennis became the
number one sports manga in Japan almost overnight. Its
cast of cool tennis players enticed legions of female readers, although it was originally intended to be a boy's comic.
The manga continues to be a success and is now on its
20th graphic novel. A hit anime series was created as well
as several video games and mountains of merchandise.

テニスの王子様

THE PRINCE OF TENNIS™

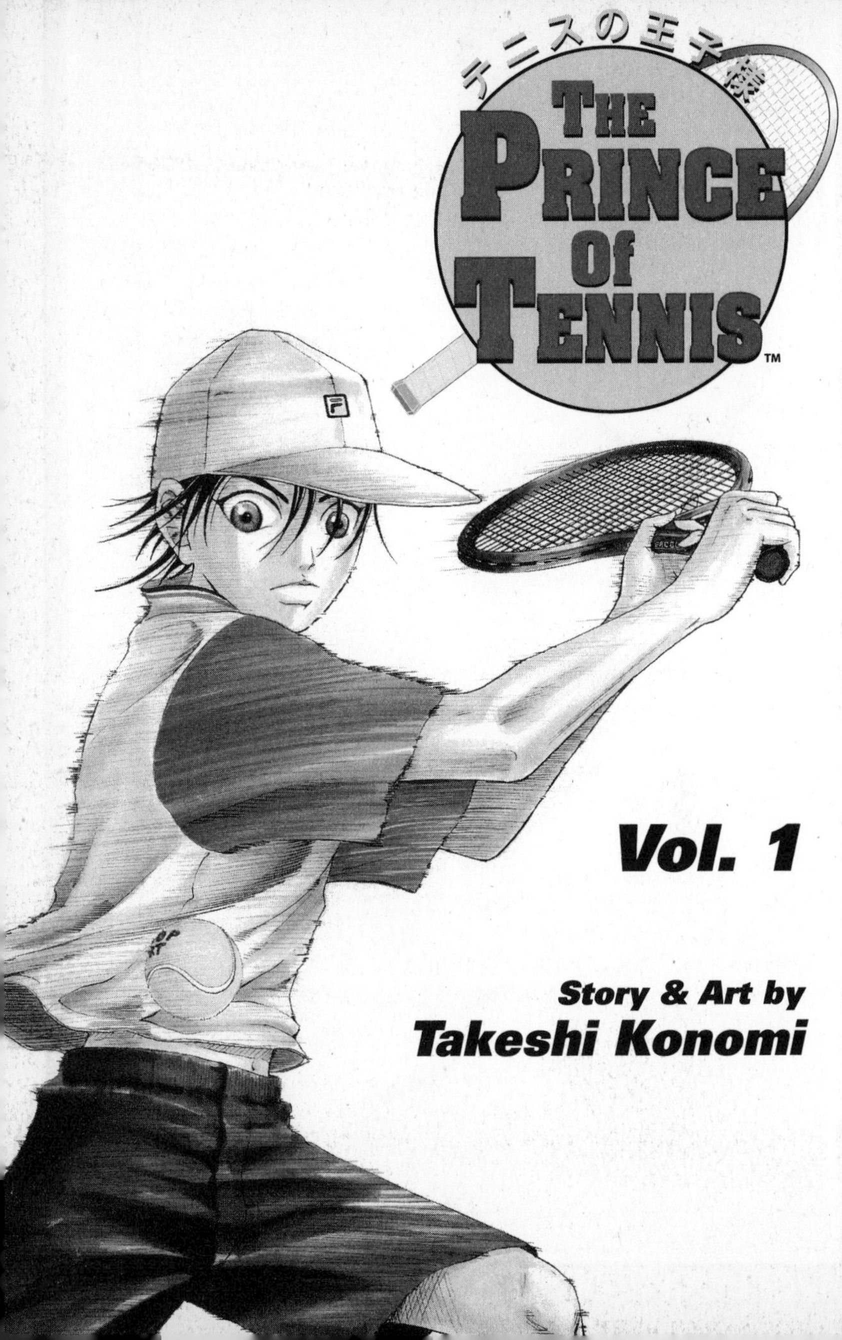

Vol. 1

Story & Art by
Takeshi Konomi

CONTENTS

Genius 1: RYOMA ECHIZEN

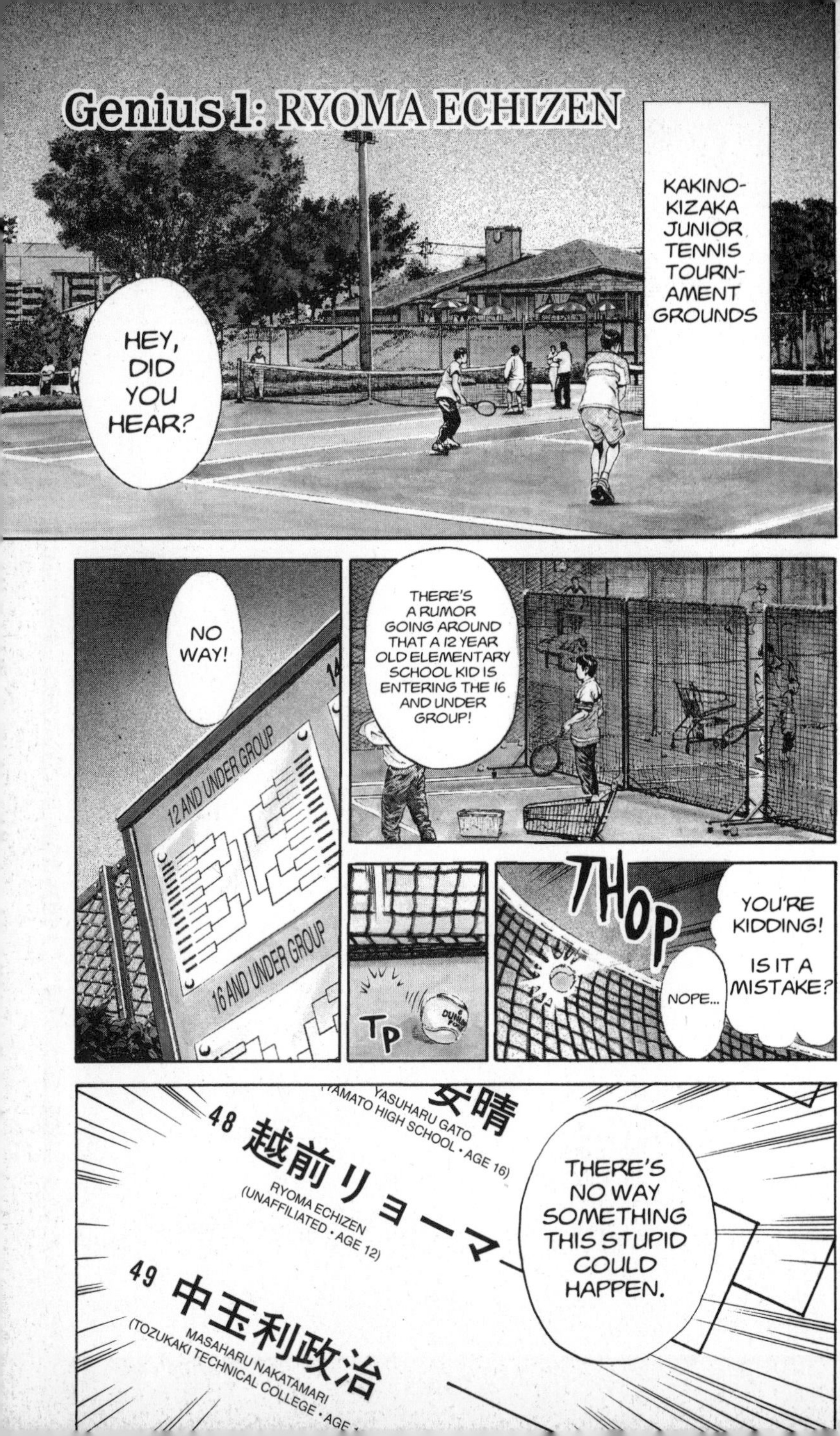

KAKINO-KIZAKA JUNIOR TENNIS TOURNAMENT GROUNDS
HEY, DID YOU HEAR?
THERE'S A RUMOR GOING AROUND THAT A 12 YEAR OLD ELEMENTARY SCHOOL KID IS ENTERING THE 16 AND UNDER GROUP!
THOP
YOU'RE KIDDING!
IS IT A MISTAKE?
NOPE...
TP
NO WAY!
12 AND UNDER GROUP
16 AND UNDER GROUP
安晴
YASUHARU GATO
(YAMATO HIGH SCHOOL • AGE 16)
48 越前リョーマ
RYOMA ECHIZEN
(UNAFFILIATED • AGE 12)
49 中玉利政治
MASAHARU NAKATAMARI
(TOZUKAKI TECHNICAL COLLEGE • AGE
THERE'S NO WAY SOMETHING THIS STUPID COULD HAPPEN.

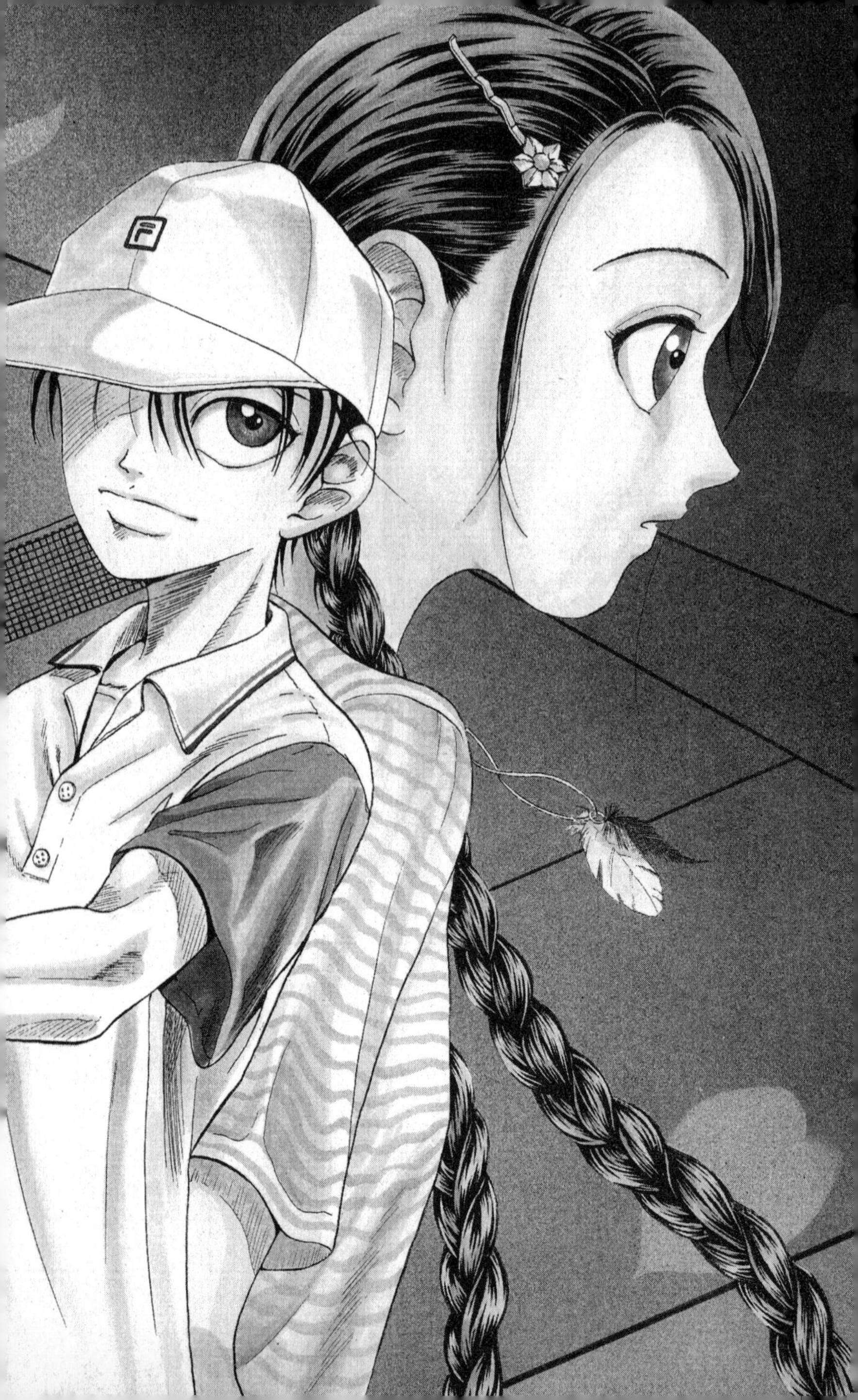

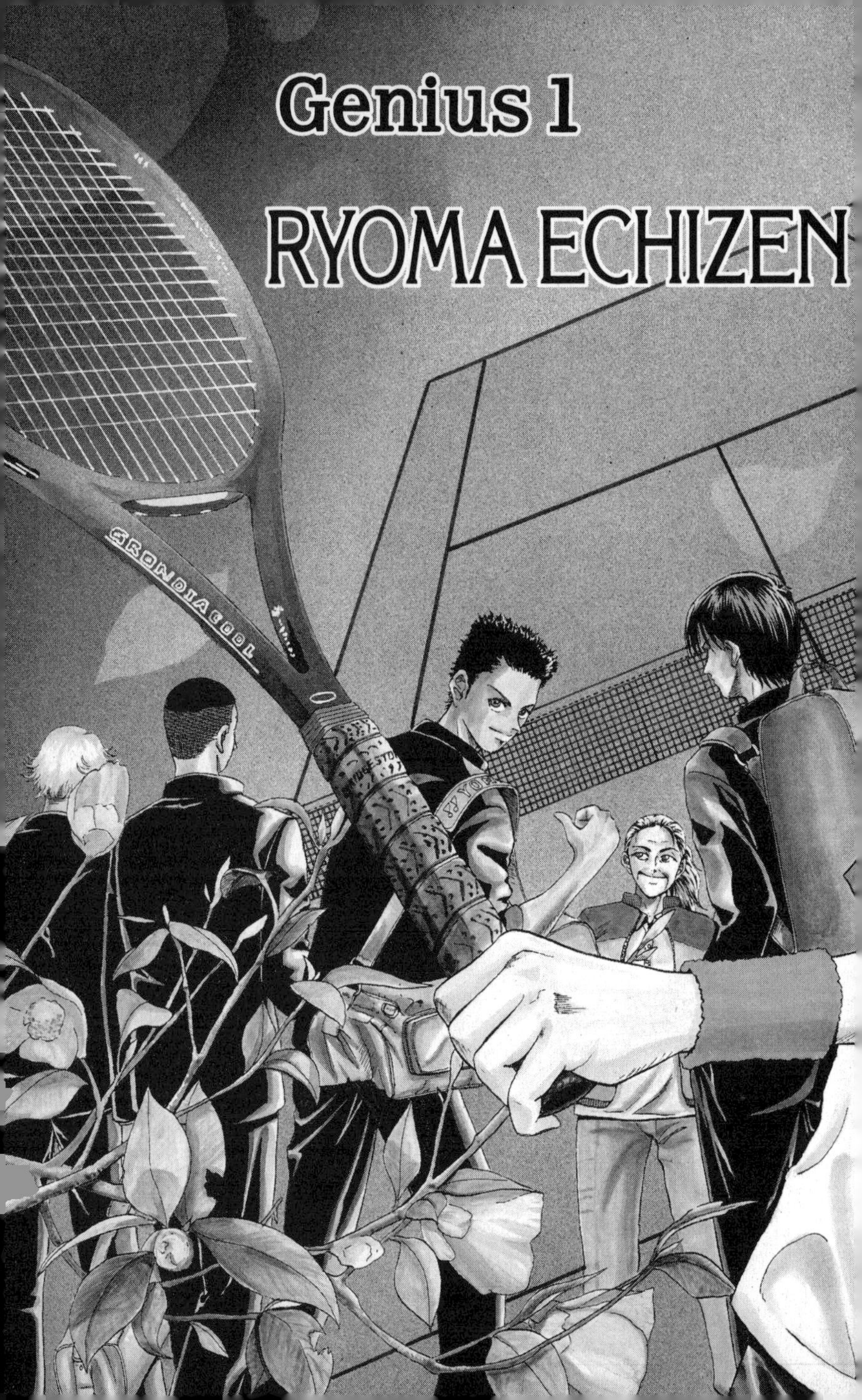
Genius 1
RYOMA ECHIZEN

テニスの王子様

THE PRINCE OF TENNIS™

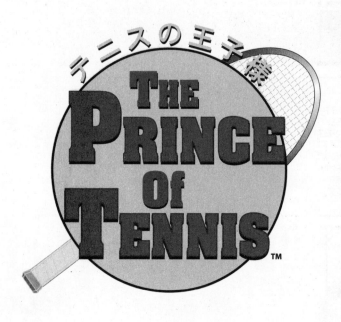

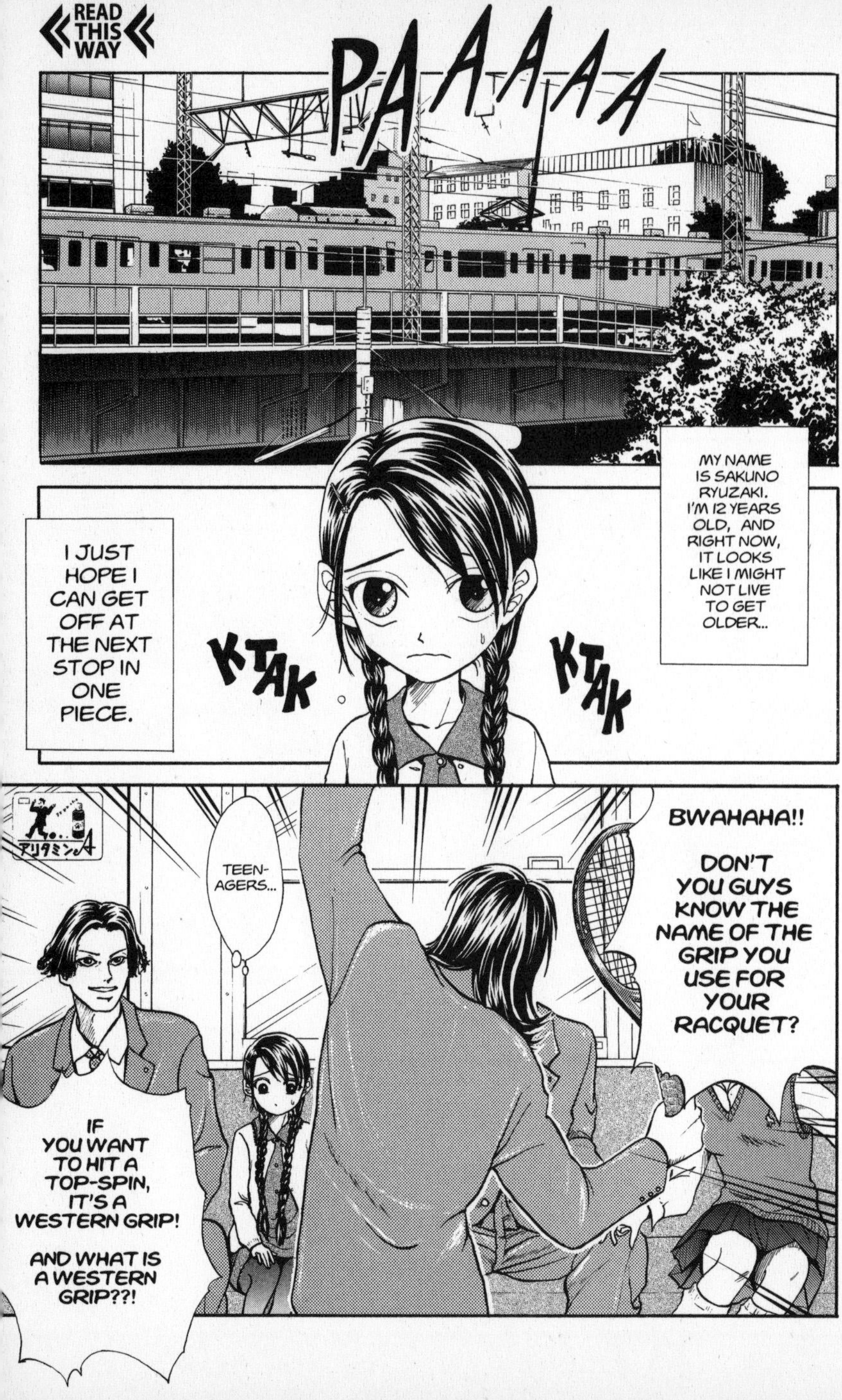

READ THIS WAY
PAAAAA
MY NAME IS SAKUNO RYUZAKI. I'M 12 YEARS OLD, AND RIGHT NOW, IT LOOKS LIKE I MIGHT NOT LIVE TO GET OLDER...
KTAK
KTAK
I JUST HOPE I CAN GET OFF AT THE NEXT STOP IN ONE PIECE.
BWAHAHA!!
DON'T YOU GUYS KNOW THE NAME OF THE GRIP YOU USE FOR YOUR RACQUET?
TEEN-AGERS...
IF YOU WANT TO HIT A TOP-SPIN, IT'S A WESTERN GRIP!
AND WHAT IS A WESTERN GRIP??!

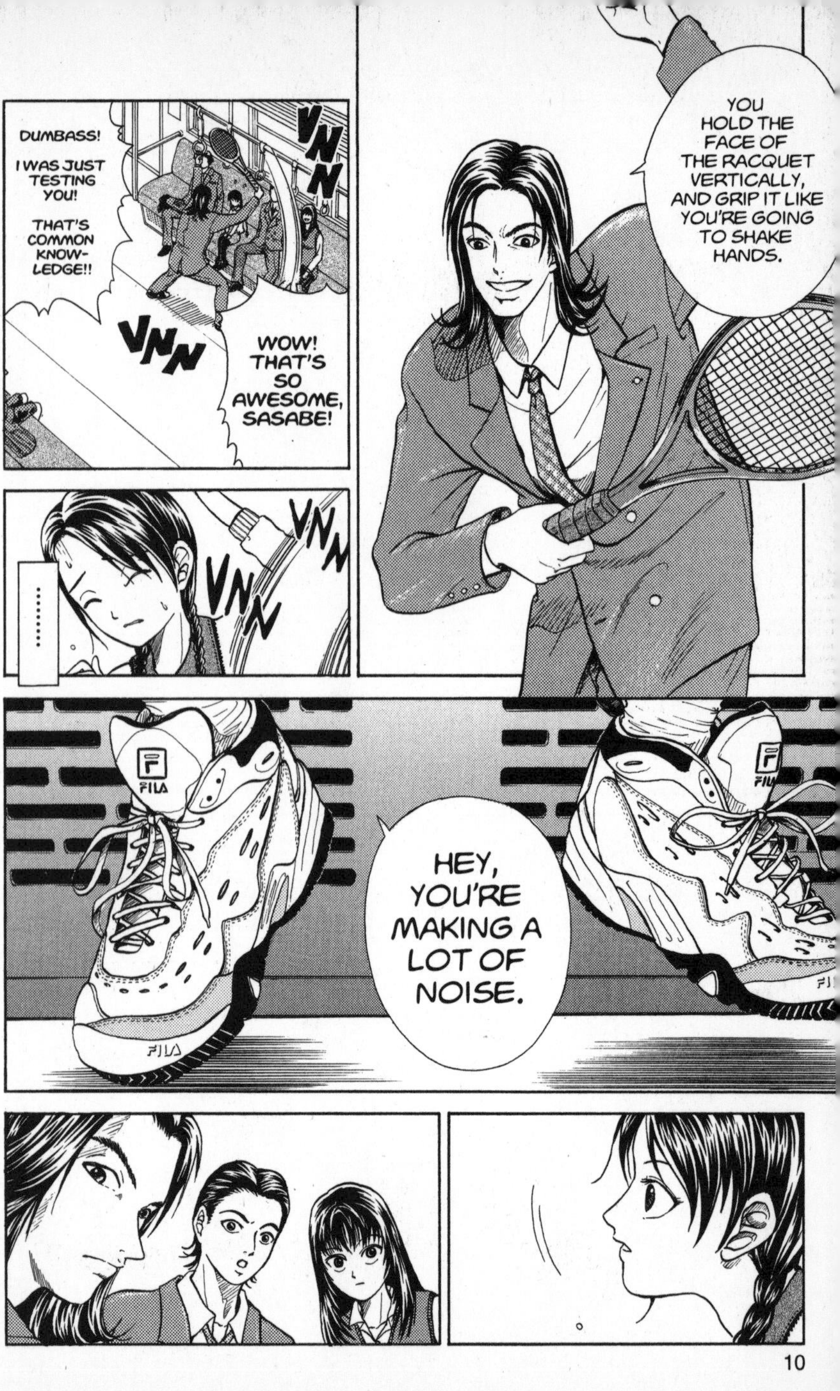

YOU HOLD THE FACE OF THE RACQUET VERTICALLY, AND GRIP IT LIKE YOU'RE GOING TO SHAKE HANDS.
VNN
DUMBASS!
I WAS JUST TESTING YOU!
THAT'S COMMON KNOW-LEDGE!!
VNN
WOW! THAT'S SO AWESOME, SASABE!
VNN
VNN
....
HEY, YOU'RE MAKING A LOT OF NOISE.

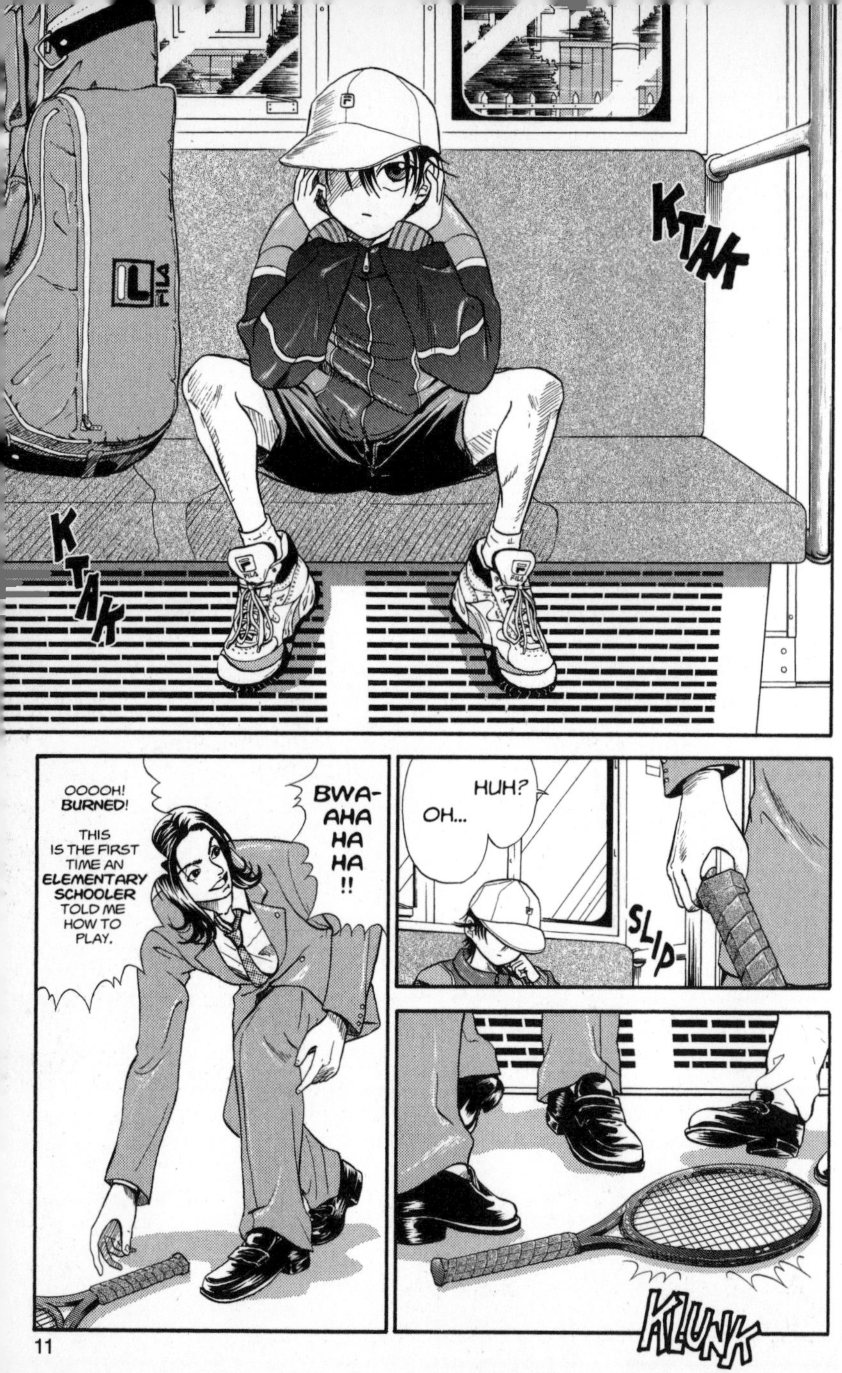
KTAK
KTAK
HUH?
OH...
SLIP
KLUNK
BWA-AHA HA HA !!
OOOOH! BURNED!
THIS IS THE FIRST TIME AN ELEMENTARY SCHOOLER TOLD ME HOW TO PLAY.

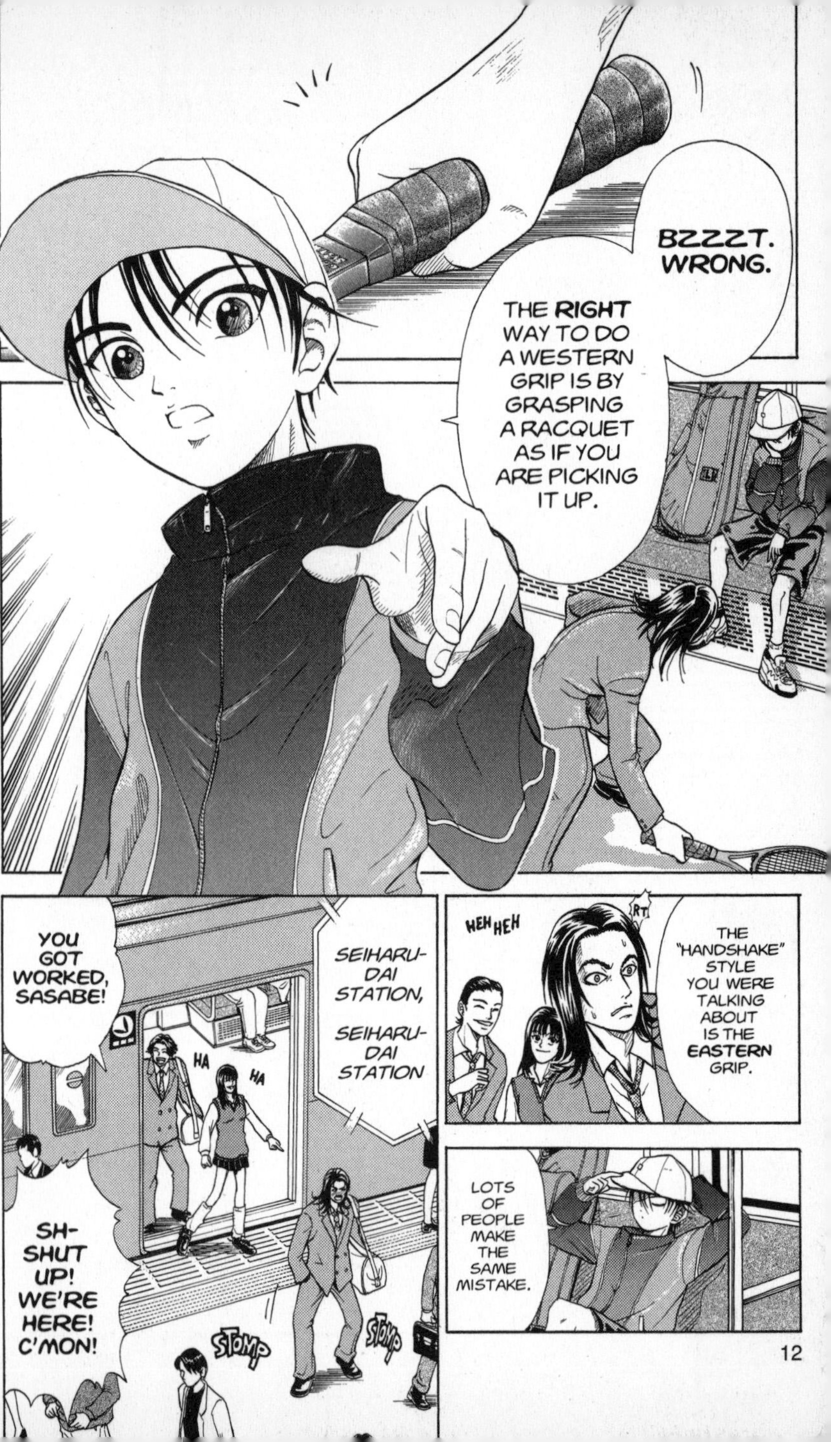

BZZZT. WRONG.
THE RIGHT WAY TO DO A WESTERN GRIP IS BY GRASPING A RACQUET AS IF YOU ARE PICKING IT UP.
HEH HEH
RT
THE "HANDSHAKE" STYLE YOU WERE TALKING ABOUT IS THE EASTERN GRIP.
LOTS OF PEOPLE MAKE THE SAME MISTAKE.
SEIHARU-DAI STATION, SEIHARU-DAI STATION
YOU GOT WORKED, SASABE!
HA HA
SH-SHUT UP! WE'RE HERE! C'MON!
STOMP
STOMP

READ THIS WAY

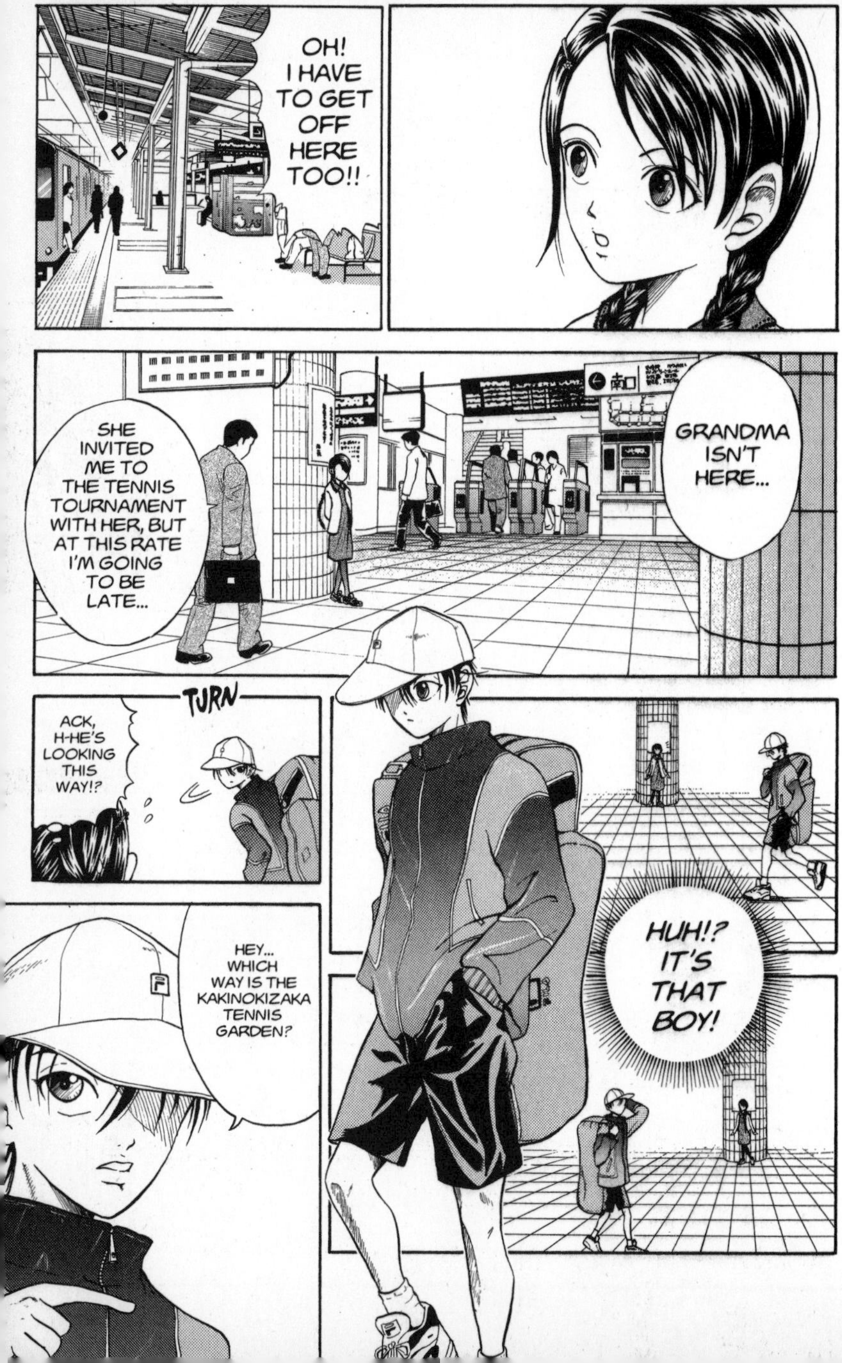
OH! I HAVE TO GET OFF HERE TOO!!
GRANDMA ISN'T HERE...
SHE INVITED ME TO THE TENNIS TOURNAMENT WITH HER, BUT AT THIS RATE I'M GOING TO BE LATE...
HUH!? IT'S THAT BOY!
TURN
ACK, H-HE'S LOOKING THIS WAY!?
HEY... WHICH WAY IS THE KAKINOKIZAKA TENNIS GARDEN?

READ THIS WAY

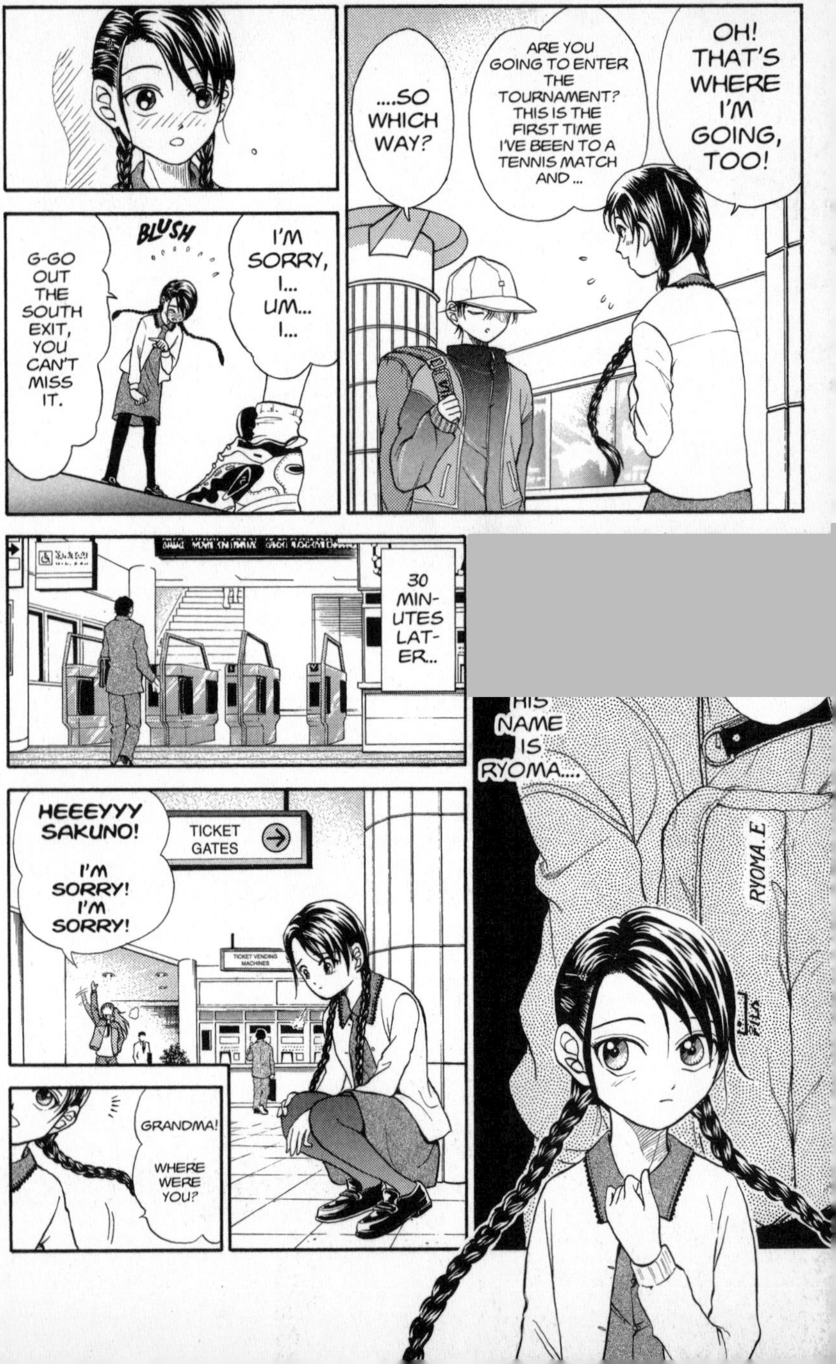
OH! THAT'S WHERE I'M GOING, TOO!
ARE YOU GOING TO ENTER THE TOURNAMENT? THIS IS THE FIRST TIME I'VE BEEN TO A TENNIS MATCH AND ...
....SO WHICH WAY?
I'M SORRY, I... UM... I...
BLUSH
G-GO OUT THE SOUTH EXIT, YOU CAN'T MISS IT.
HIS NAME IS RYOMA....
RYOMA.E
30 MINUTES LATER...
TICKET GATES
HEEEYYY SAKUNO!
I'M SORRY! I'M SORRY!
TICKET VENDING MACHINES
GRANDMA!
WHERE WERE YOU?

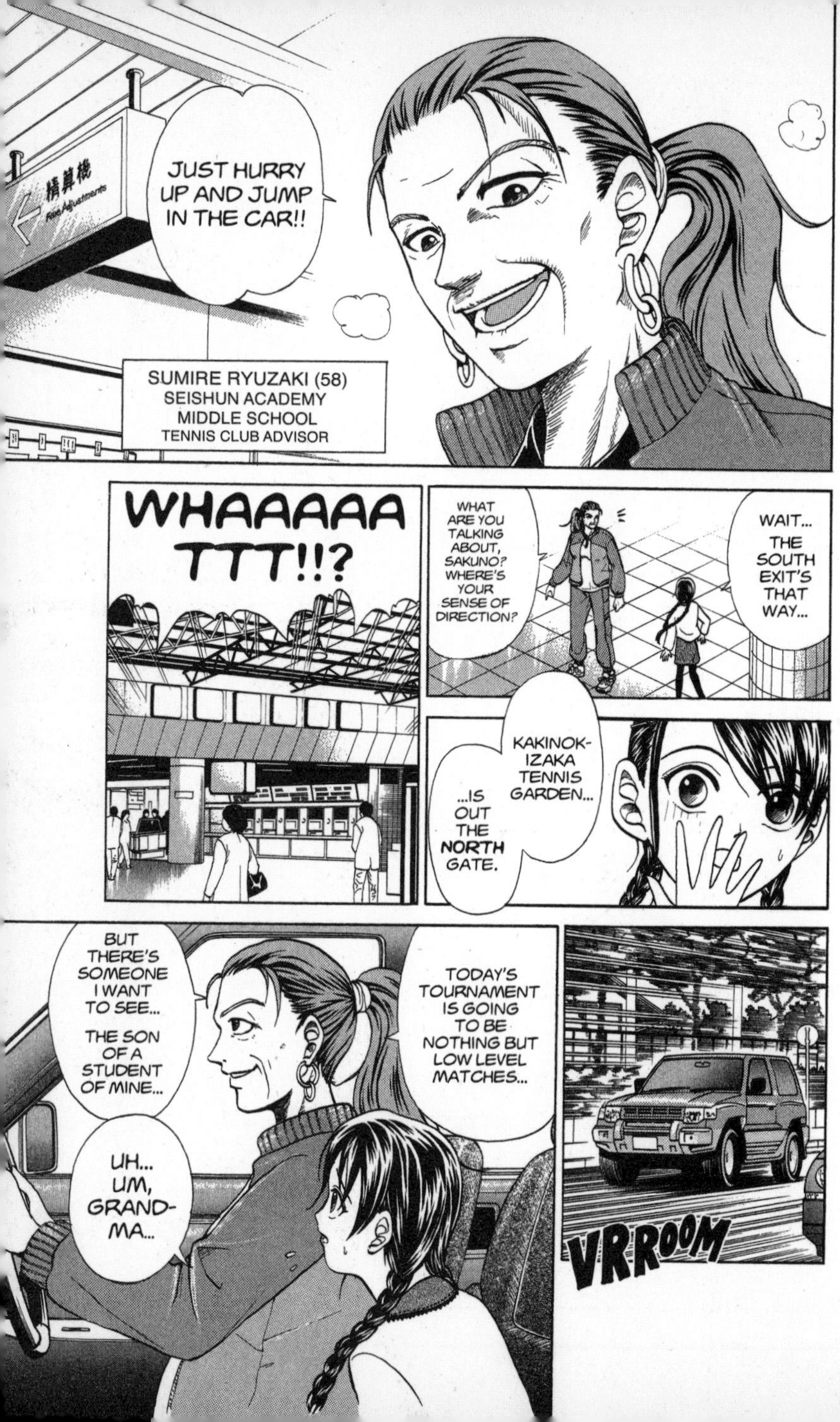
精算機
Fare Adjustments
JUST HURRY UP AND JUMP IN THE CAR!!
SUMIRE RYUZAKI (58)
SEISHUN ACADEMY MIDDLE SCHOOL
TENNIS CLUB ADVISOR
WAIT... THE SOUTH EXIT'S THAT WAY...
WHAT ARE YOU TALKING ABOUT, SAKUNO? WHERE'S YOUR SENSE OF DIRECTION?
KAKINOKIZAKA TENNIS GARDEN...
...IS OUT THE NORTH GATE.
WHAAAAAATTT!!?
VRROOM
TODAY'S TOURNAMENT IS GOING TO BE NOTHING BUT LOW LEVEL MATCHES...
BUT THERE'S SOMEONE I WANT TO SEE...
THE SON OF A STUDENT OF MINE...
UH... UM, GRANDMA...

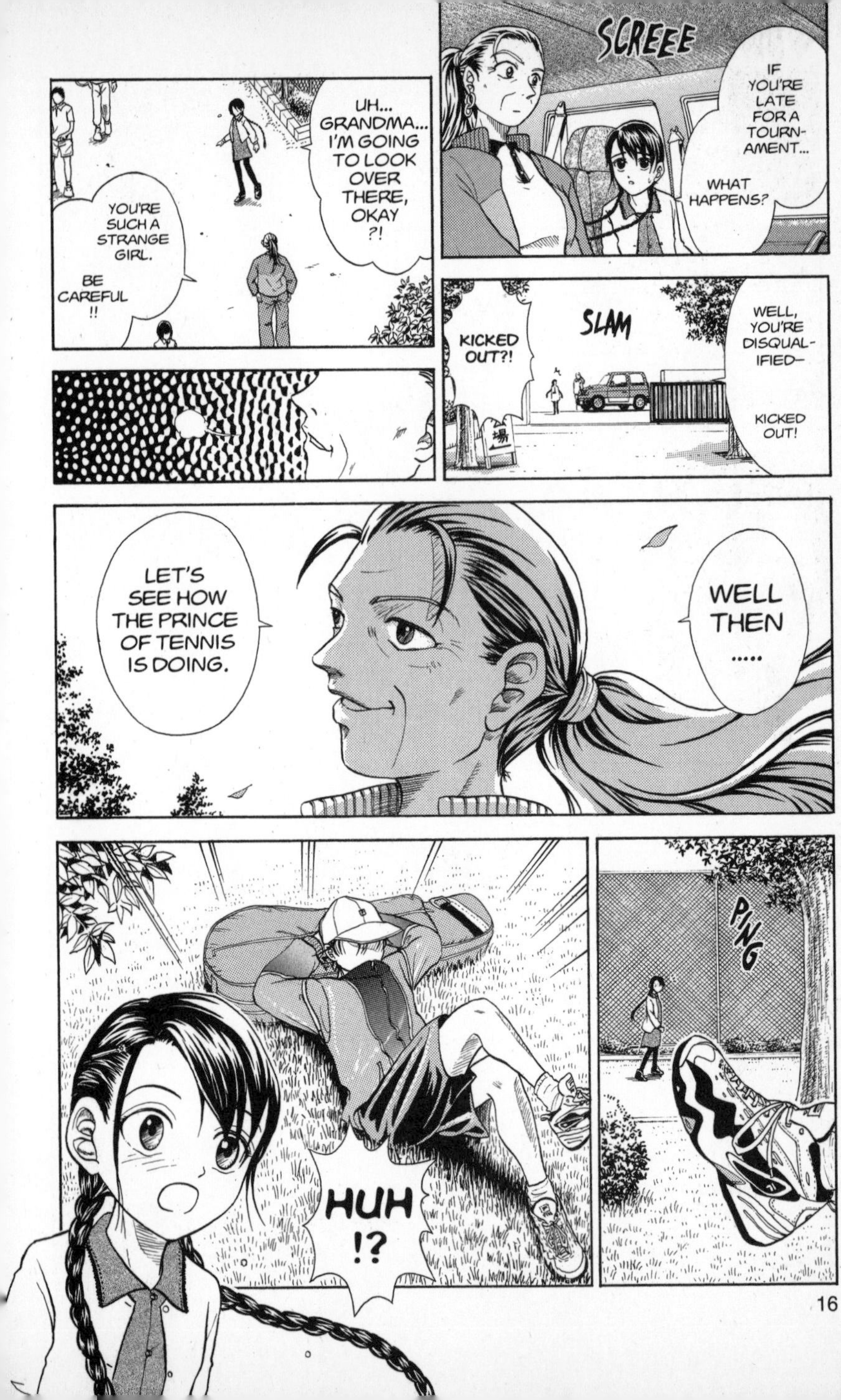
SCREEE
IF YOU'RE LATE FOR A TOURNAMENT...
WHAT HAPPENS?
WELL, YOU'RE DISQUALIFIED—
KICKED OUT!
SLAM
KICKED OUT?!
UH... GRANDMA... I'M GOING TO LOOK OVER THERE, OKAY?!
YOU'RE SUCH A STRANGE GIRL.
BE CAREFUL!!
WELL THEN .....
LET'S SEE HOW THE PRINCE OF TENNIS IS DOING.
PING
HUH!?

READ THIS WAY

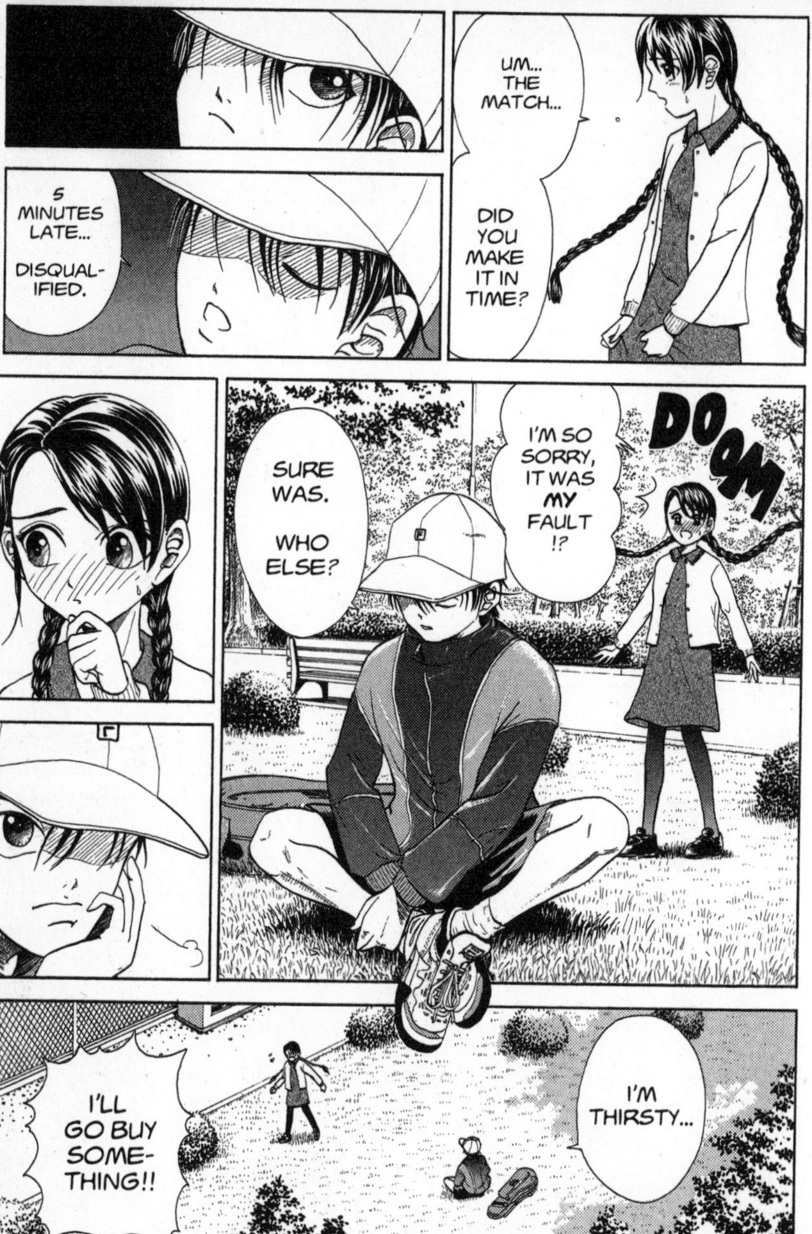
UM... THE MATCH...
DID YOU MAKE IT IN TIME?
5 MINUTES LATE...
DISQUAL-IFIED.
DOOM
I'M SO SORRY, IT WAS MY FAULT !?
SURE WAS.
WHO ELSE?
I'M THIRSTY...
I'LL GO BUY SOME-THING!!

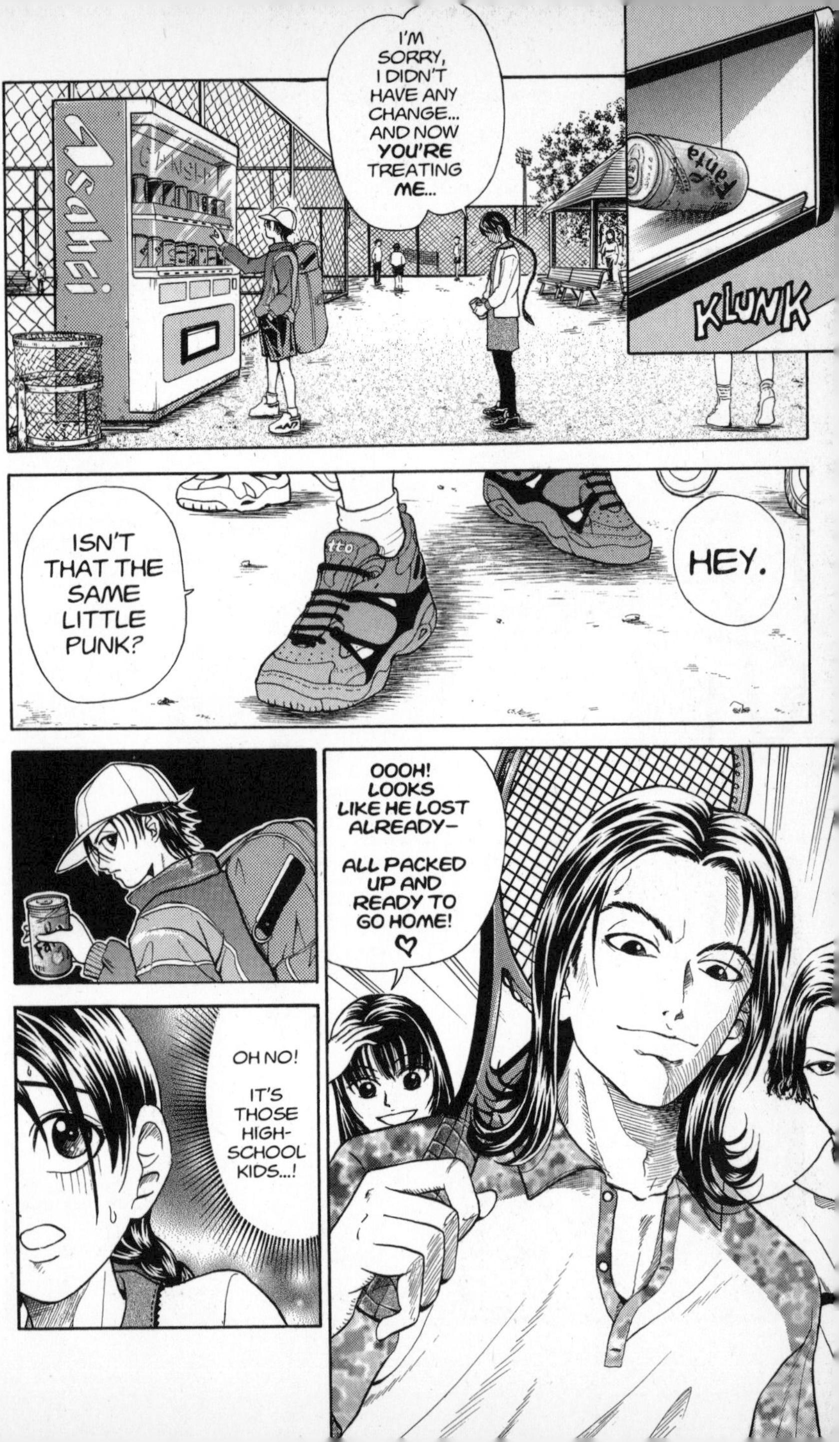

KLUNK
I'M SORRY, I DIDN'T HAVE ANY CHANGE... AND NOW YOU'RE TREATING ME...
HEY.
ISN'T THAT THE SAME LITTLE PUNK?
OOOH! LOOKS LIKE HE LOST ALREADY– ALL PACKED UP AND READY TO GO HOME! ♡
OH NO! IT'S THOSE HIGH-SCHOOL KIDS...!

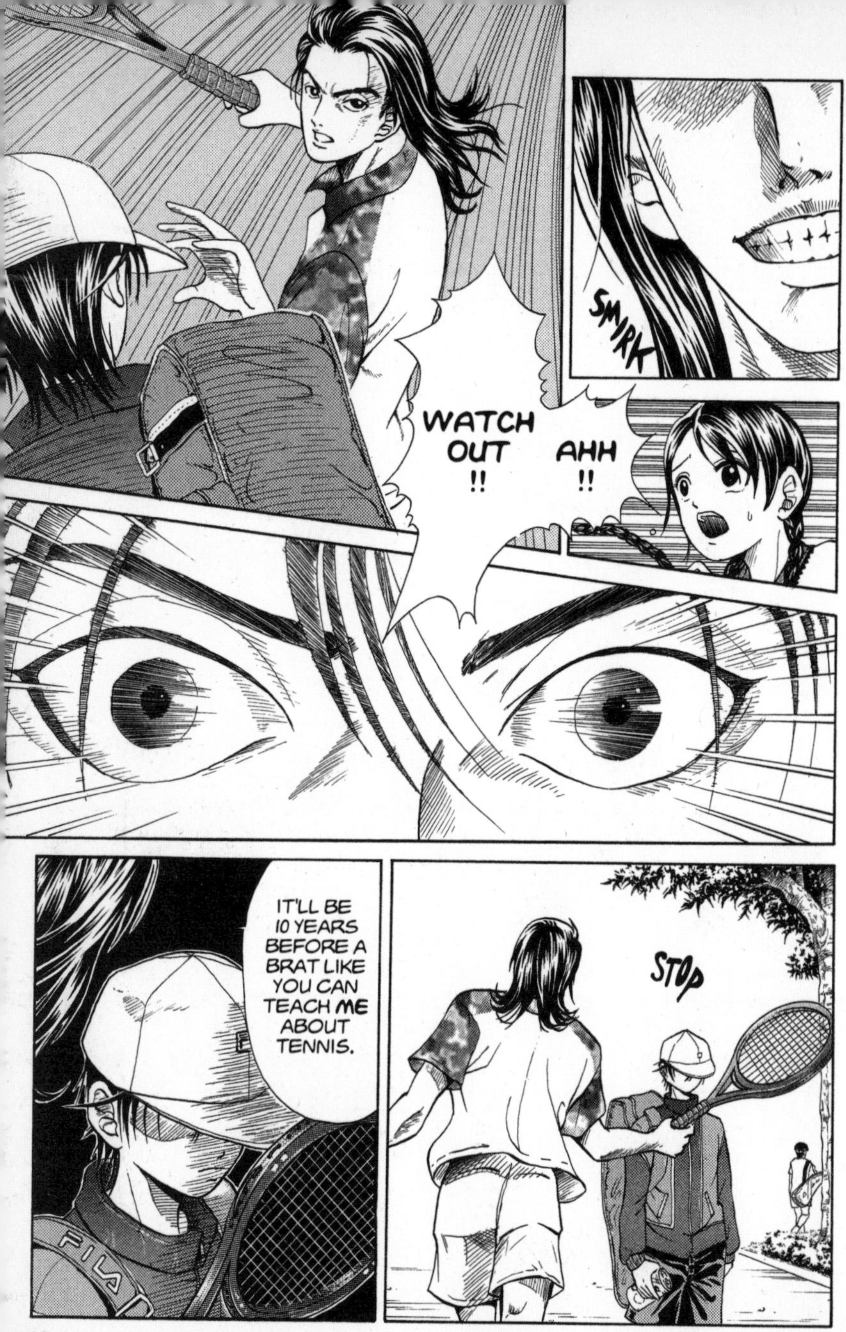
SMIRK
WATCH OUT !!
AHH !!
STOP
IT'LL BE 10 YEARS BEFORE A BRAT LIKE YOU CAN TEACH **ME** ABOUT TENNIS.

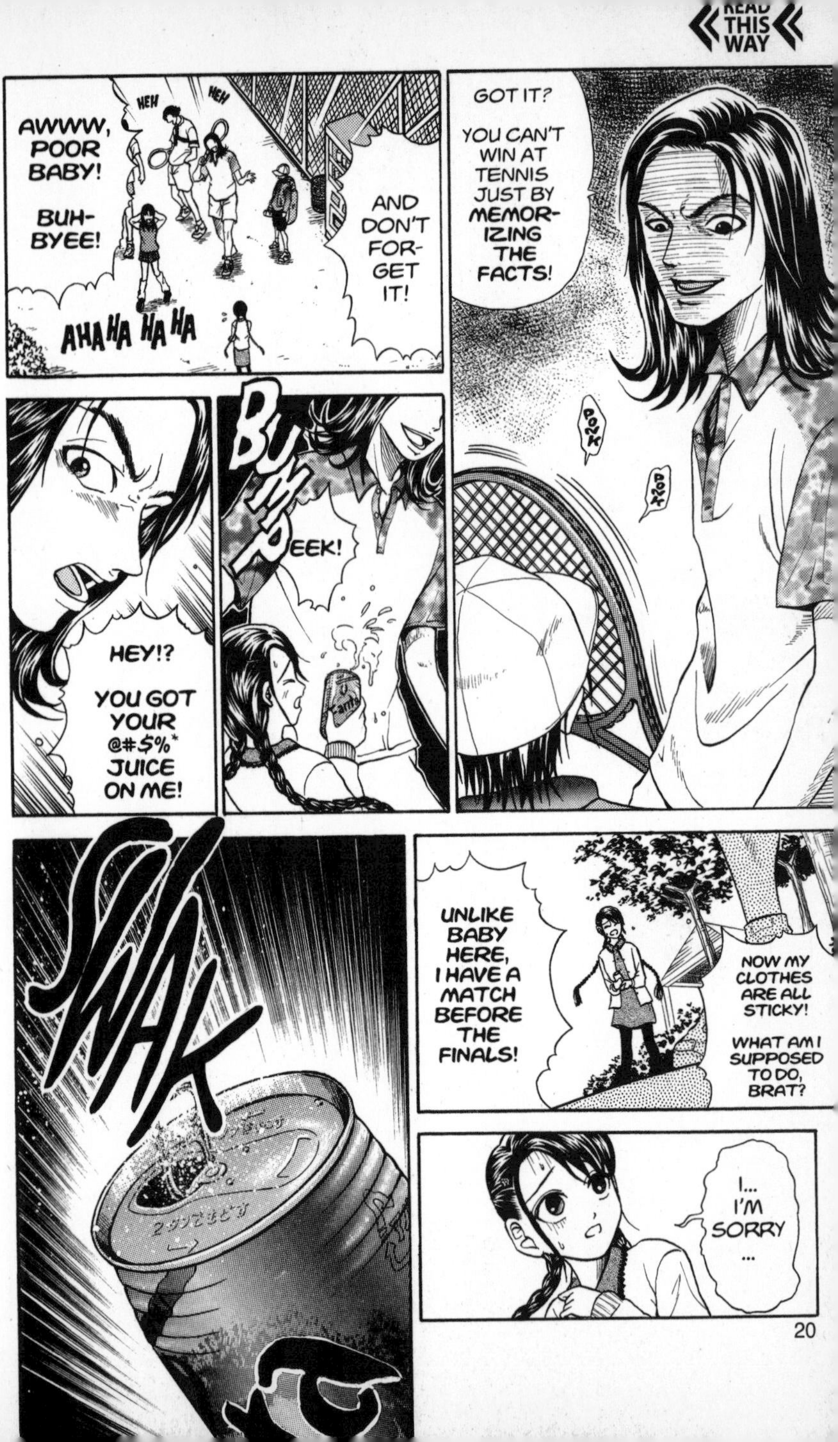

READ THIS WAY
GOT IT?
YOU CAN'T WIN AT TENNIS JUST BY MEMORIZING THE FACTS!
DONK
DONK
AND DON'T FORGET IT!
HEH
HEH
AWWW, POOR BABY!
BUH-BYEE!
AHAHA HA HA
BUMP
EEK!
HEY!?
YOU GOT YOUR @#$%* JUICE ON ME!
UNLIKE BABY HERE, I HAVE A MATCH BEFORE THE FINALS!
NOW MY CLOTHES ARE ALL STICKY!
WHAT AM I SUPPOSED TO DO, BRAT?
I... I'M SORRY ...
SPLAK

READ THIS WAY

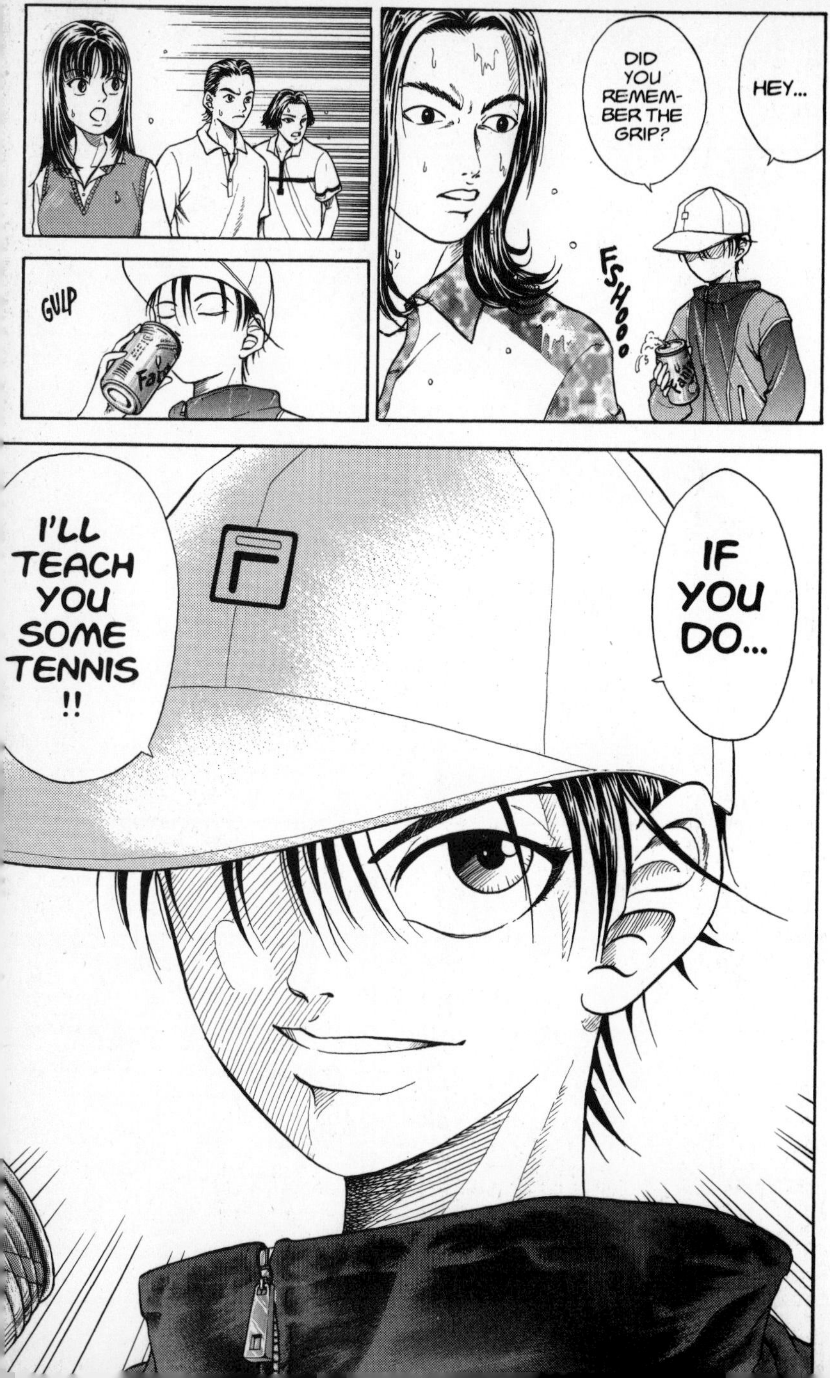
HEY...
DID YOU REMEMBER THE GRIP?
FSHOOO
GULP
IF YOU DO...
I'LL TEACH YOU SOME TENNIS!!

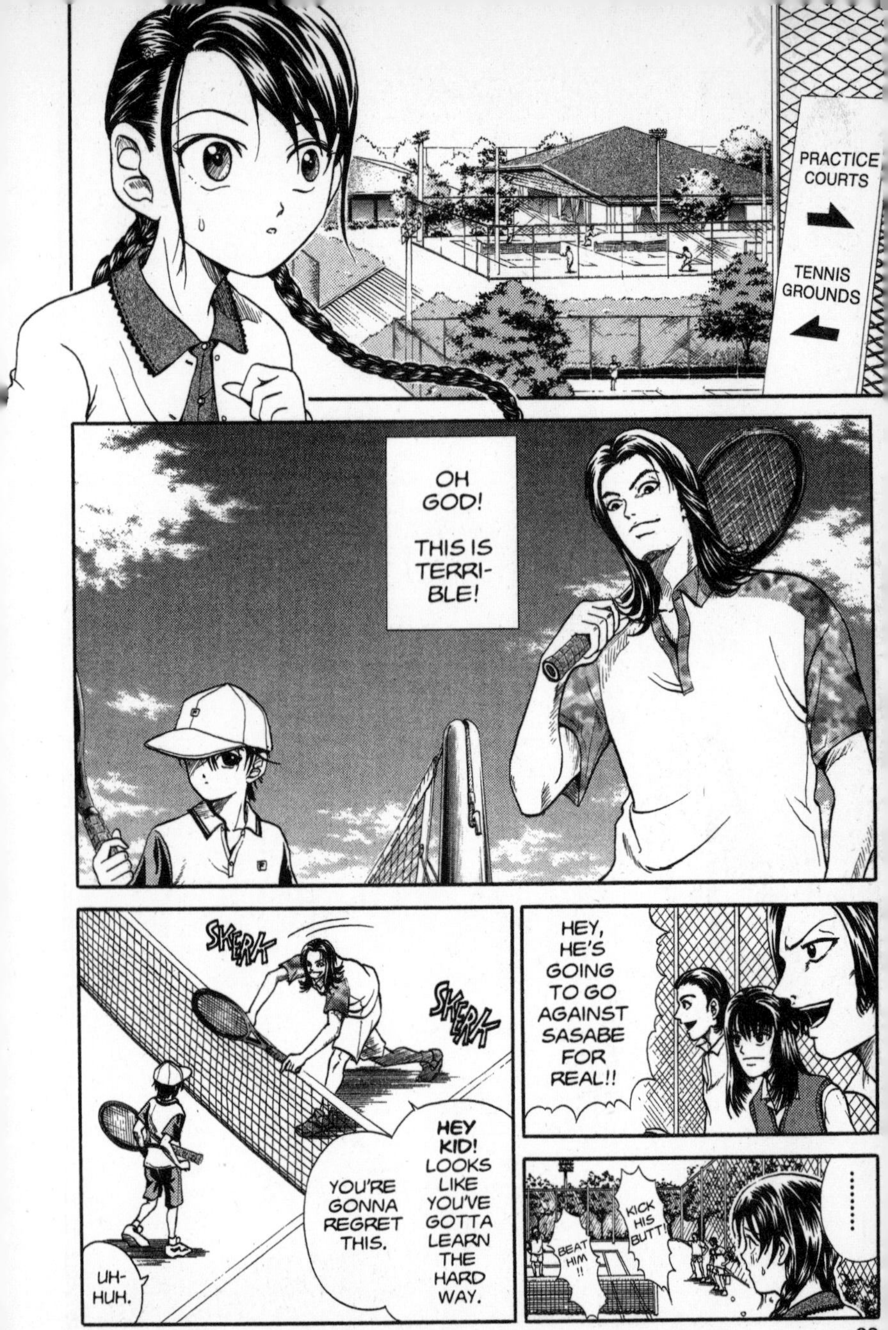

PRACTICE COURTS
TENNIS GROUNDS
OH GOD! THIS IS TERRIBLE!
HEY, HE'S GOING TO GO AGAINST SASABE FOR REAL!!
......
KICK HIS BUTT!
BEAT HIM!!
SKERK
SKERK
HEY KID! LOOKS LIKE YOU'VE GOTTA LEARN THE HARD WAY.
YOU'RE GONNA REGRET THIS.
UH-HUH.

READ THIS WAY

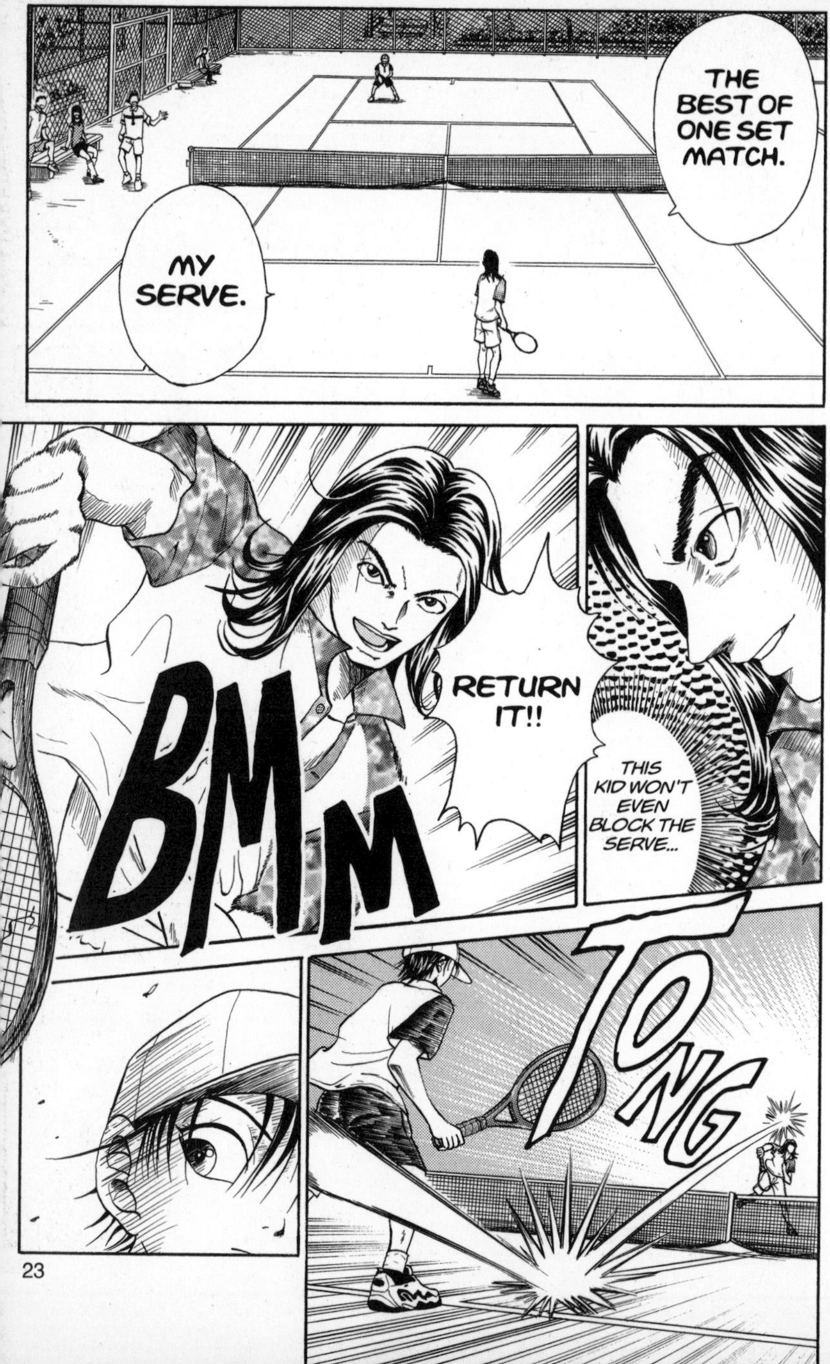
THE BEST OF ONE SET MATCH.
MY SERVE.
THIS KID WON'T EVEN BLOCK THE SERVE...
RETURN IT!!
BMM
TONG

READ THIS WAY

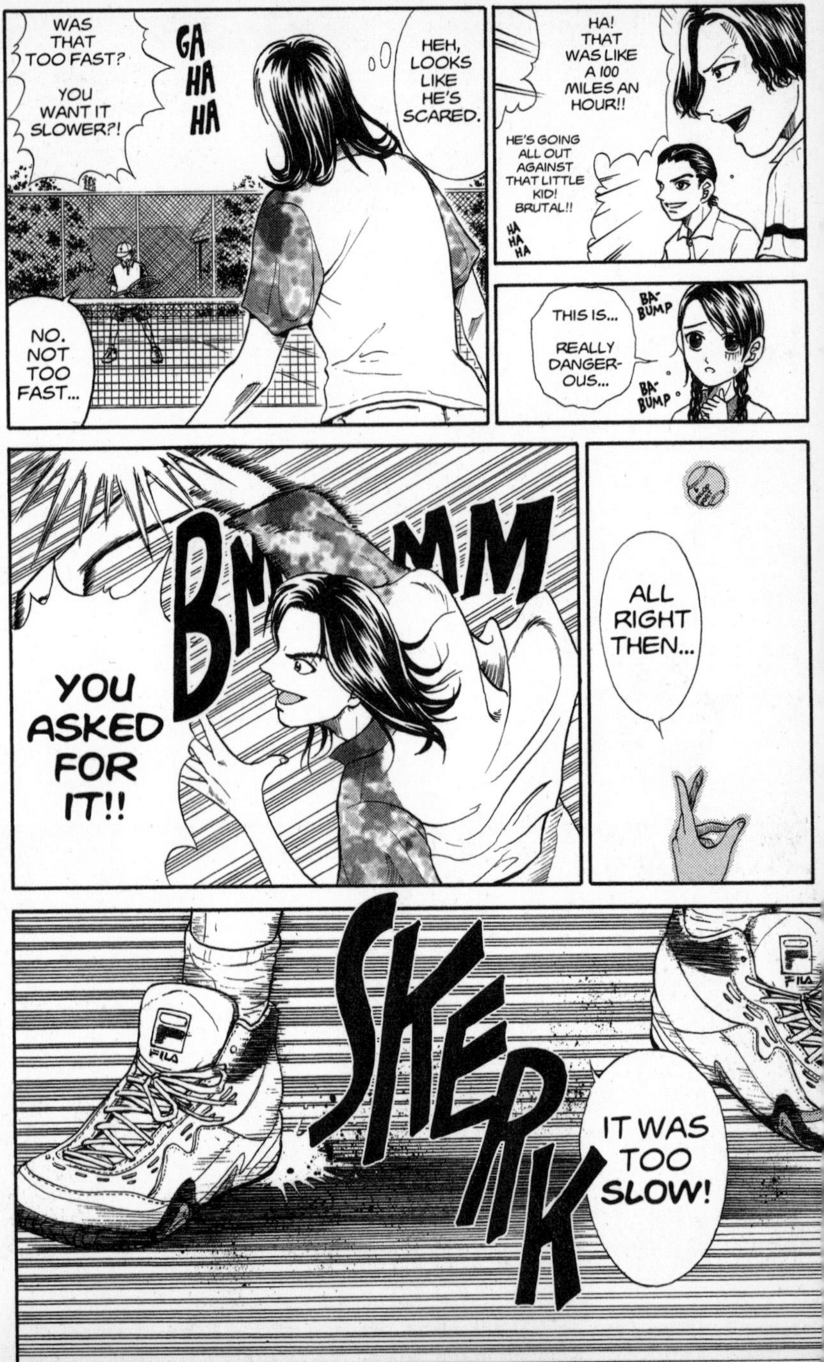
HA! THAT WAS LIKE A 100 MILES AN HOUR!!
HE'S GOING ALL OUT AGAINST THAT LITTLE KID! BRUTAL!!
HA HA HA
BA-BUMP
THIS IS... REALLY DANGER-OUS...
BA-BUMP
HEH, LOOKS LIKE HE'S SCARED.
GA HA HA
WAS THAT TOO FAST? YOU WANT IT SLOWER?!
NO. NOT TOO FAST...
ALL RIGHT THEN...
BMMMM
YOU ASKED FOR IT!!
SKERRK
IT WAS TOO SLOW!

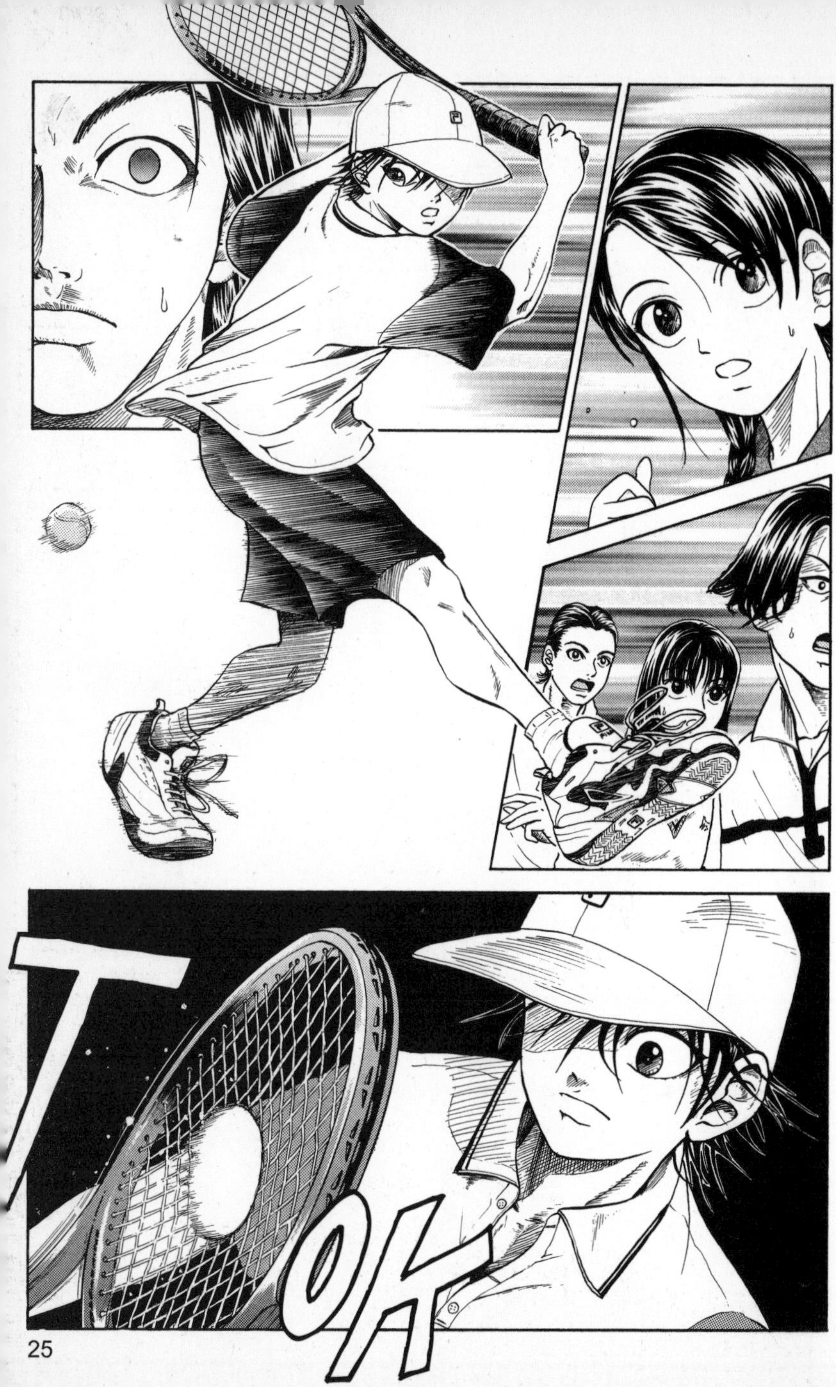
TOK

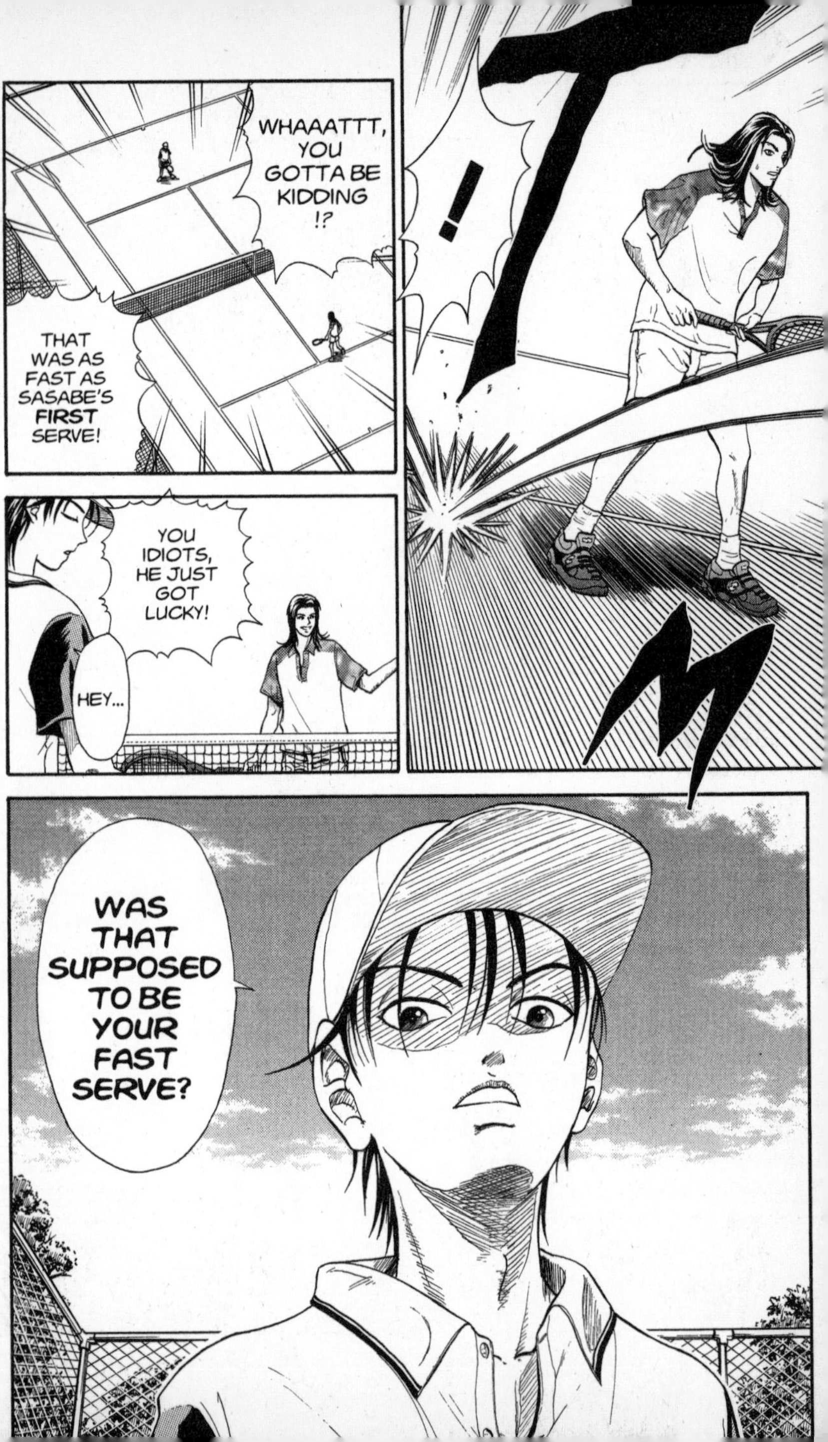
!
WHAAATTT, YOU GOTTA BE KIDDING !?
THAT WAS AS FAST AS SASABE'S **FIRST** SERVE!
YOU IDIOTS, HE JUST GOT LUCKY!
HEY...
WAS THAT SUPPOSED TO BE YOUR FAST SERVE?

READ THIS WAY

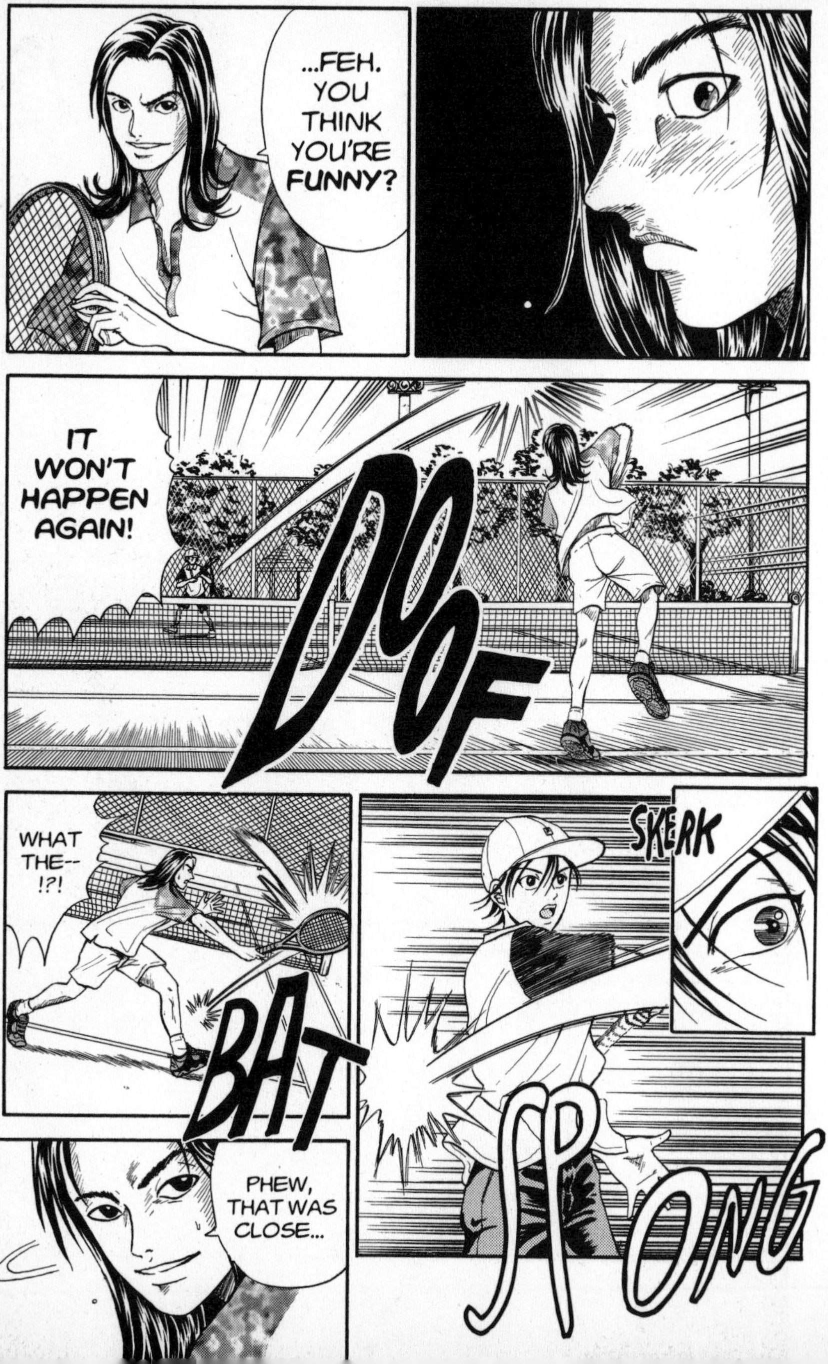
...FEH. YOU THINK YOU'RE FUNNY?
IT WON'T HAPPEN AGAIN!
DOOF
SKERK
SPONG
WHAT THE-- !?!
BAT
PHEW, THAT WAS CLOSE...

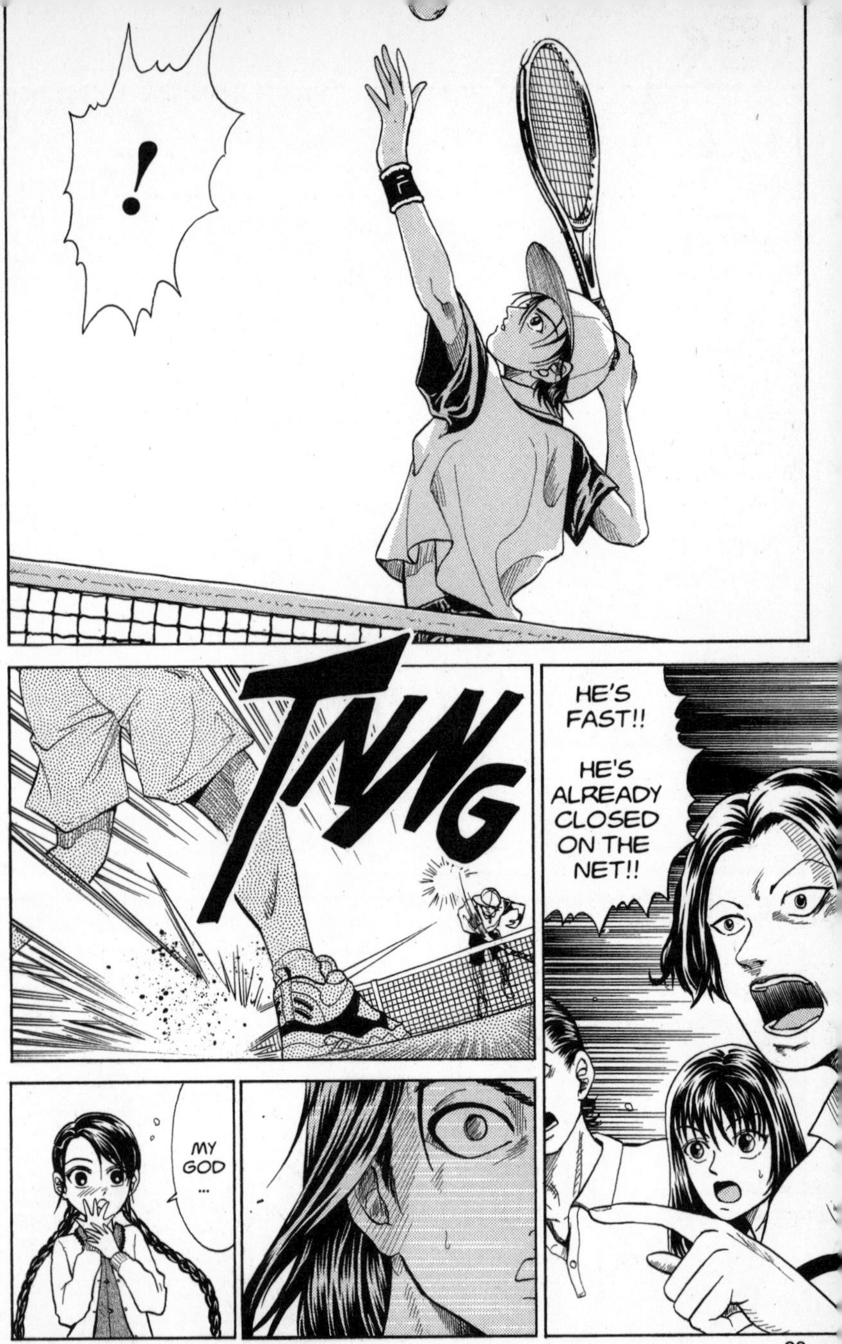
!
HE'S FAST!!
HE'S ALREADY CLOSED ON THE NET!!
TNNG
MY GOD ...

READ THIS WAY

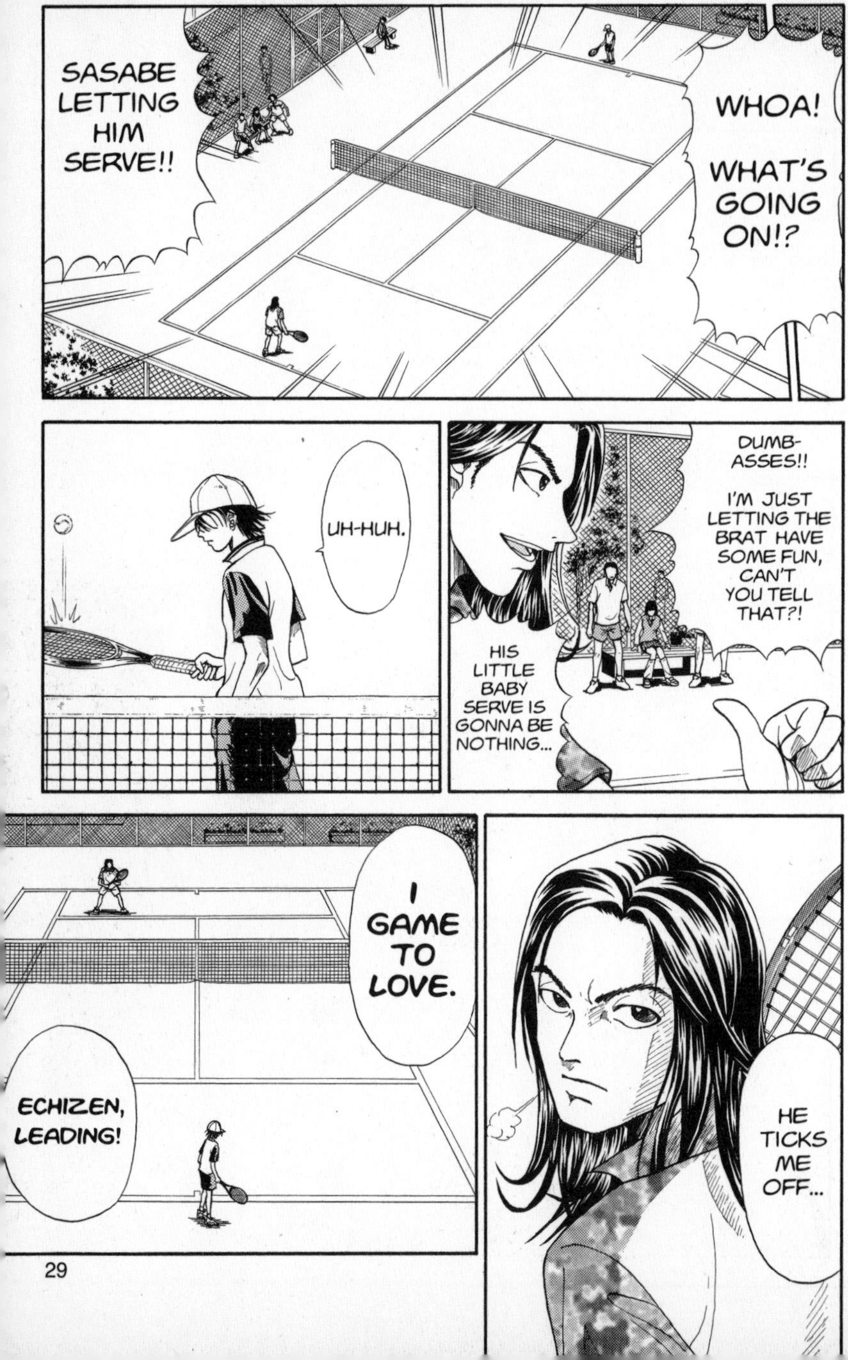
WHOA!
WHAT'S GOING ON!?
SASABE LETTING HIM SERVE!!
DUMB-ASSES!!
I'M JUST LETTING THE BRAT HAVE SOME FUN, CAN'T YOU TELL THAT?!
HIS LITTLE BABY SERVE IS GONNA BE NOTHING...
UH-HUH.
HE TICKS ME OFF...
1 GAME TO LOVE.
ECHIZEN, LEADING!

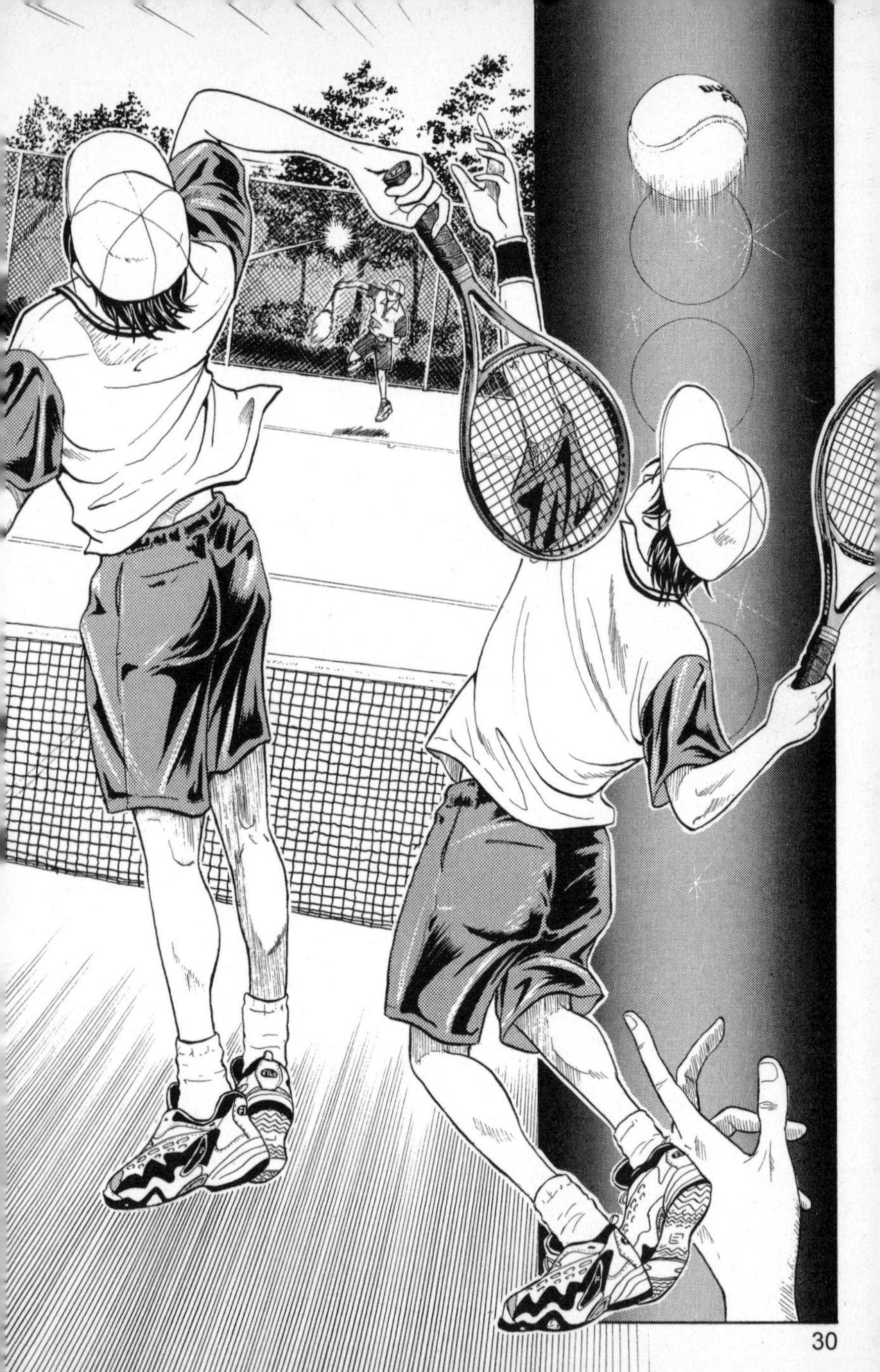

READ THIS WAY

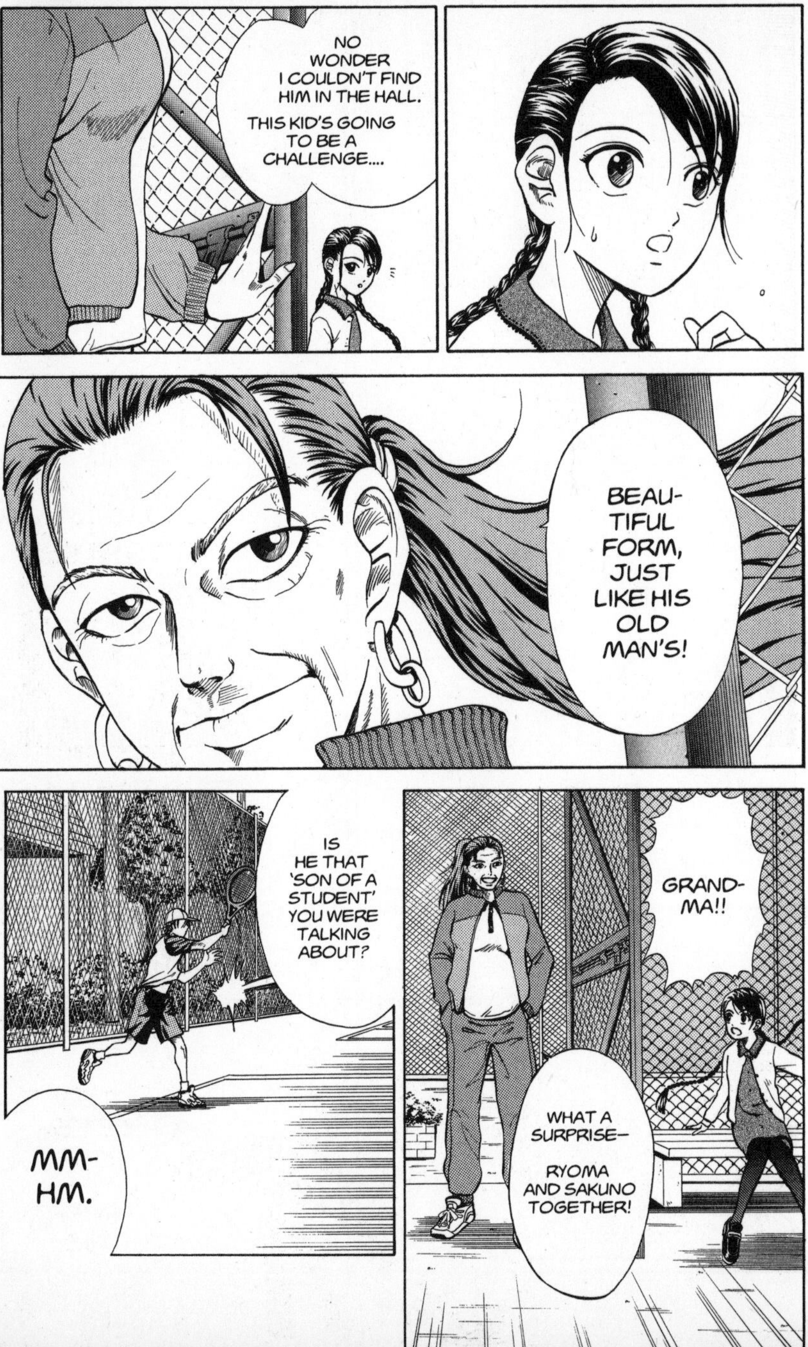
NO WONDER I COULDN'T FIND HIM IN THE HALL.
THIS KID'S GOING TO BE A CHALLENGE....
BEAU-TIFUL FORM, JUST LIKE HIS OLD MAN'S!
GRAND-MA!!
WHAT A SURPRISE— RYOMA AND SAKUNO TOGETHER!
IS HE THAT 'SON OF A STUDENT' YOU WERE TALKING ABOUT?
MM-HM.

READ THIS WAY

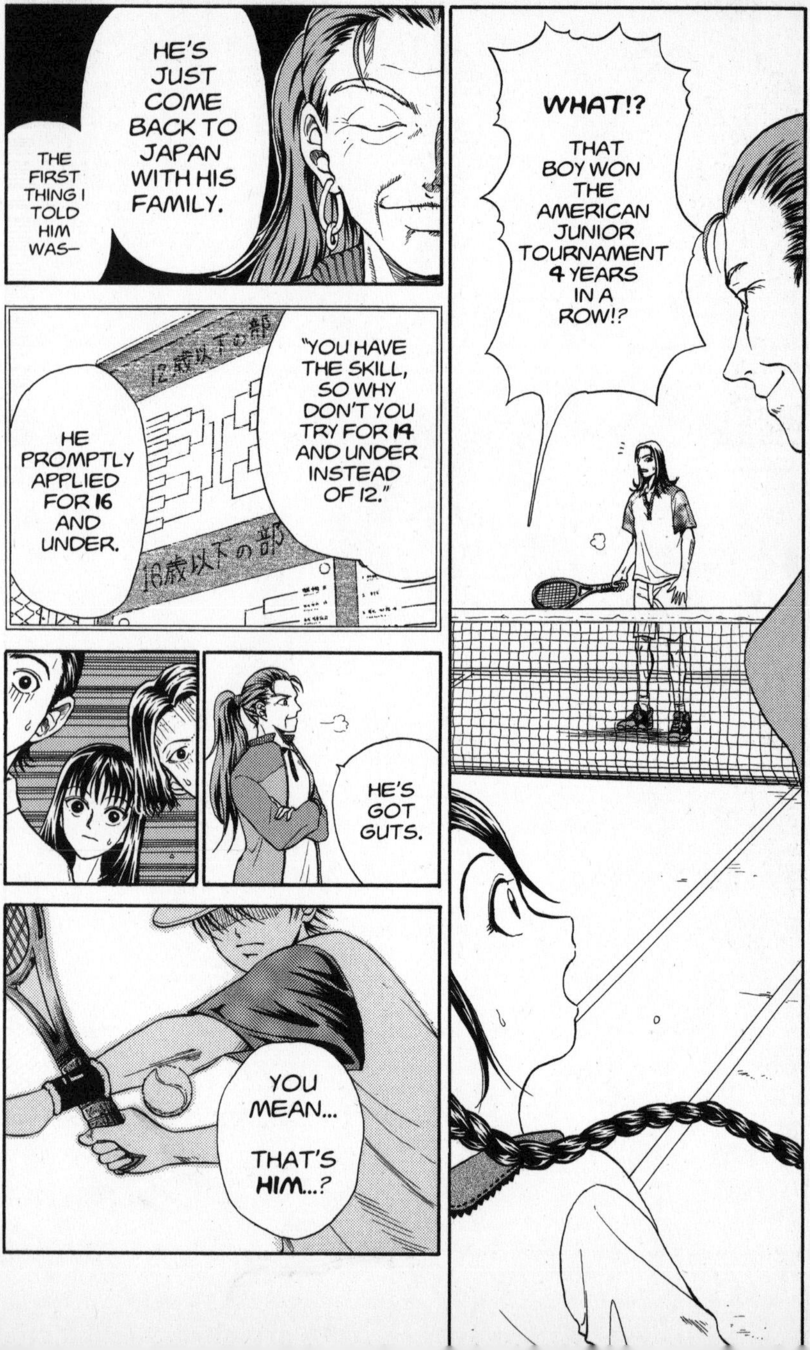

WHAT!?
THAT BOY WON THE AMERICAN JUNIOR TOURNAMENT 4 YEARS IN A ROW!?
HE'S JUST COME BACK TO JAPAN WITH HIS FAMILY.
THE FIRST THING I TOLD HIM WAS—
"YOU HAVE THE SKILL, SO WHY DON'T YOU TRY FOR 14 AND UNDER INSTEAD OF 12."
HE PROMPTLY APPLIED FOR 16 AND UNDER.
12歳以下の部
18歳以下の部
HE'S GOT GUTS.
YOU MEAN... THAT'S HIM...?

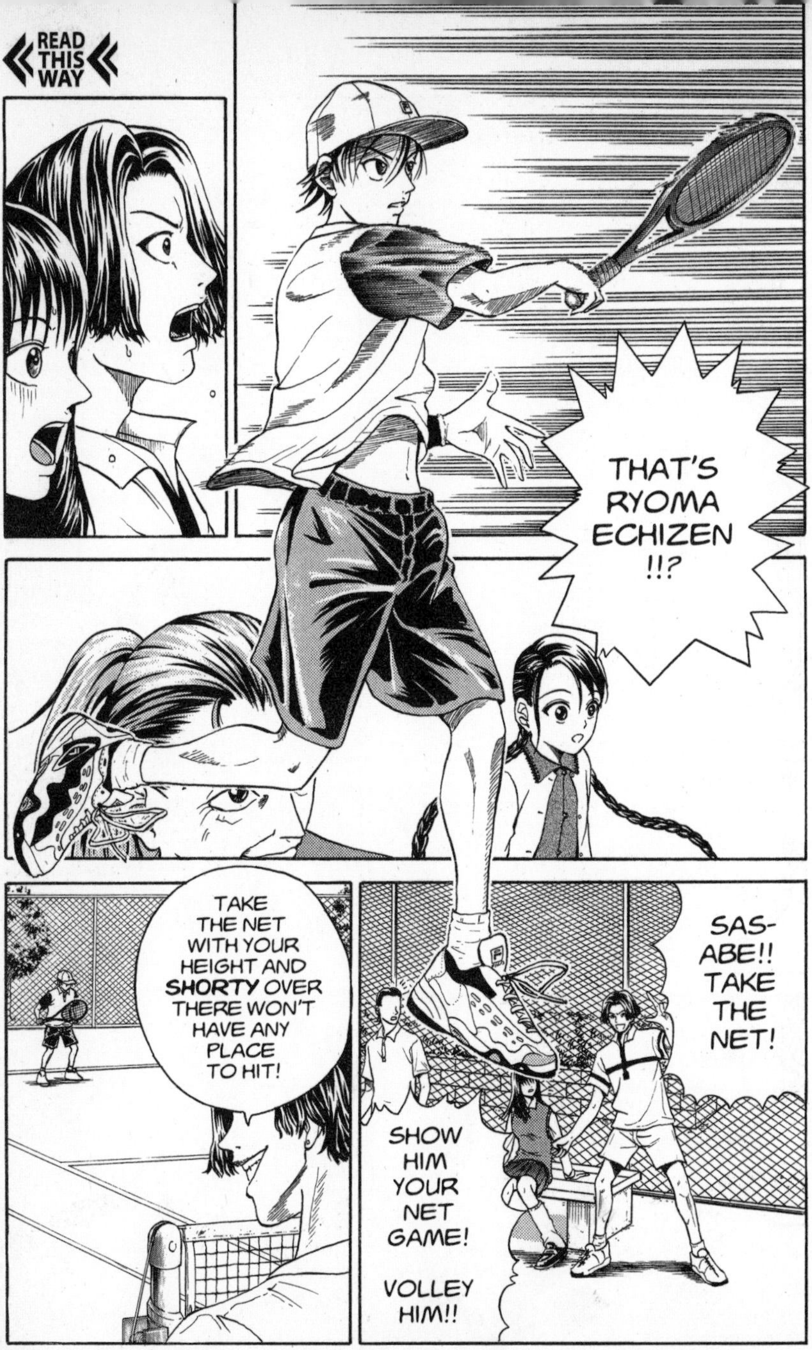
READ THIS WAY
THAT'S RYOMA ECHIZEN !!?
SAS-ABE!! TAKE THE NET!
SHOW HIM YOUR NET GAME!
VOLLEY HIM!!
TAKE THE NET WITH YOUR HEIGHT AND **SHORTY** OVER THERE WON'T HAVE ANY PLACE TO HIT!

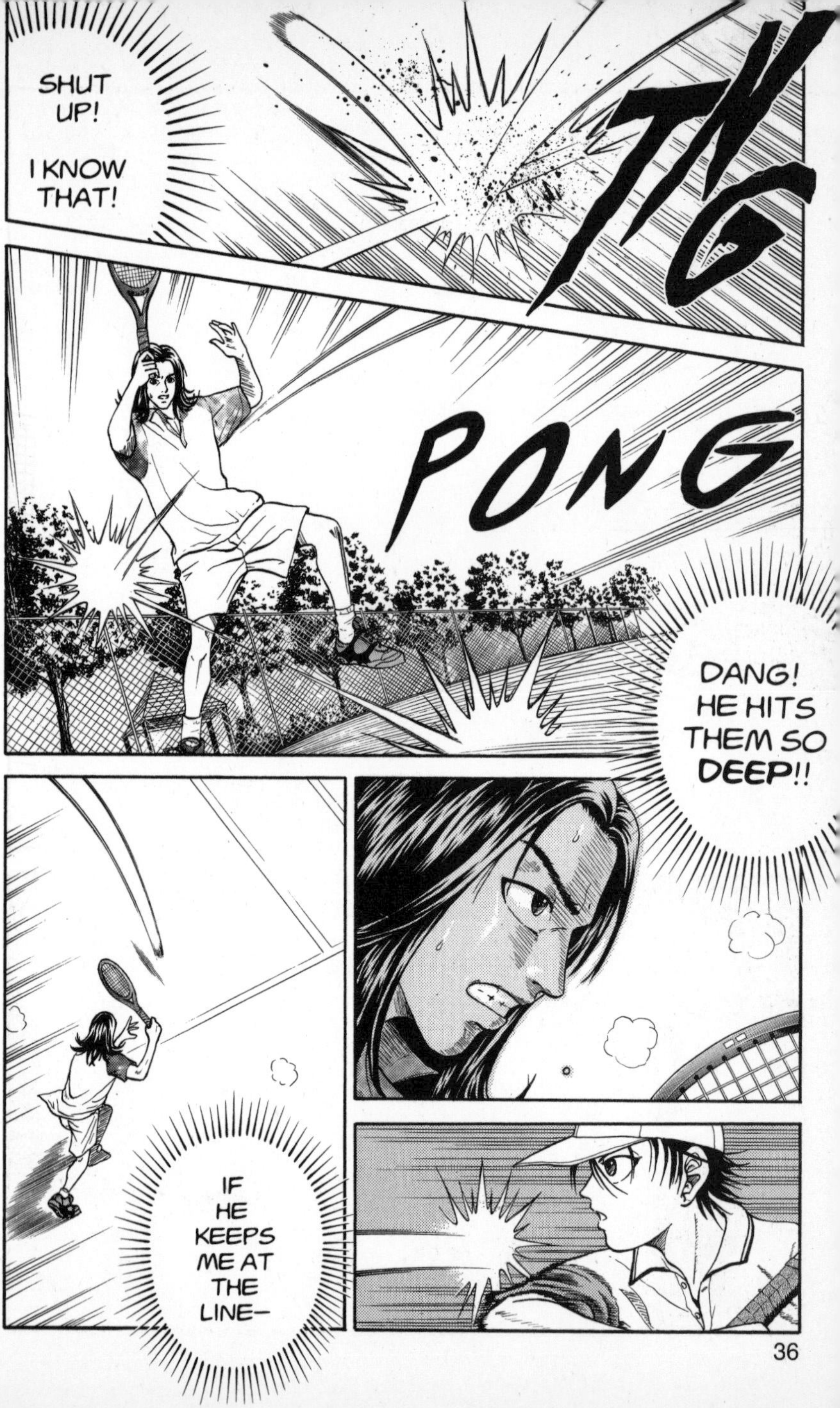
SHUT UP!
I KNOW THAT!
PONG
DANG! HE HITS THEM SO DEEP!!
IF HE KEEPS ME AT THE LINE—

READ THIS WAY

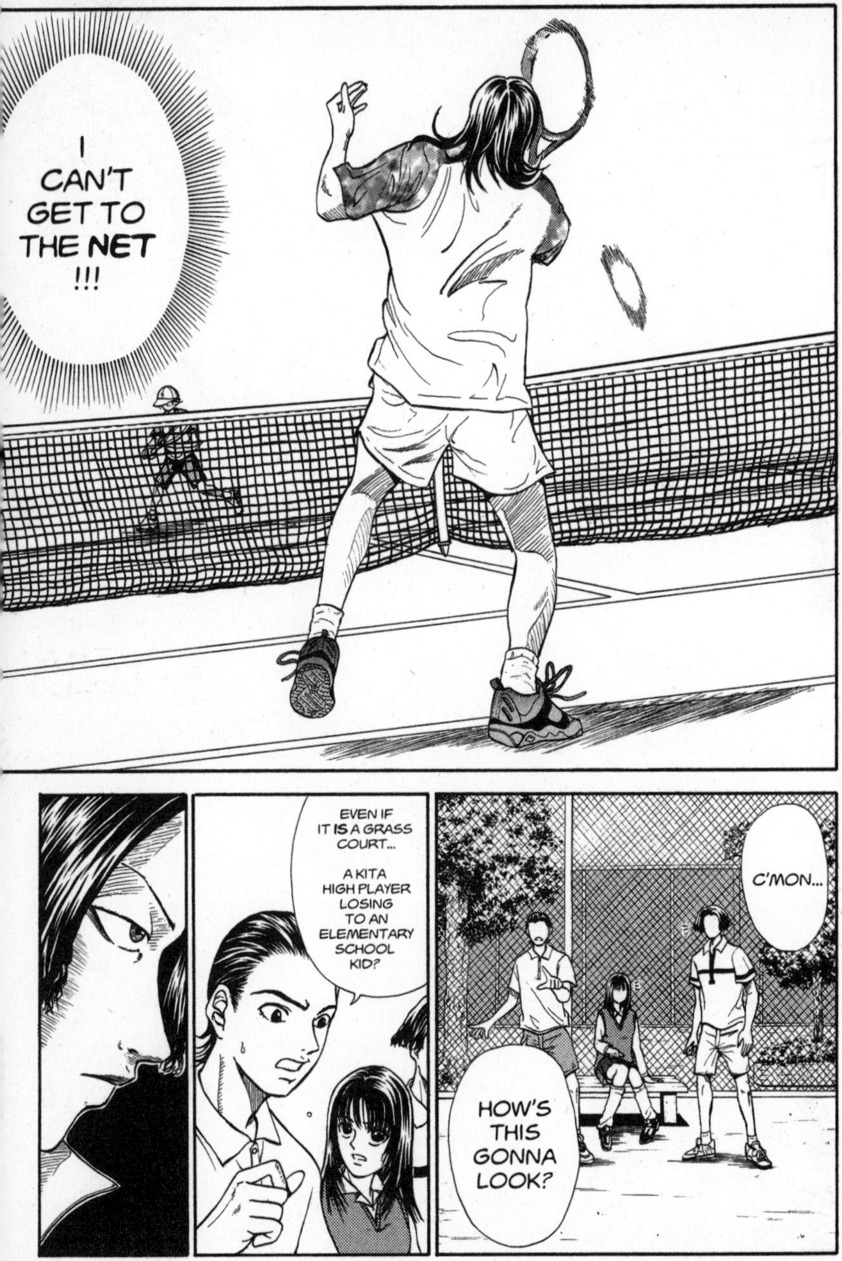
I CAN'T GET TO THE NET !!!
C'MON...
HOW'S THIS GONNA LOOK?
EVEN IF IT IS A GRASS COURT...
A KITA HIGH PLAYER LOSING TO AN ELEMENTARY SCHOOL KID?

READ THIS WAY

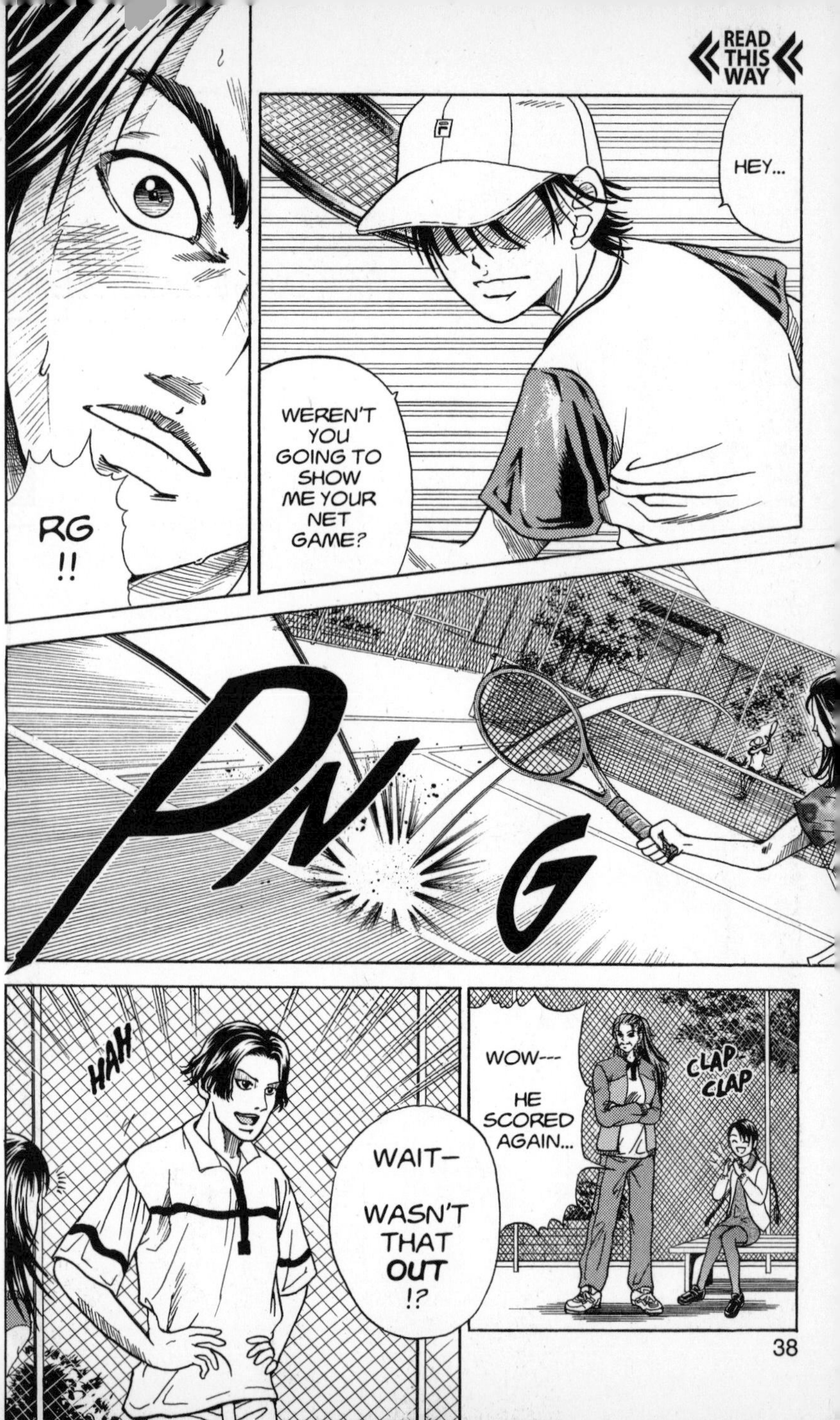
HEY...
WEREN'T YOU GOING TO SHOW ME YOUR NET GAME?
RG !!
PNG
WOW---
HE SCORED AGAIN...
CLAP CLAP
HAH
WAIT—
WASN'T THAT **OUT** !?

READ THIS WAY

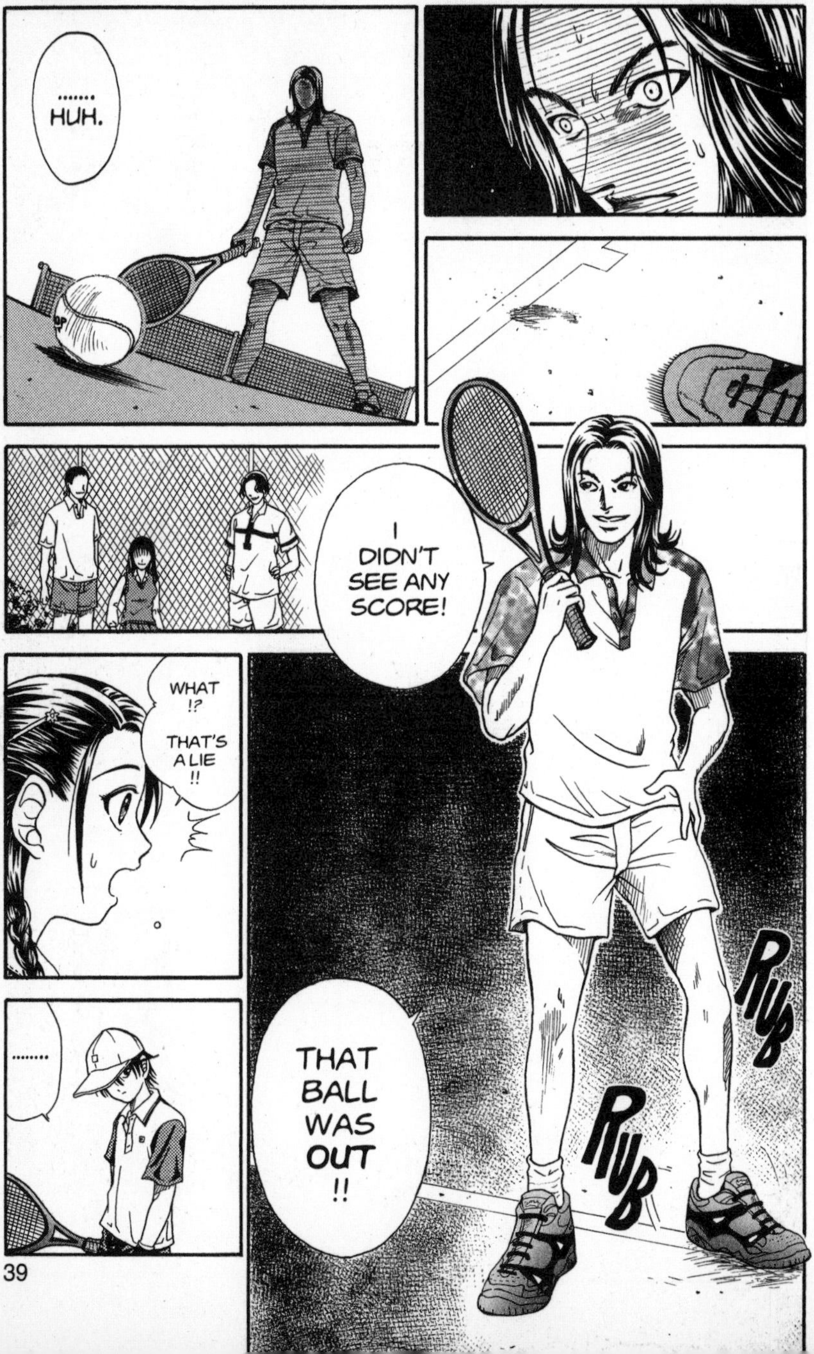
.... HUH.
I DIDN'T SEE ANY SCORE!
THAT BALL WAS OUT !!
RUB
RUB
WHAT !? THAT'S A LIE !!
....

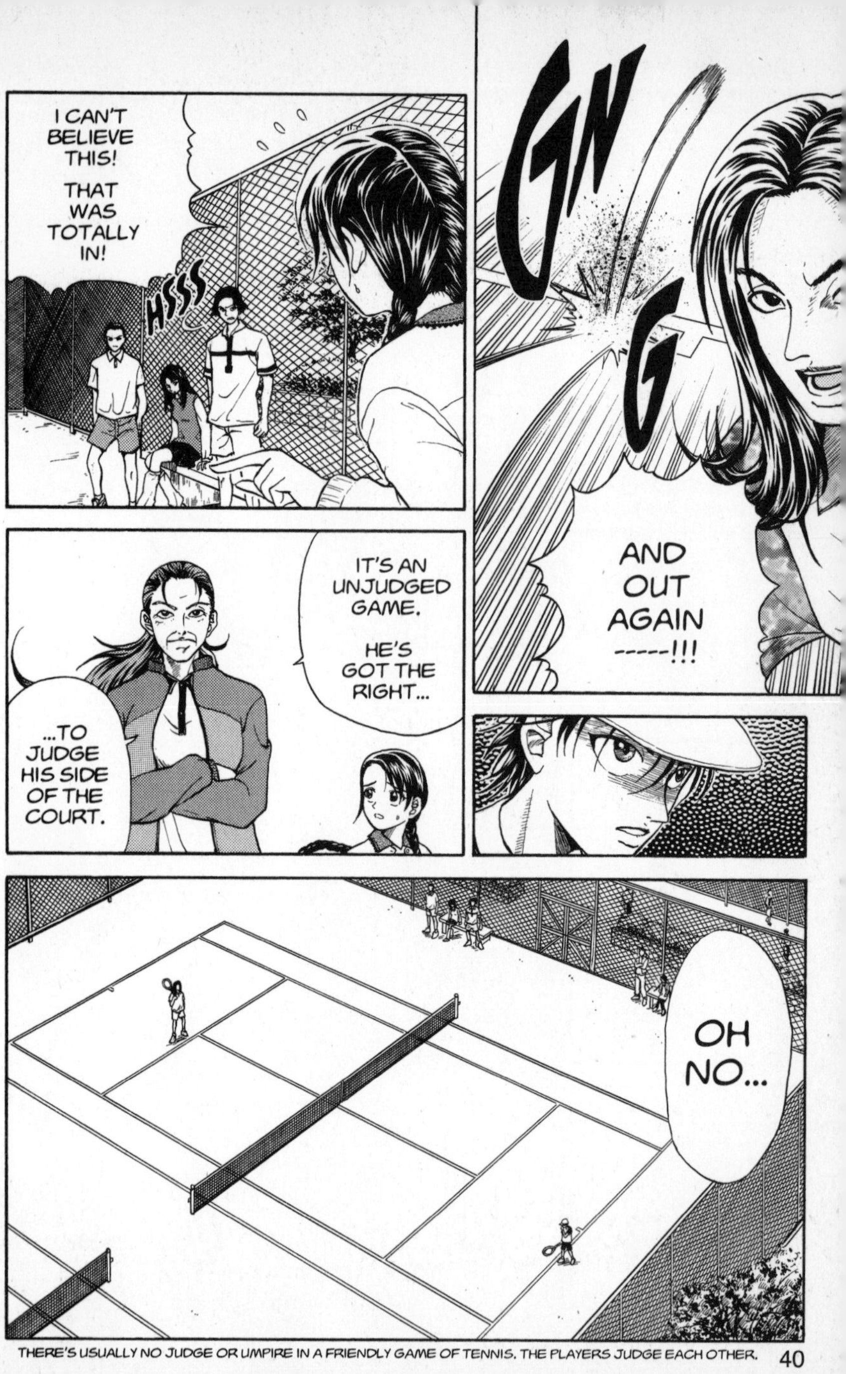
GN G
AND OUT AGAIN -----!!!
I CAN'T BELIEVE THIS!
THAT WAS TOTALLY IN!
HSSS
IT'S AN UNJUDGED GAME.
HE'S GOT THE RIGHT...
...TO JUDGE HIS SIDE OF THE COURT.
OH NO...

THERE'S USUALLY NO JUDGE OR UMPIRE IN A FRIENDLY GAME OF TENNIS. THE PLAYERS JUDGE EACH OTHER.

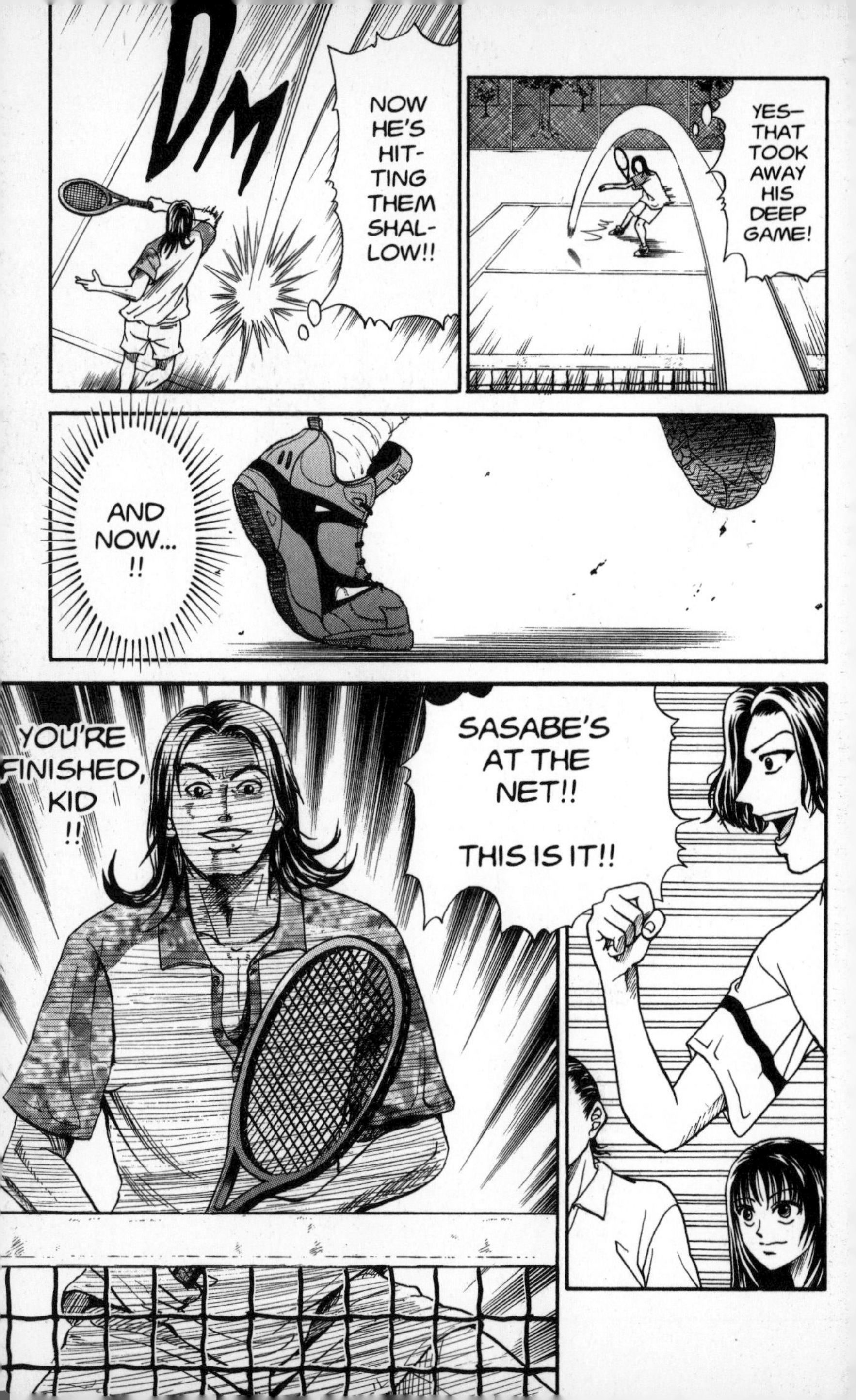
DM
NOW HE'S HIT-TING THEM SHAL-LOW!!
YES— THAT TOOK AWAY HIS DEEP GAME!
AND NOW... !!
SASABE'S AT THE NET!!
THIS IS IT!!
YOU'RE FINISHED, KID !!

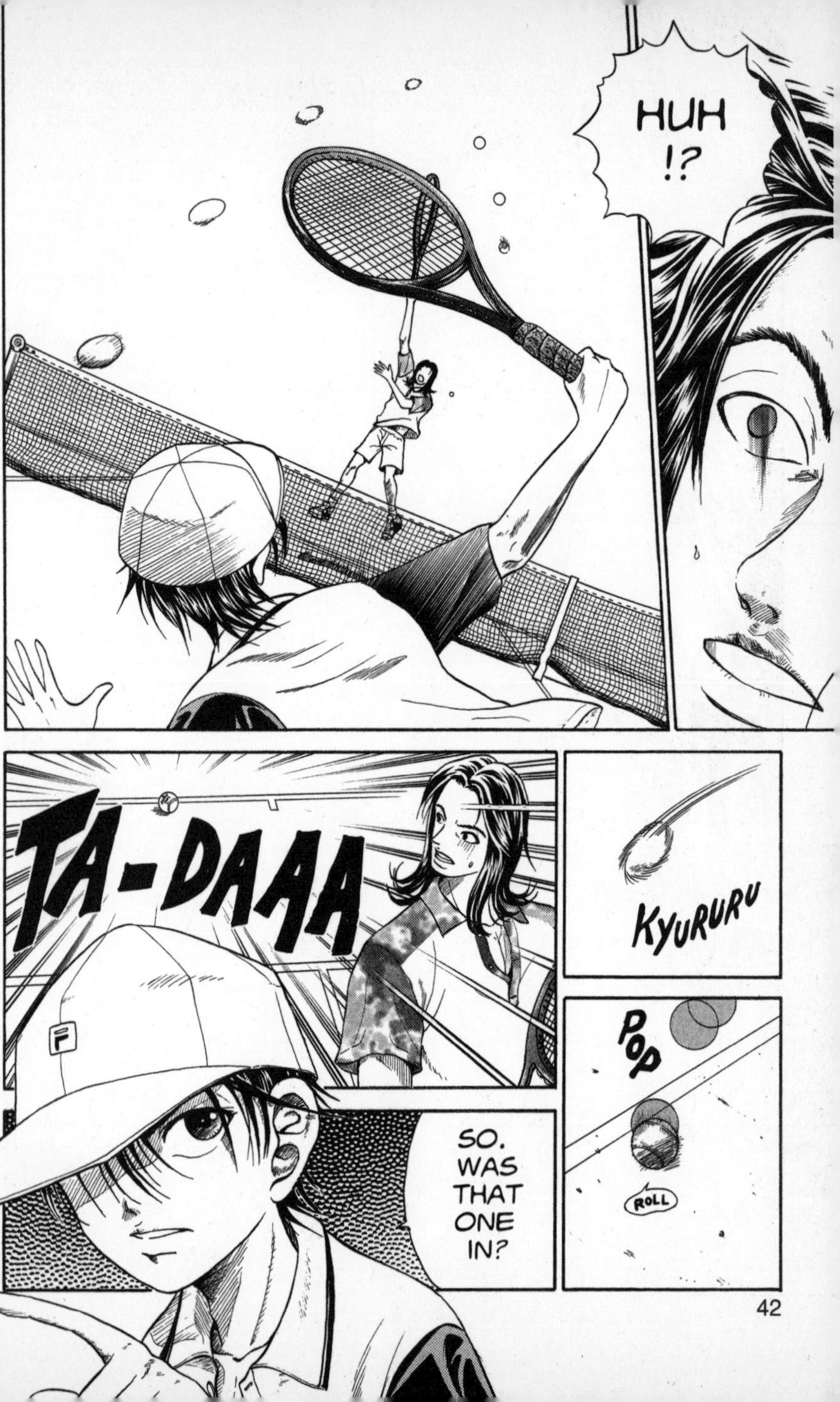
HUH !?
KYURURU
POP
ROLL
TA-DAAA
SO. WAS THAT ONE IN?

READ THIS WAY

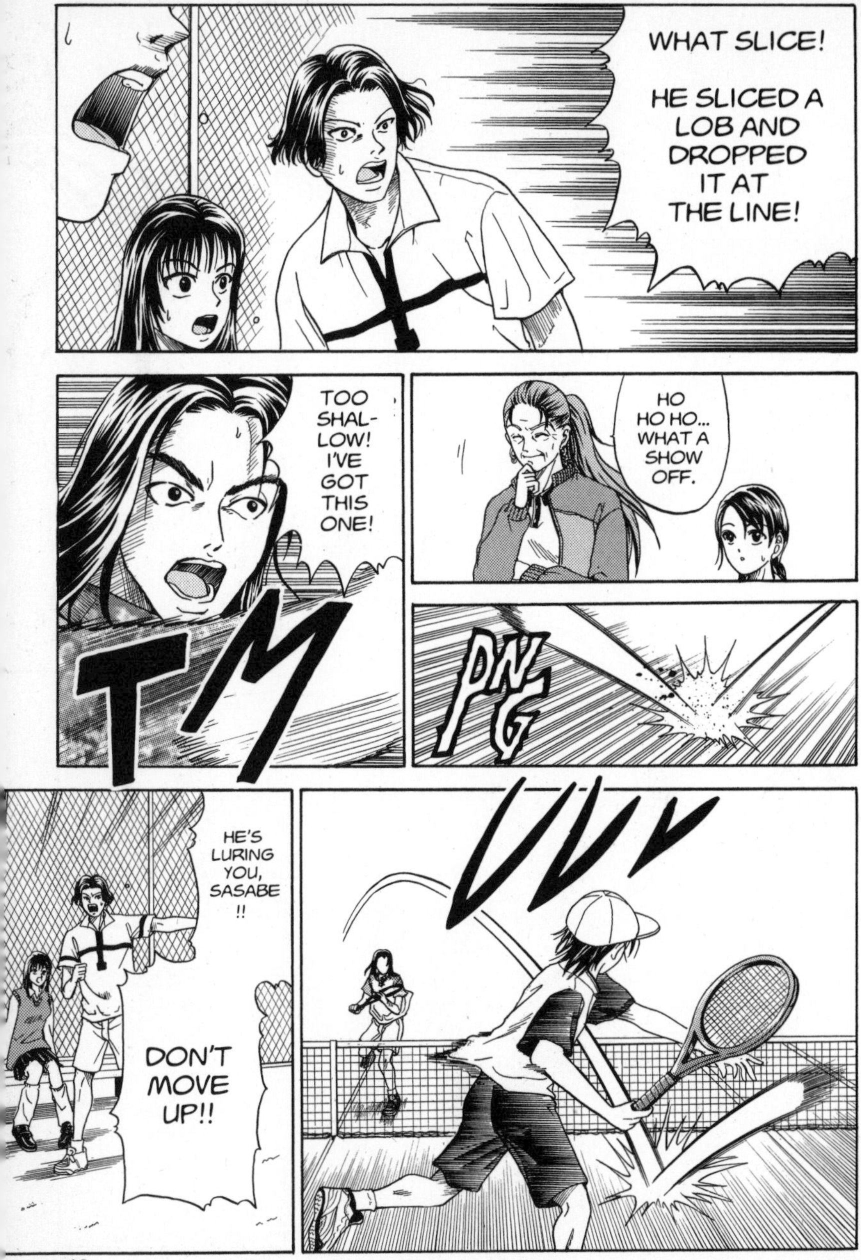
WHAT SLICE!
HE SLICED A LOB AND DROPPED IT AT THE LINE!
HO HO HO... WHAT A SHOW OFF.
PNG
TOO SHAL-LOW! I'VE GOT THIS ONE!
TM
VVVV
HE'S LURING YOU, SASABE!!
DON'T MOVE UP!!

READ THIS WAY

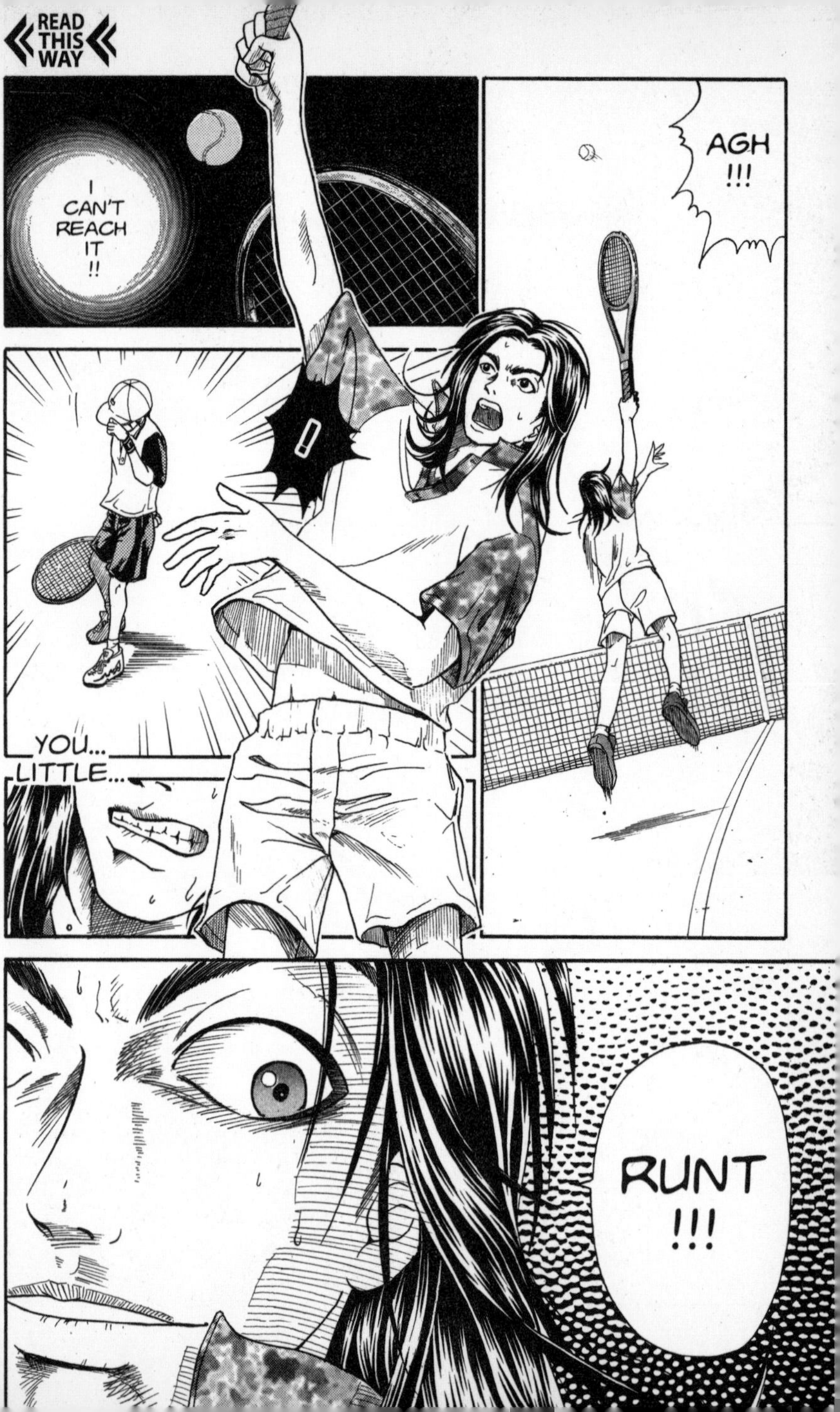
AGH!!!
I CAN'T REACH IT!!
!
YOU... LITTLE...
RUNT!!!

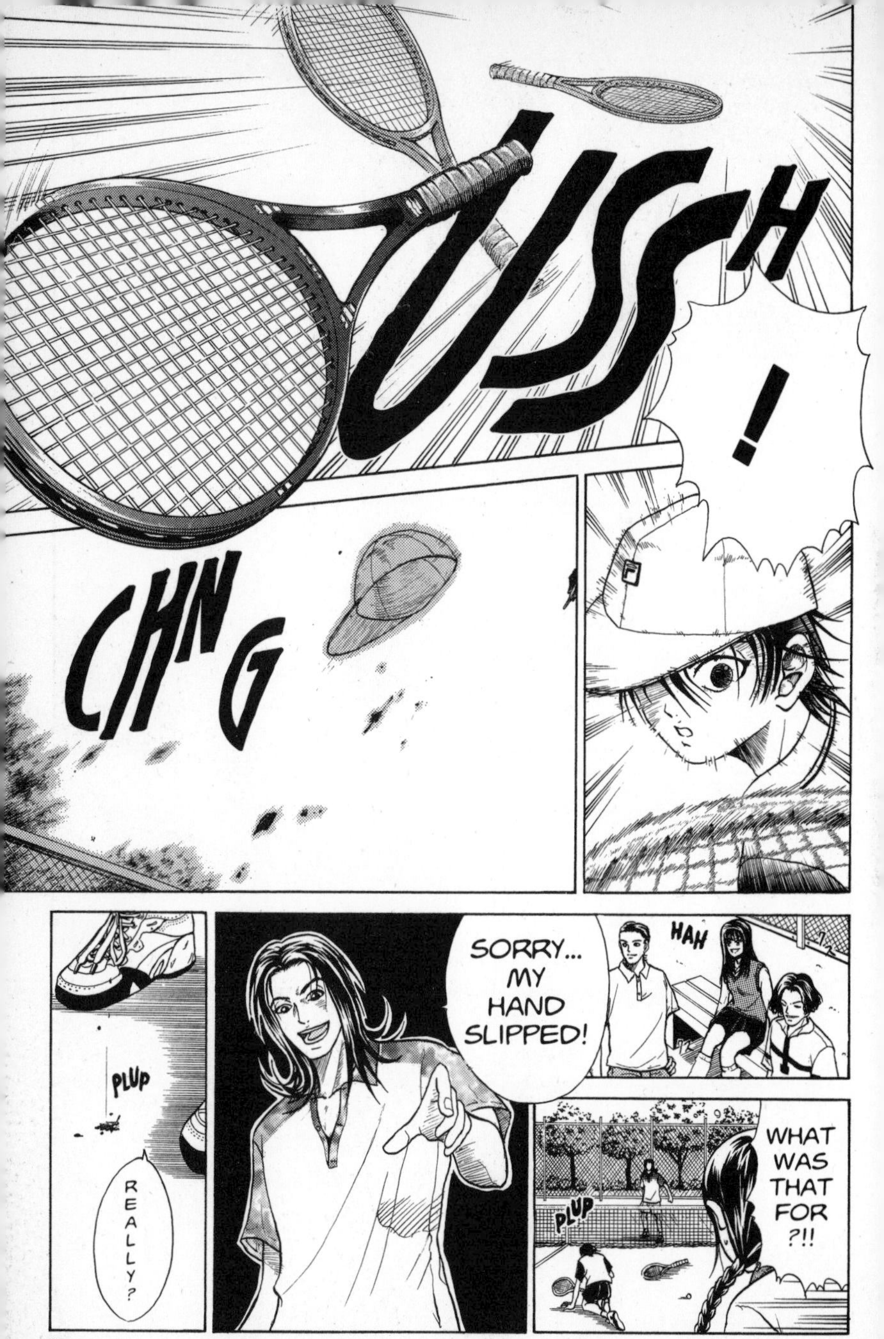
WUSH
!
CHING
HAH
WHAT WAS THAT FOR ?!!
PLUP
SORRY... MY HAND SLIPPED!
PLUP
REALLY?

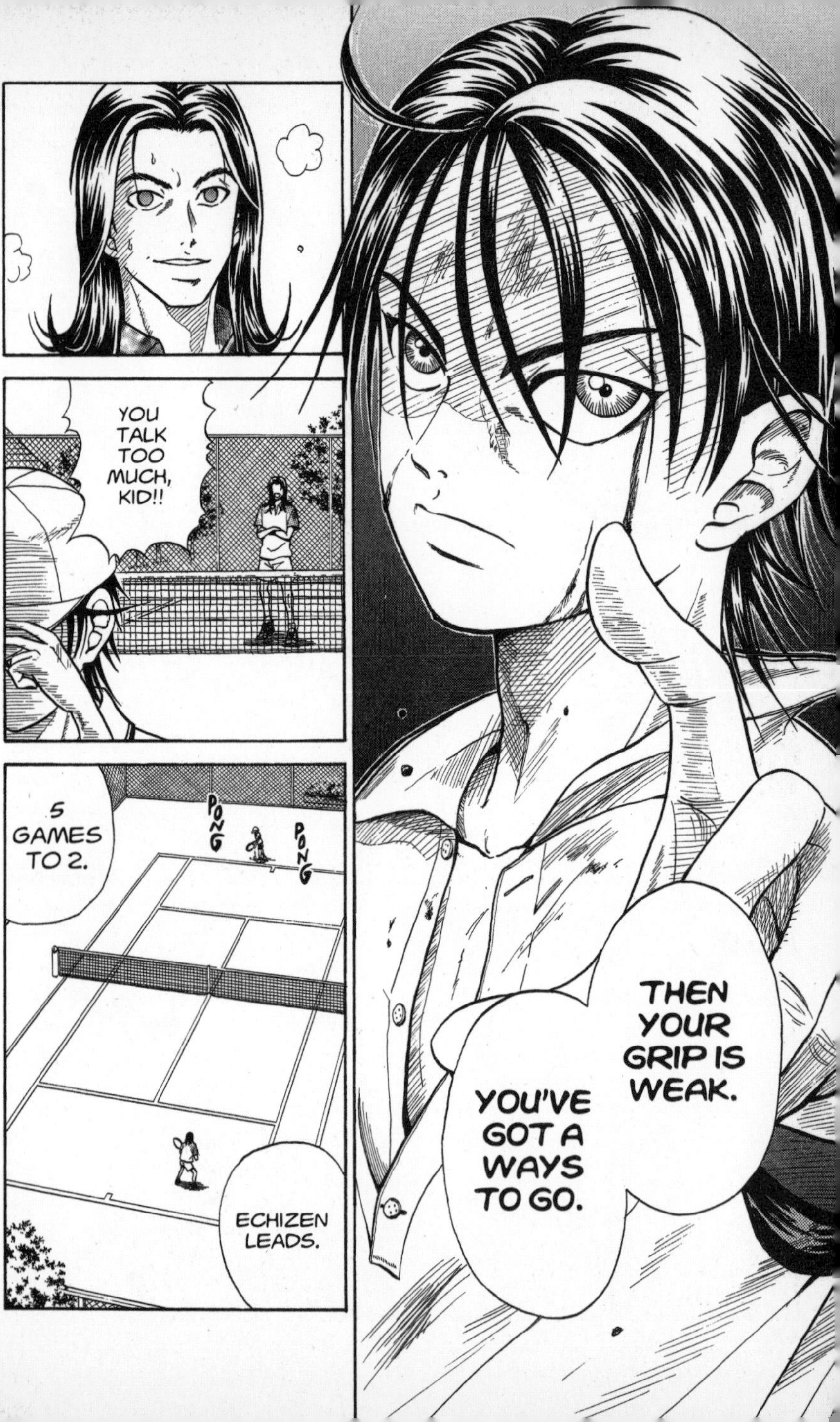
THEN YOUR GRIP IS WEAK.
YOU'VE GOT A WAYS TO GO.
YOU TALK TOO MUCH, KID!!
PONG
PONG
5 GAMES TO 2.
ECHIZEN LEADS.

READ THIS WAY

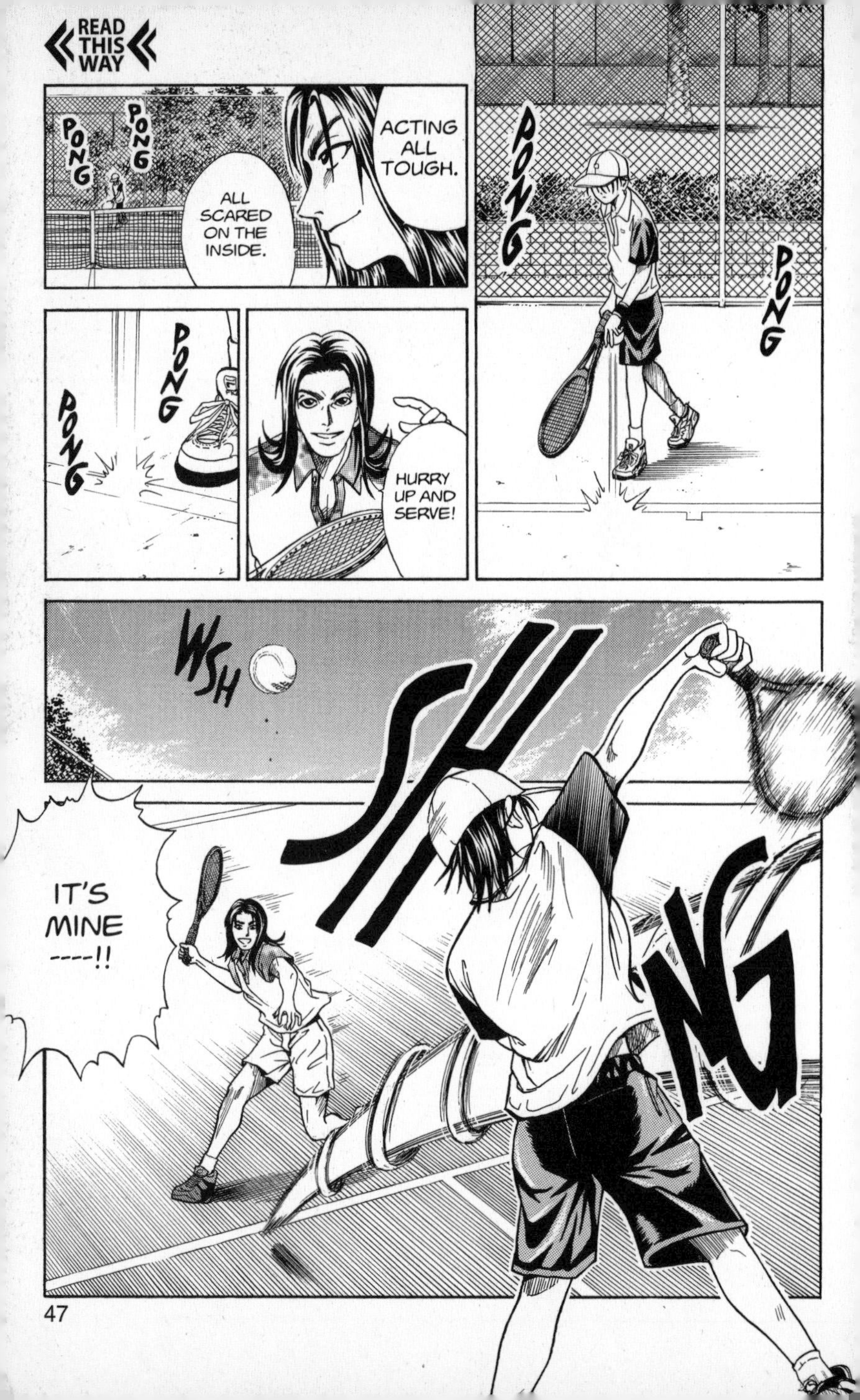

PONG
PONG
ACTING ALL TOUGH.
ALL SCARED ON THE INSIDE.
PONG
PONG
HURRY UP AND SERVE!
PONG
PONG
WSH
SHING
IT'S MINE ----!!

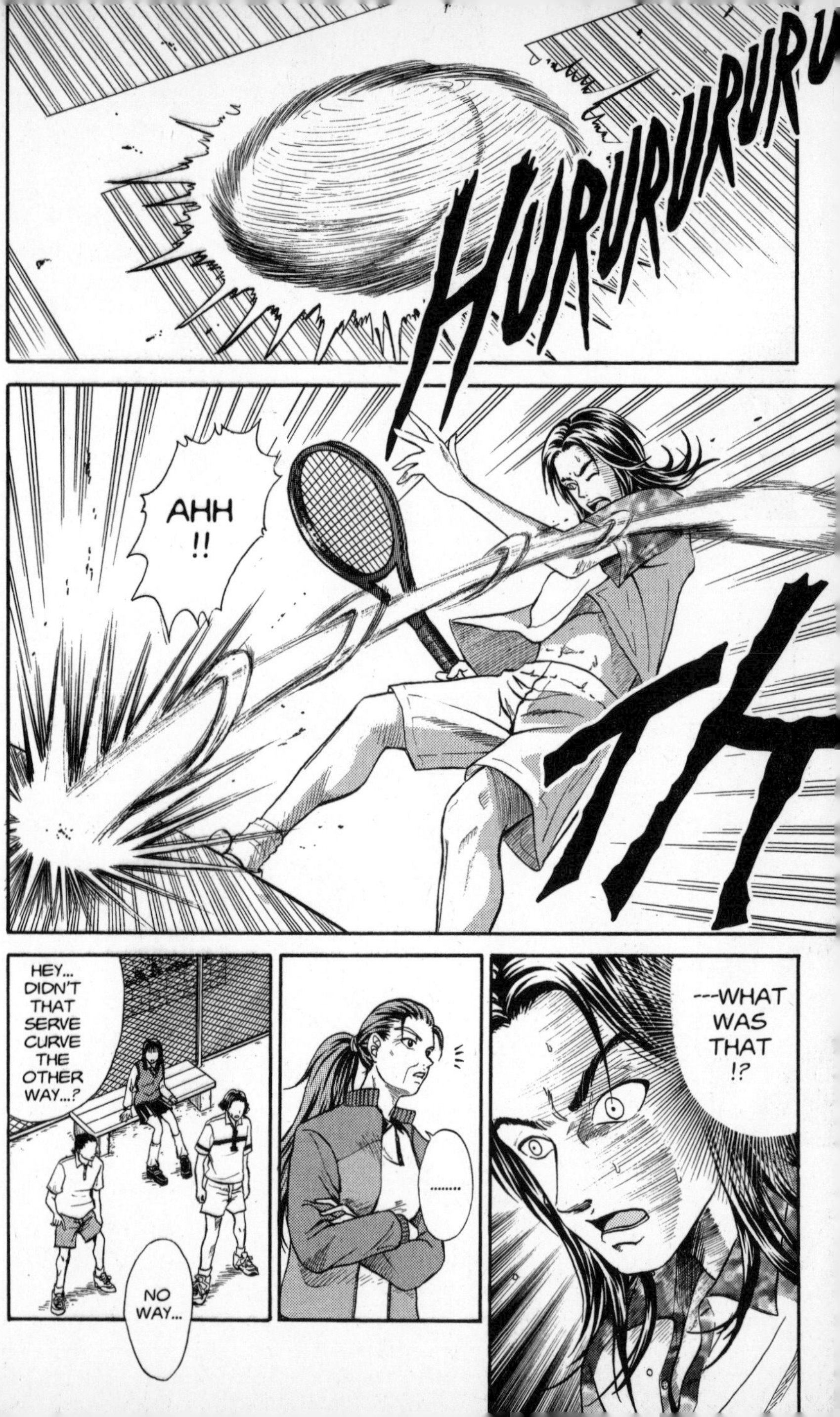
HURURURURURU
AHH !!
TH
---WHAT WAS THAT !?
....
HEY... DIDN'T THAT SERVE CURVE THE OTHER WAY...?
NO WAY...

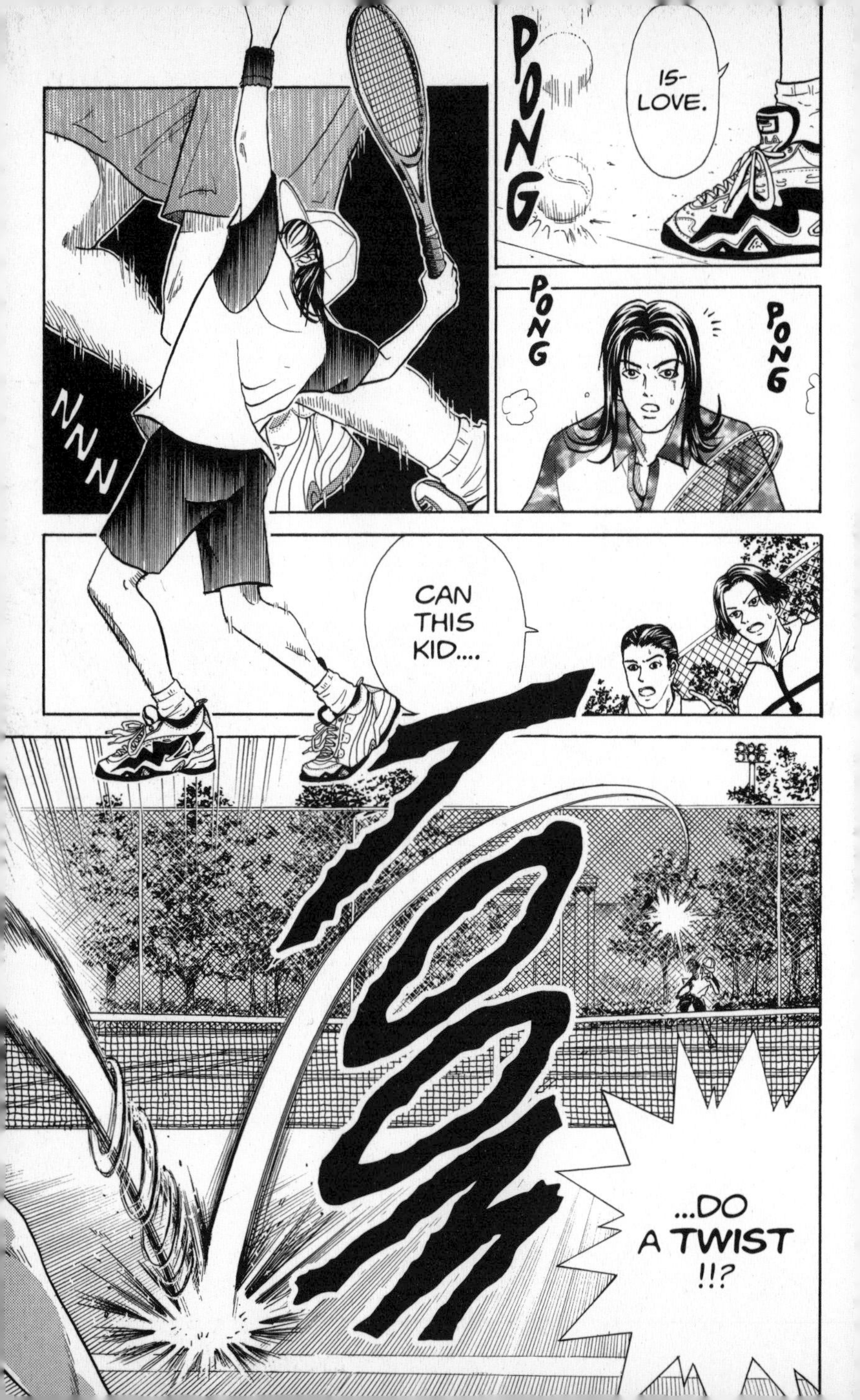
PONG
IS-LOVE.
PONG
PONG
NNN
CAN THIS KID....
...DO A TWIST !!?

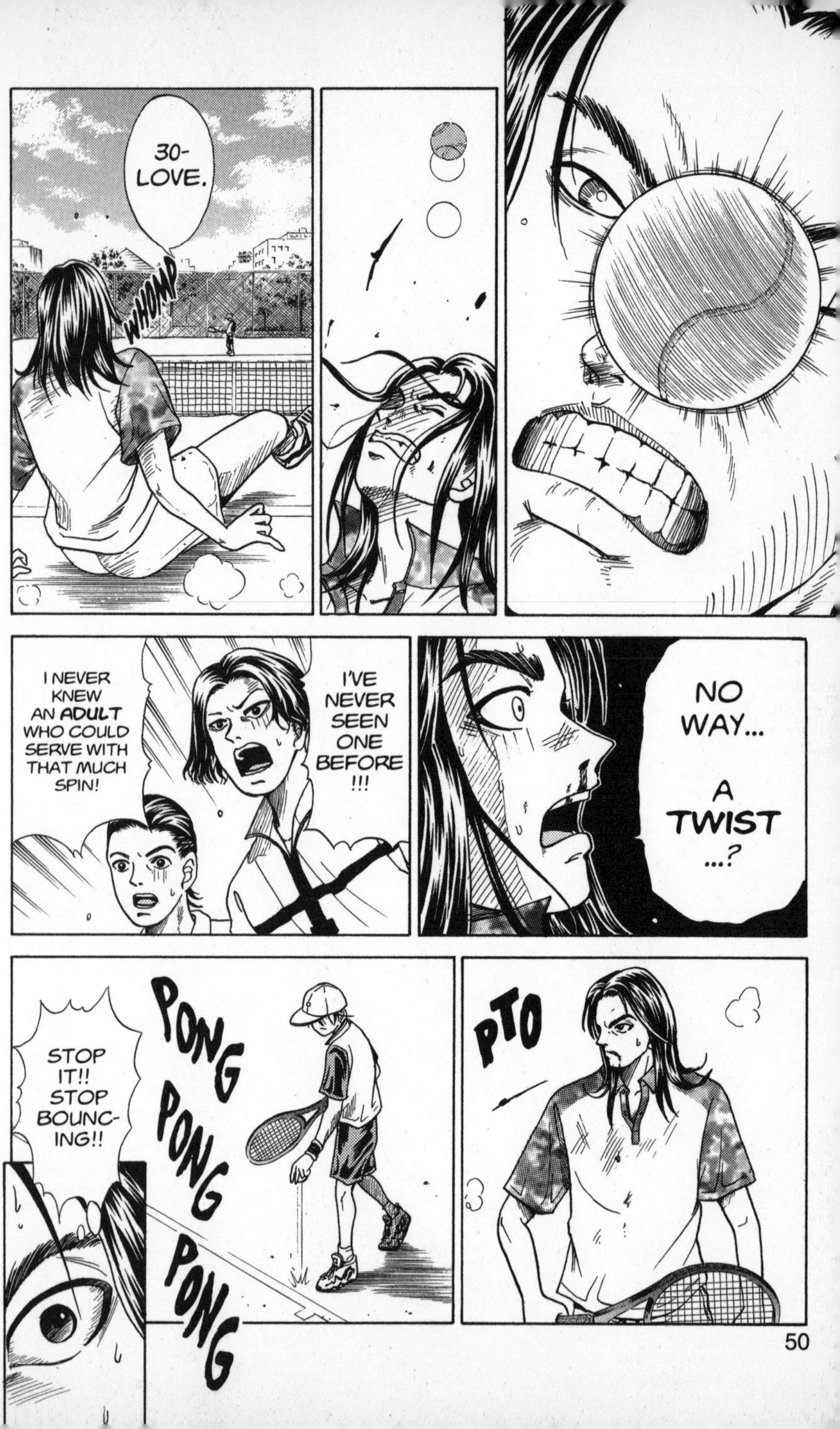
30-LOVE.
WHOMP
NO WAY... A TWIST ...?
I'VE NEVER SEEN ONE BEFORE !!!
I NEVER KNEW AN ADULT WHO COULD SERVE WITH THAT MUCH SPIN!
PTO
PONG PONG PONG PONG
STOP IT!! STOP BOUNC-ING!!

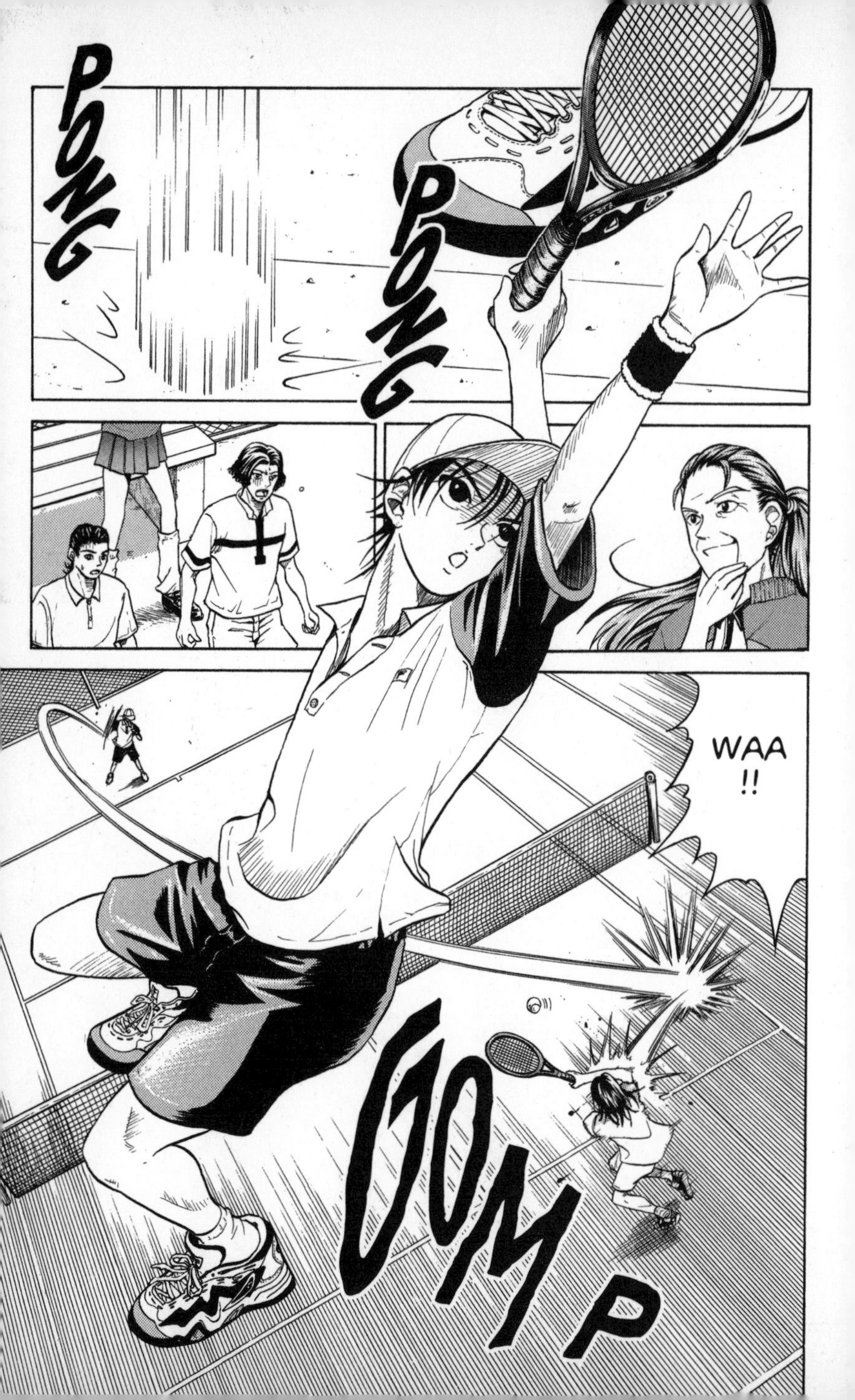
PONG
PONG
WAA !!
COMP

READ THIS WAY

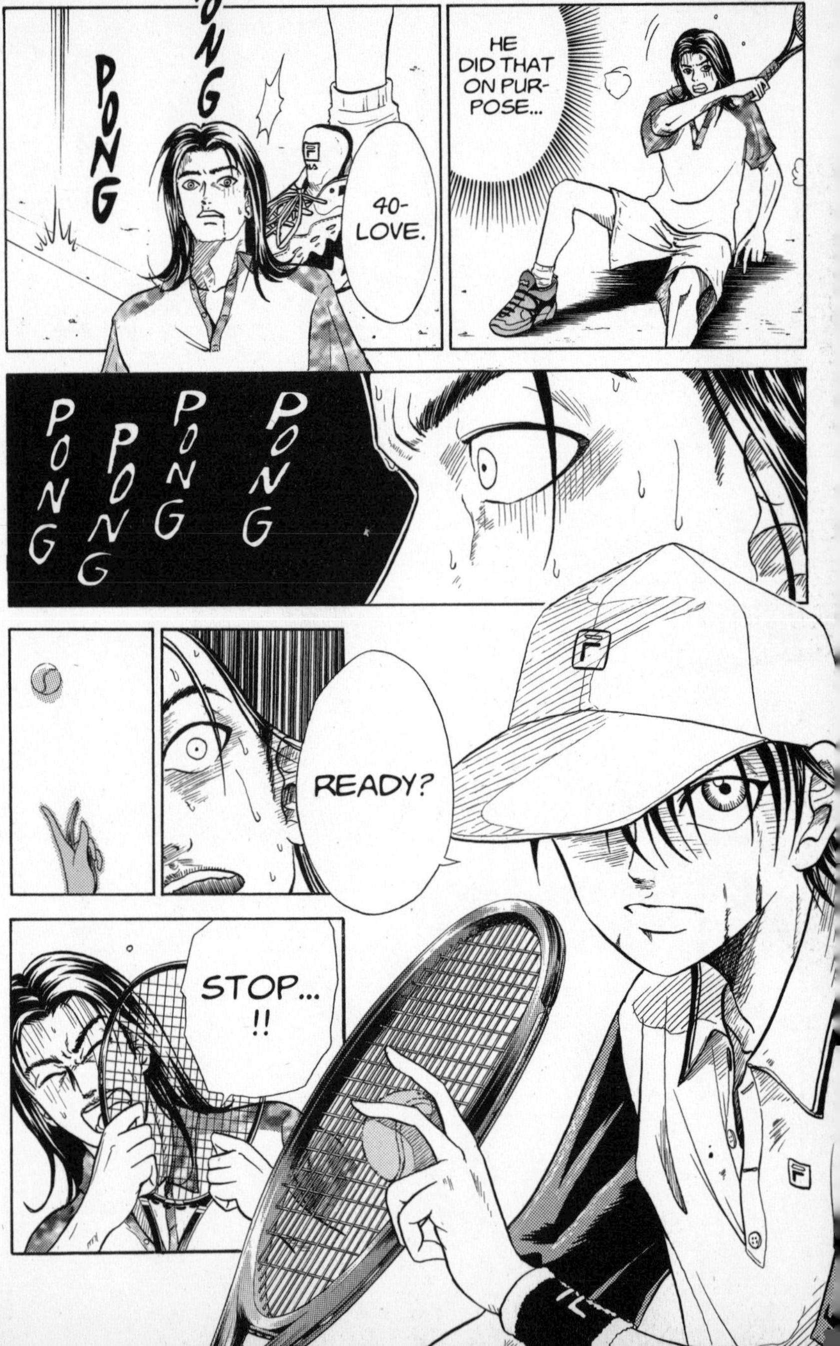
HE DID THAT ON PURPOSE...
PONG
PONG
40-LOVE.
PONG PONG PONG PONG
READY?
STOP... !!

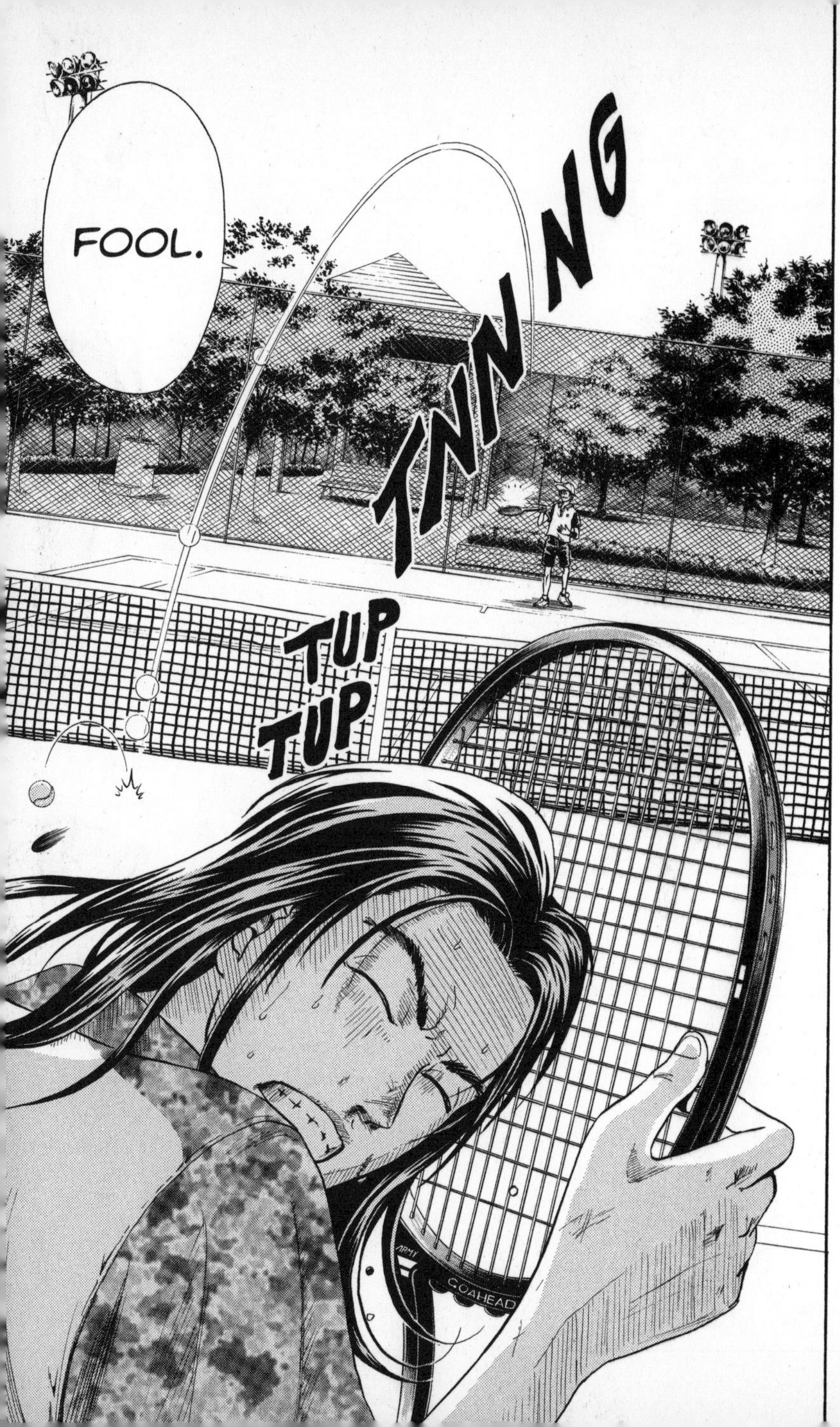
FOOL.
TNNNG
TUP TUP

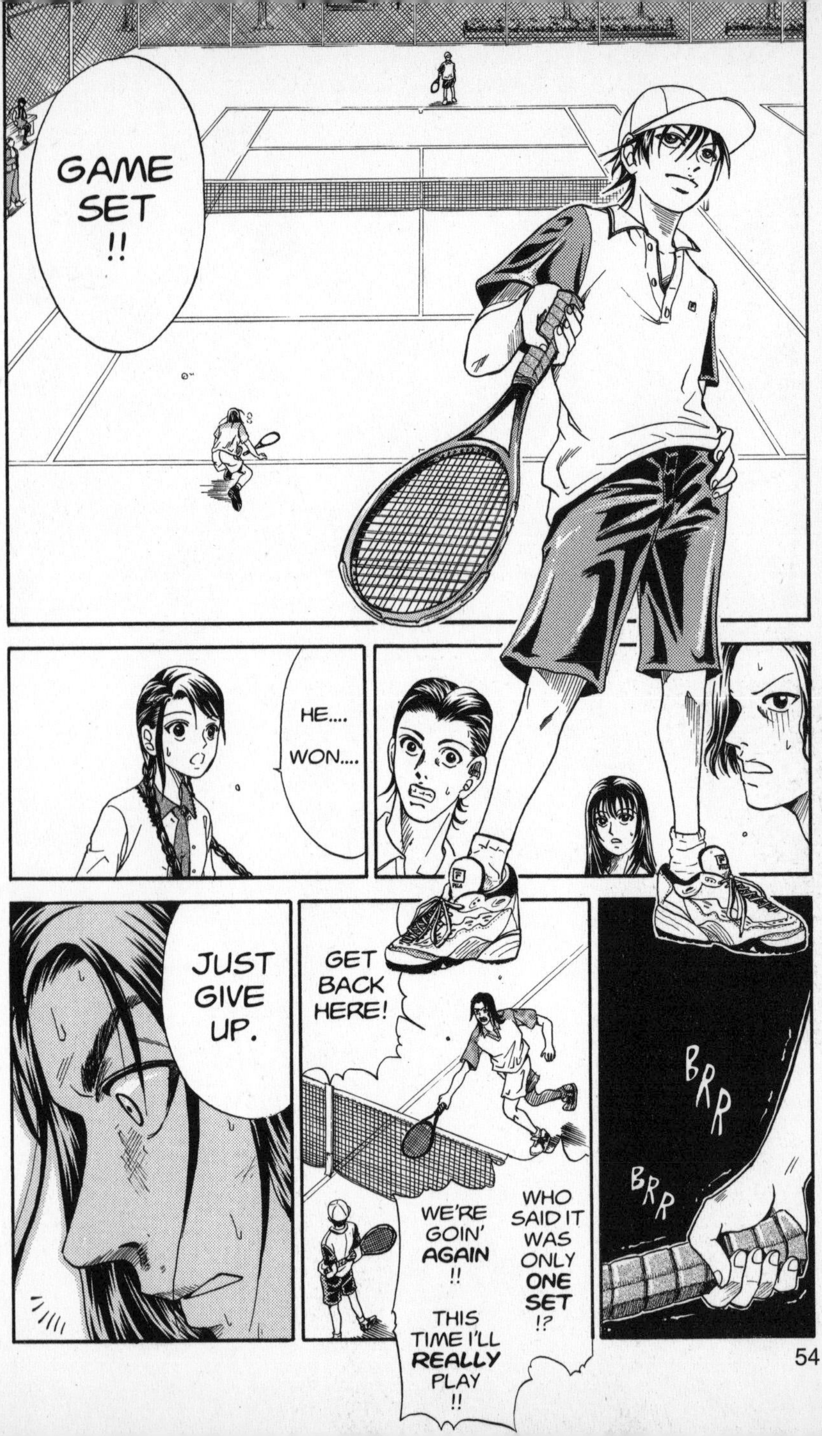
GAME SET !!
HE.... WON....
BRR
BRR
GET BACK HERE!
WHO SAID IT WAS ONLY ONE SET !?
WE'RE GOIN' AGAIN !!
THIS TIME I'LL REALLY PLAY !!
JUST GIVE UP.

READ THIS WAY

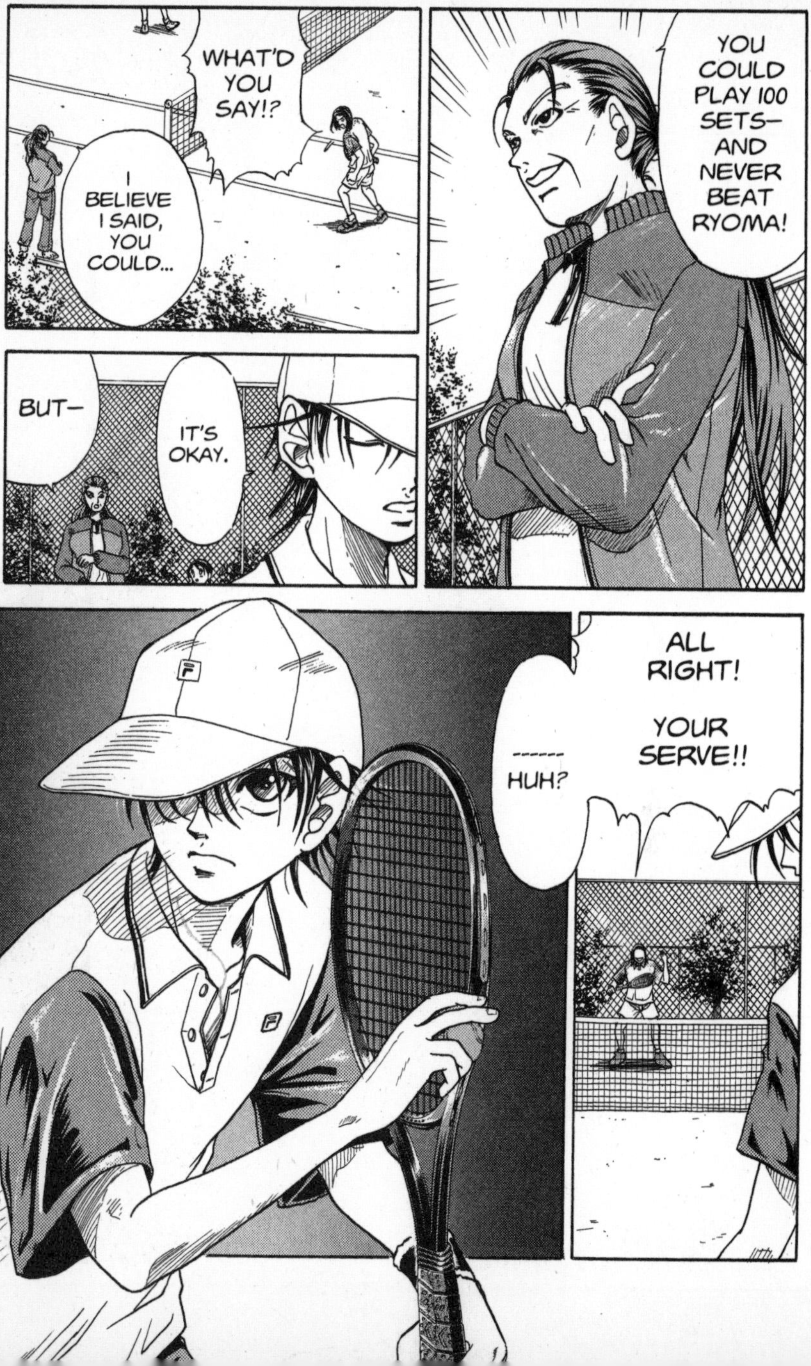
WHAT'D YOU SAY!?
I BELIEVE I SAID, YOU COULD...
YOU COULD PLAY 100 SETS— AND NEVER BEAT RYOMA!
IT'S OKAY.
BUT—
ALL RIGHT! YOUR SERVE!!
------ HUH?

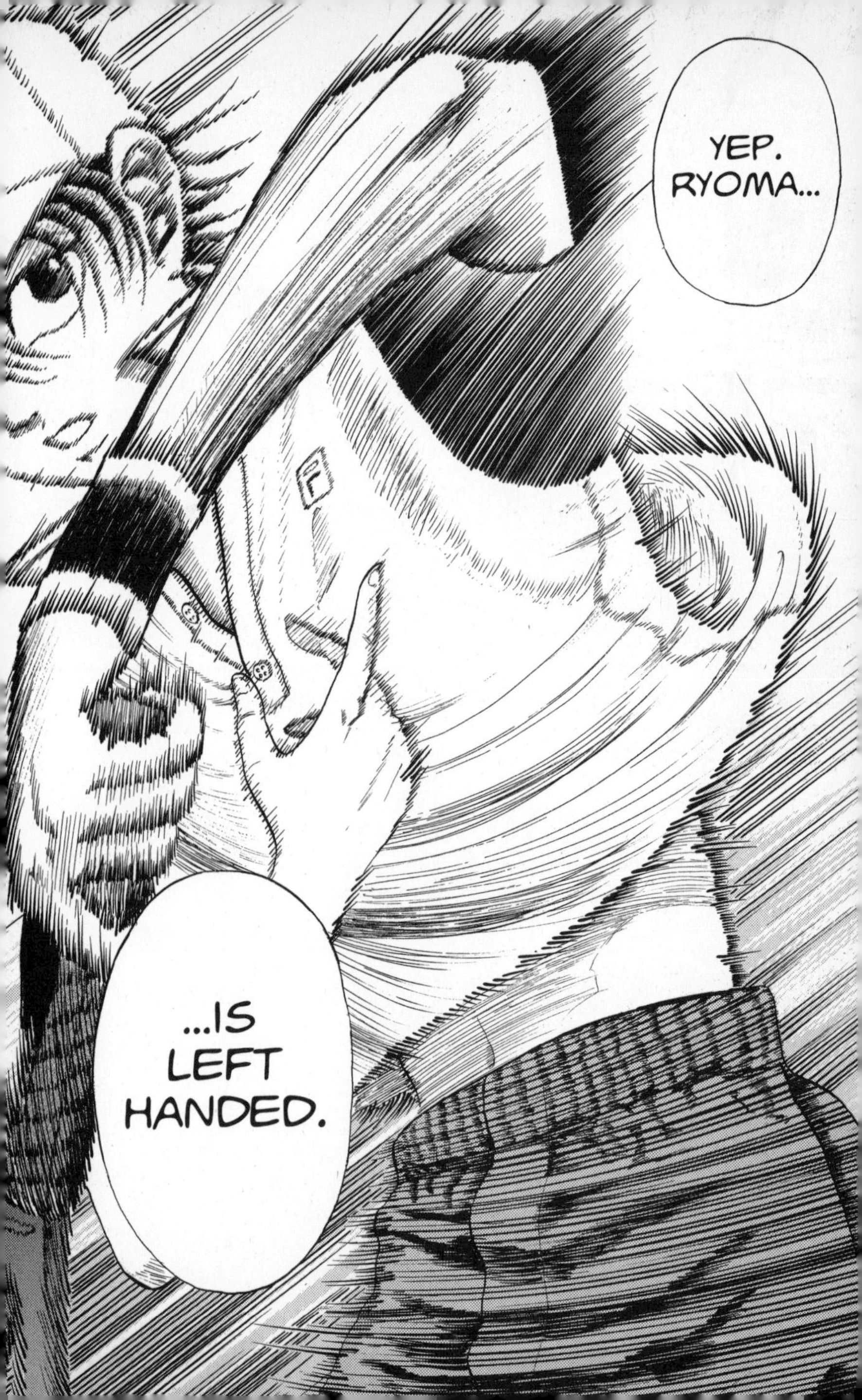
YEP. RYOMA...
...IS LEFT HANDED.

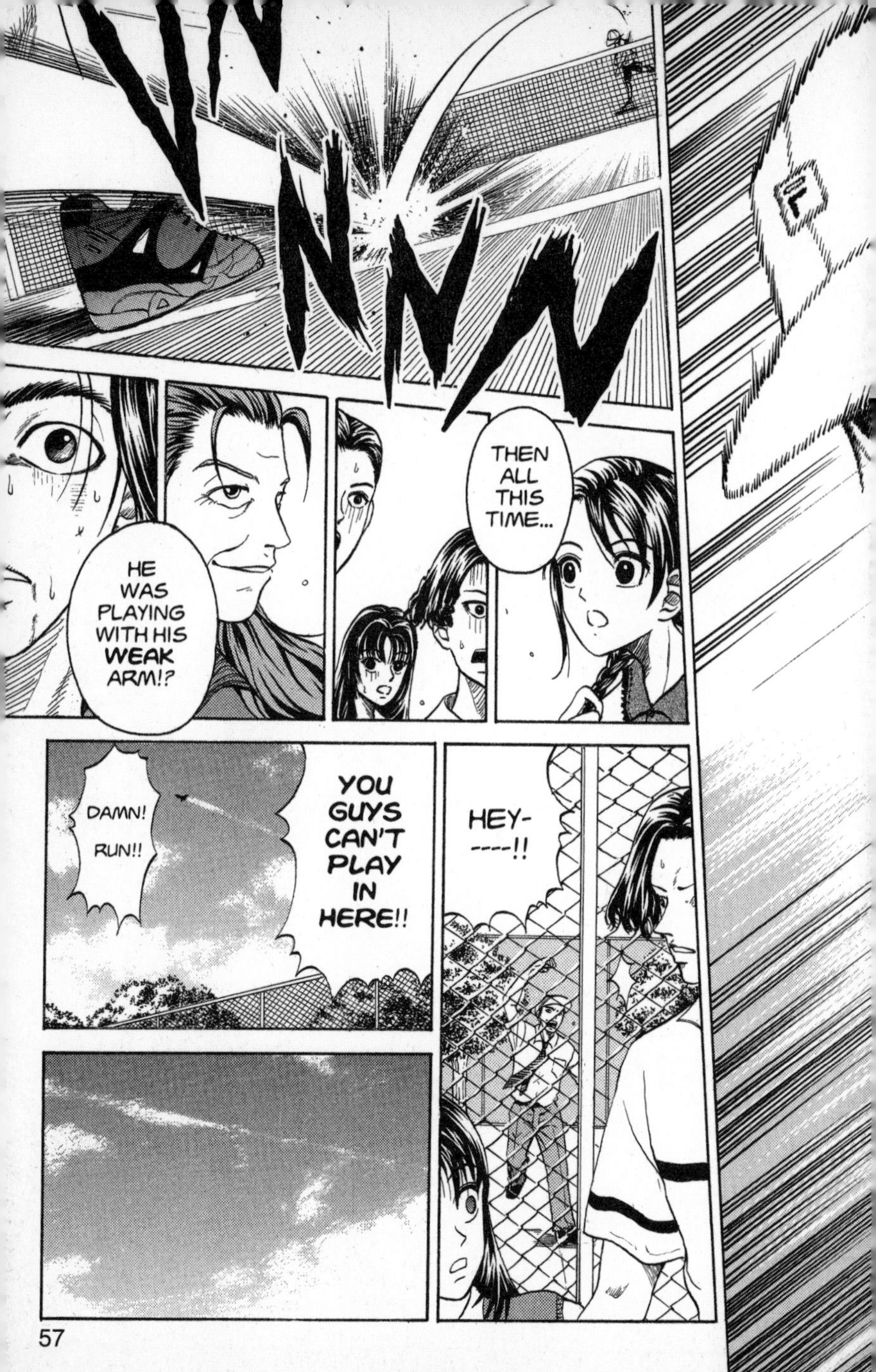
THEN ALL THIS TIME...
HE WAS PLAYING WITH HIS WEAK ARM!?
HEY-----!!
YOU GUYS CAN'T PLAY IN HERE!!
DAMN! RUN!!

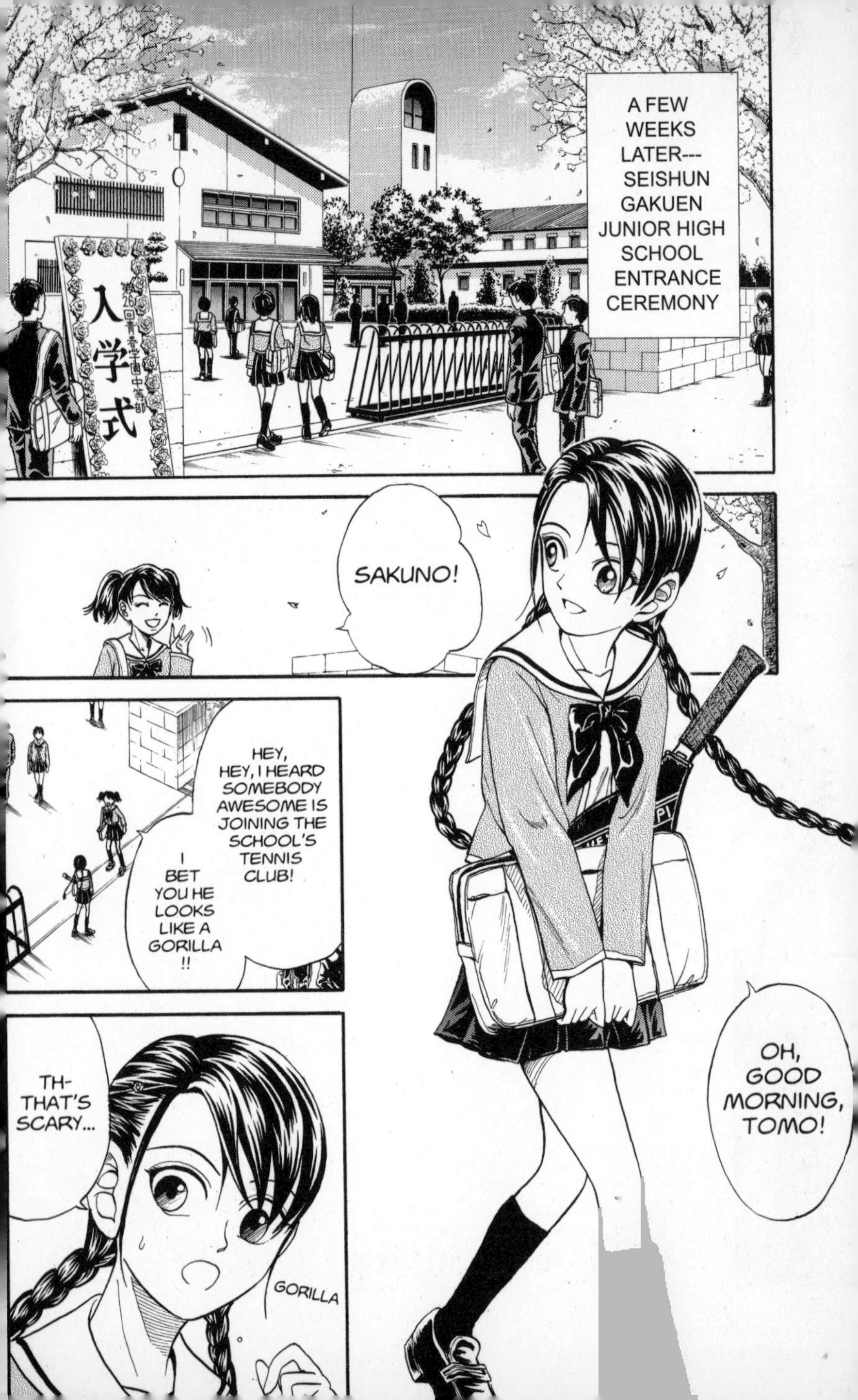
A FEW WEEKS LATER--- SEISHUN GAKUEN JUNIOR HIGH SCHOOL ENTRANCE CEREMONY
第26回青春学園中等部
入学式
SAKUNO!
OH, GOOD MORNING, TOMO!
HEY, HEY, I HEARD SOMEBODY AWESOME IS JOINING THE SCHOOL'S TENNIS CLUB!
I BET YOU HE LOOKS LIKE A GORILLA !!
TH- THAT'S SCARY...
GORILLA

READ THIS WAY

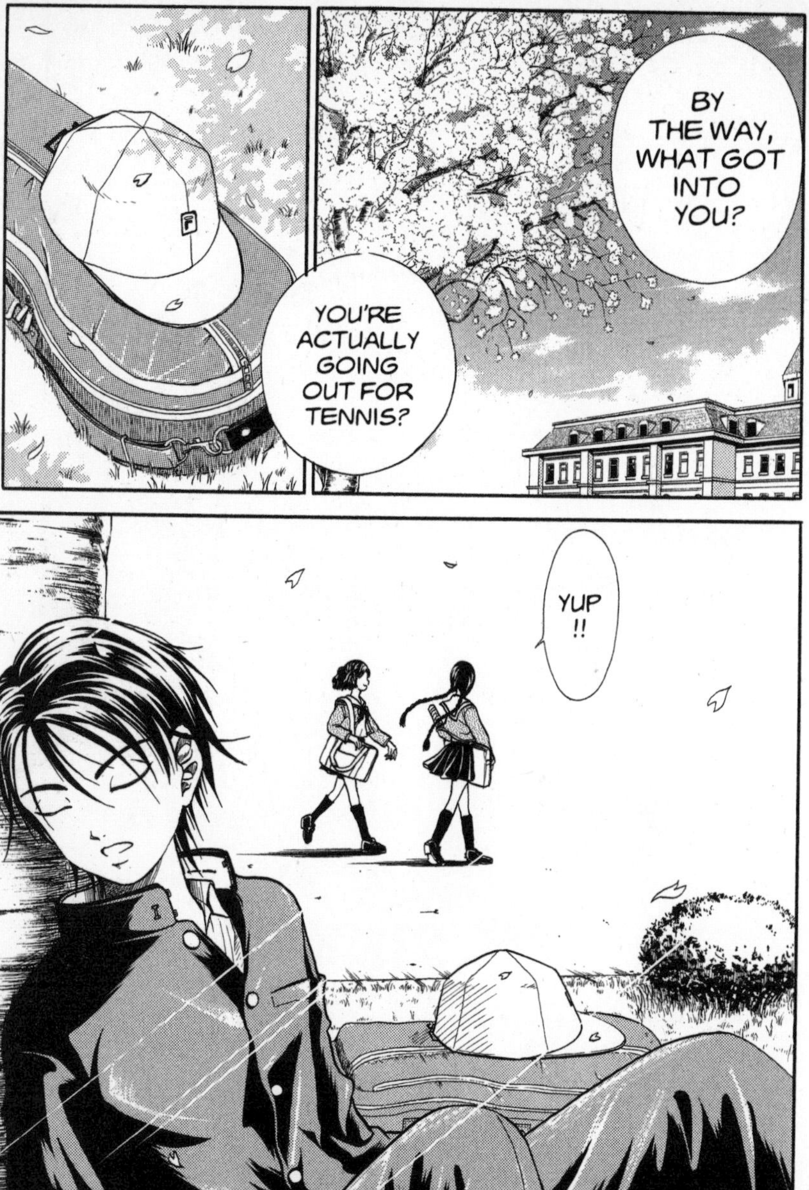
BY THE WAY, WHAT GOT INTO YOU?
YOU'RE ACTUALLY GOING OUT FOR TENNIS?
YUP !!

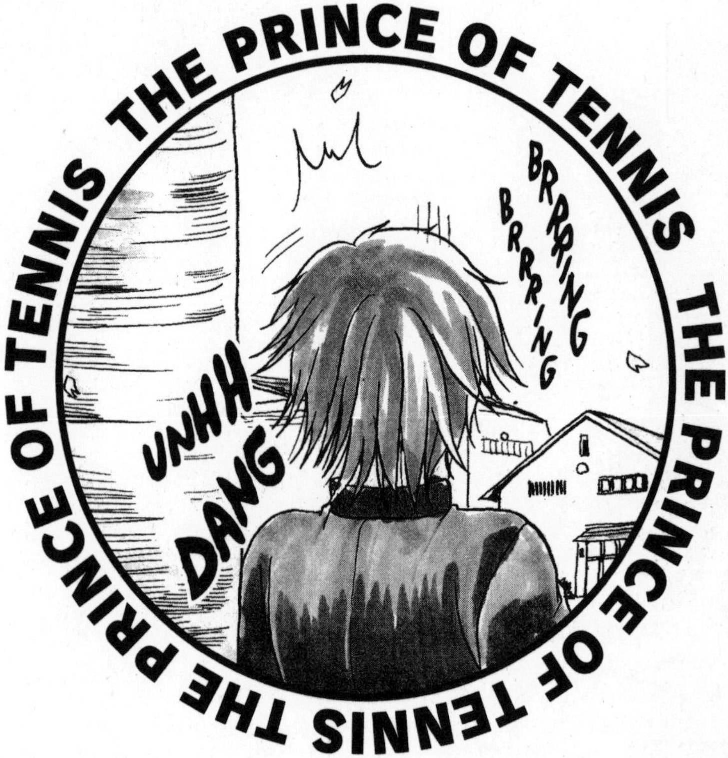
THE PRINCE OF TENNIS THE PRINCE OF TENNIS THE PRINCE OF TENNIS
BRRRRING
BRRRRING
UNHH
DANG

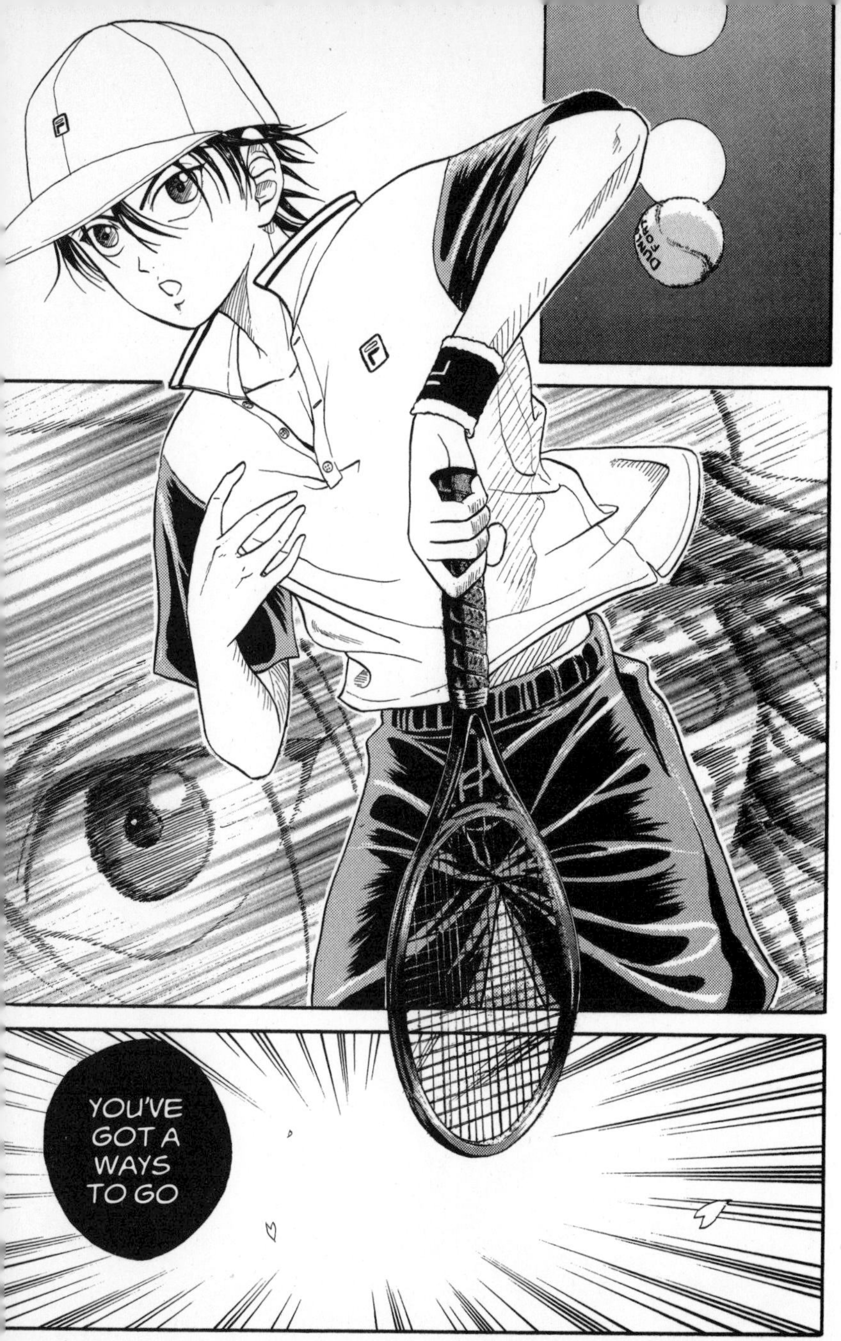
YOU'VE GOT A WAYS TO GO

Genius 2 WOLF IN SHEEP'S CLOTHING

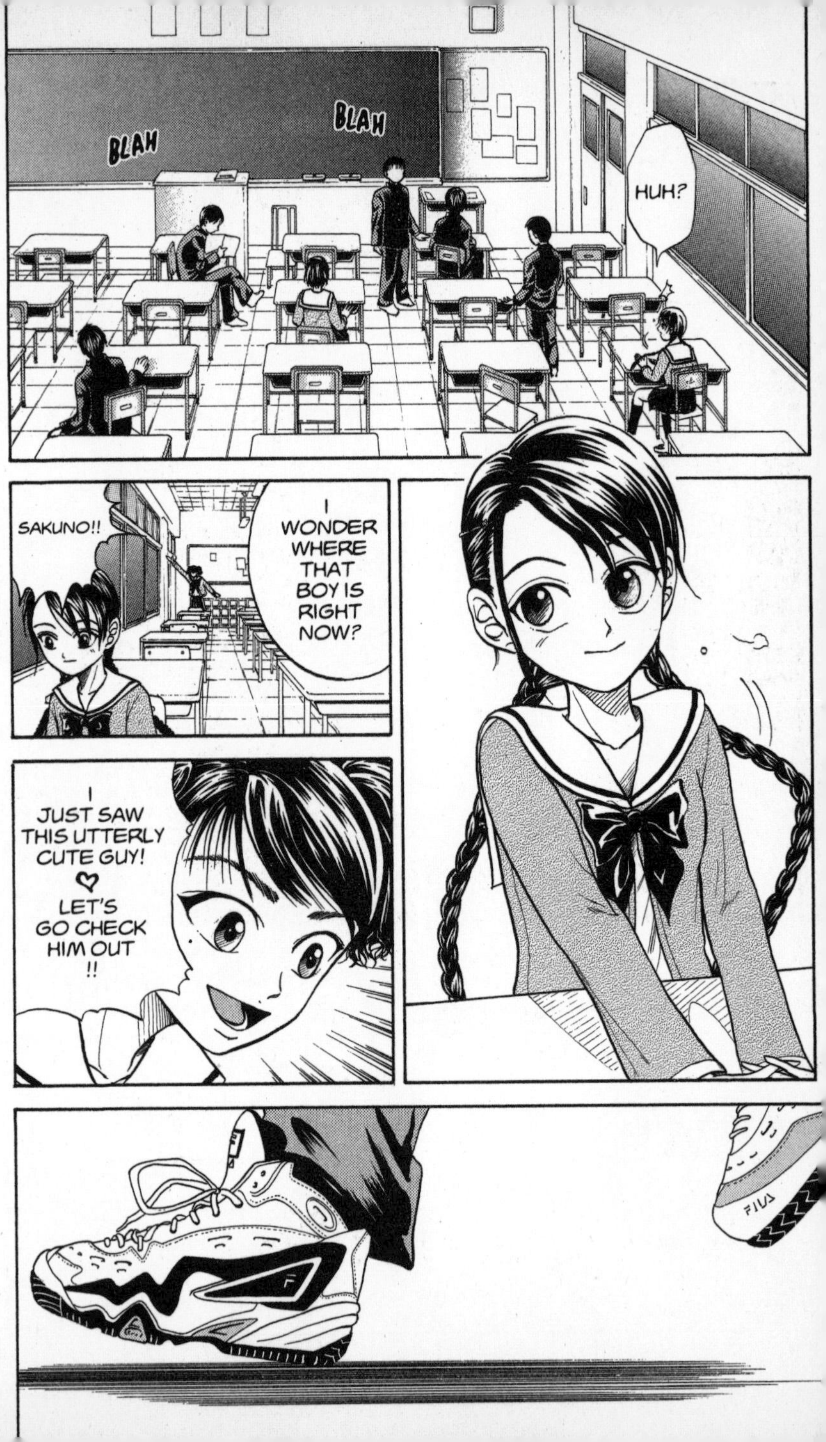
HUH?
BLAH
BLAH
I WONDER WHERE THAT BOY IS RIGHT NOW?
SAKUNO!!
I JUST SAW THIS UTTERLY CUTE GUY! ♡ LET'S GO CHECK HIM OUT !!

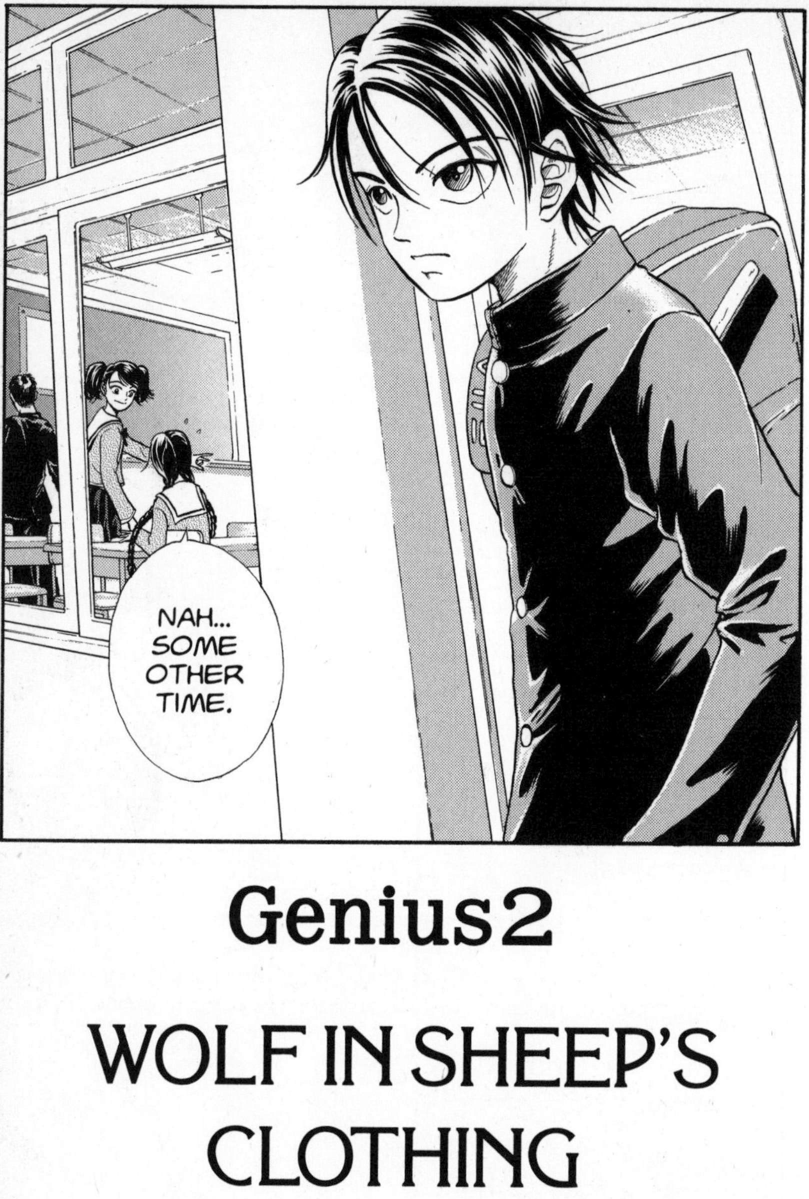
NAH... SOME OTHER TIME.

Genius 2

WOLF IN SHEEP'S CLOTHING

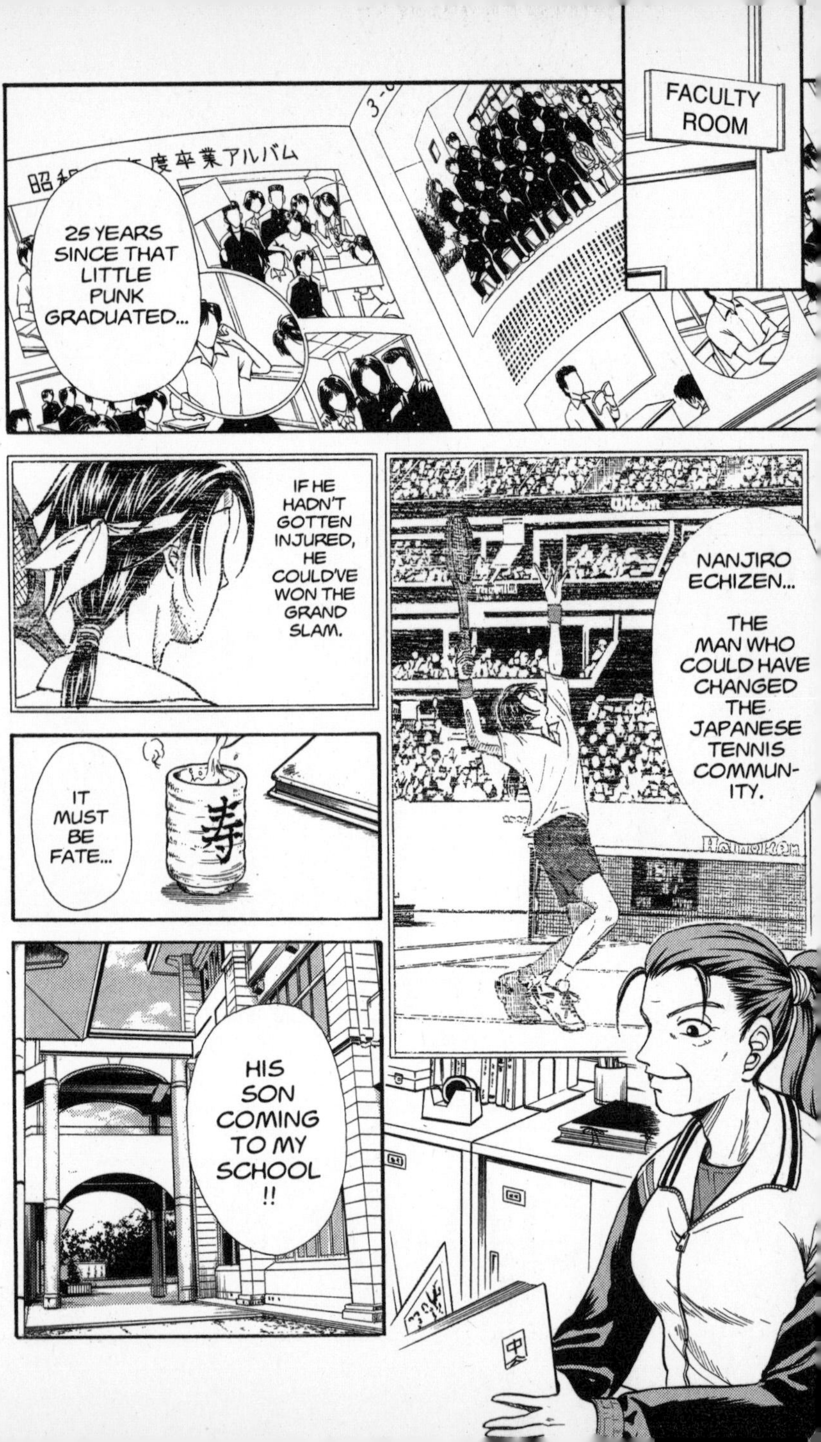
FACULTY ROOM
25 YEARS SINCE THAT LITTLE PUNK GRADUATED...
NANJIRO ECHIZEN... THE MAN WHO COULD HAVE CHANGED THE JAPANESE TENNIS COMMUN-ITY.
IF HE HADN'T GOTTEN INJURED, HE COULD'VE WON THE GRAND SLAM.
IT MUST BE FATE...
HIS SON COMING TO MY SCHOOL !!

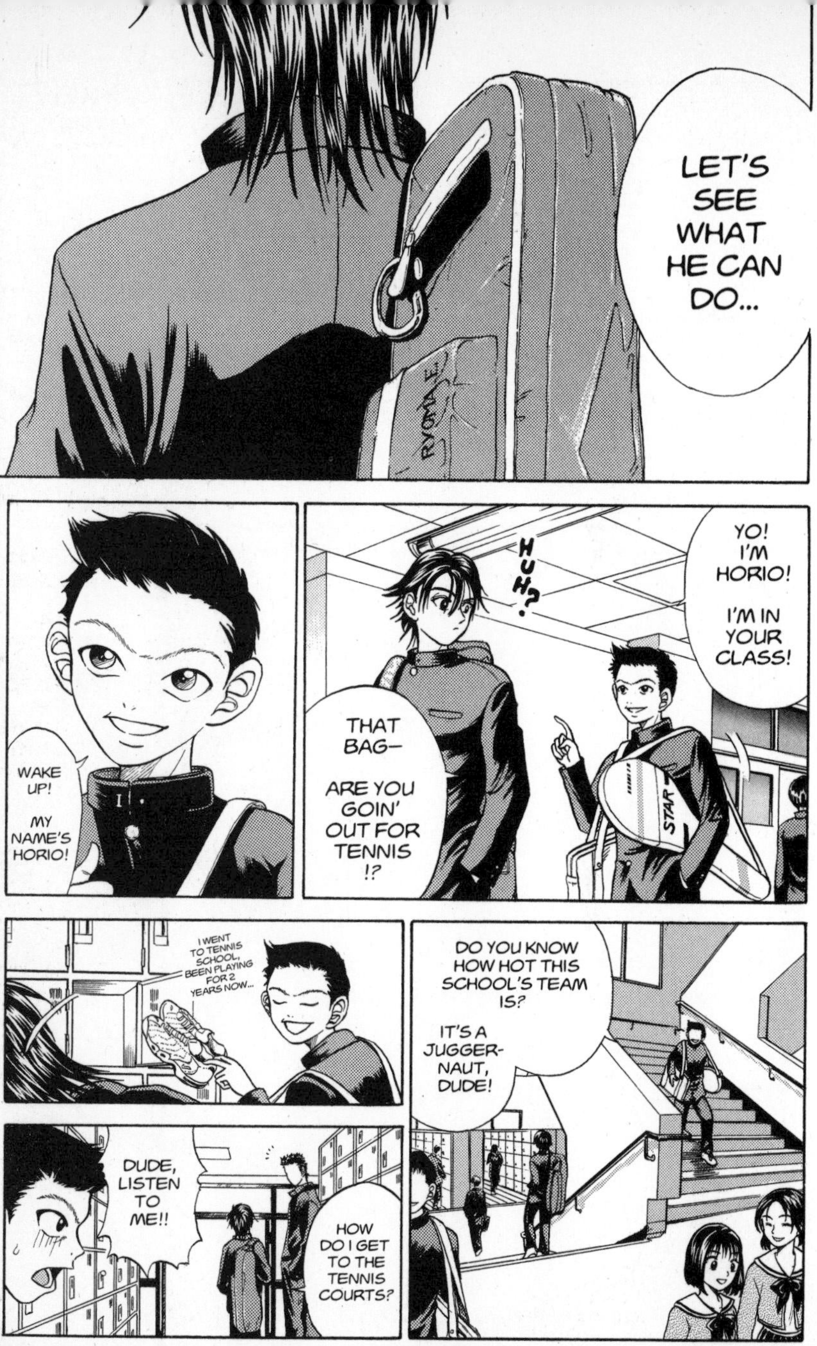
LET'S SEE WHAT HE CAN DO...
YO! I'M HORIO!
I'M IN YOUR CLASS!
HUH?
THAT BAG—
ARE YOU GOIN' OUT FOR TENNIS !?
WAKE UP!
MY NAME'S HORIO!
DO YOU KNOW HOW HOT THIS SCHOOL'S TEAM IS?
IT'S A JUGGER-NAUT, DUDE!
I WENT TO TENNIS SCHOOL, BEEN PLAYING FOR 2 YEARS NOW...
HOW DO I GET TO THE TENNIS COURTS?
DUDE, LISTEN TO ME!!

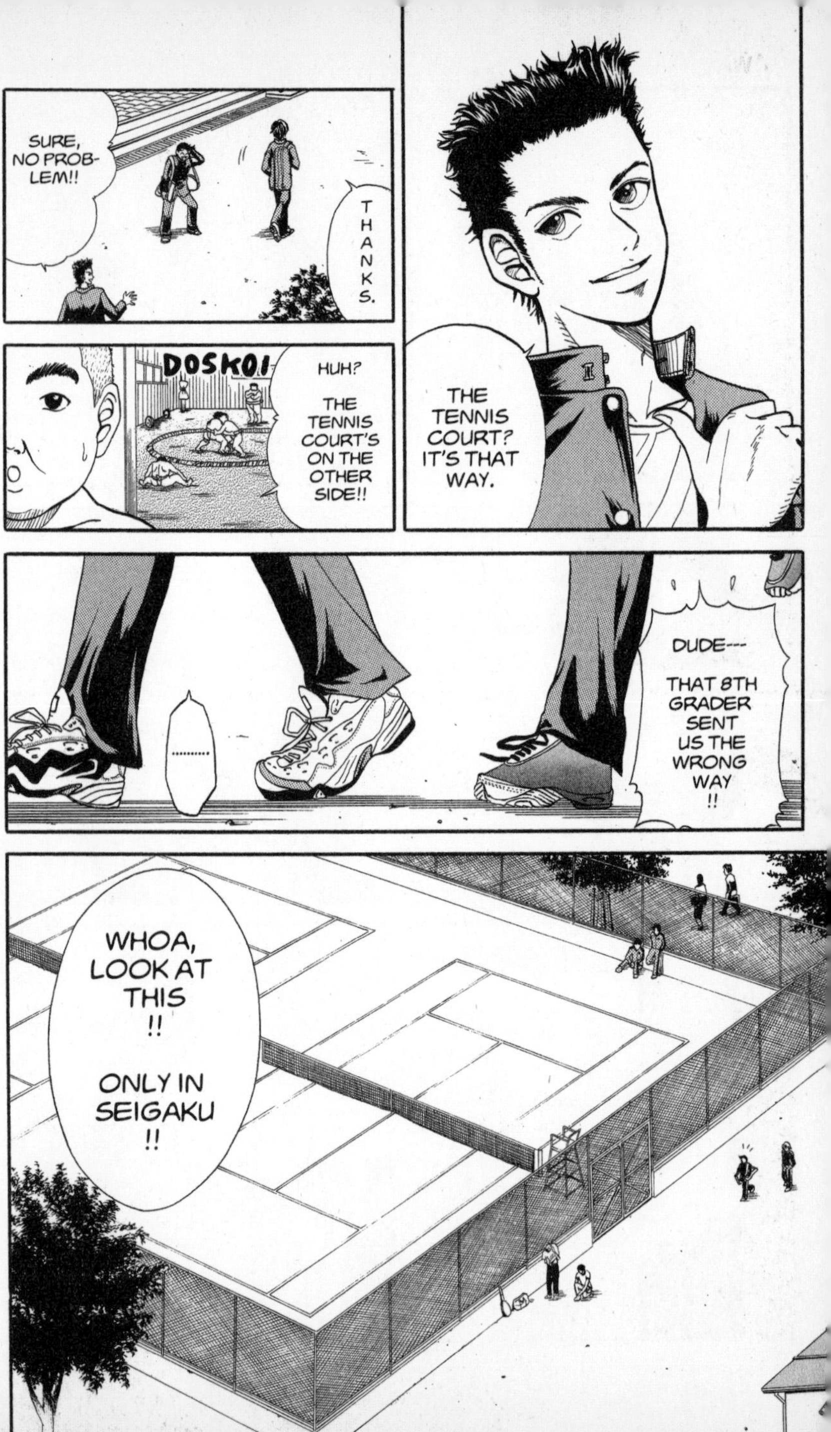
THE TENNIS COURT? IT'S THAT WAY.
THANKS.
SURE, NO PROB-LEM!!
DOSKOI
HUH? THE TENNIS COURT'S ON THE OTHER SIDE!!
DUDE--- THAT 8TH GRADER SENT US THE WRONG WAY !!
....
WHOA, LOOK AT THIS !! ONLY IN SEIGAKU !!

READ THIS WAY

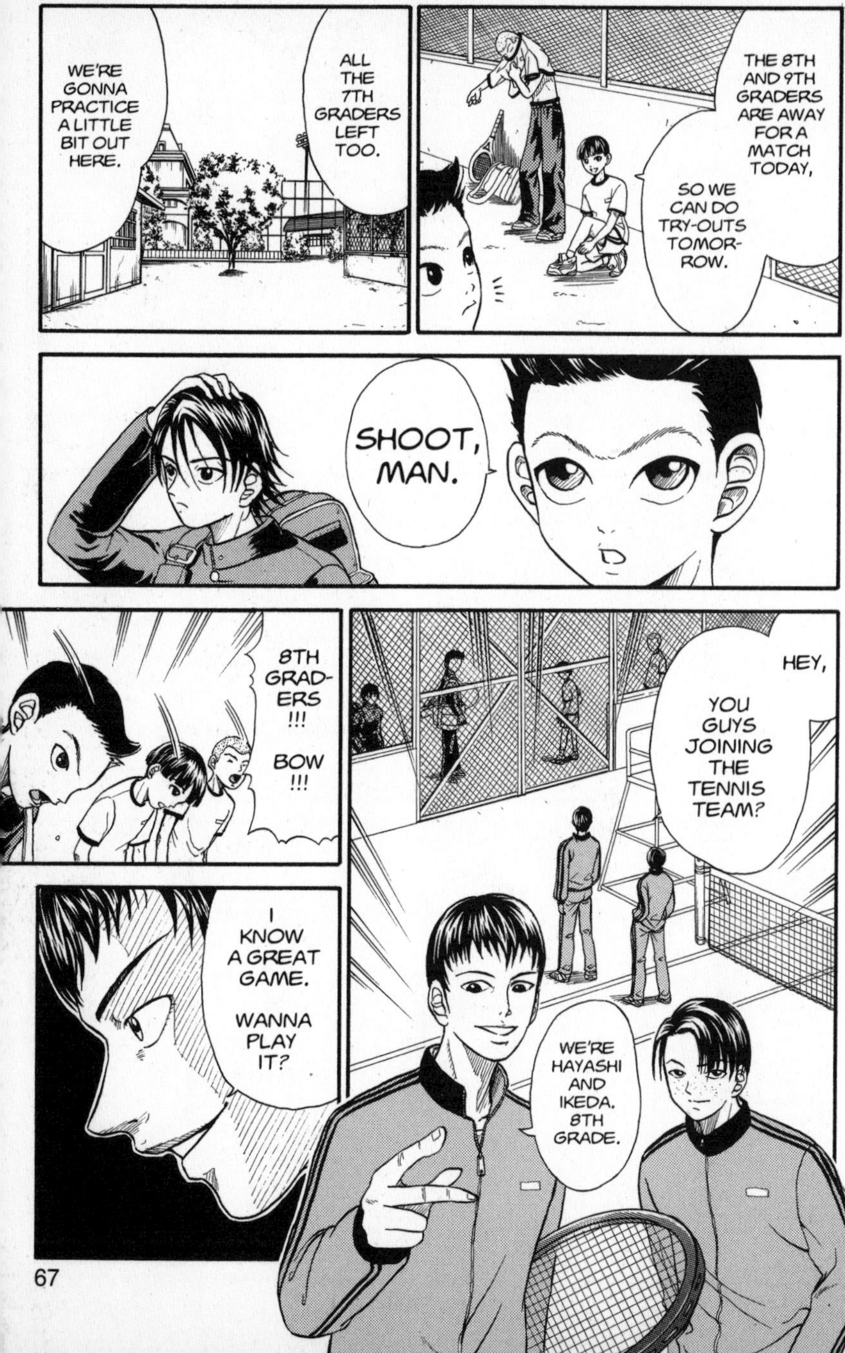

THE 8TH AND 9TH GRADERS ARE AWAY FOR A MATCH TODAY,
SO WE CAN DO TRY-OUTS TOMOR-ROW.
ALL THE 7TH GRADERS LEFT TOO.
WE'RE GONNA PRACTICE A LITTLE BIT OUT HERE.
SHOOT, MAN.
HEY,
YOU GUYS JOINING THE TENNIS TEAM?
WE'RE HAYASHI AND IKEDA. 8TH GRADE.
8TH GRAD-ERS !!!
BOW !!!
I KNOW A GREAT GAME.
WANNA PLAY IT?

READ THIS WAY

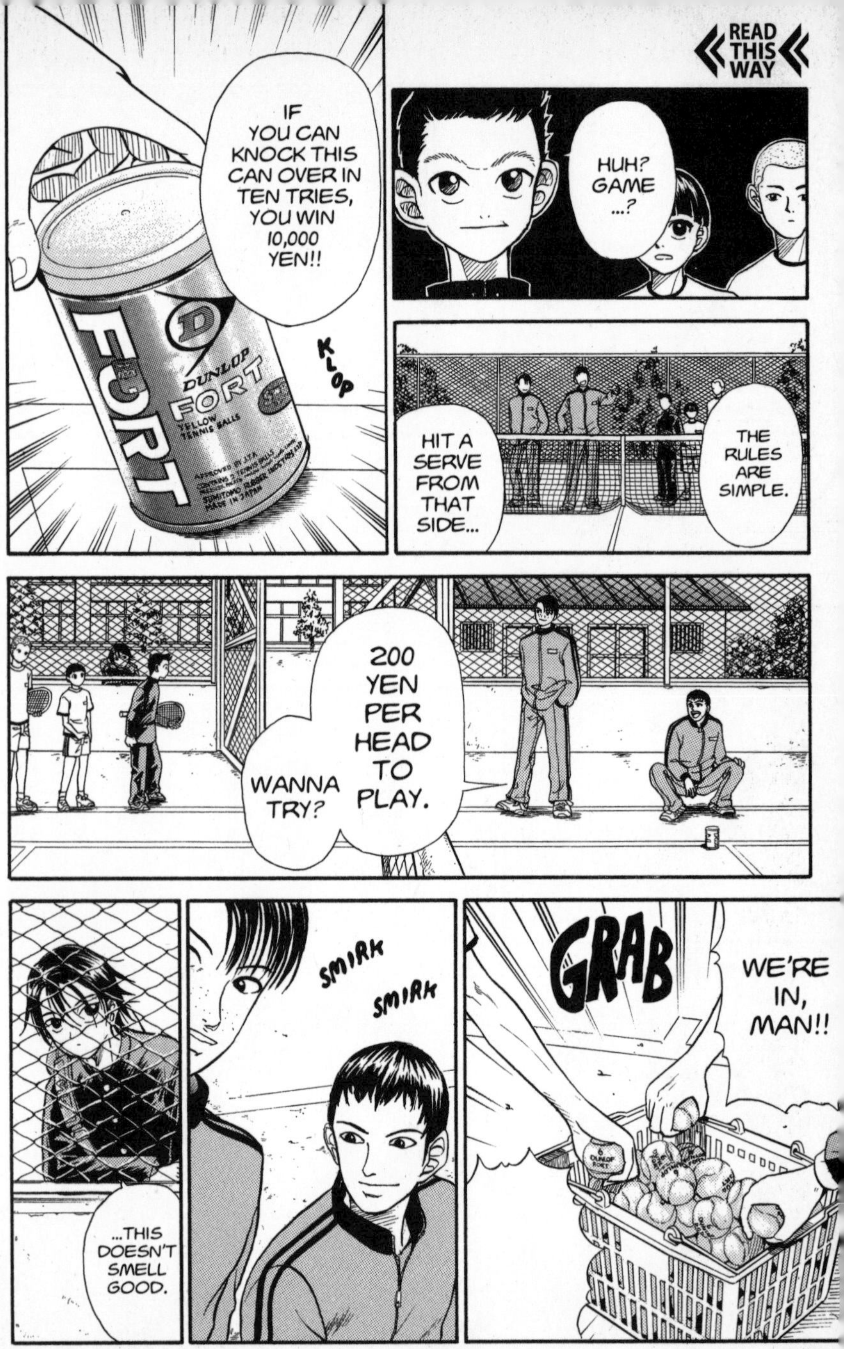
HUH? GAME ...?
THE RULES ARE SIMPLE.
HIT A SERVE FROM THAT SIDE...
IF YOU CAN KNOCK THIS CAN OVER IN TEN TRIES, YOU WIN 10,000 YEN!!
KLOP
DUNLOP FORT YELLOW TENNIS BALLS
200 YEN PER HEAD TO PLAY.
WANNA TRY?
WE'RE IN, MAN!!
GRAB
SMIRK
SMIRK
...THIS DOESN'T SMELL GOOD.

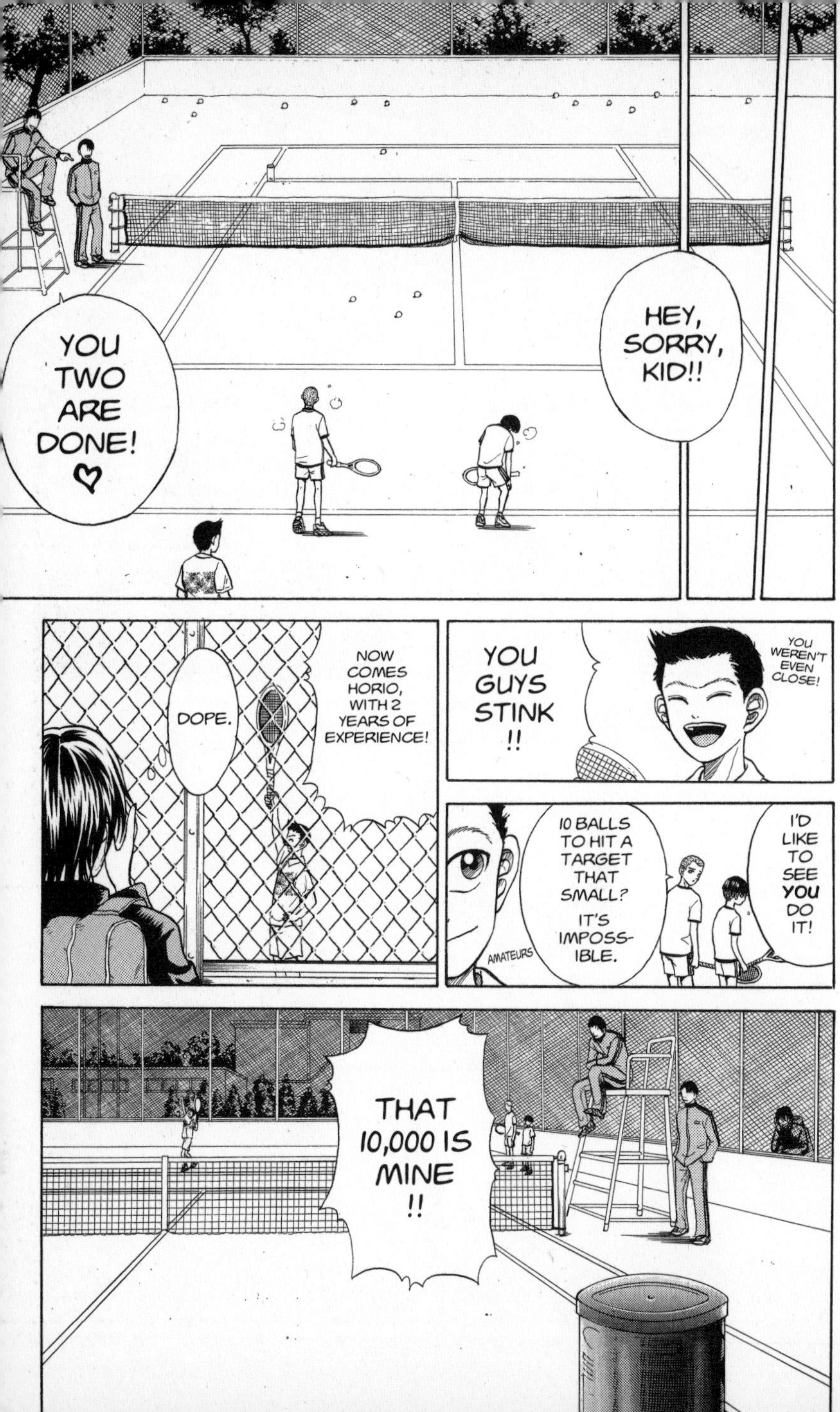
HEY, SORRY, KID!!
YOU TWO ARE DONE! ♡
YOU WEREN'T EVEN CLOSE!
YOU GUYS STINK!!
I'D LIKE TO SEE **YOU** DO IT!
10 BALLS TO HIT A TARGET THAT SMALL? IT'S IMPOSSIBLE.
AMATEURS
NOW COMES HORIO, WITH 2 YEARS OF EXPERIENCE!
DOPE.
THAT 10,000 IS MINE!!

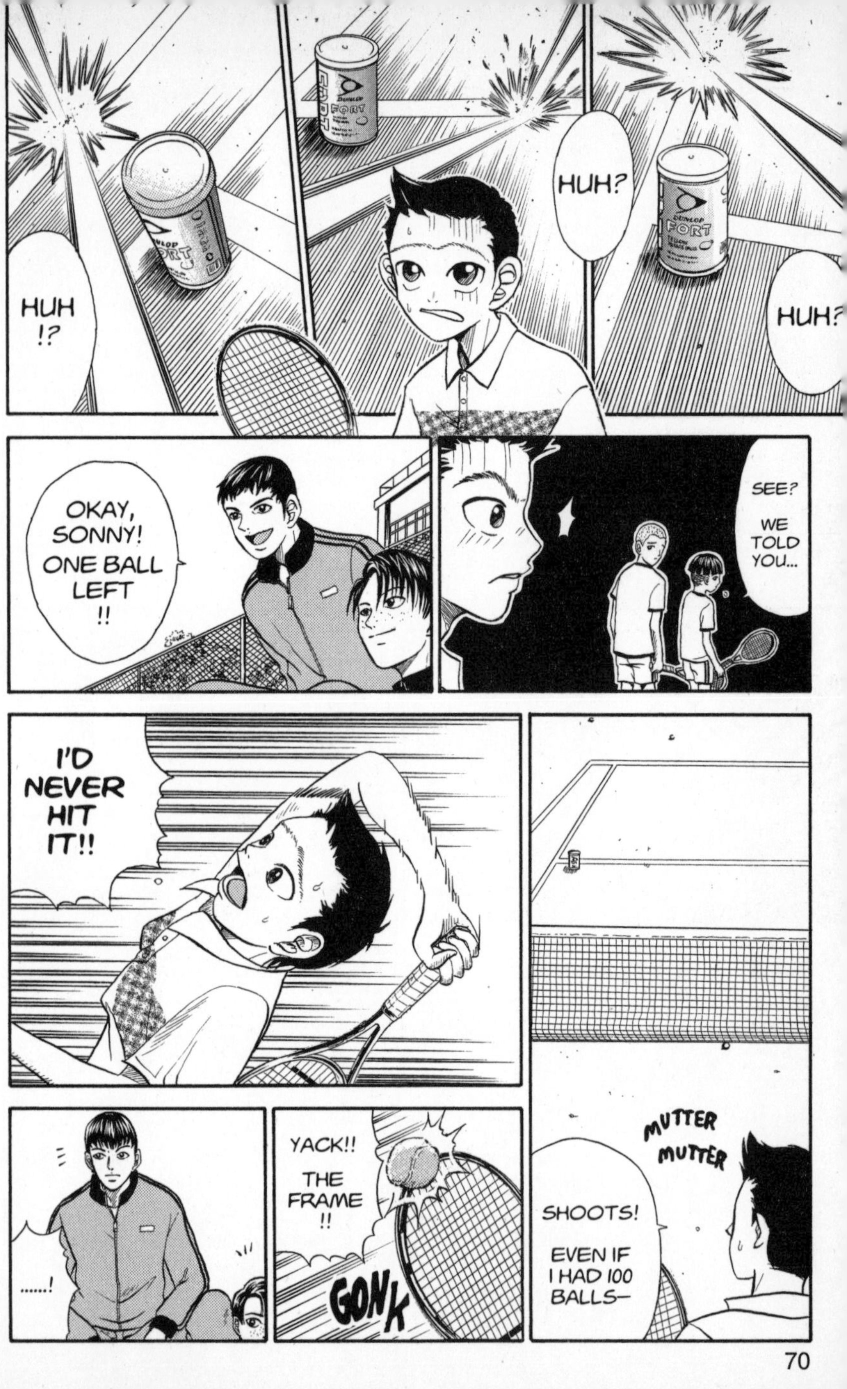
HUH?
HUH?
HUH !?
SEE? WE TOLD YOU...
OKAY, SONNY! ONE BALL LEFT !!
MUTTER MUTTER
SHOOTS! EVEN IF I HAD 100 BALLS—
I'D NEVER HIT IT!!
YACK!! THE FRAME !!
GONK
......!

READ THIS WAY

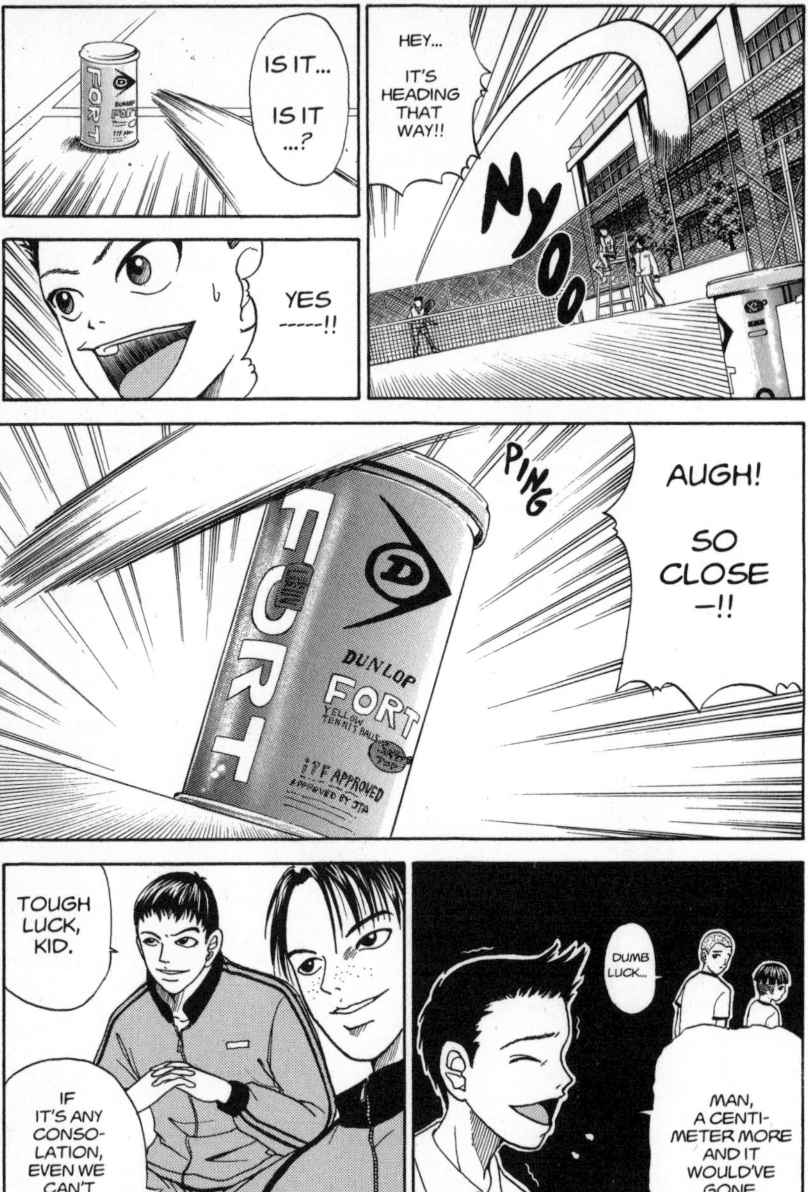
HEY... IT'S HEADING THAT WAY!!
NYOOO
IS IT... IS IT ...?
YES -----!!
PING
AUGH! SO CLOSE —!!
DUNLOP
FORT
YELLOW TENNIS BALLS
ITF APPROVED
DUMB LUCK...
MAN, A CENTI-METER MORE AND IT WOULD'VE GONE DOWN~~
TOUGH LUCK, KID.
IF IT'S ANY CONSO-LATION, EVEN WE CAN'T DO IT.

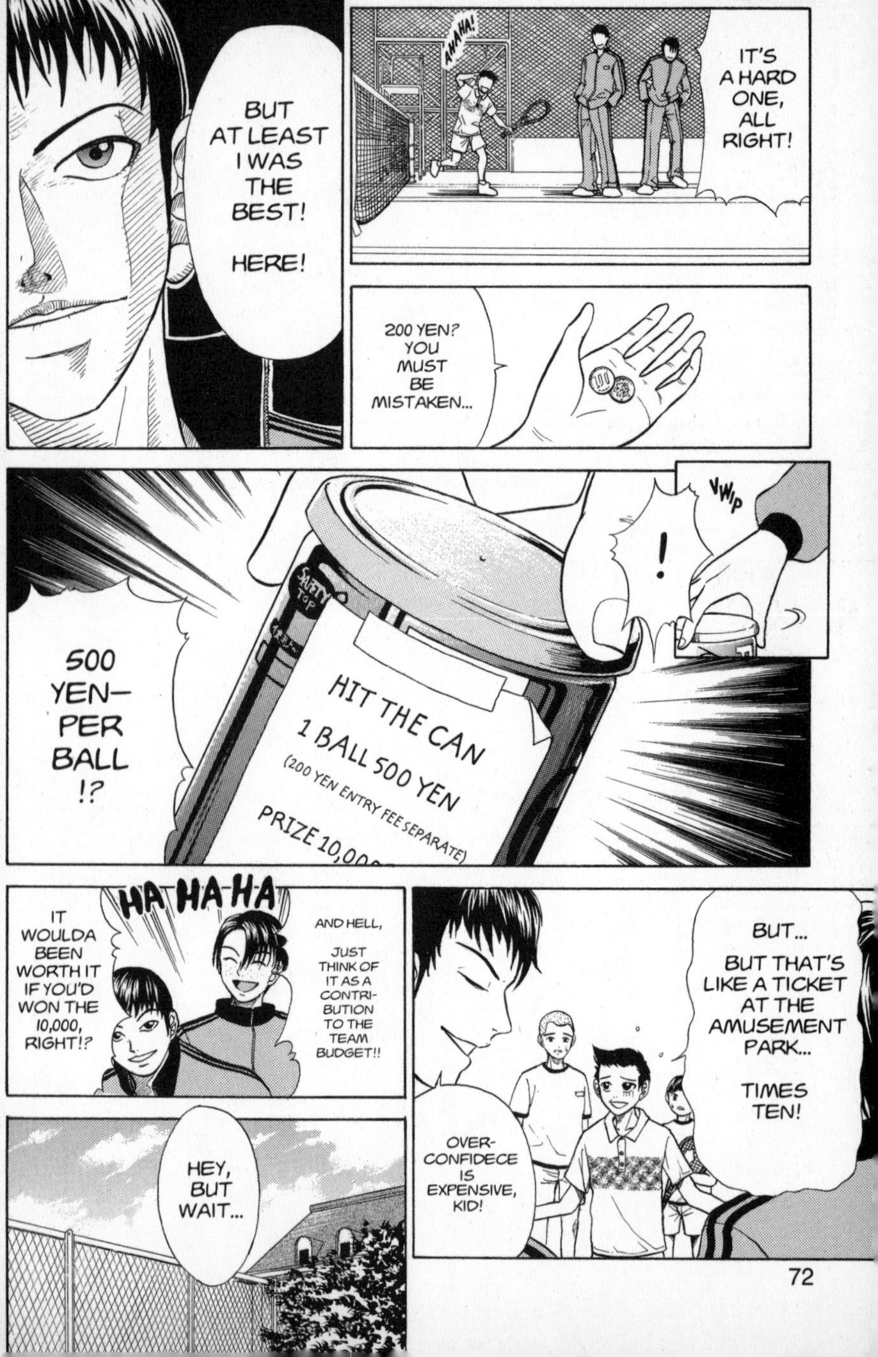
READ THIS WAY
AHAHA!
IT'S A HARD ONE, ALL RIGHT!
200 YEN? YOU MUST BE MISTAKEN...
BUT AT LEAST I WAS THE BEST!
HERE!
VWIP
!
500 YEN— PER BALL !?
HIT THE CAN
1 BALL 500 YEN
(200 YEN ENTRY FEE SEPARATE)
PRIZE 10,000
SAFETY TOP
BUT... BUT THAT'S LIKE A TICKET AT THE AMUSEMENT PARK...
TIMES TEN!
OVER-CONFIDECE IS EXPENSIVE, KID!
HA HA HA
AND HELL, JUST THINK OF IT AS A CONTRIBUTION TO THE TEAM BUDGET!!
IT WOULDA BEEN WORTH IT IF YOU'D WON THE 10,000, RIGHT!?
HEY, BUT WAIT...

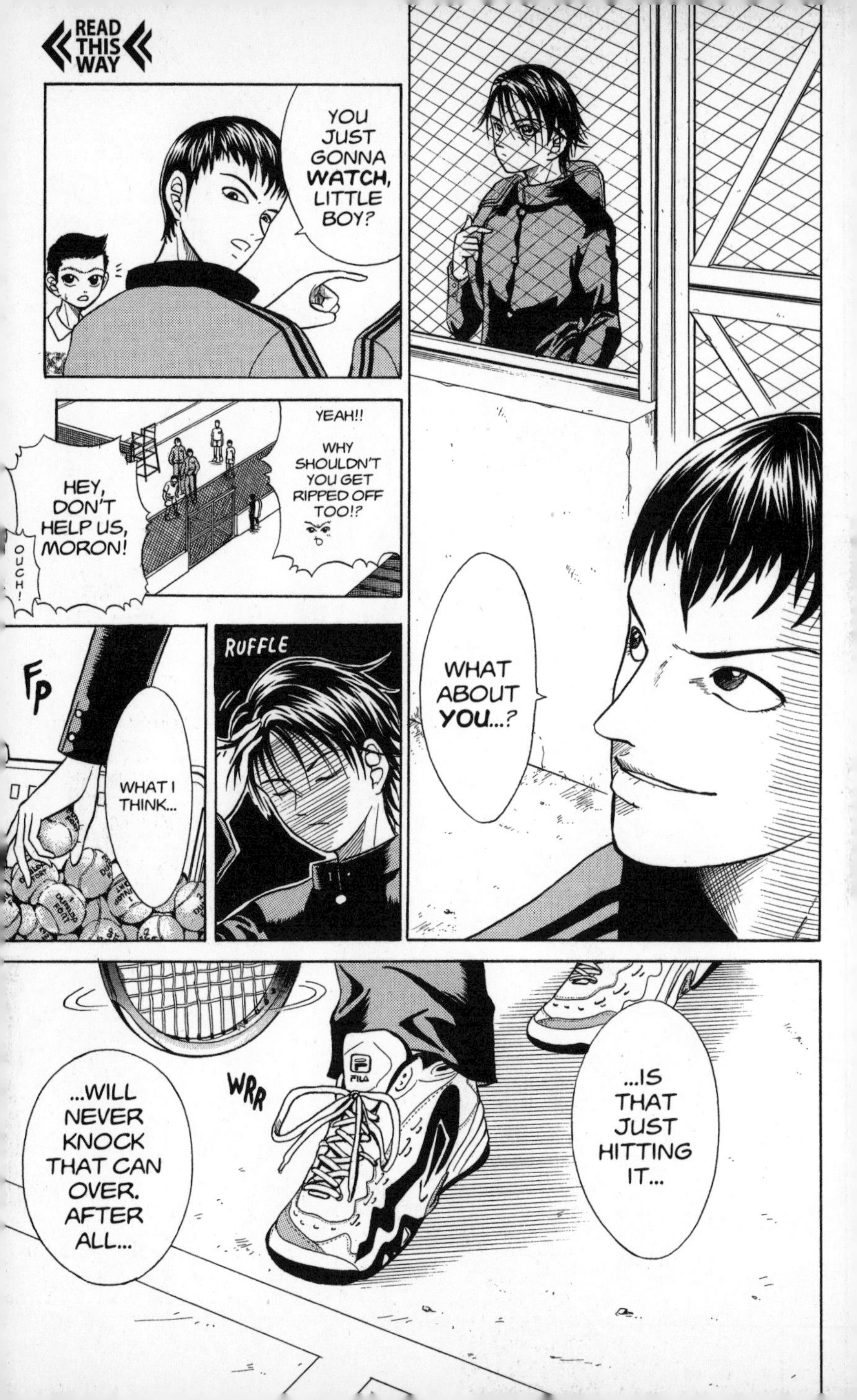
READ THIS WAY
YOU JUST GONNA WATCH, LITTLE BOY?
YEAH!! WHY SHOULDN'T YOU GET RIPPED OFF TOO!?
HEY, DON'T HELP US, MORON!
OUCH!
WHAT ABOUT YOU...?
RUFFLE
FP
WHAT I THINK...
...IS THAT JUST HITTING IT...
WRR
...WILL NEVER KNOCK THAT CAN OVER. AFTER ALL...

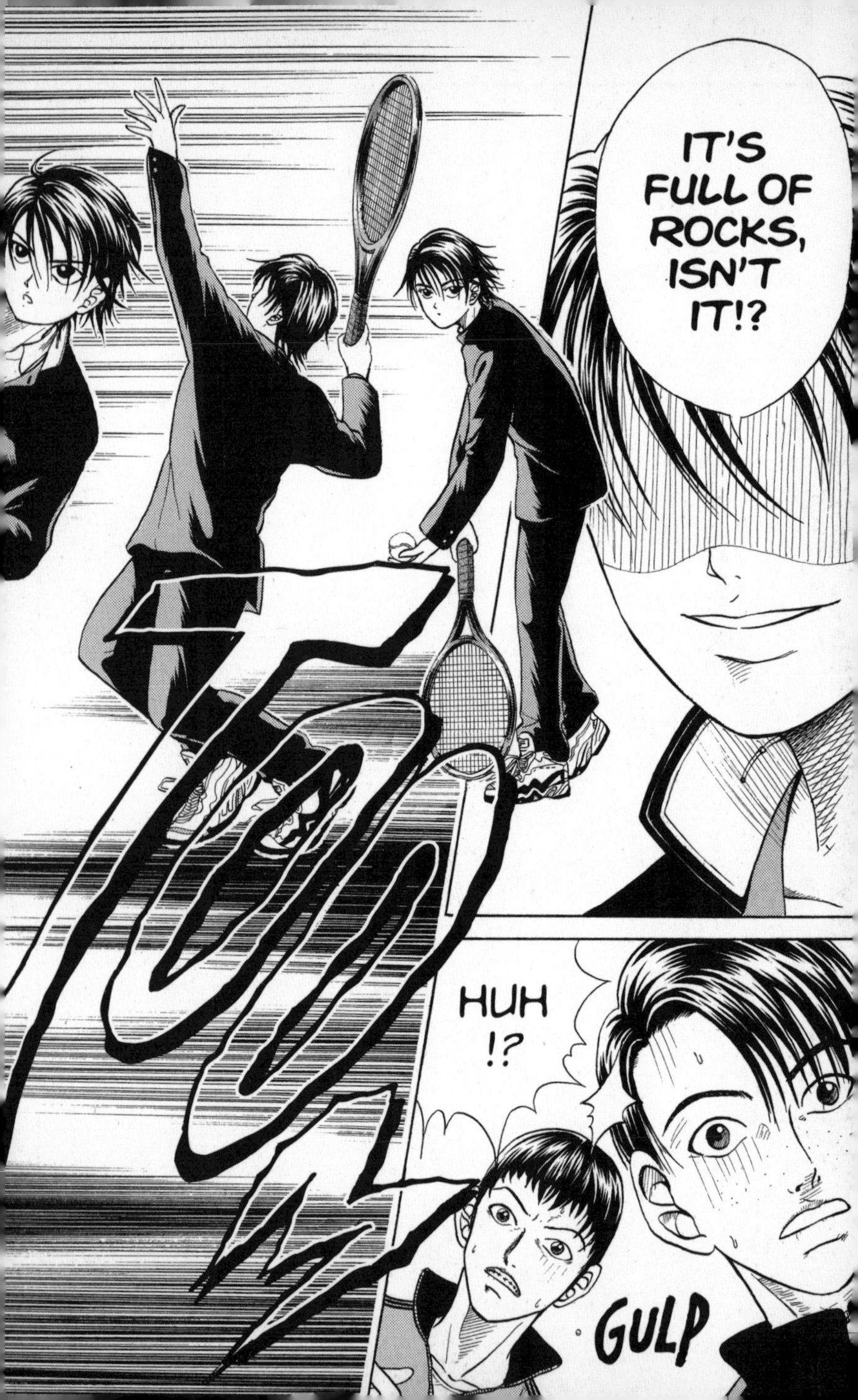
IT'S FULL OF ROCKS, ISN'T IT!?
HUH !?
GULP

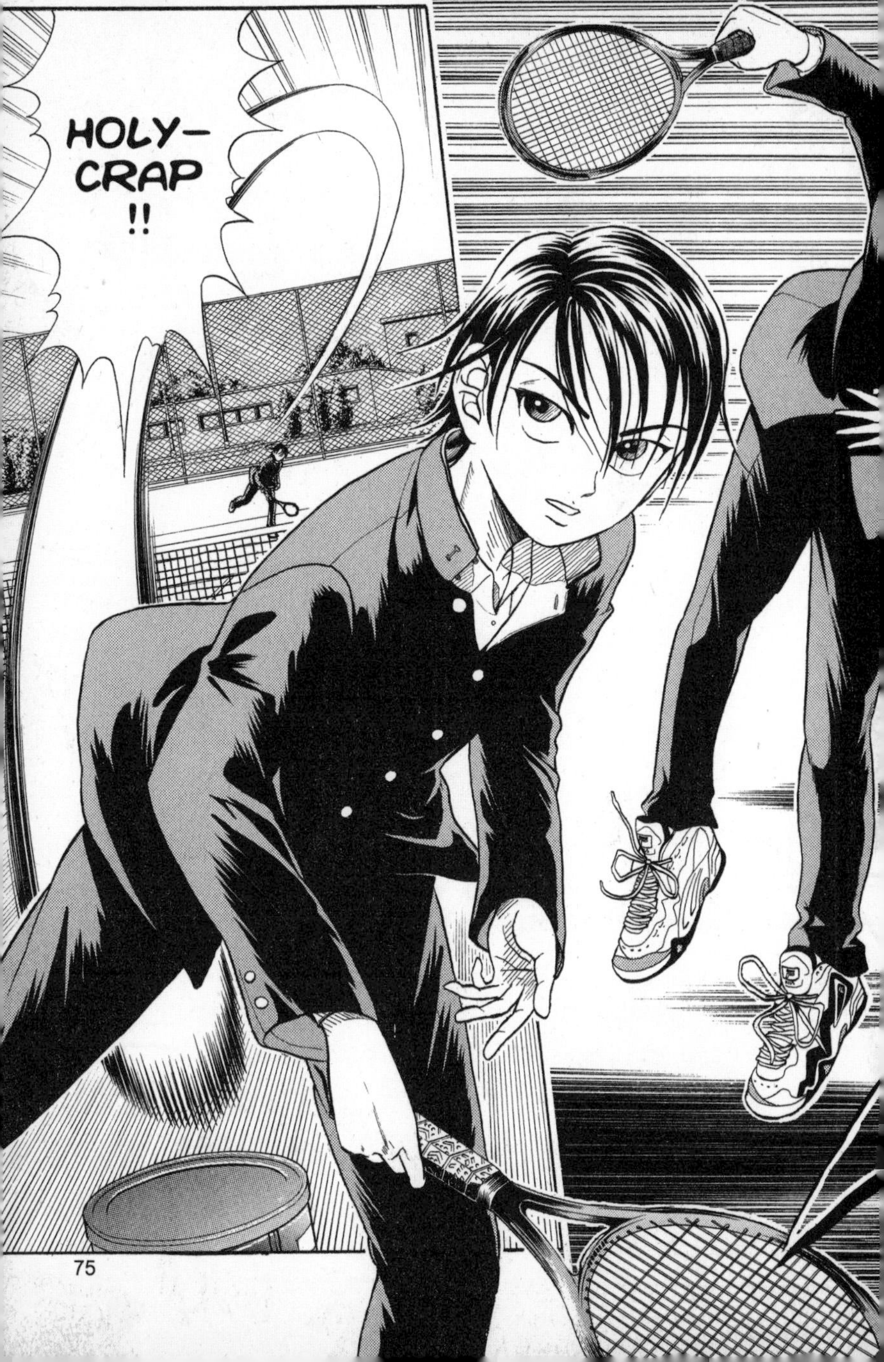
HOLY-
CRAP
!!

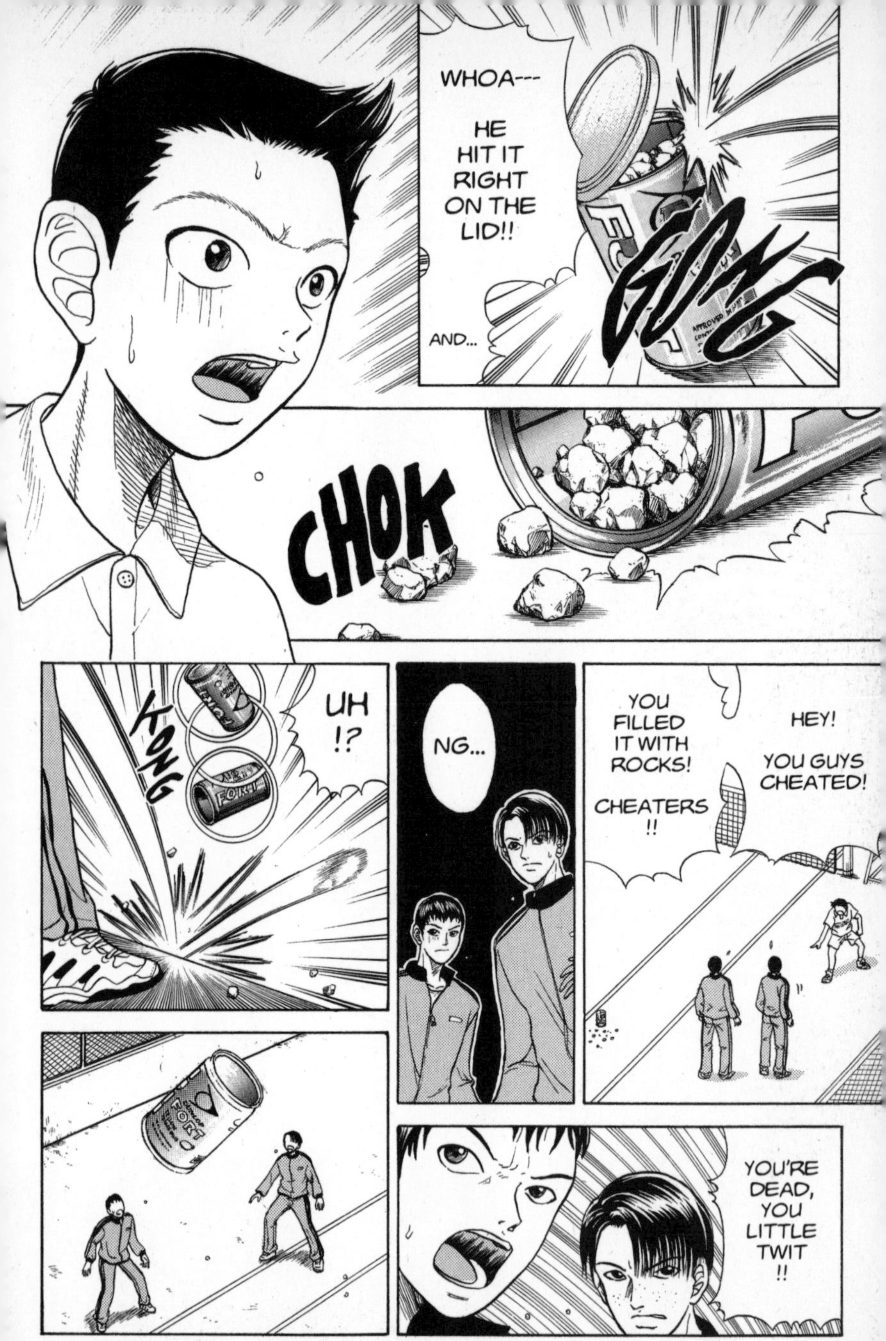
WHOA---
HE HIT IT RIGHT ON THE LID!!
AND...
GONG
CHOK
HEY!
YOU GUYS CHEATED!
YOU FILLED IT WITH ROCKS!
CHEATERS !!
NG...
UH !?
KONG
YOU'RE DEAD, YOU LITTLE TWIT !!

READ THIS WAY

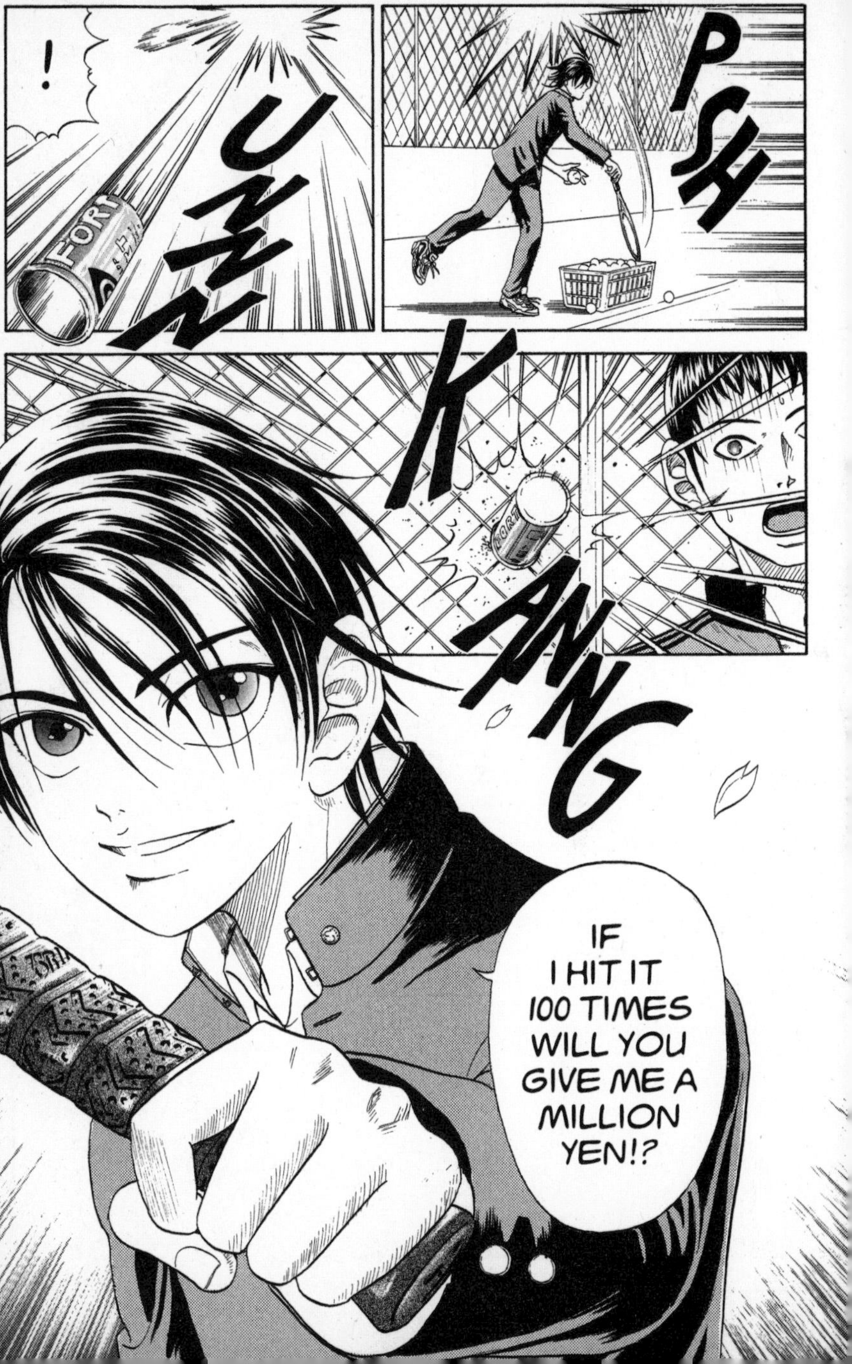
PSH
!
UNNN
KANG
IF I HIT IT 100 TIMES WILL YOU GIVE ME A MILLION YEN!?

READ THIS WAY

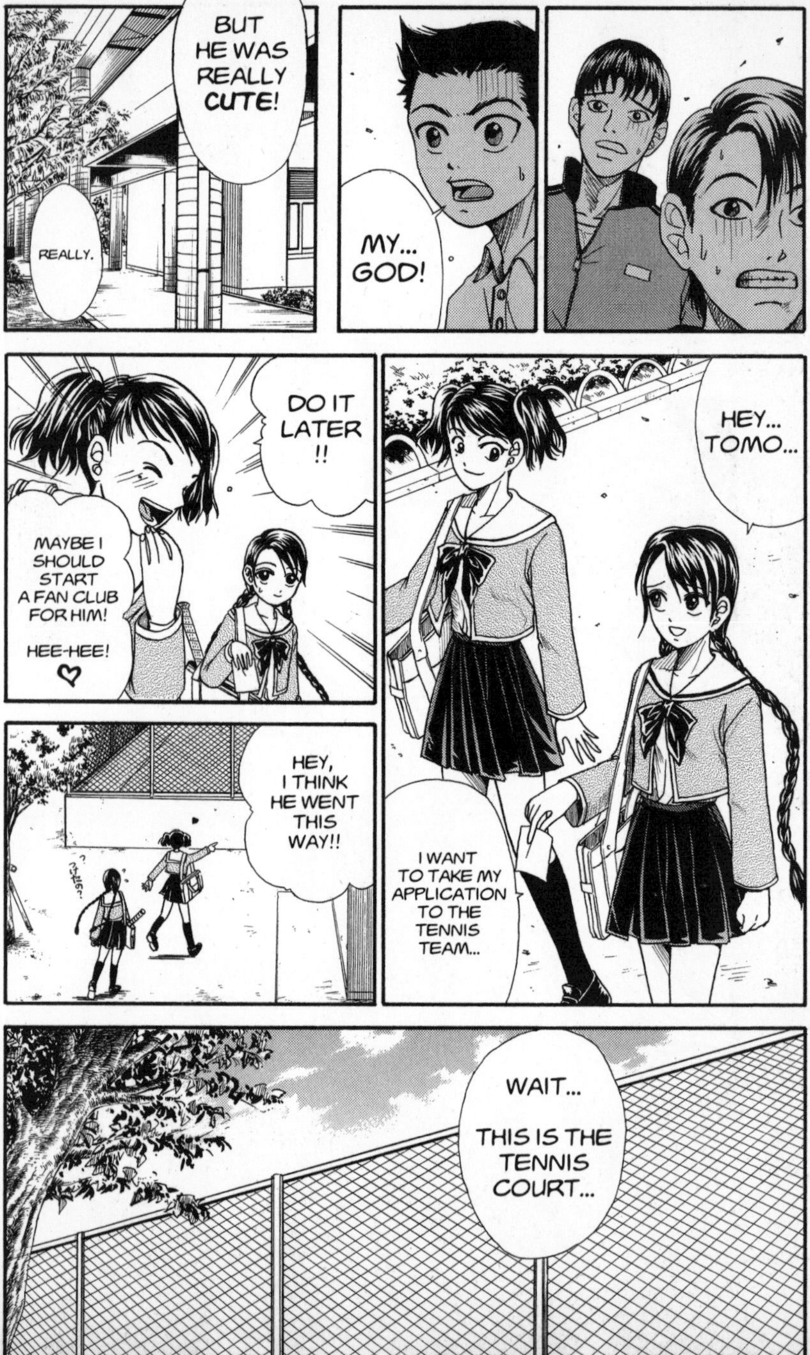
MY... GOD!
BUT HE WAS REALLY CUTE!
REALLY.
HEY... TOMO...
I WANT TO TAKE MY APPLICATION TO THE TENNIS TEAM...
DO IT LATER!!
MAYBE I SHOULD START A FAN CLUB FOR HIM! HEE-HEE! ♡
HEY, I THINK HE WENT THIS WAY!!
WAIT... THIS IS THE TENNIS COURT...

READ THIS WAY

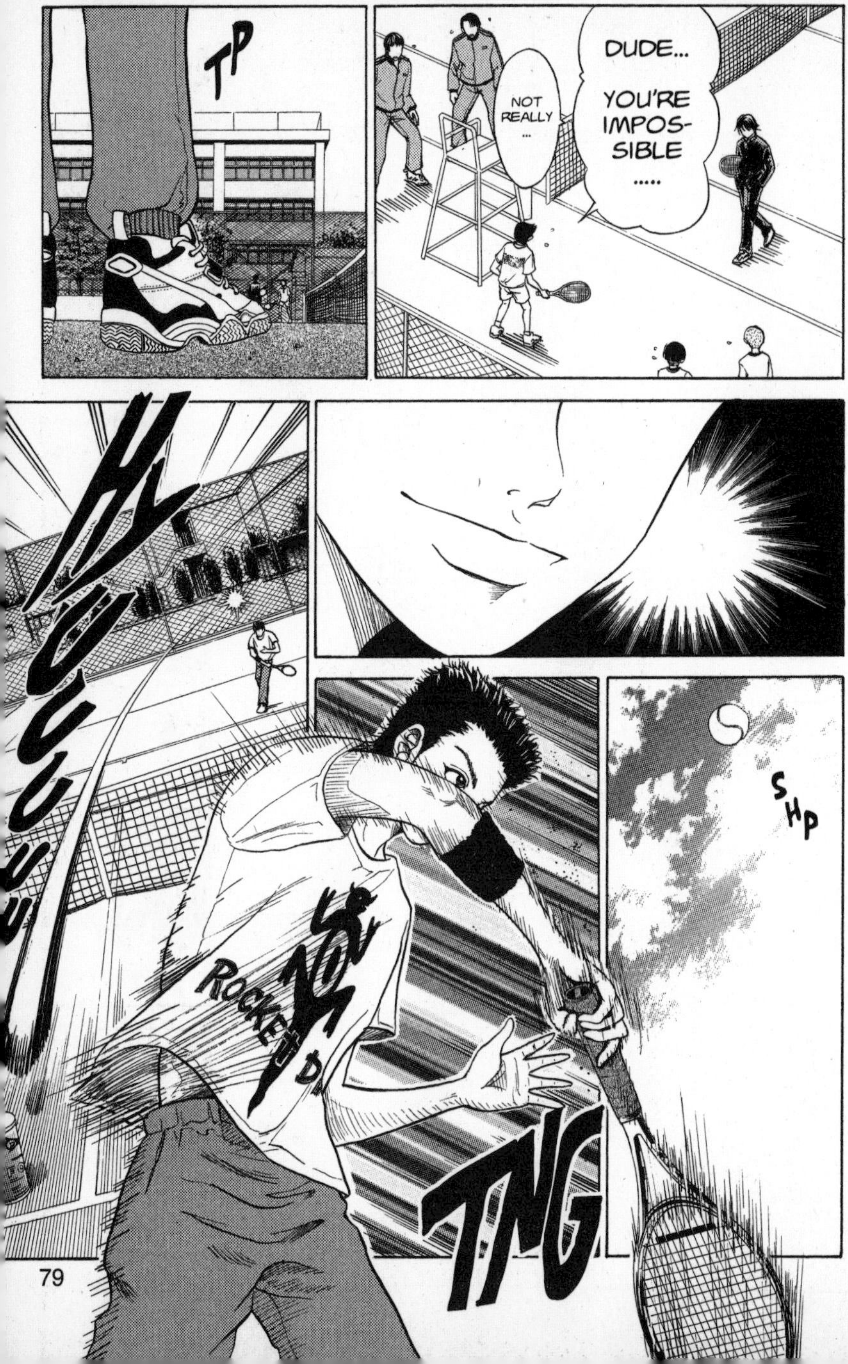
DUDE... YOU'RE IMPOSSIBLE .....
NOT REALLY ...
TP
SHP
TNG
ROCKET D
HYUUUUUU

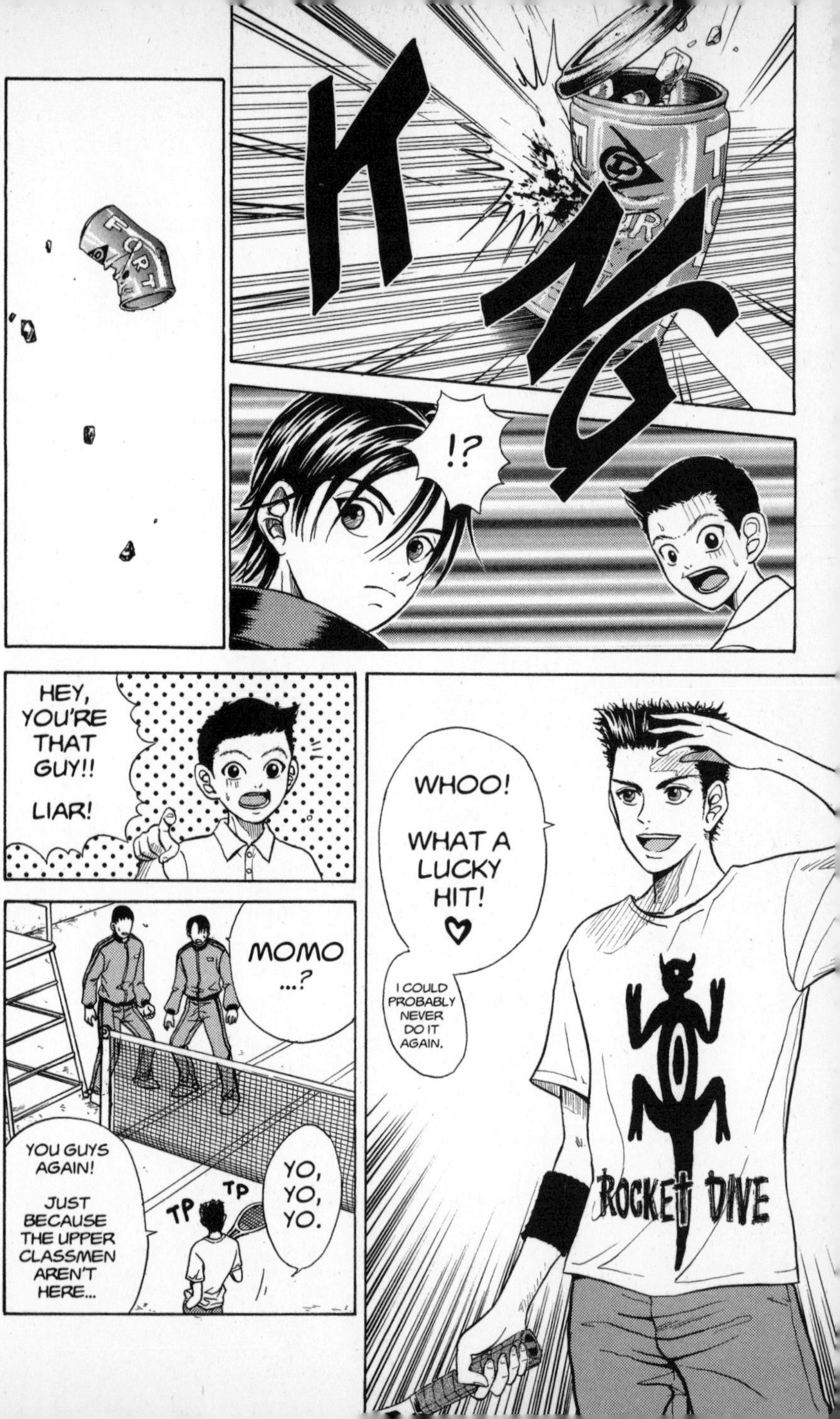
KNG
!?
FORT
WHOO! WHAT A LUCKY HIT! ♥
I COULD PROBABLY NEVER DO IT AGAIN.
ROCKET DIVE
HEY, YOU'RE THAT GUY!! LIAR!
MOMO ...?
YO, YO, YO.
YOU GUYS AGAIN! JUST BECAUSE THE UPPER CLASSMEN AREN'T HERE...
TP TP

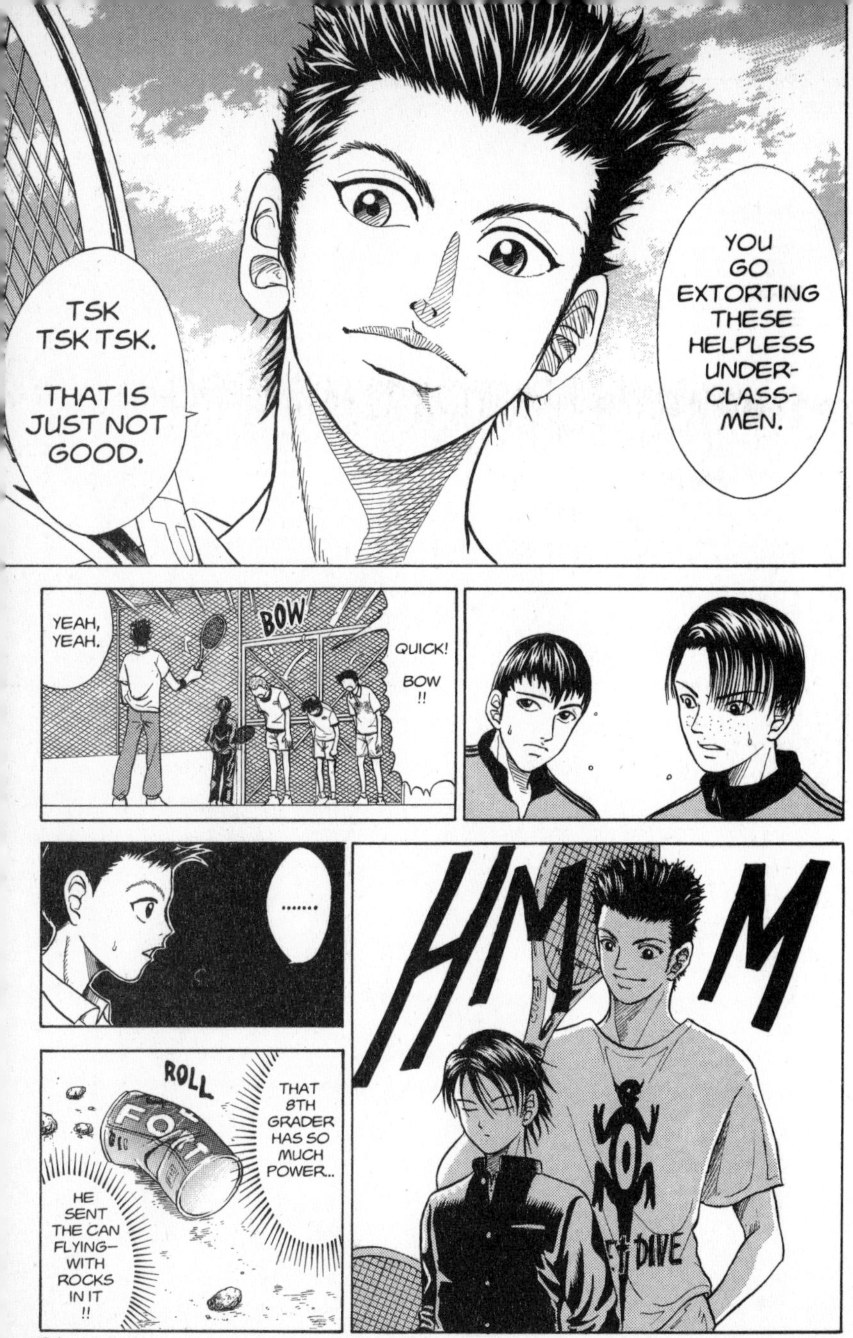
YOU GO EXTORTING THESE HELPLESS UNDER-CLASSMEN.
TSK TSK TSK.
THAT IS JUST NOT GOOD.
QUICK! BOW !!
BOW
YEAH, YEAH.
HMM
......
THAT 8TH GRADER HAS SO MUCH POWER...
ROLL
HE SENT THE CAN FLYING—WITH ROCKS IN IT !!

READ THIS WAY

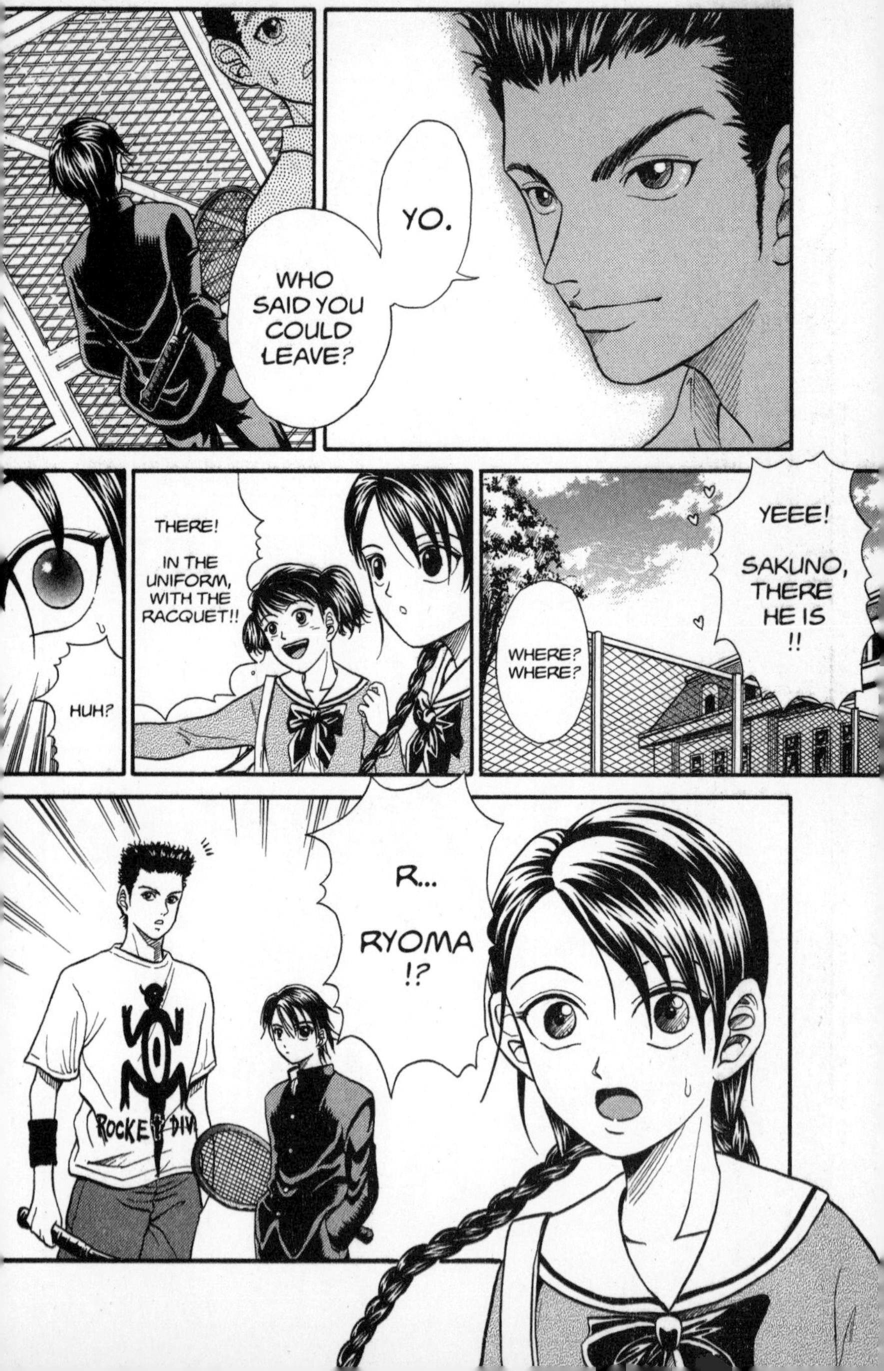
YO.
WHO SAID YOU COULD LEAVE?
YEEE! SAKUNO, THERE HE IS !!
WHERE? WHERE?
THERE! IN THE UNIFORM, WITH THE RACQUET!!
HUH?
R... RYOMA !?

READ THIS WAY

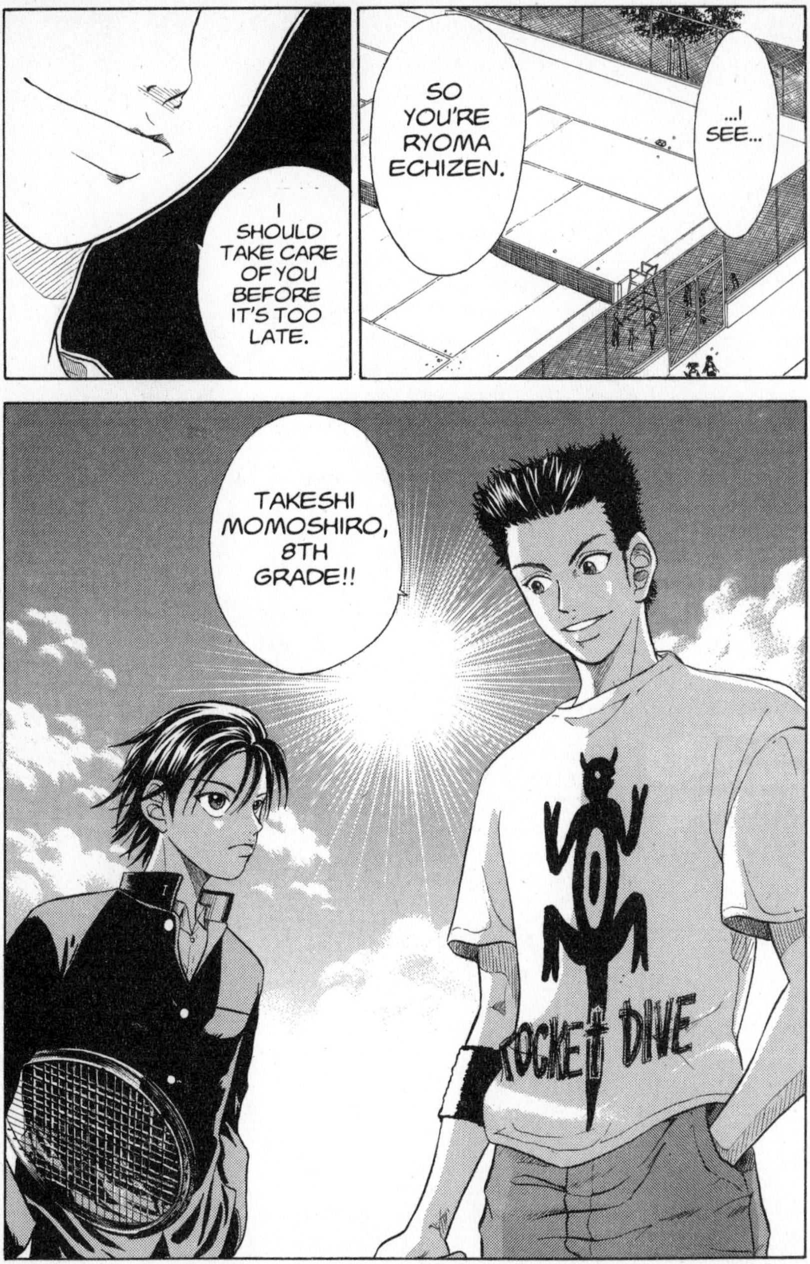
...I SEE...
SO YOU'RE RYOMA ECHIZEN.
I SHOULD TAKE CARE OF YOU BEFORE IT'S TOO LATE.
TAKESHI MOMOSHIRO, 8TH GRADE!!
ROCKET DIVE

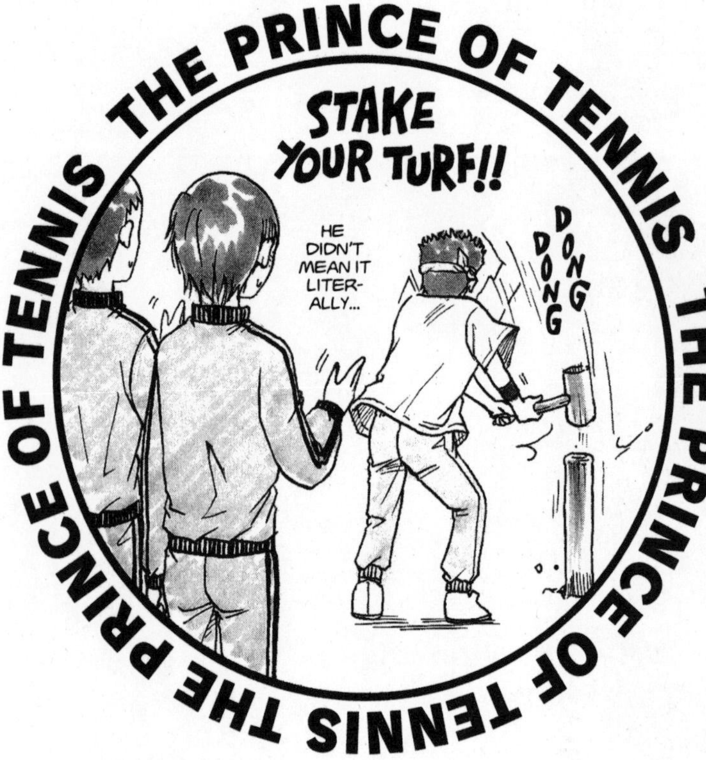
THE PRINCE OF TENNIS THE PRINCE OF TENNIS THE PRINCE OF TENNIS
STAKE YOUR TURF!!
DONG DONG
HE DIDN'T MEAN IT LITER-ALLY...

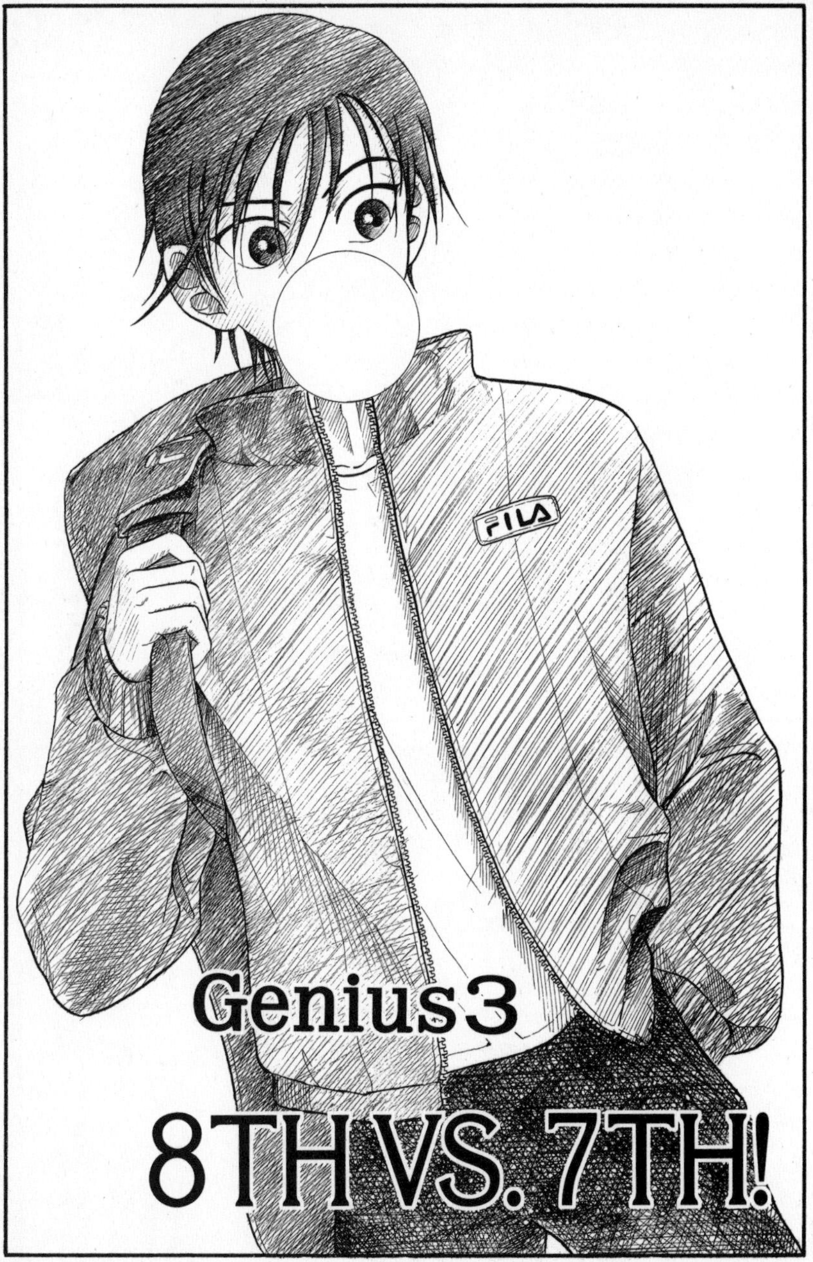
FILA

Genius 3

8TH VS. 7TH!

READ THIS WAY

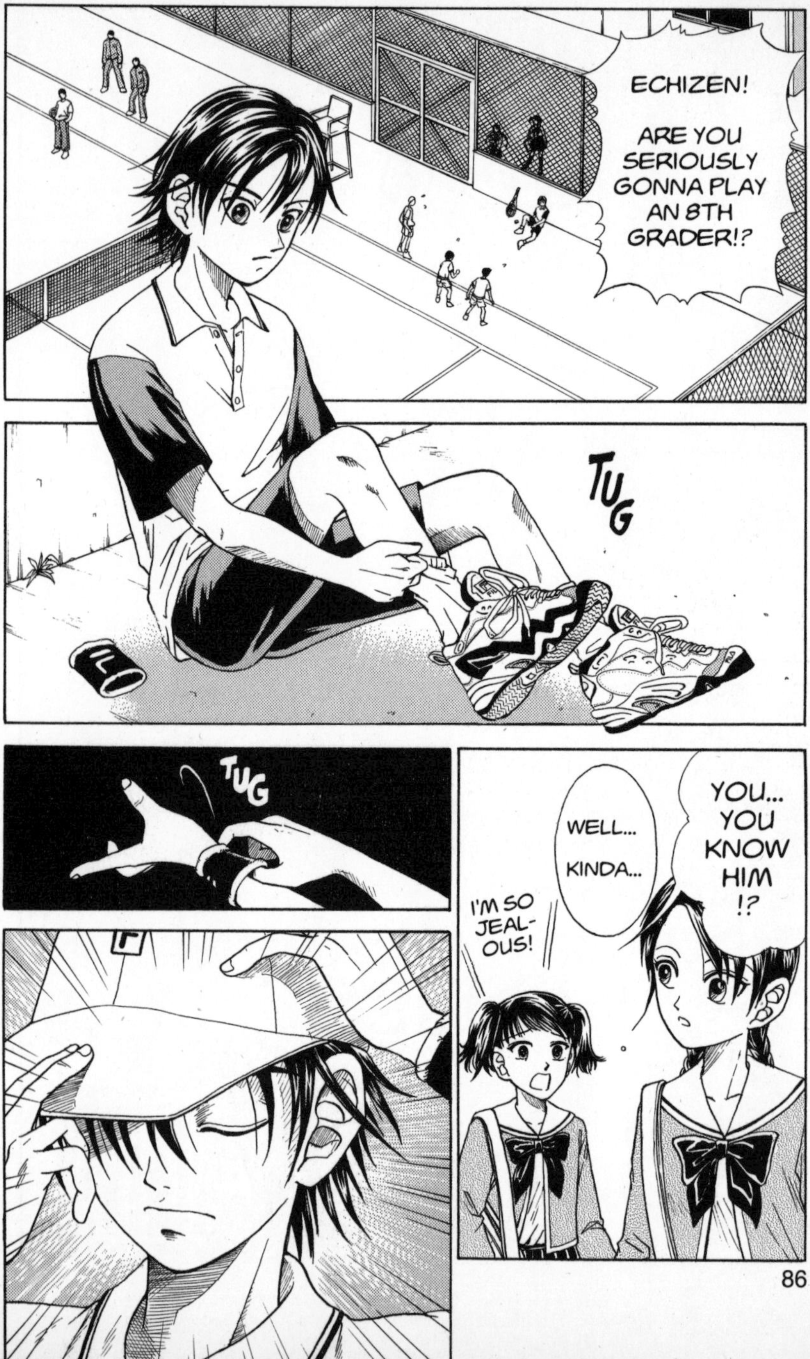
ECHIZEN!
ARE YOU SERIOUSLY GONNA PLAY AN 8TH GRADER!?
TUG
YOU... YOU KNOW HIM!?
WELL... KINDA...
I'M SO JEAL-OUS!
TUG

READ THIS WAY

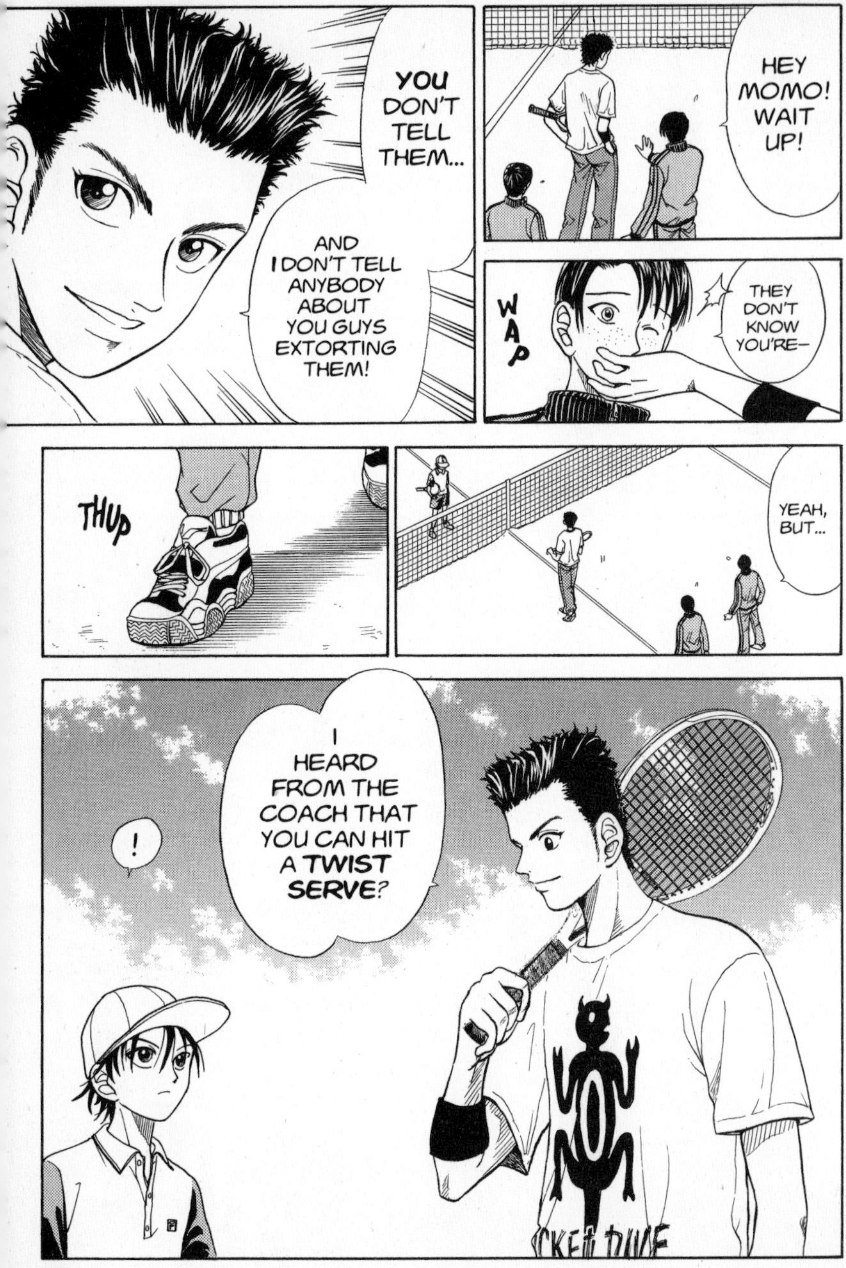
HEY MOMO! WAIT UP!
THEY DON'T KNOW YOU'RE—
WAP
YOU DON'T TELL THEM...
AND I DON'T TELL ANYBODY ABOUT YOU GUYS EXTORTING THEM!
YEAH, BUT...
THUP
I HEARD FROM THE COACH THAT YOU CAN HIT A TWIST SERVE?
!

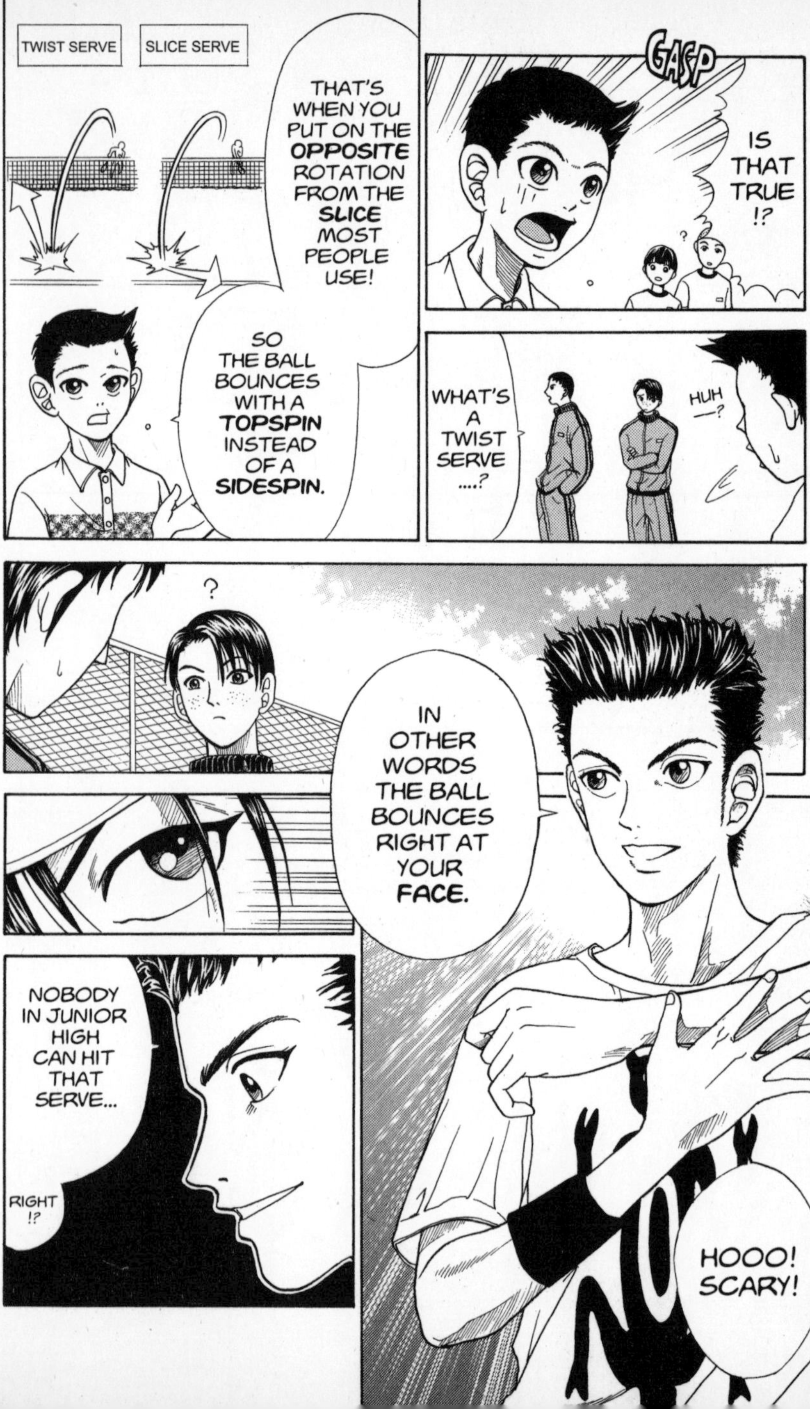
GASP
IS THAT TRUE !?
WHAT'S A TWIST SERVE ....?
HUH —?
TWIST SERVE
SLICE SERVE
THAT'S WHEN YOU PUT ON THE OPPOSITE ROTATION FROM THE SLICE MOST PEOPLE USE!
SO THE BALL BOUNCES WITH A TOPSPIN INSTEAD OF A SIDESPIN.
IN OTHER WORDS THE BALL BOUNCES RIGHT AT YOUR FACE.
HOOO! SCARY!
?
NOBODY IN JUNIOR HIGH CAN HIT THAT SERVE...
RIGHT !?

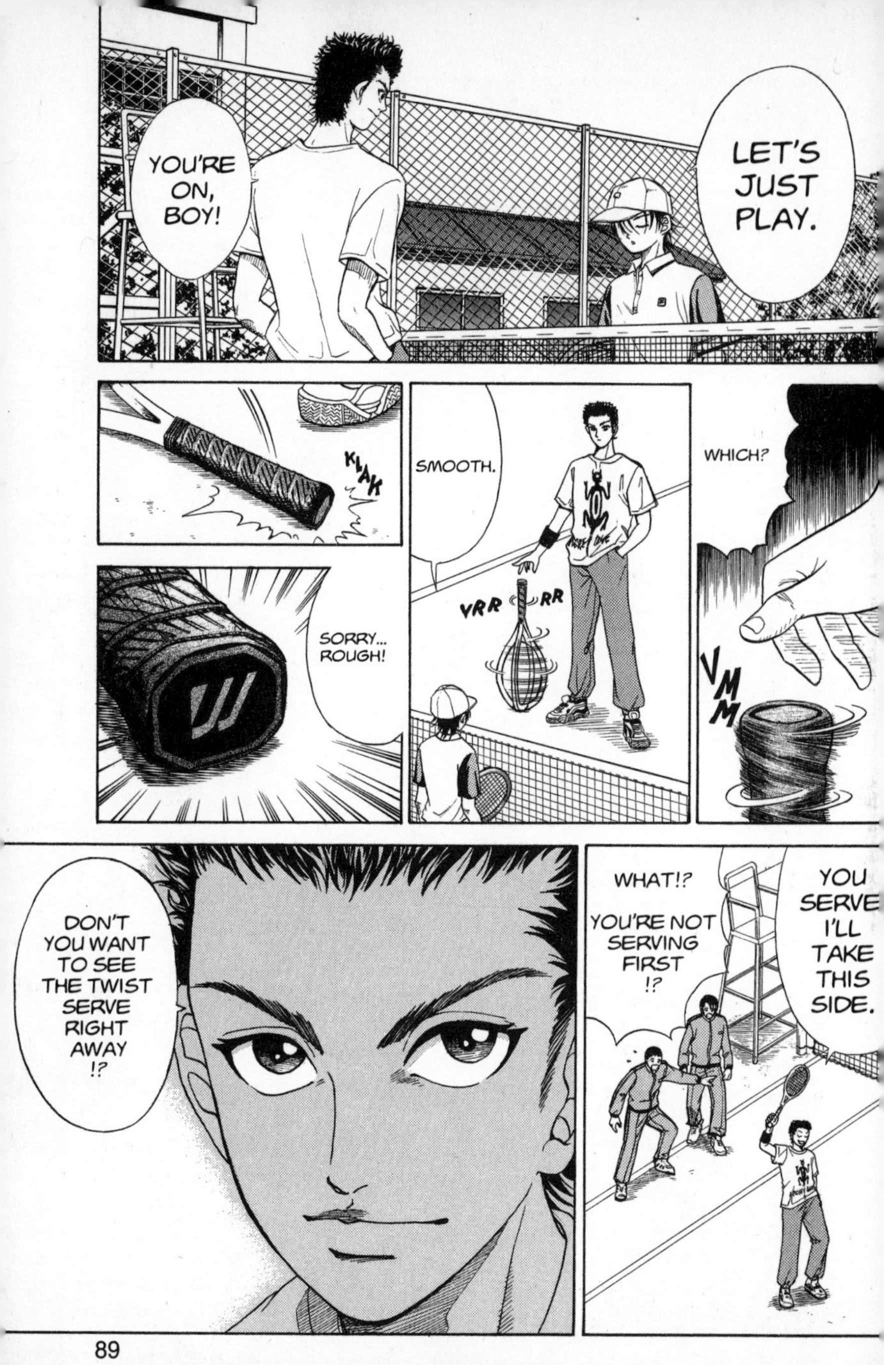
LET'S JUST PLAY.
YOU'RE ON, BOY!
WHICH?
VMM
SMOOTH.
VRR RR
KLAK
SORRY... ROUGH!
YOU SERVE I'LL TAKE THIS SIDE.
WHAT!?
YOU'RE NOT SERVING FIRST !?
DON'T YOU WANT TO SEE THE TWIST SERVE RIGHT AWAY !?

READ THIS WAY

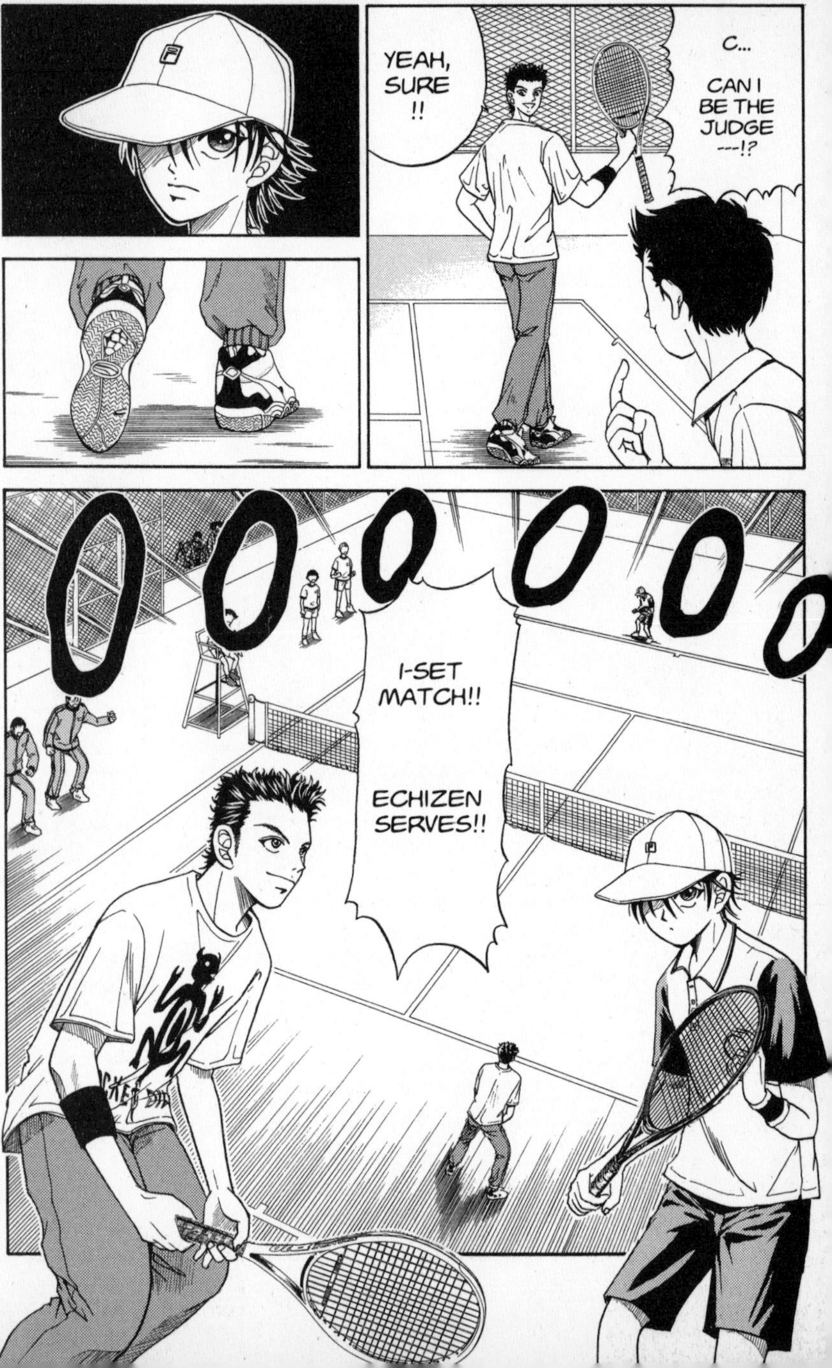
C...
CAN I BE THE JUDGE ---!?
YEAH, SURE !!
OOOOOOO
1-SET MATCH!!
ECHIZEN SERVES!!

READ THIS WAY

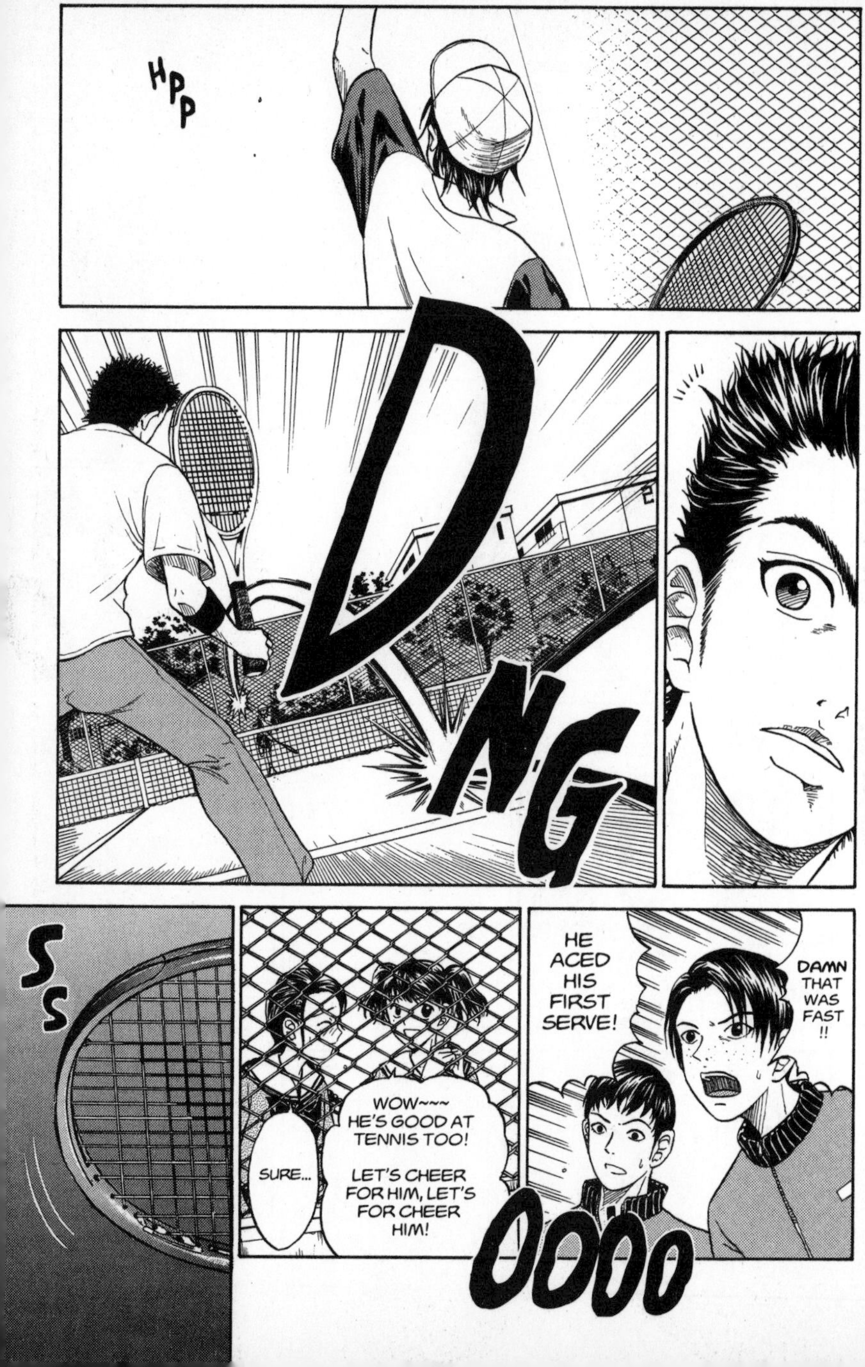
HPP
DNG
DAMN THAT WAS FAST!!
HE ACED HIS FIRST SERVE!
OOOO
WOW~~~ HE'S GOOD AT TENNIS TOO!
LET'S CHEER FOR HIM, LET'S FOR CHEER HIM!
SURE...
SS

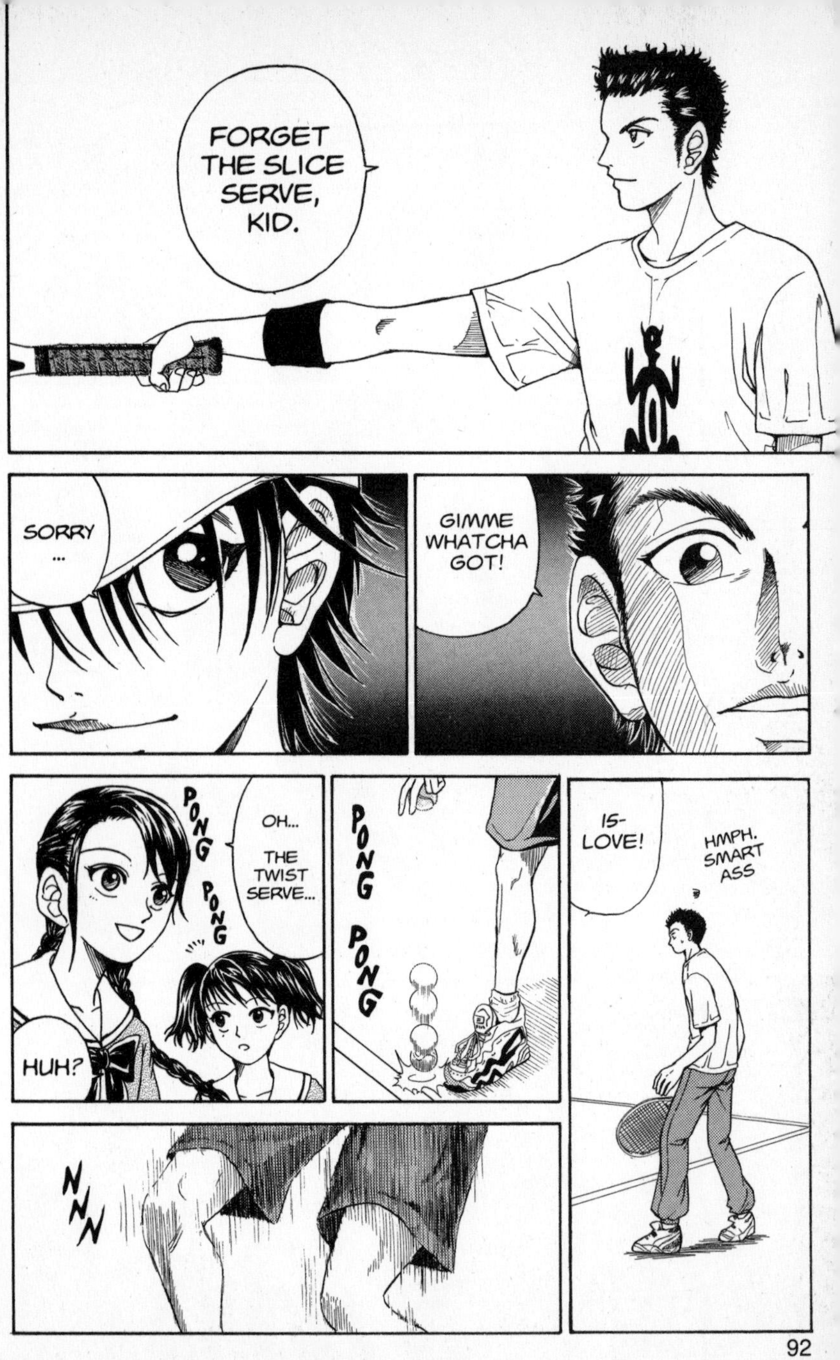
FORGET THE SLICE SERVE, KID.
GIMME WHATCHA GOT!
SORRY ...
15-LOVE!
HMPH. SMART ASS
PONG PONG
OH... THE TWIST SERVE...
PONG PONG
HUH?
NNN

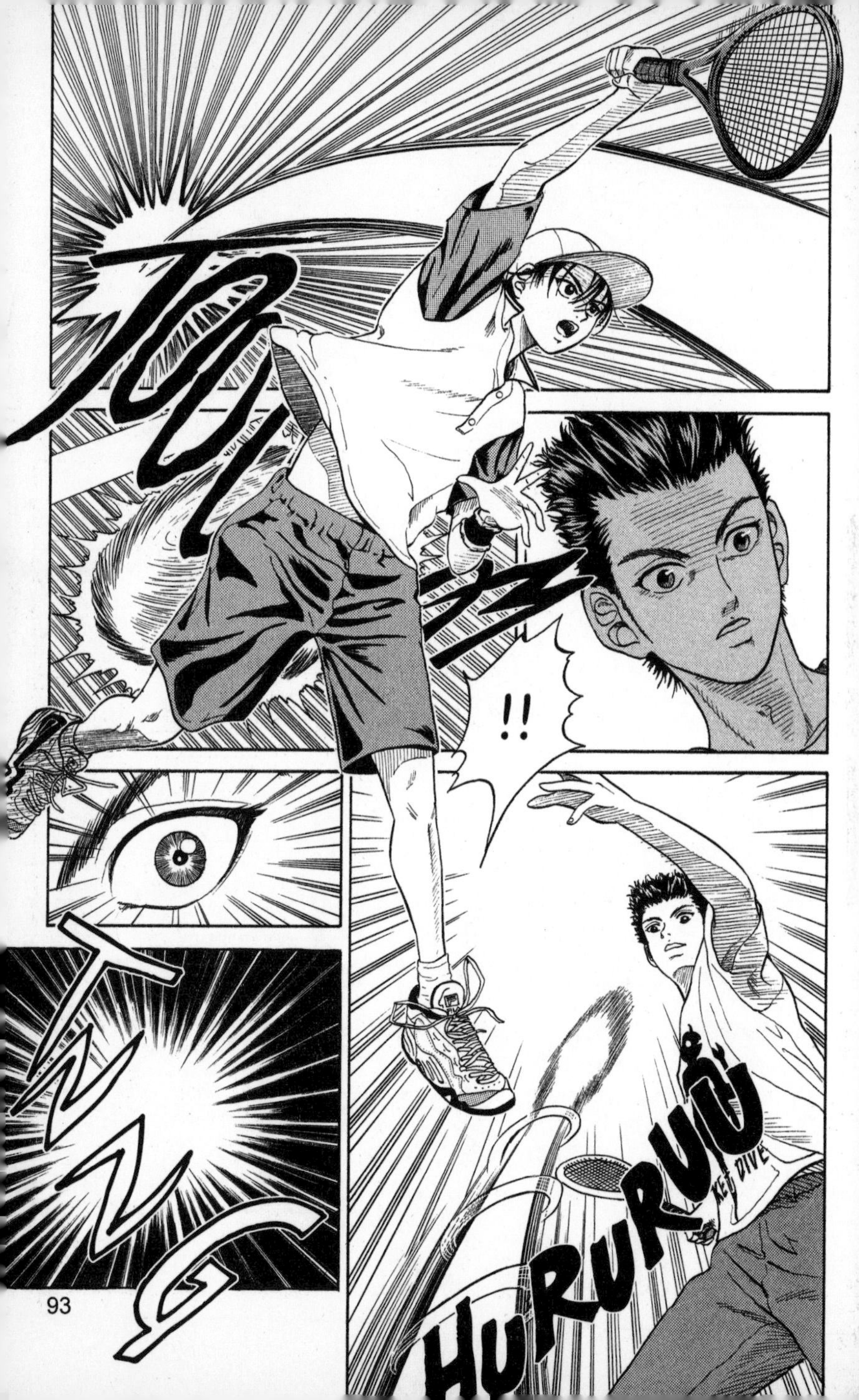
!!

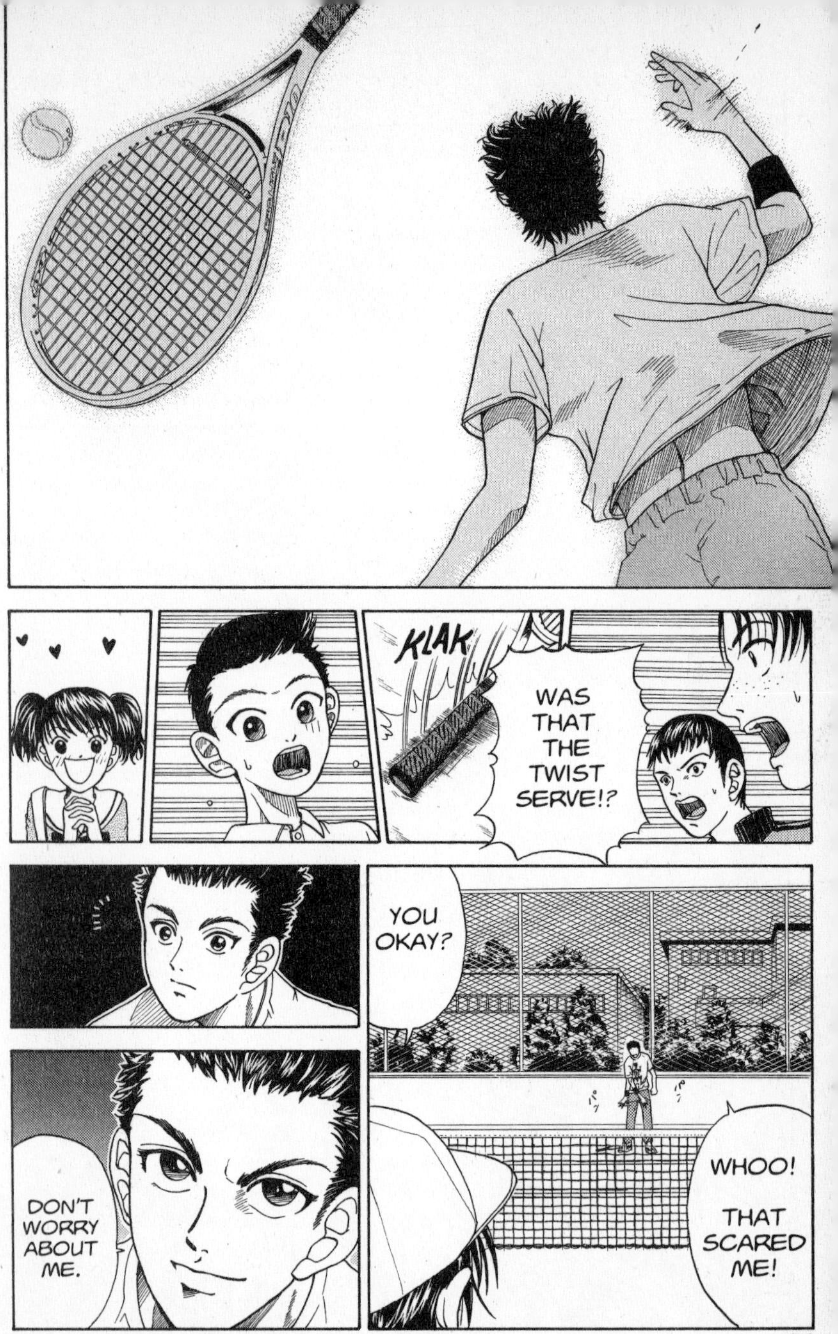
KLAK
WAS THAT THE TWIST SERVE!?
YOU OKAY?
WHOO! THAT SCARED ME!
DON'T WORRY ABOUT ME.

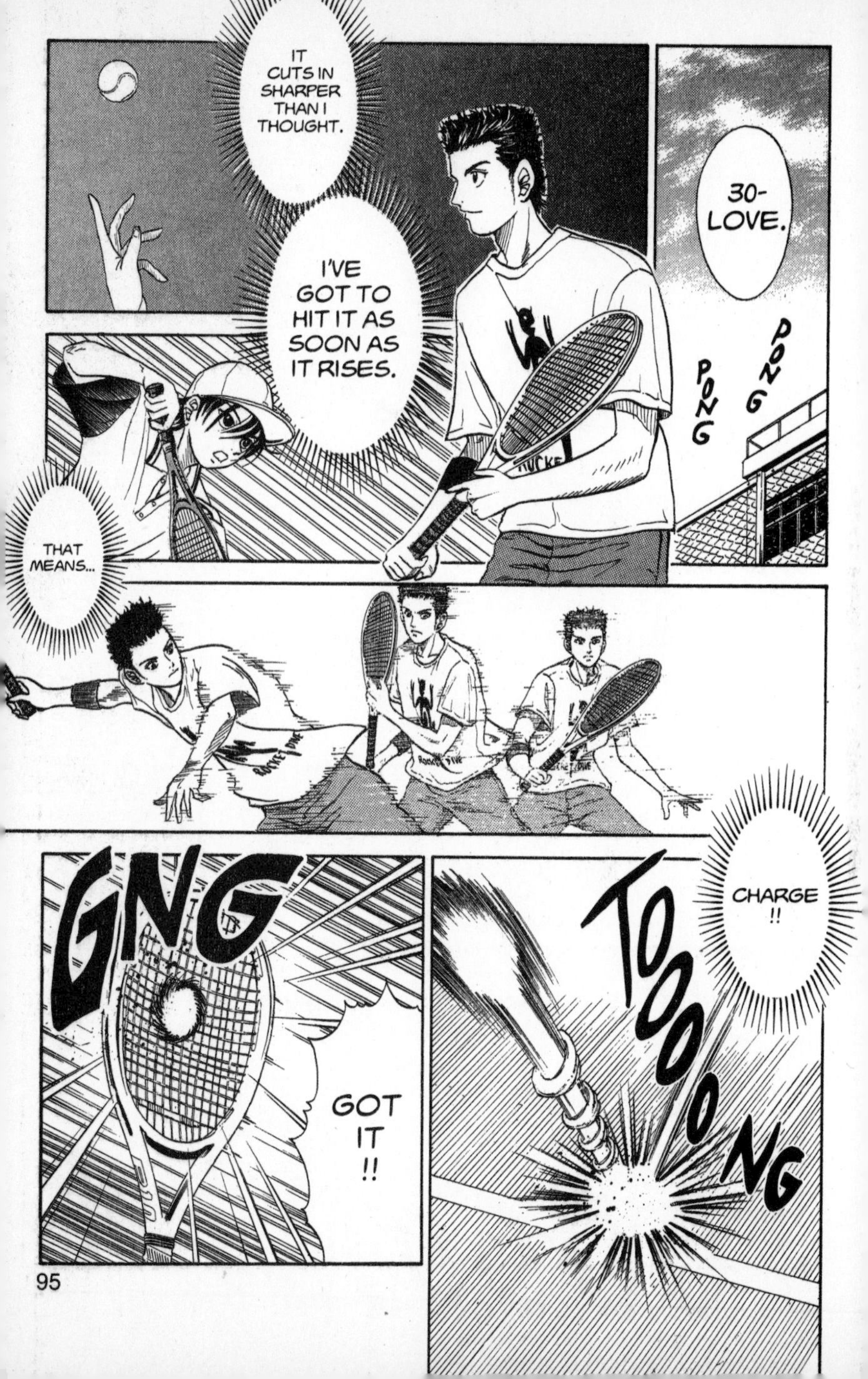
30-LOVE.
PONG
PONG
IT CUTS IN SHARPER THAN I THOUGHT.
I'VE GOT TO HIT IT AS SOON AS IT RISES.
THAT MEANS...
CHARGE!!
TOOOOONG
GNG
GOT IT!!

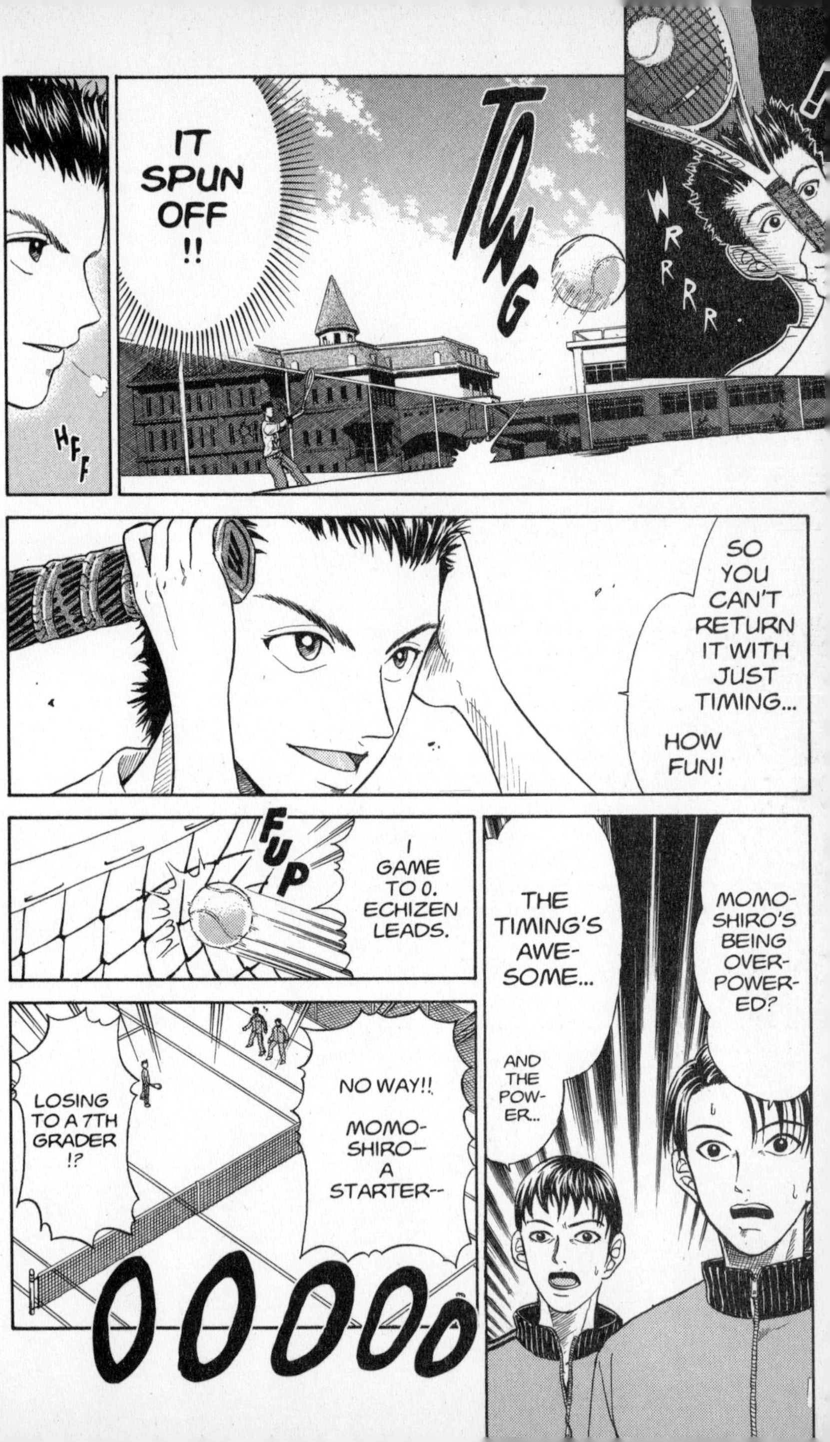
WRRRR
IT SPUN OFF!!
TONG
HFF
SO YOU CAN'T RETURN IT WITH JUST TIMING...
HOW FUN!
MOMOSHIRO'S BEING OVERPOWERED?
THE TIMING'S AWESOME...
AND THE POWER...
FUP
1 GAME TO 0. ECHIZEN LEADS.
NO WAY!!
MOMOSHIRO— A STARTER--
LOSING TO A 7TH GRADER !?
OOOOO

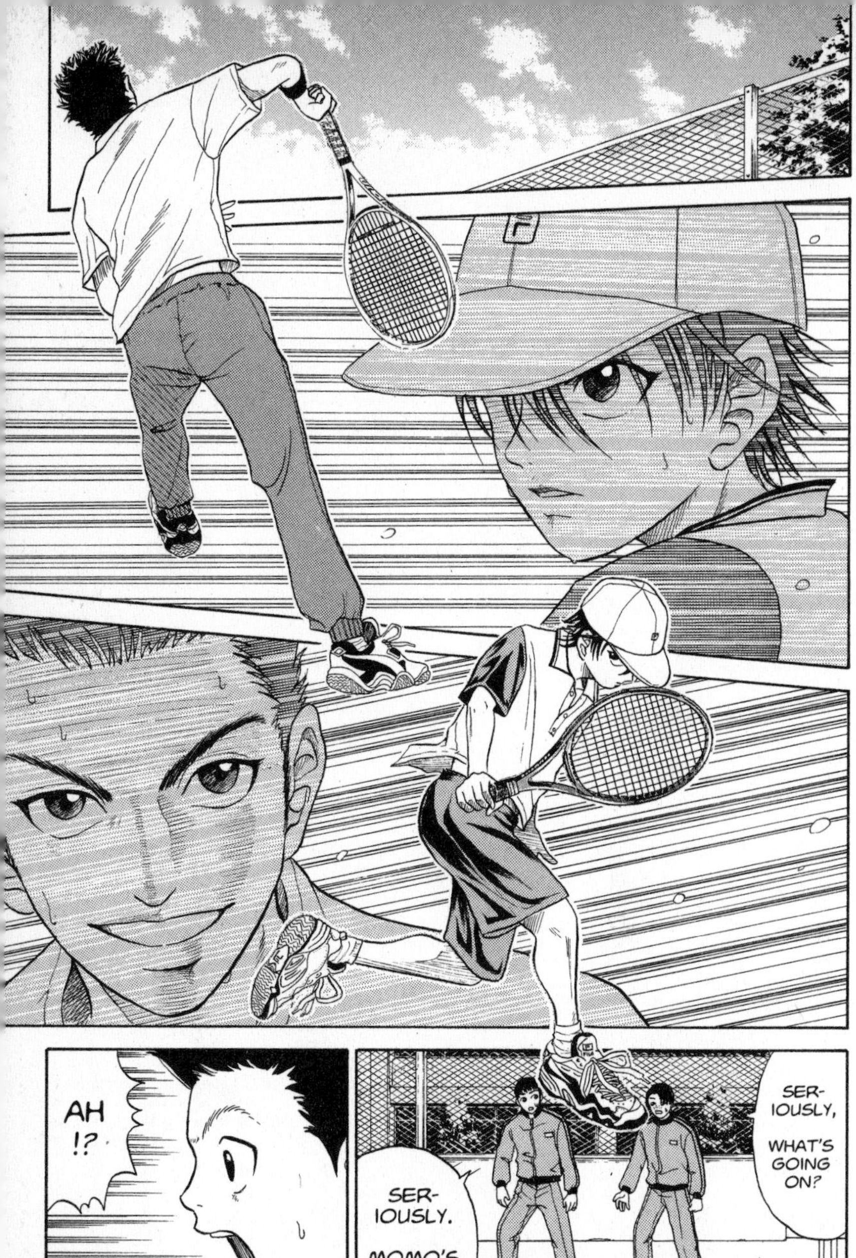
SER-IOUSLY, WHAT'S GOING ON?
SER-IOUSLY. MOMO'S LOSING.
AH !?

READ THIS WAY

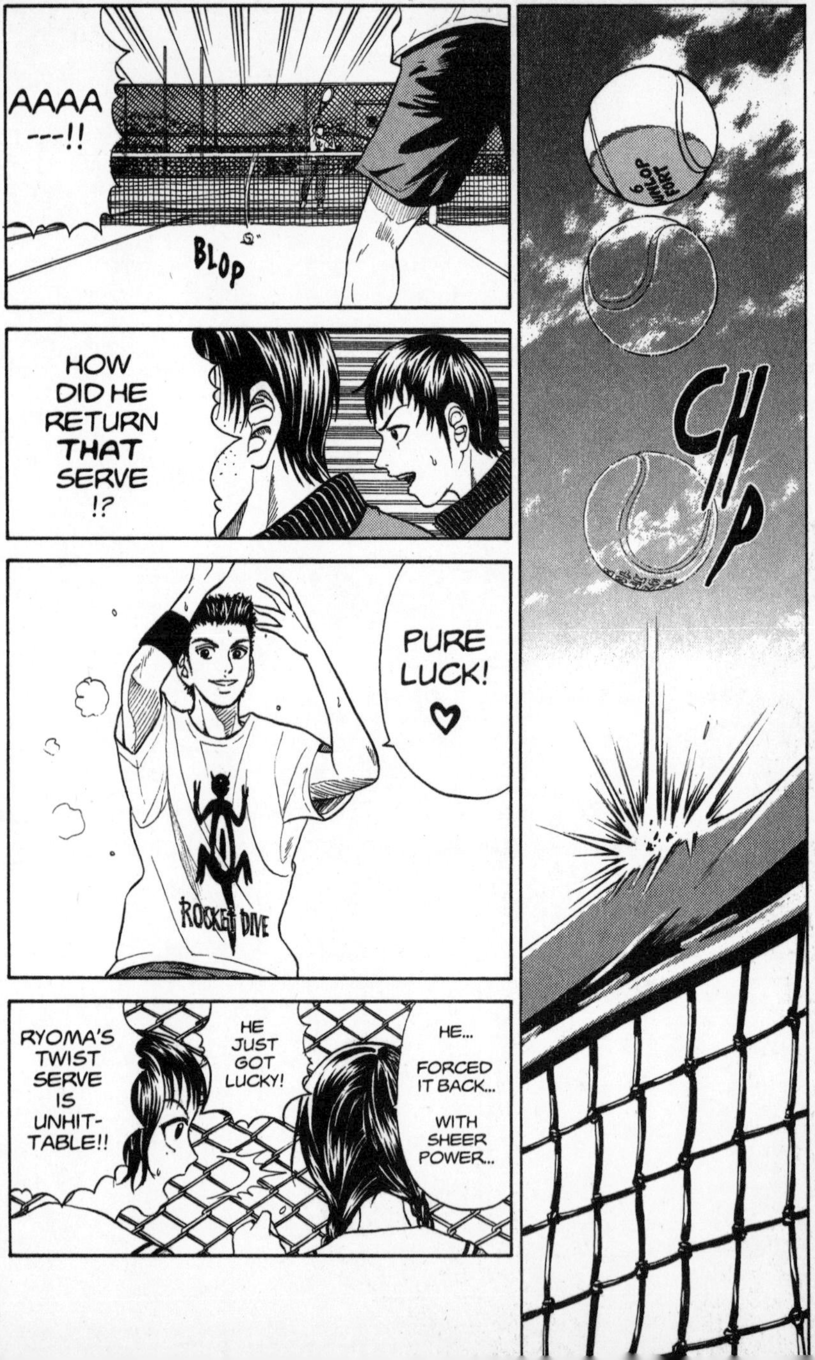

CHP
AAAA---!!
BLOP
HOW DID HE RETURN THAT SERVE !?
PURE LUCK! ♥
HE... FORCED IT BACK... WITH SHEER POWER...
HE JUST GOT LUCKY!
RYOMA'S TWIST SERVE IS UNHIT-TABLE!!
ROCKET DIVE

READ THIS WAY

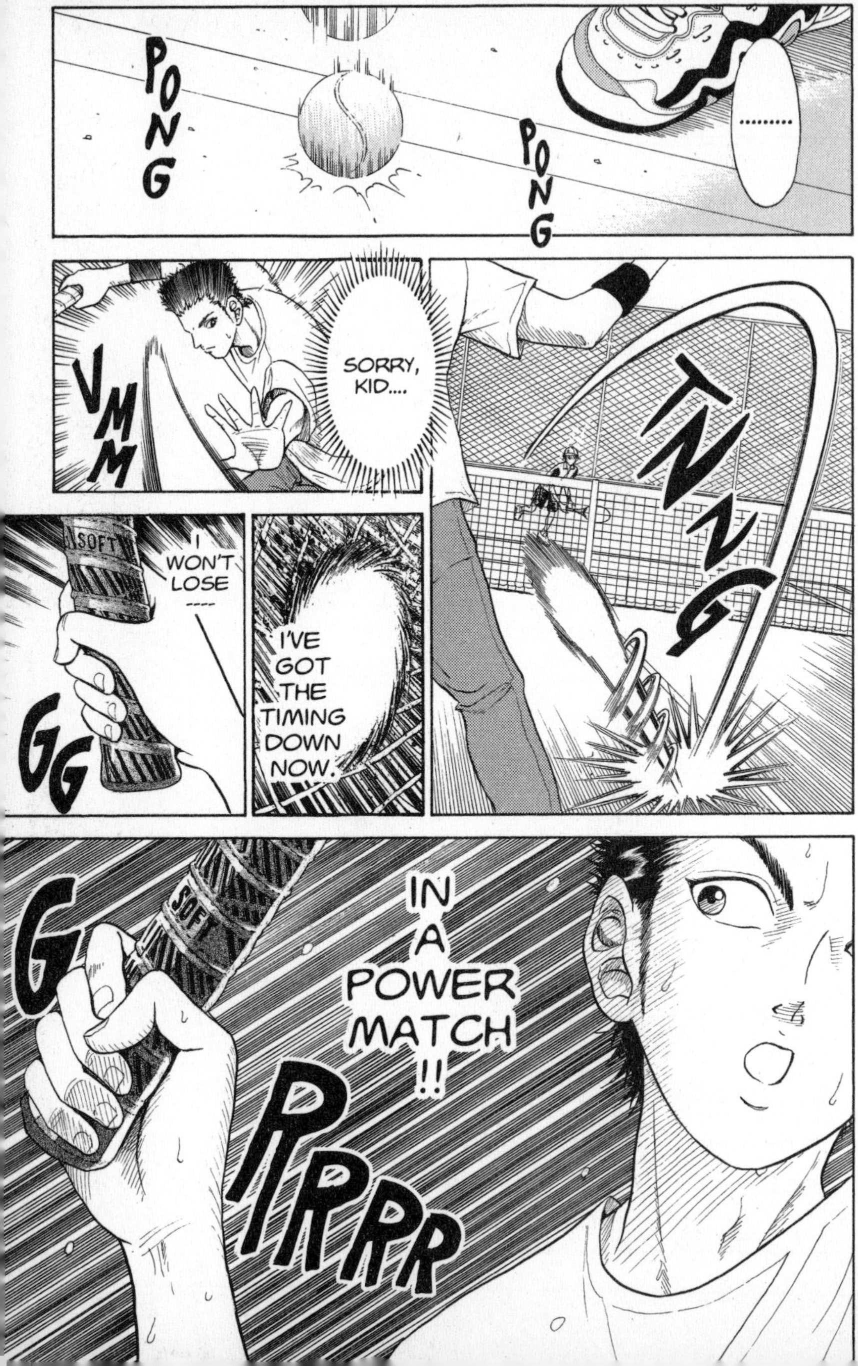
....
PONG
PONG
TNNG
SORRY, KID....
VMM
I'VE GOT THE TIMING DOWN NOW.
I WON'T LOSE ----
GG
IN A POWER MATCH !!
PRRRR
GG

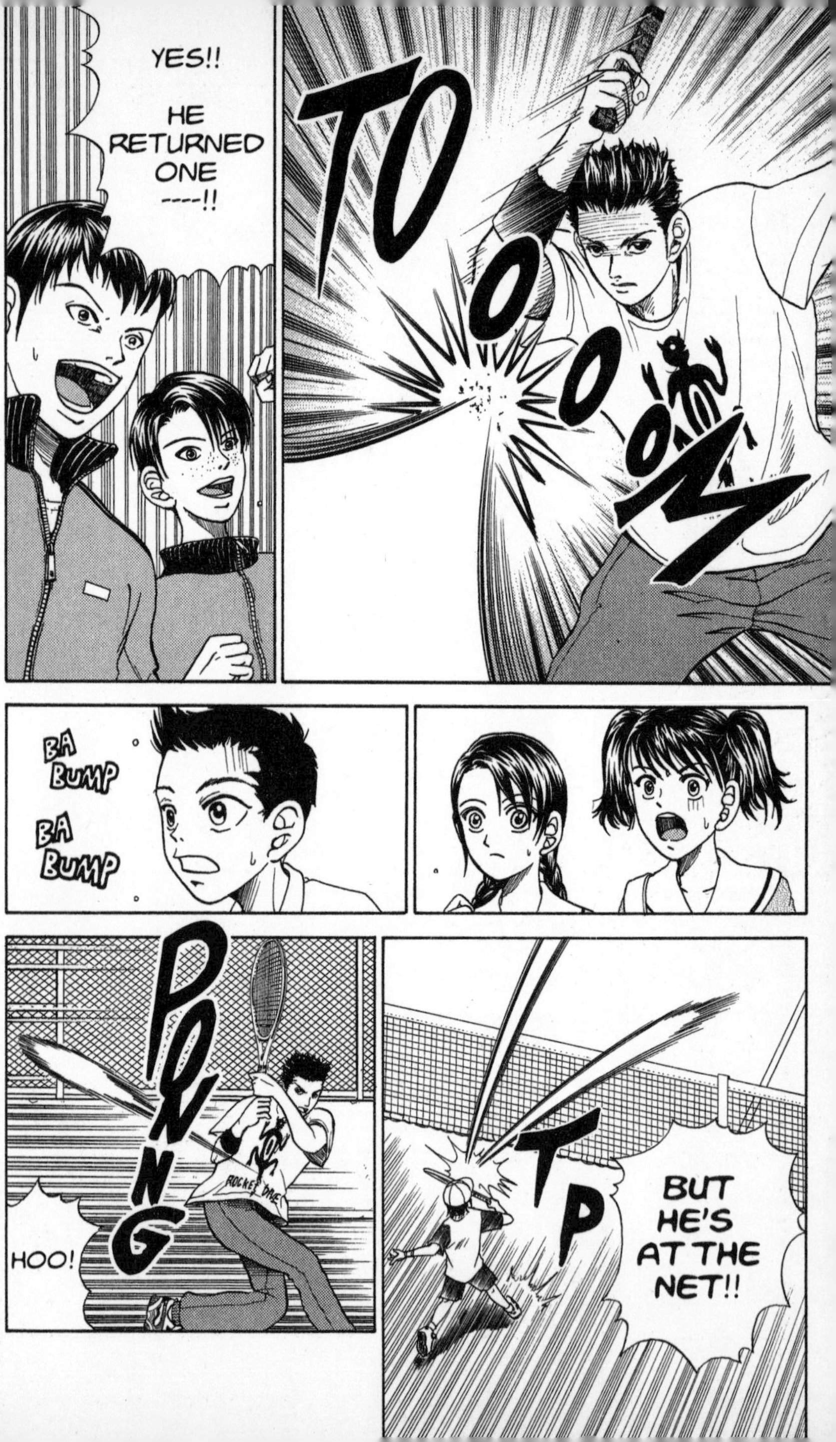
TOOOOM
YES!! HE RETURNED ONE ----!!
BA BUMP BA BUMP
TP
BUT HE'S AT THE NET!!
PONG
HOO!

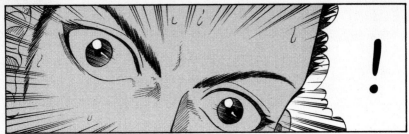

LOB

HE'S NOT GOING DOWN EASY !!

A DROP VOLLEY !!

YOU CAN DO THAT TOO ...?

PLOP

READ THIS WAY

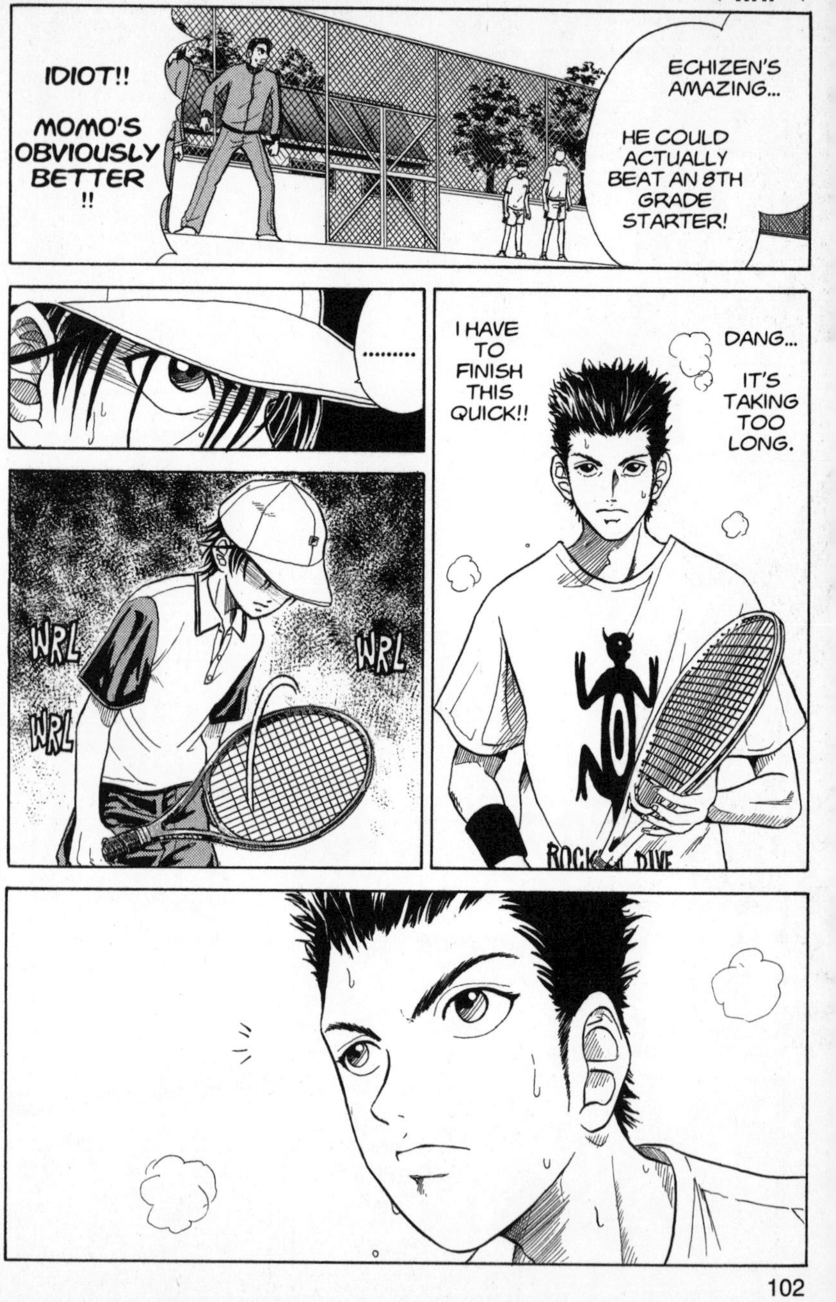
ECHIZEN'S AMAZING...
HE COULD ACTUALLY BEAT AN 8TH GRADE STARTER!
IDIOT!!
MOMO'S OBVIOUSLY BETTER!!
DANG...
IT'S TAKING TOO LONG.
I HAVE TO FINISH THIS QUICK!!
....
WRL
WRL
WRL

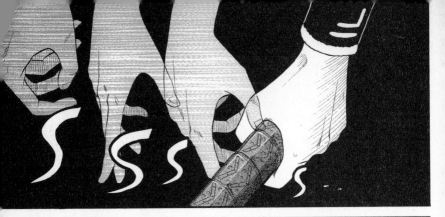

OH...

THAT'S RIGHT.....

OY.

103

READ THIS WAY

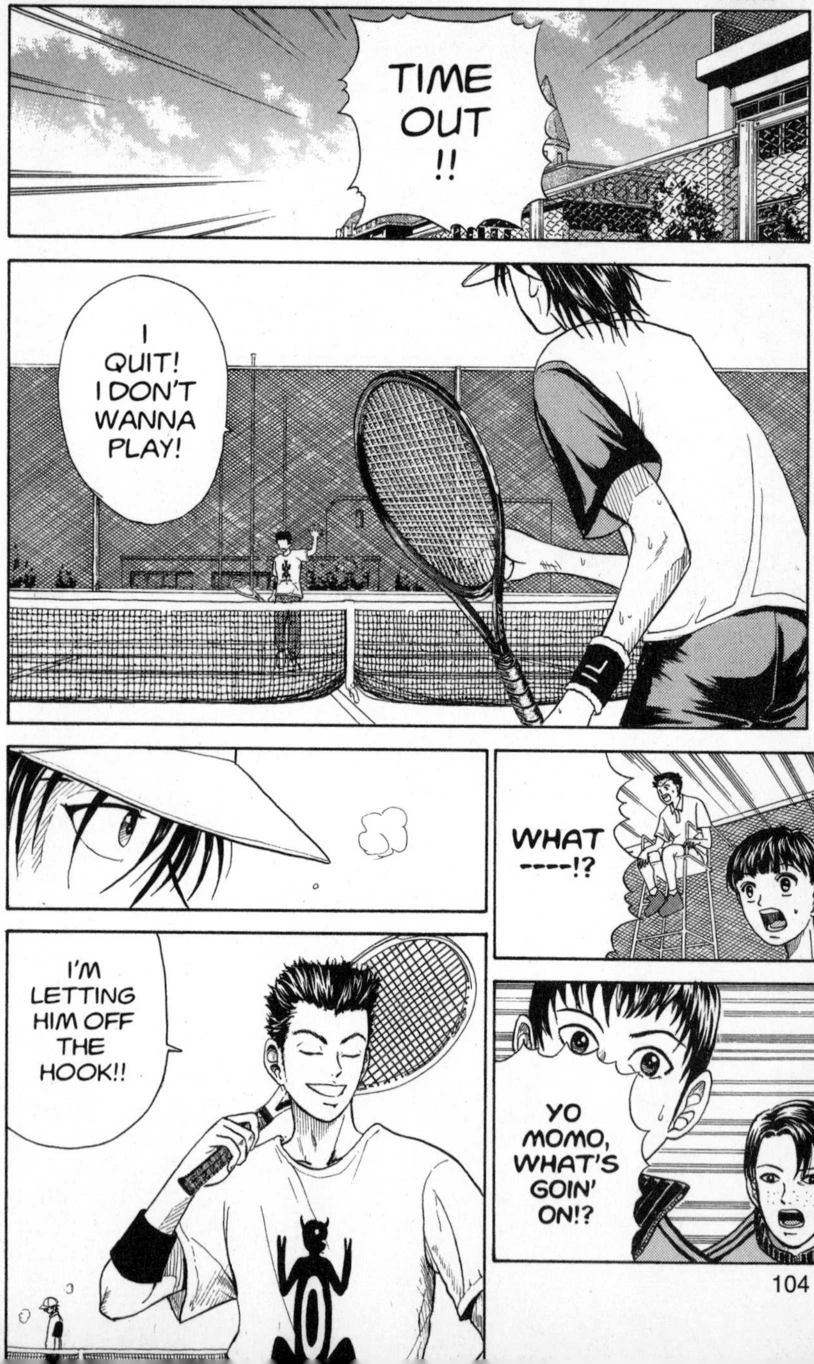
TIME OUT !!
I QUIT! I DON'T WANNA PLAY!
WHAT ----!?
YO MOMO, WHAT'S GOIN' ON!?
I'M LETTING HIM OFF THE HOOK!!

READ THIS WAY

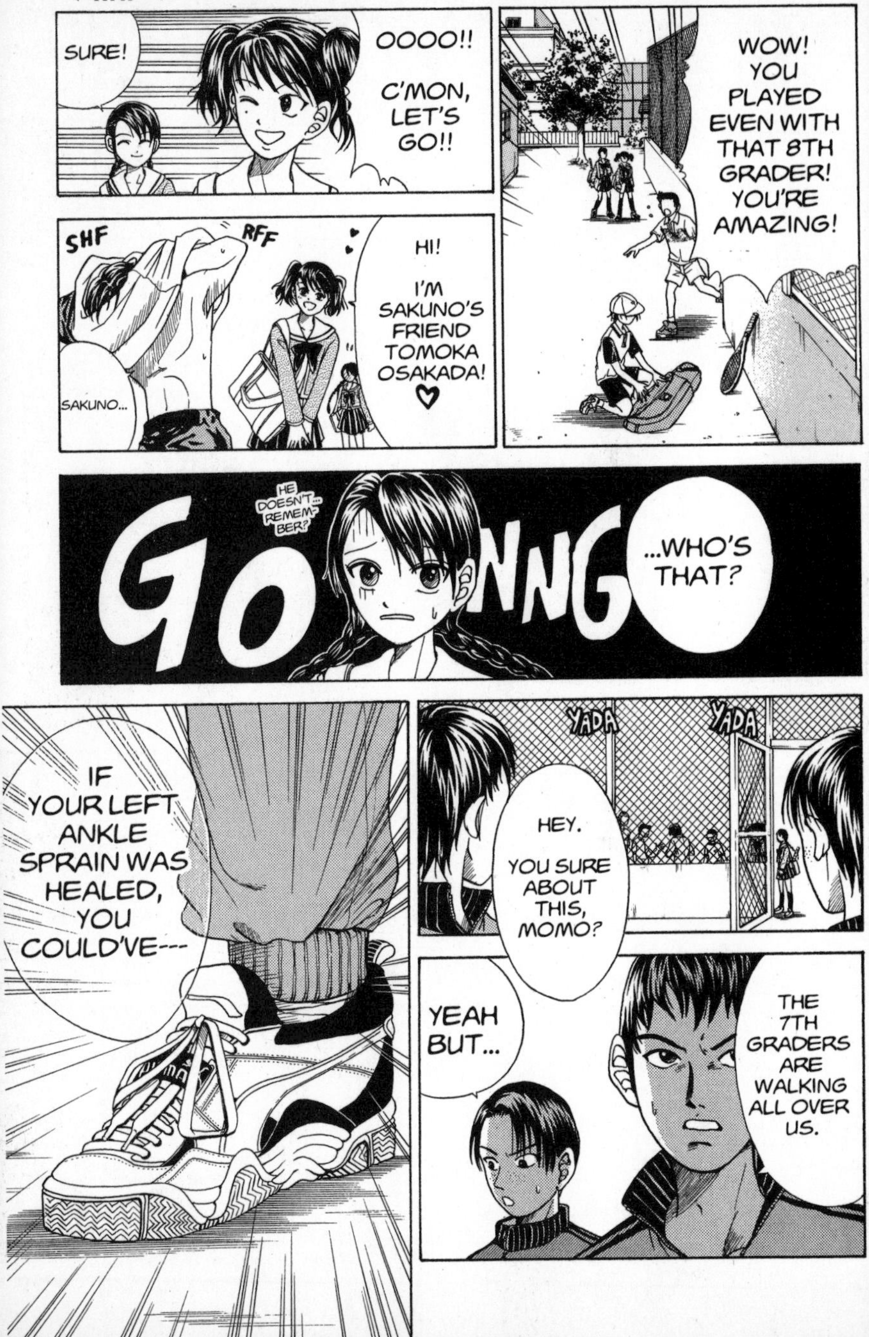
WOW! YOU PLAYED EVEN WITH THAT 8TH GRADER! YOU'RE AMAZING!
OOOO!!
C'MON, LET'S GO!!
SURE!
RFF
SHF
HI!
I'M SAKUNO'S FRIEND TOMOKA OSAKADA! ♥
SAKUNO...
...WHO'S THAT?
GONNG
HE DOESN'T... REMEMBER?
YADA
YADA
HEY.
YOU SURE ABOUT THIS, MOMO?
THE 7TH GRADERS ARE WALKING ALL OVER US.
YEAH BUT...
IF YOUR LEFT ANKLE SPRAIN WAS HEALED, YOU COULD'VE---

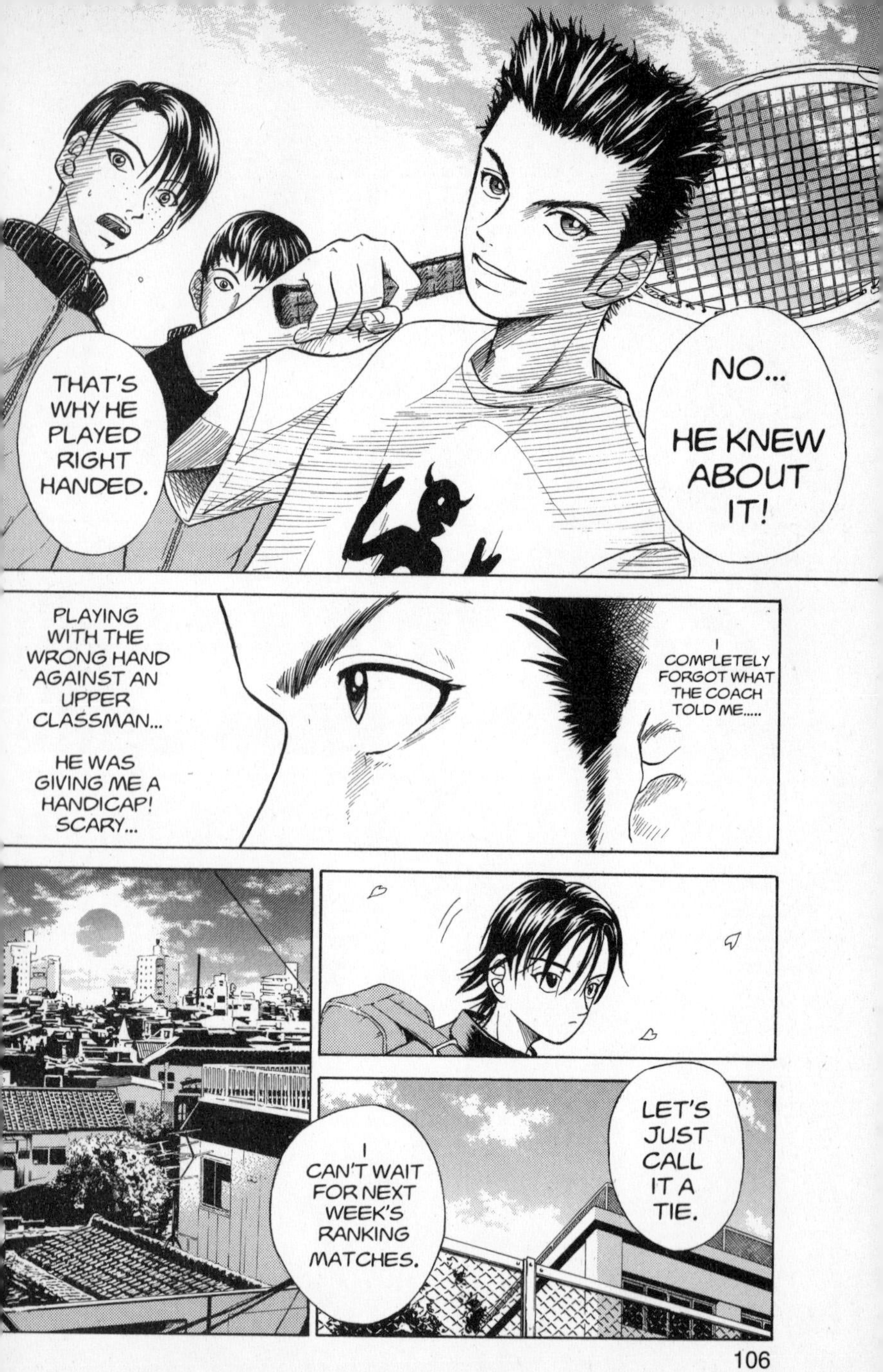
NO... HE KNEW ABOUT IT!
THAT'S WHY HE PLAYED RIGHT HANDED.
I COMPLETELY FORGOT WHAT THE COACH TOLD ME.....
PLAYING WITH THE WRONG HAND AGAINST AN UPPER CLASSMAN...
HE WAS GIVING ME A HANDICAP! SCARY...
LET'S JUST CALL IT A TIE.
I CAN'T WAIT FOR NEXT WEEK'S RANKING MATCHES.

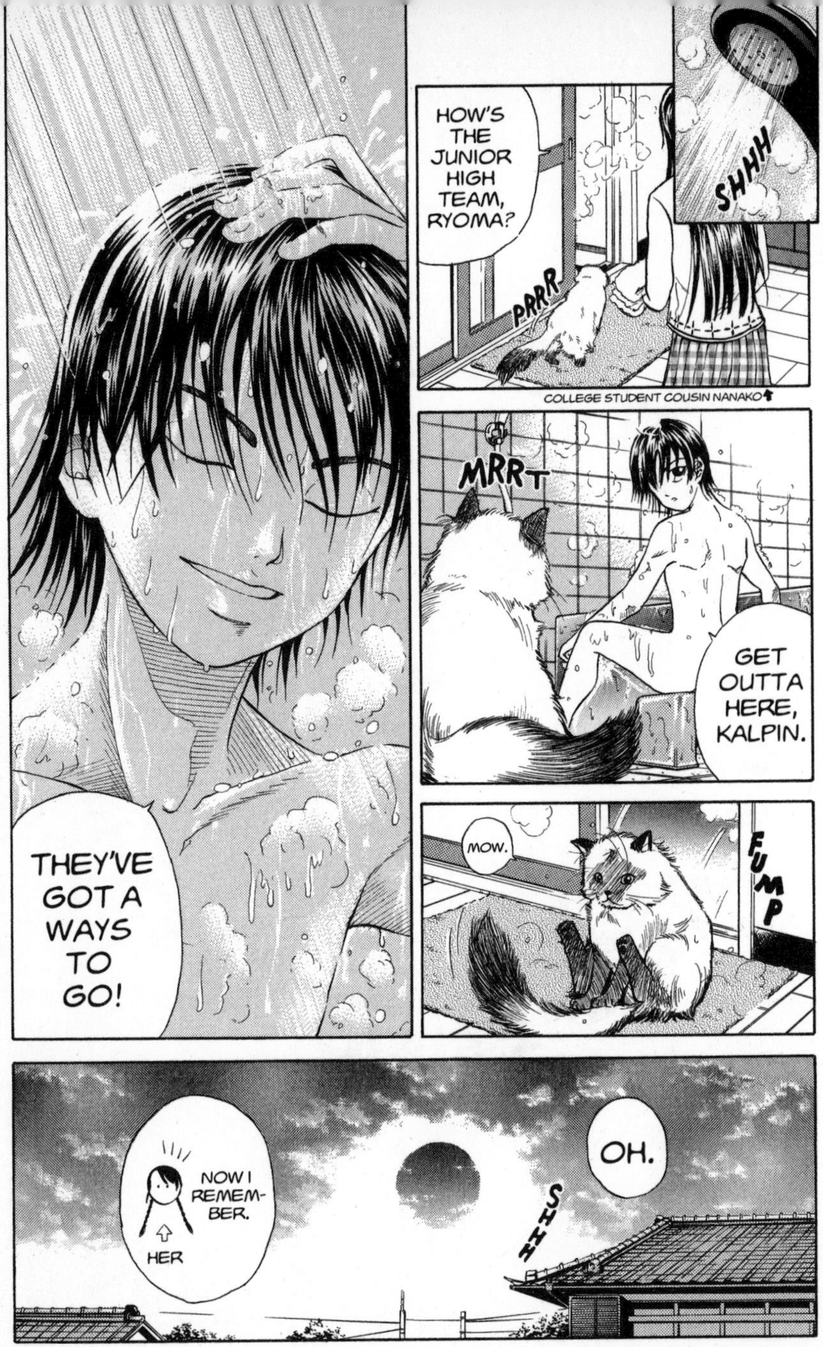

SHHH
HOW'S THE JUNIOR HIGH TEAM, RYOMA?
PRRR
COLLEGE STUDENT COUSIN NANAKO
MRRT
GET OUTTA HERE, KALPIN.
FUMP
MOW.
THEY'VE GOT A WAYS TO GO!
OH.
SHHH
NOW I REMEMBER.
HER

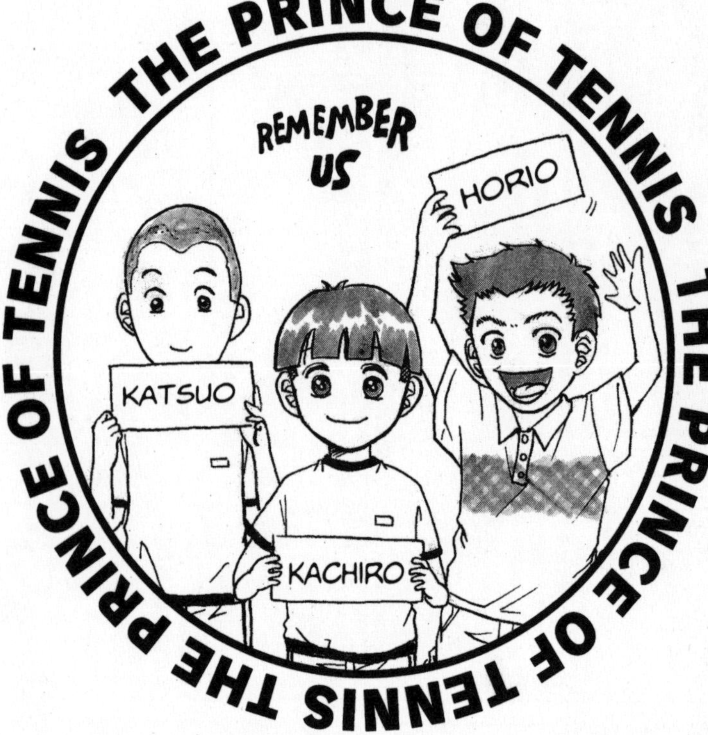
THE PRINCE OF TENNIS THE PRINCE OF TENNIS THE PRINCE OF TENNIS
REMEMBER US
HORIO
KATSUO
KACHIRO

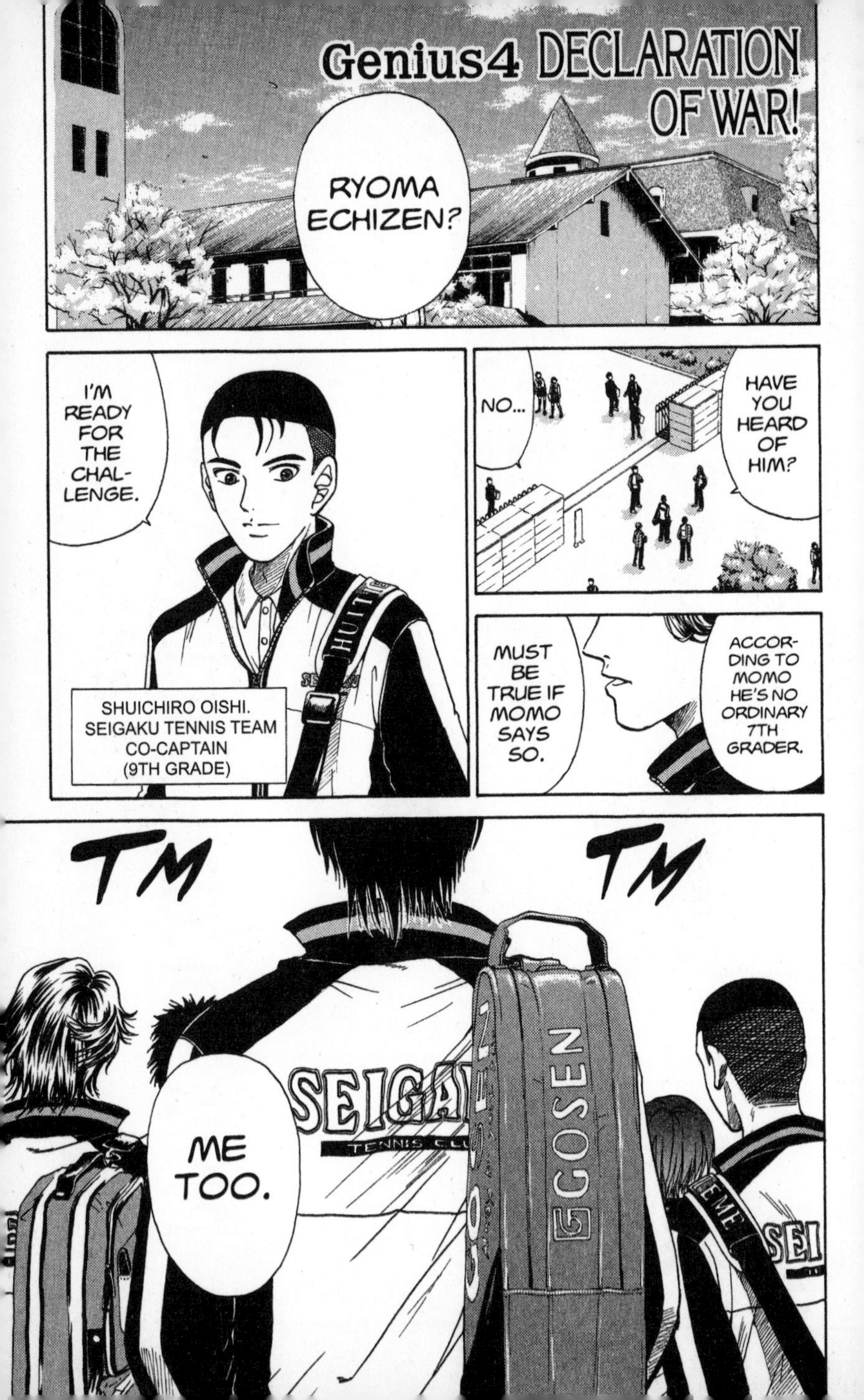
Genius 4 DECLARATION OF WAR!
RYOMA ECHIZEN?
HAVE YOU HEARD OF HIM?
NO...
ACCORDING TO MOMO HE'S NO ORDINARY 7TH GRADER.
MUST BE TRUE IF MOMO SAYS SO.
I'M READY FOR THE CHALLENGE.
SHUICHIRO OISHI. SEIGAKU TENNIS TEAM CO-CAPTAIN (9TH GRADE)
TM
TM
ME TOO.

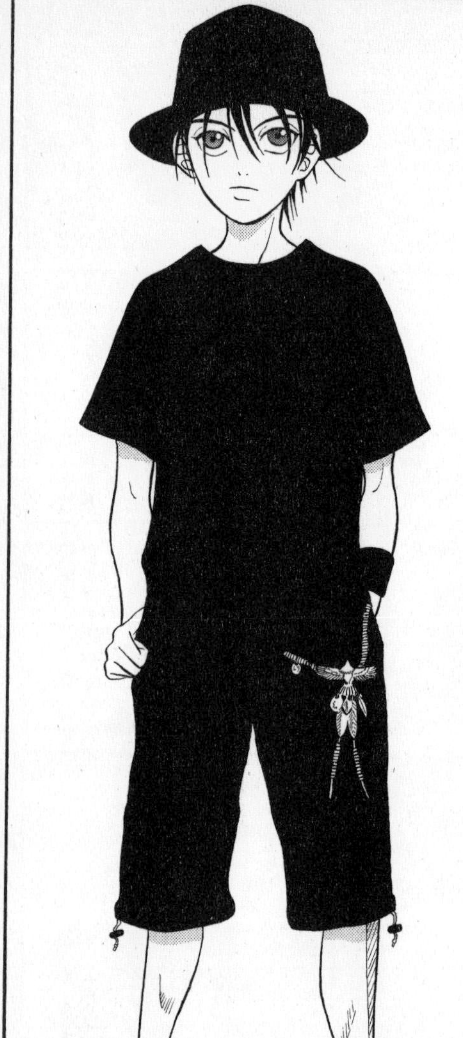

Genius 4 DECLARATION OF WAR!

READ THIS WAY

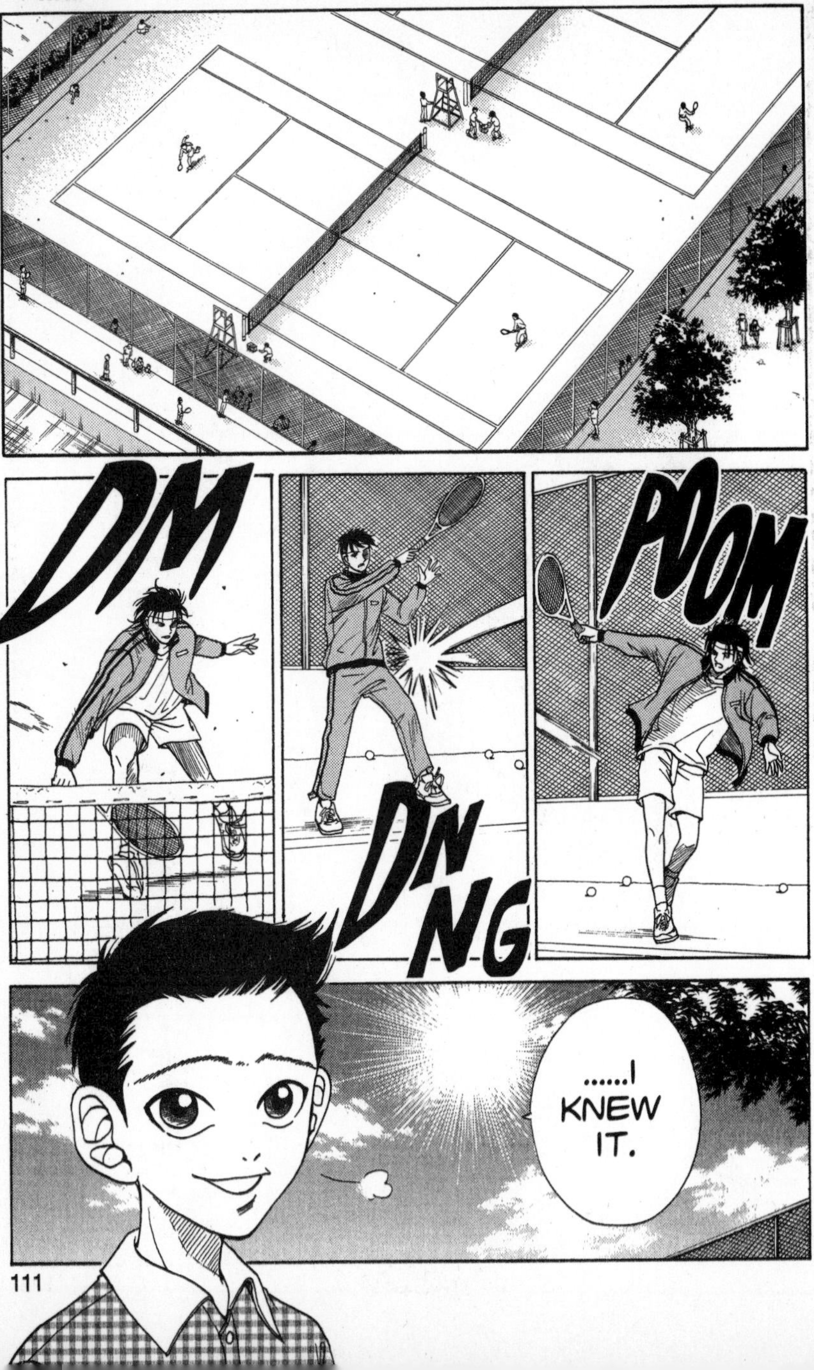
POOM
DING
DM
......I KNEW IT.

READ THIS WAY

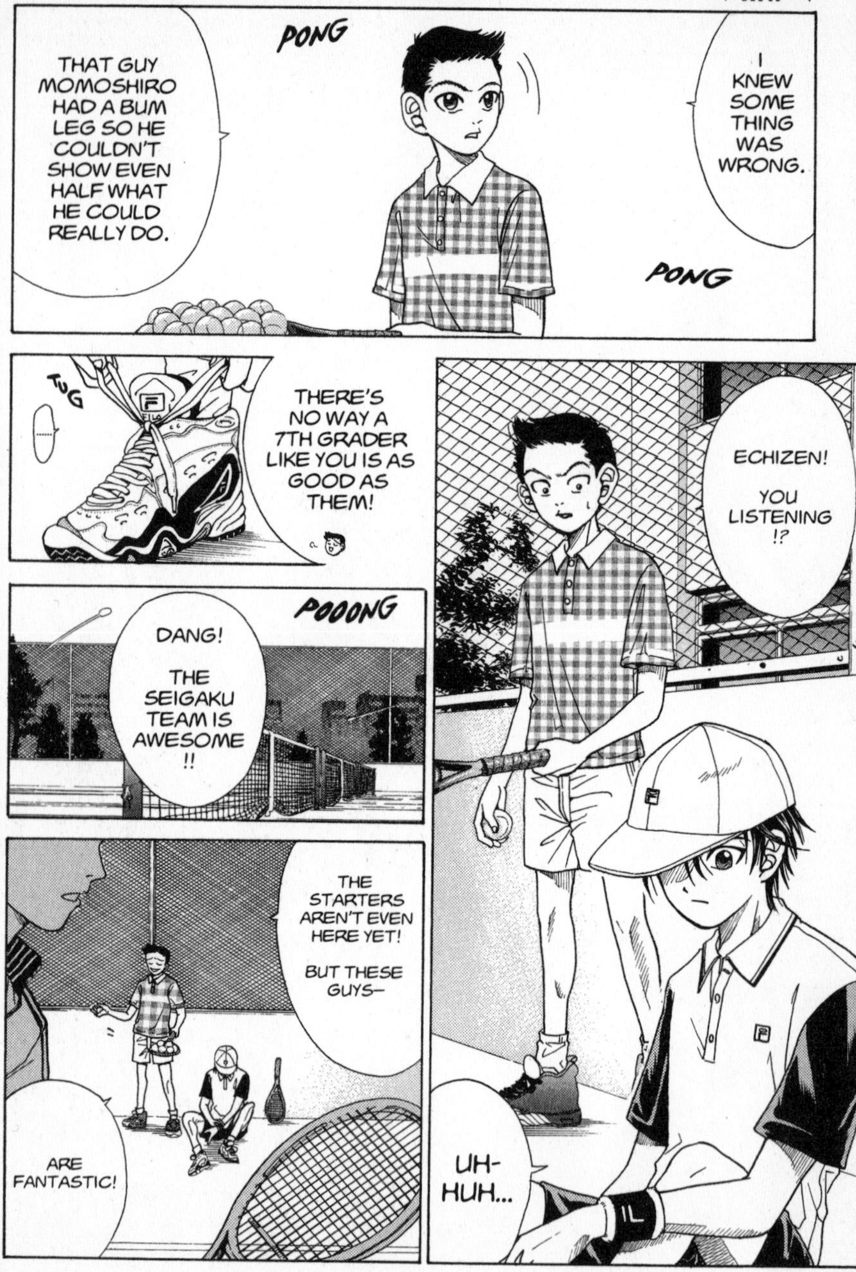
I KNEW SOMETHING WAS WRONG.
PONG
THAT GUY MOMOSHIRO HAD A BUM LEG SO HE COULDN'T SHOW EVEN HALF WHAT HE COULD REALLY DO.
PONG
ECHIZEN! YOU LISTENING!?
UH-HUH...
THERE'S NO WAY A 7TH GRADER LIKE YOU IS AS GOOD AS THEM!
TUG
......
POOONG
DANG! THE SEIGAKU TEAM IS AWESOME!!
THE STARTERS AREN'T EVEN HERE YET! BUT THESE GUYS—
ARE FANTASTIC!

READ THIS WAY

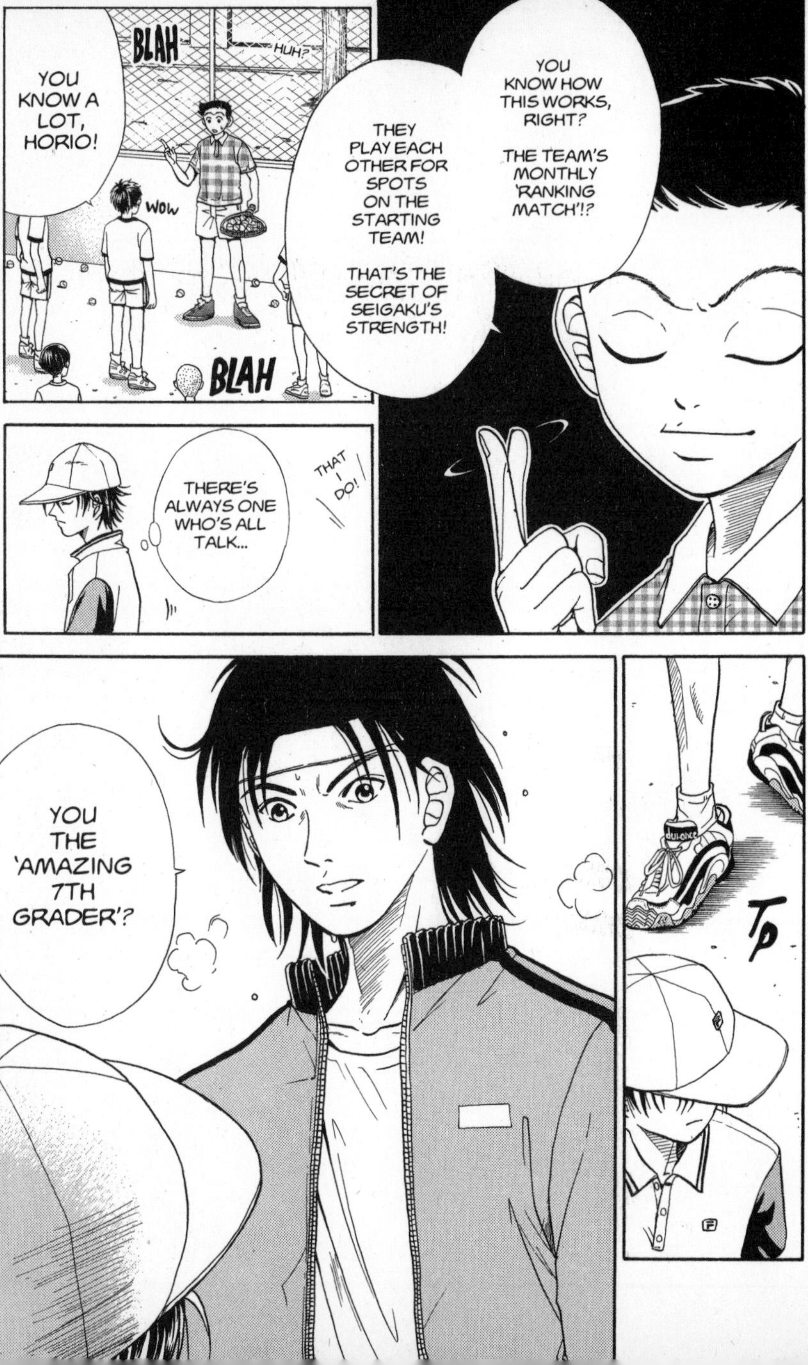
YOU KNOW HOW THIS WORKS, RIGHT?
THE TEAM'S MONTHLY 'RANKING MATCH'!?
THEY PLAY EACH OTHER FOR SPOTS ON THE STARTING TEAM!
THAT'S THE SECRET OF SEIGAKU'S STRENGTH!
HUH?
BLAH
YOU KNOW A LOT, HORIO!
WOW
BLAH
THAT I DO!
THERE'S ALWAYS ONE WHO'S ALL TALK...
TP
YOU THE 'AMAZING 7TH GRADER'?

READ THIS WAY

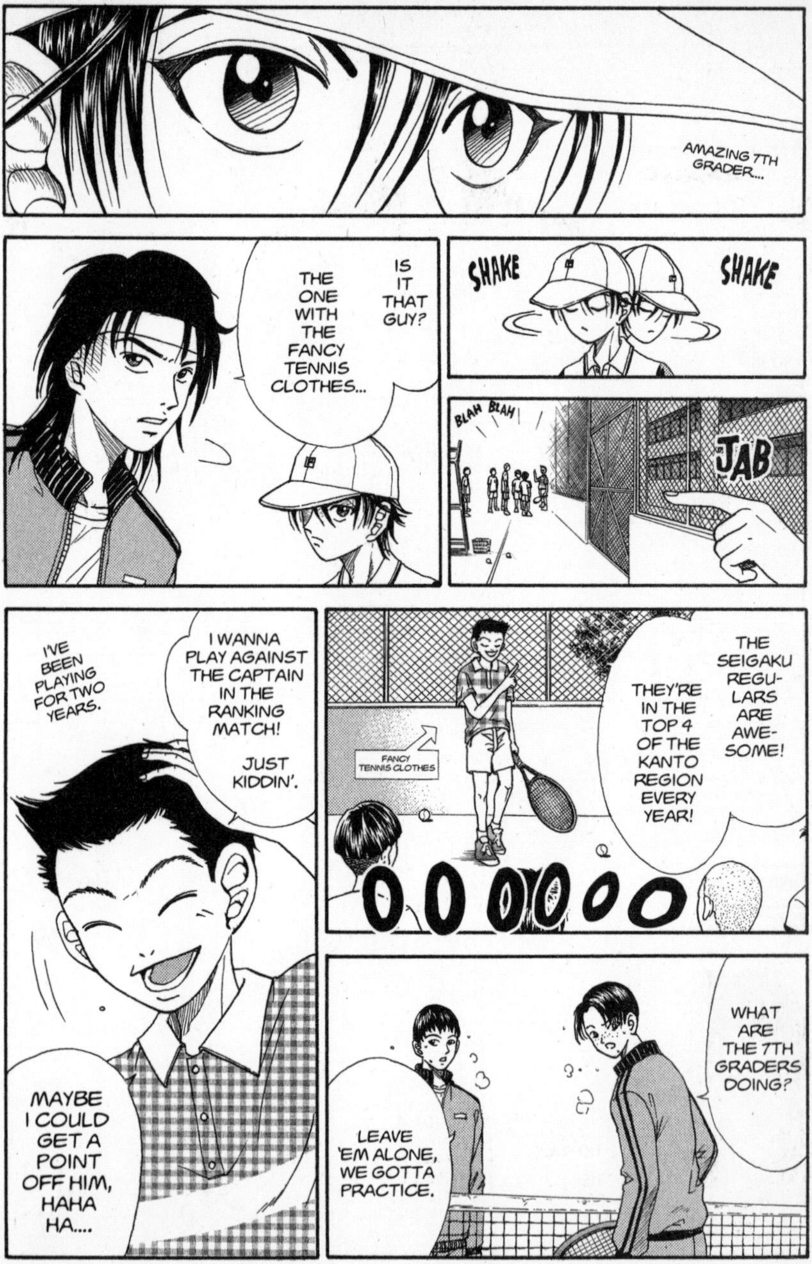
AMAZING 7TH GRADER...
SHAKE
SHAKE
BLAH BLAH
JAB
IS IT THAT GUY?
THE ONE WITH THE FANCY TENNIS CLOTHES...
THE SEIGAKU REGULARS ARE AWESOME!
THEY'RE IN THE TOP 4 OF THE KANTO REGION EVERY YEAR!
FANCY TENNIS CLOTHES
OOOOOO
WHAT ARE THE 7TH GRADERS DOING?
LEAVE 'EM ALONE, WE GOTTA PRACTICE.
I WANNA PLAY AGAINST THE CAPTAIN IN THE RANKING MATCH!
JUST KIDDIN'.
I'VE BEEN PLAYING FOR TWO YEARS.
MAYBE I COULD GET A POINT OFF HIM, HAHA HA....

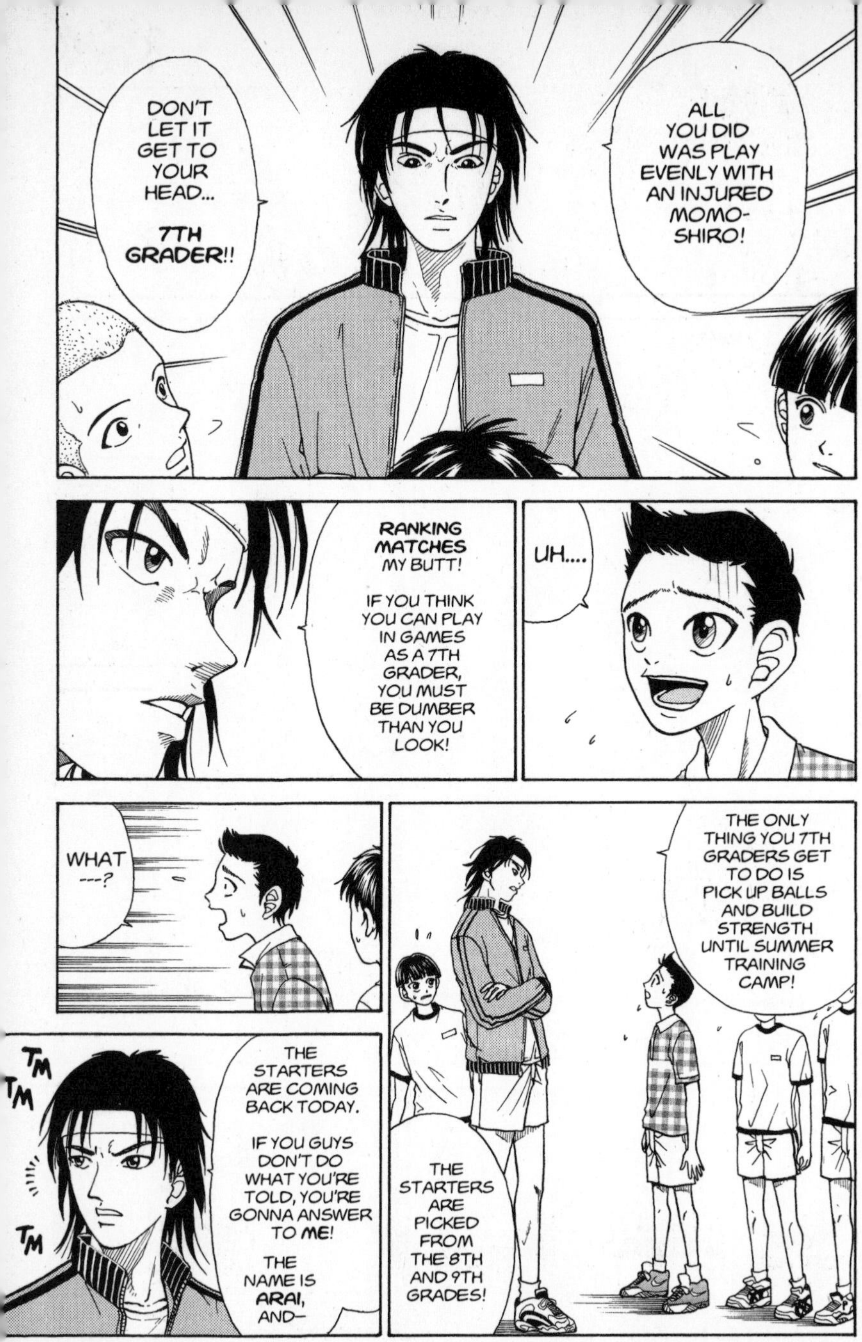
ALL YOU DID WAS PLAY EVENLY WITH AN INJURED MOMO-SHIRO!
DON'T LET IT GET TO YOUR HEAD... 7TH GRADER!!
UH....
RANKING MATCHES MY BUTT! IF YOU THINK YOU CAN PLAY IN GAMES AS A 7TH GRADER, YOU MUST BE DUMBER THAN YOU LOOK!
THE ONLY THING YOU 7TH GRADERS GET TO DO IS PICK UP BALLS AND BUILD STRENGTH UNTIL SUMMER TRAINING CAMP!
THE STARTERS ARE PICKED FROM THE 8TH AND 9TH GRADES!
WHAT ---?
TM
TM
TM
THE STARTERS ARE COMING BACK TODAY.
IF YOU GUYS DON'T DO WHAT YOU'RE TOLD, YOU'RE GONNA ANSWER TO ME!
THE NAME IS ARAI, AND—

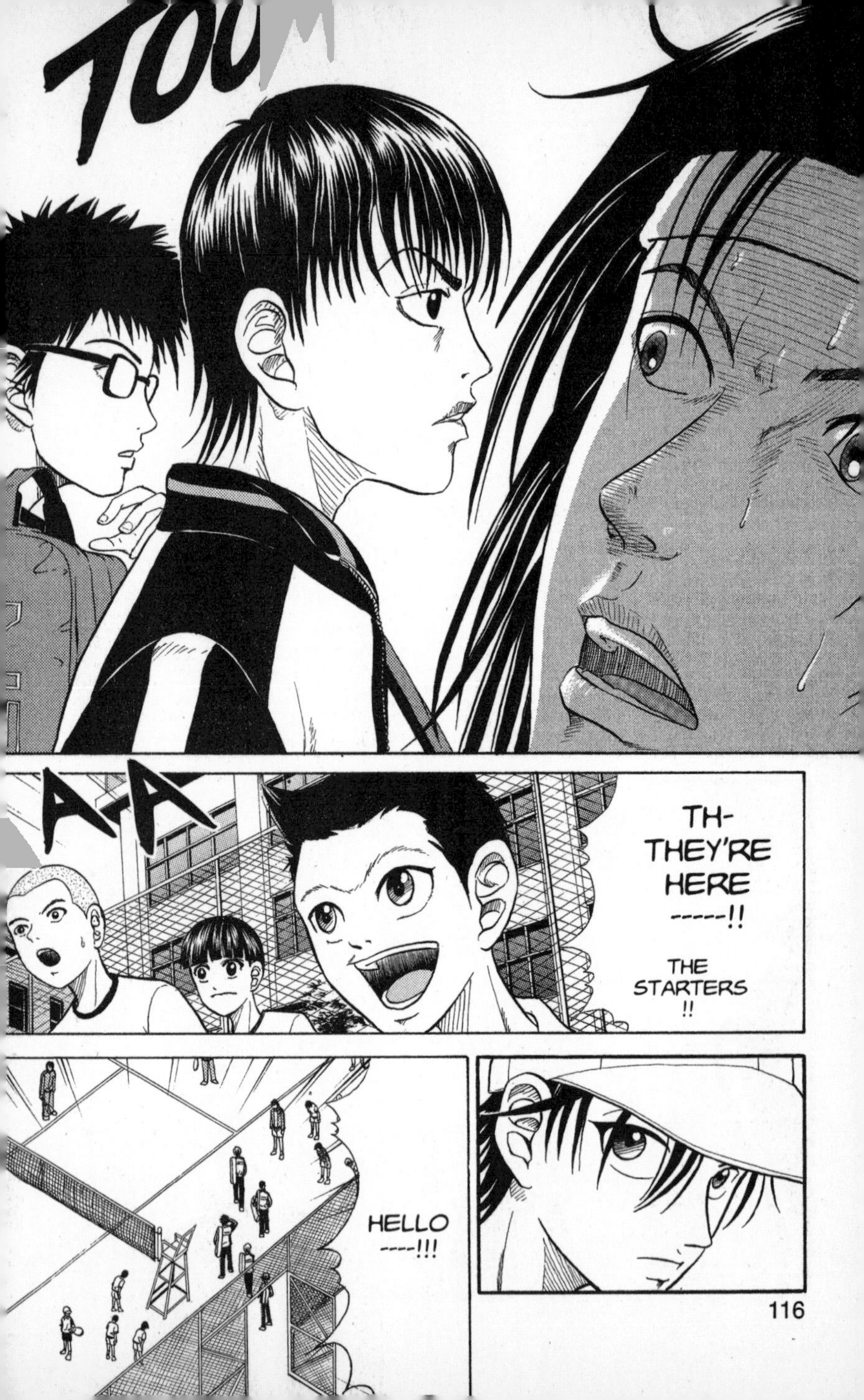
TOU
TH- THEY'RE HERE -----!!
THE STARTERS !!
AA
HELLO ----!!!

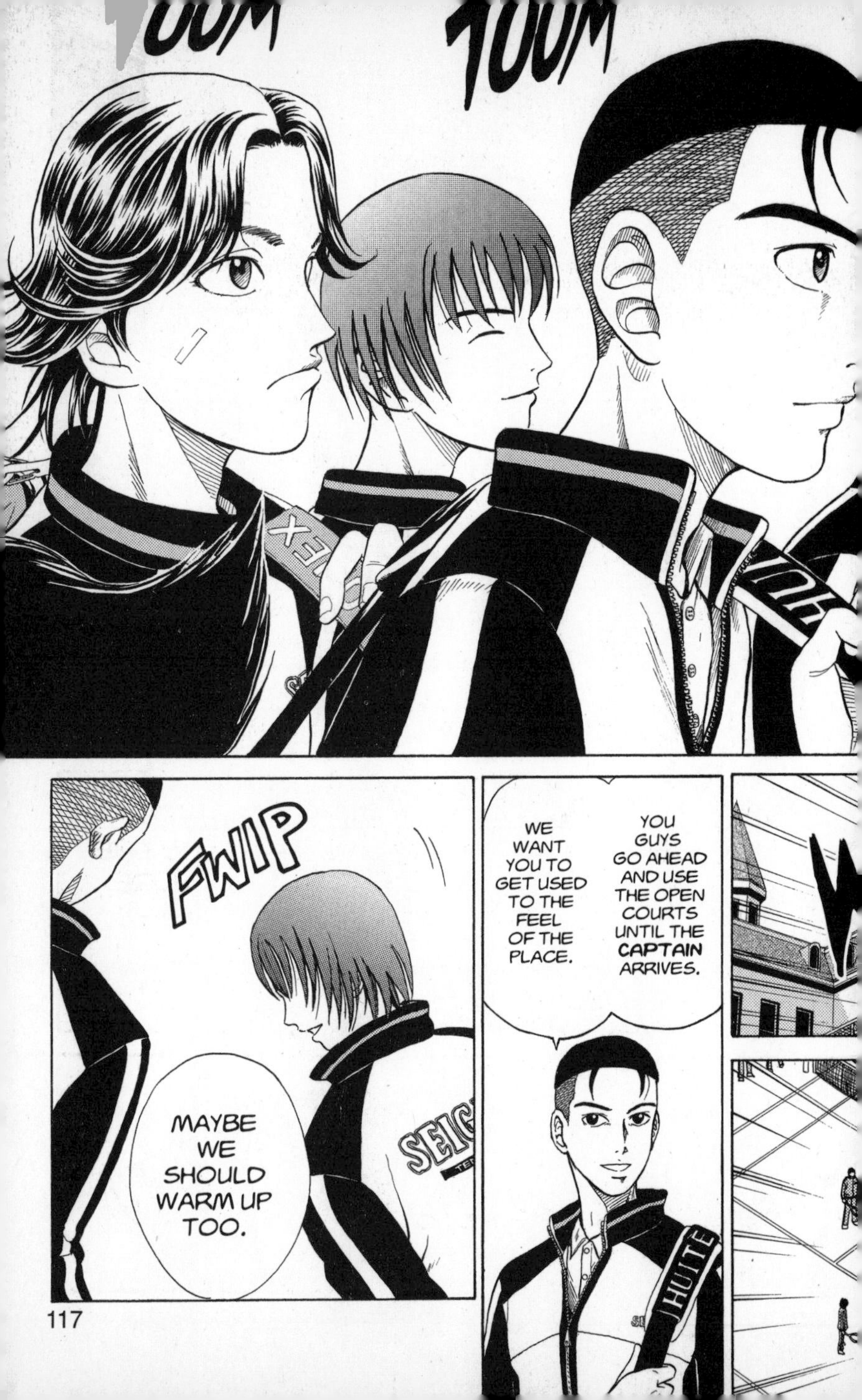
VOOM
VOOM
YOU GUYS GO AHEAD AND USE THE OPEN COURTS UNTIL THE **CAPTAIN** ARRIVES.
WE WANT YOU TO GET USED TO THE FEEL OF THE PLACE.
FWIP
MAYBE WE SHOULD WARM UP TOO.

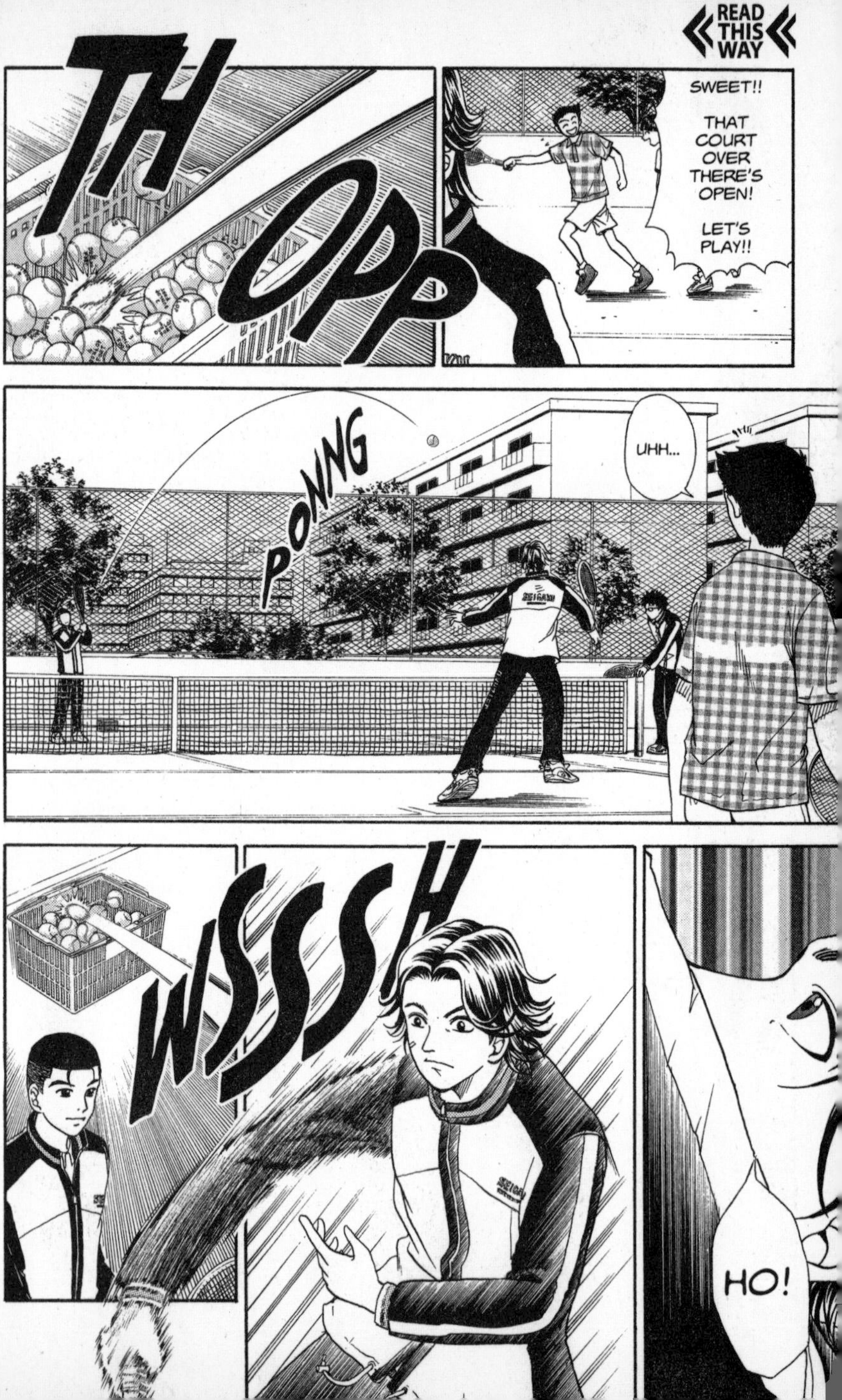
READ THIS WAY
SWEET!!
THAT COURT OVER THERE'S OPEN!
LET'S PLAY!!
THOPP
UHH...
PONNG
HO!
WSSSH

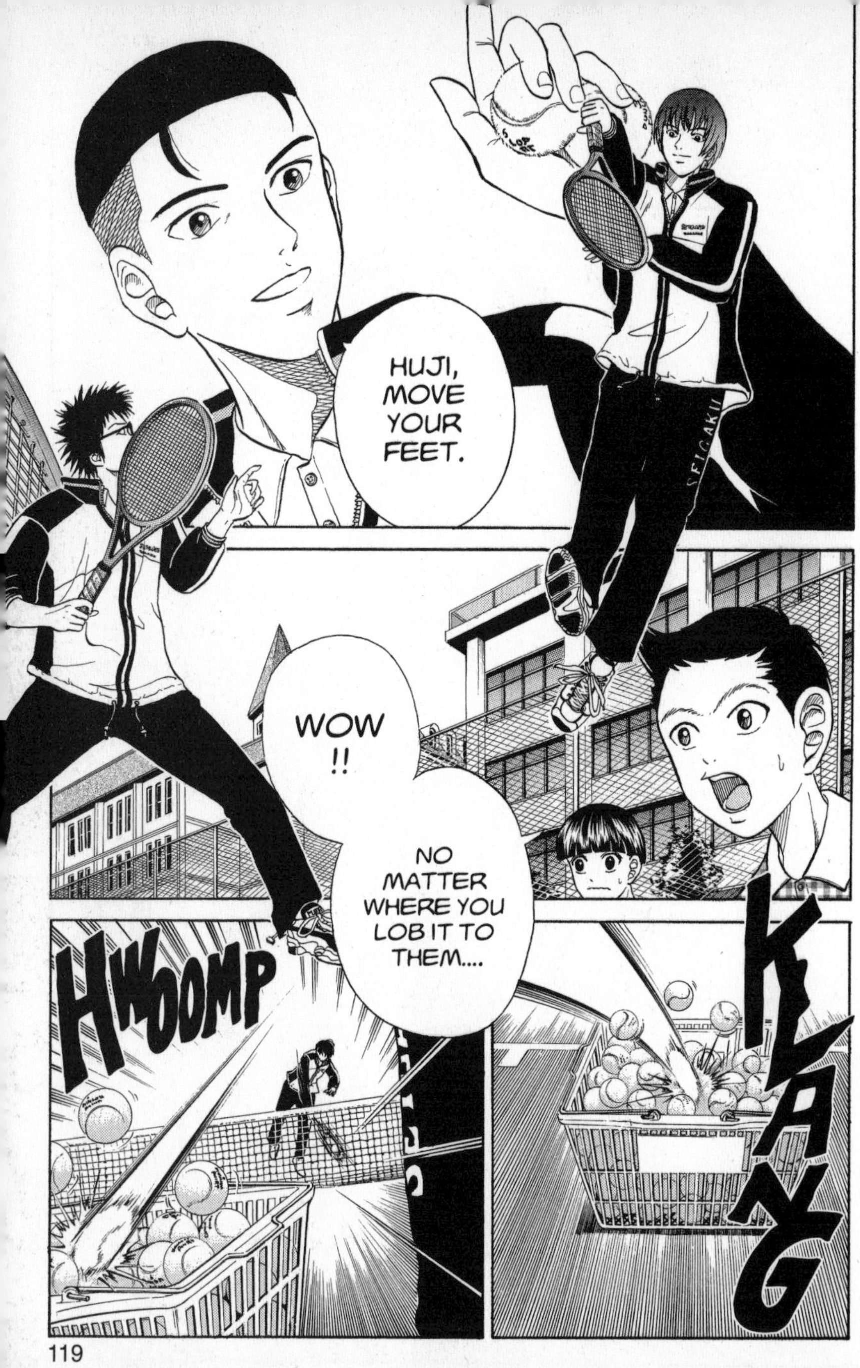
HUJI, MOVE YOUR FEET.
WOW !!
NO MATTER WHERE YOU LOB IT TO THEM....
KLANG
HWOOMP

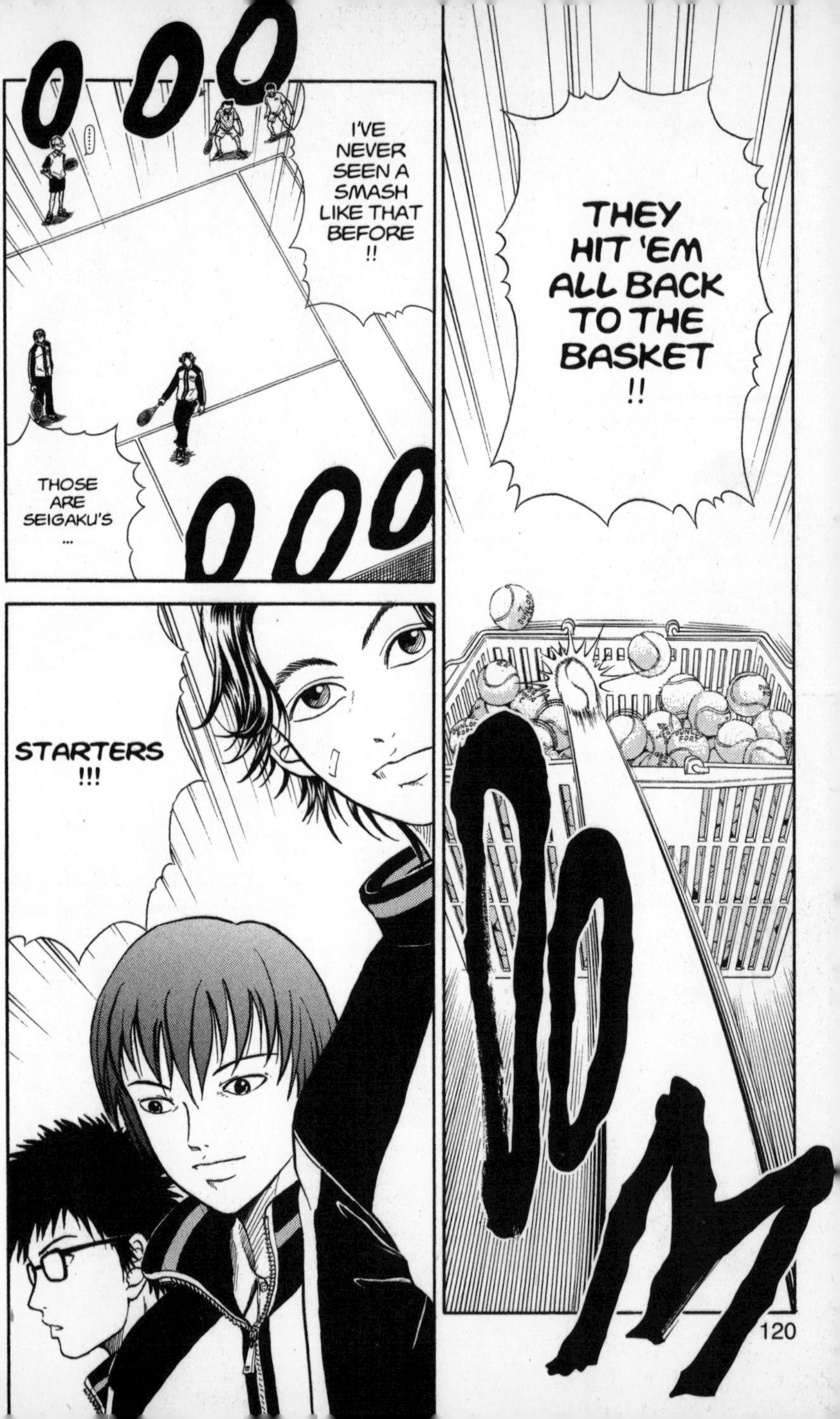
THEY HIT 'EM ALL BACK TO THE BASKET !!
I'VE NEVER SEEN A SMASH LIKE THAT BEFORE !!
...
THOSE ARE SEIGAKU'S ...
STARTERS !!!

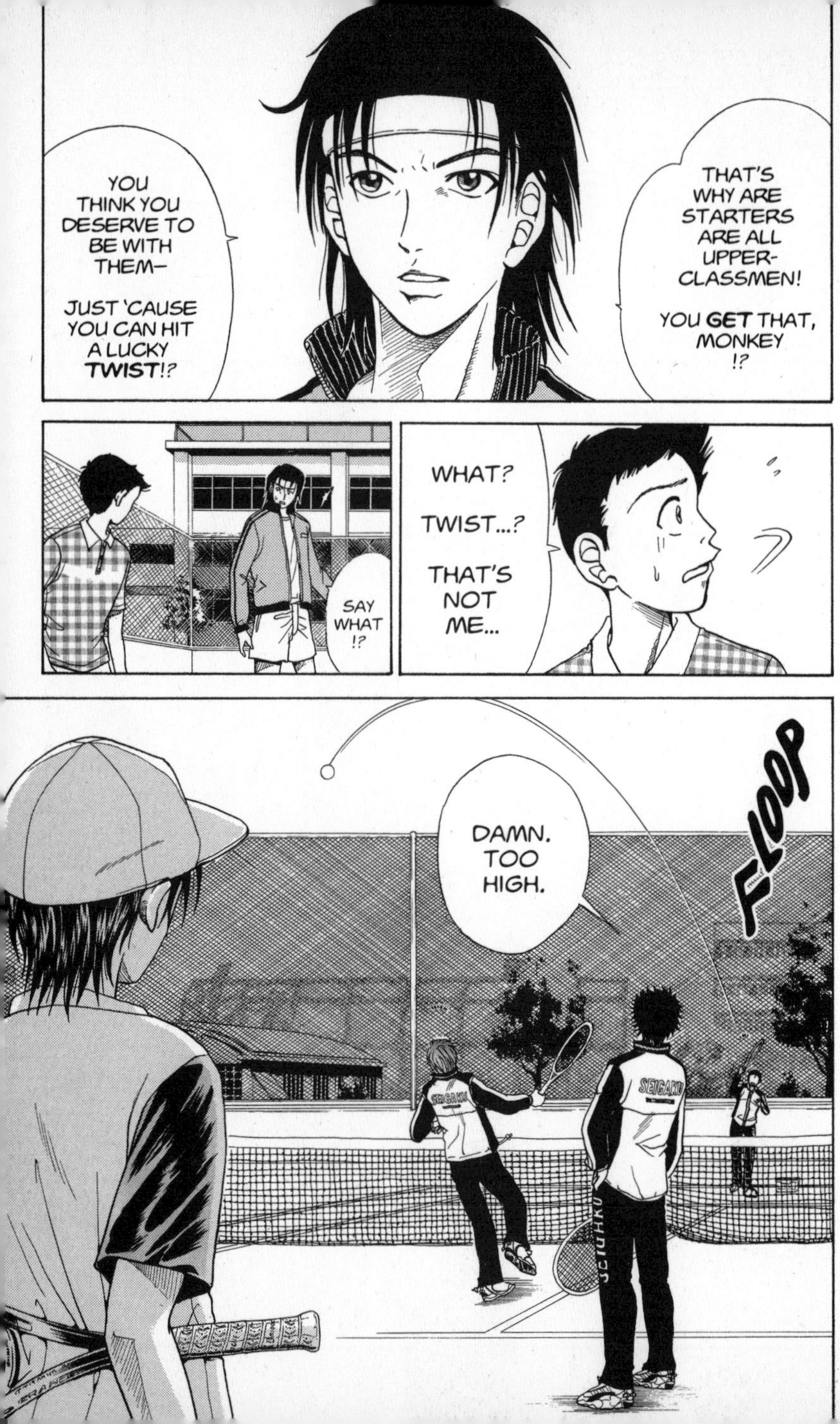
THAT'S WHY ARE STARTERS ARE ALL UPPER-CLASSMEN! YOU **GET** THAT, MONKEY !?
YOU THINK YOU DESERVE TO BE WITH THEM– JUST 'CAUSE YOU CAN HIT A LUCKY **TWIST**!?
WHAT? TWIST...? THAT'S NOT ME...
SAY WHAT !?
FLOOP
DAMN. TOO HIGH.
SEIGAKU
SEIGAKU

READ THIS WAY

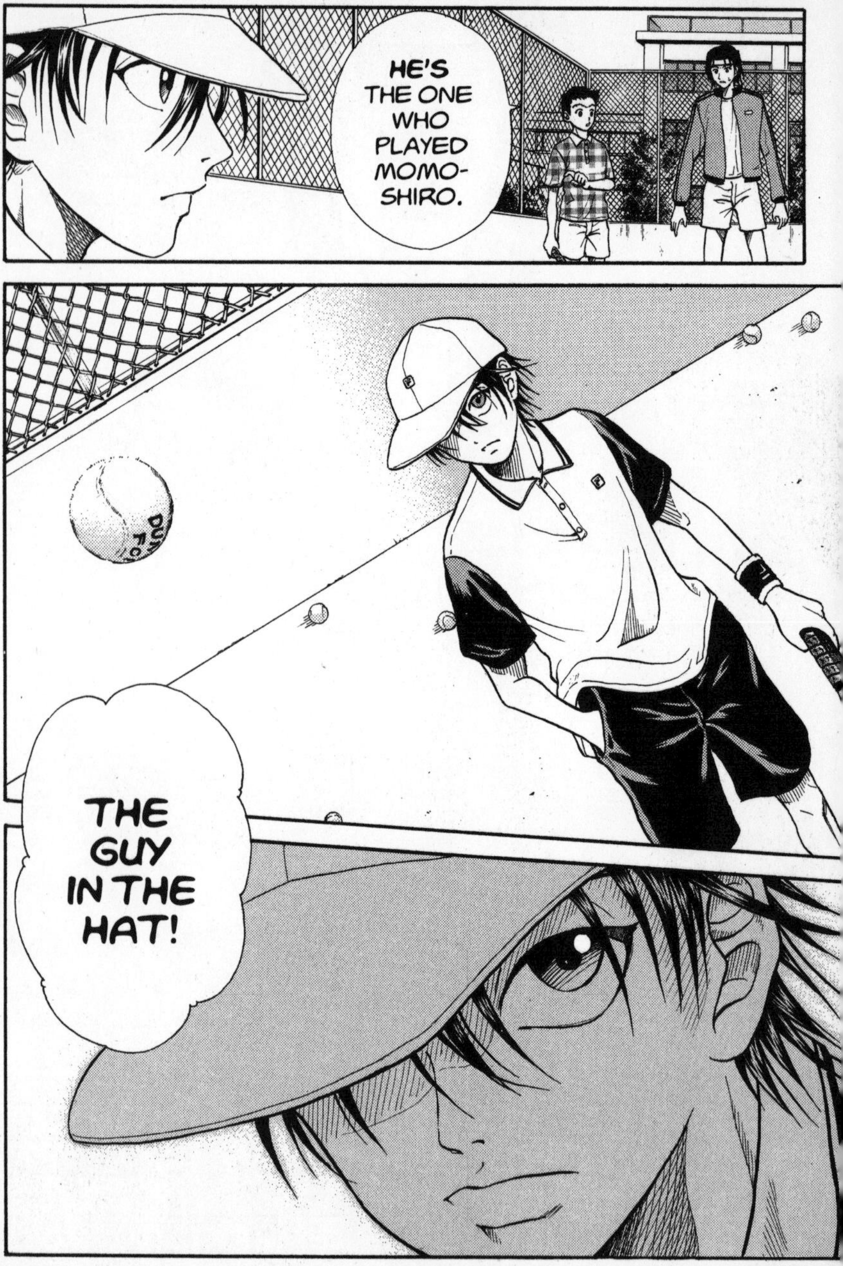
HE'S THE ONE WHO PLAYED MOMO-SHIRO.
THE GUY IN THE HAT!

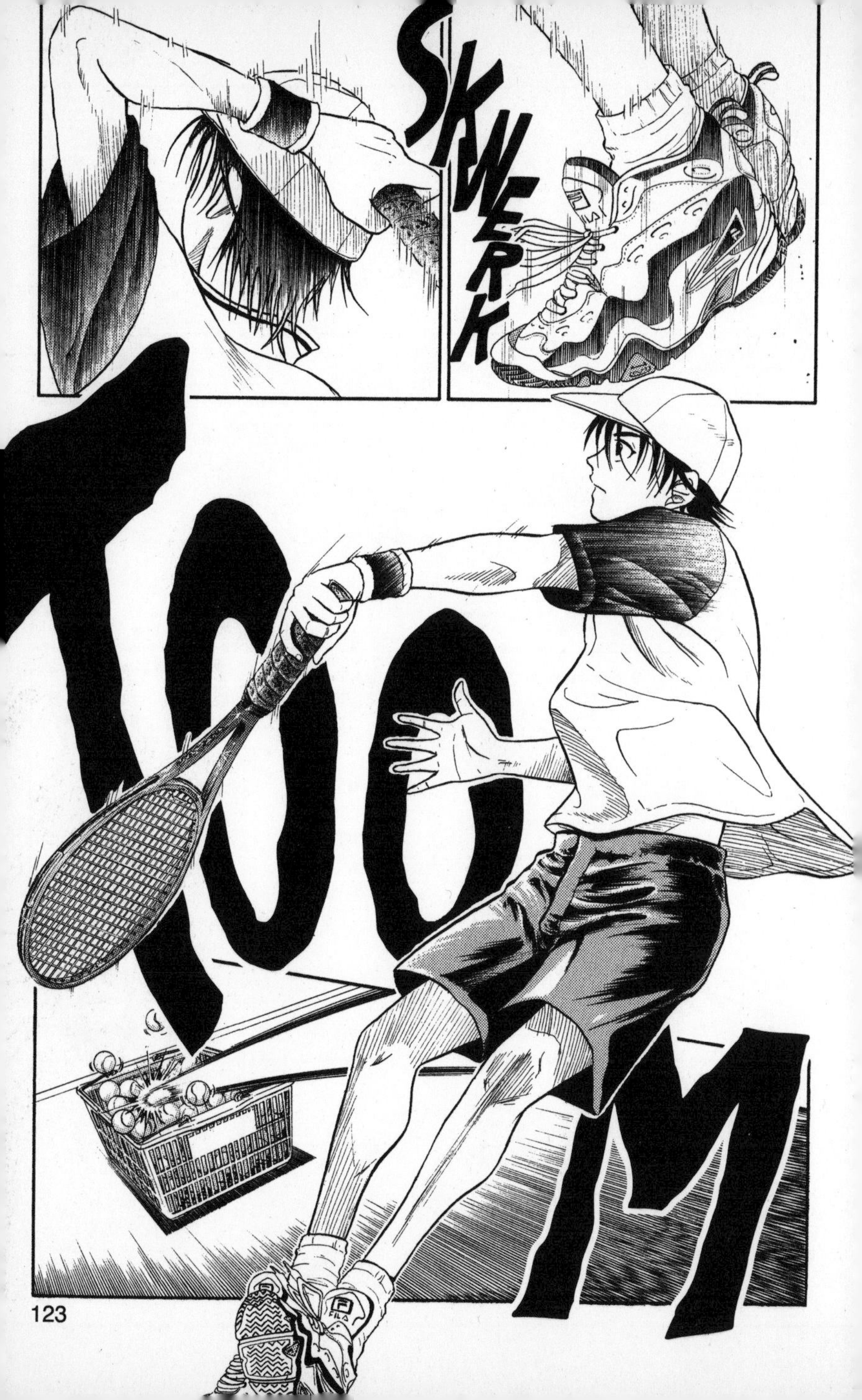
SKWERK
VOOM

READ THIS WAY

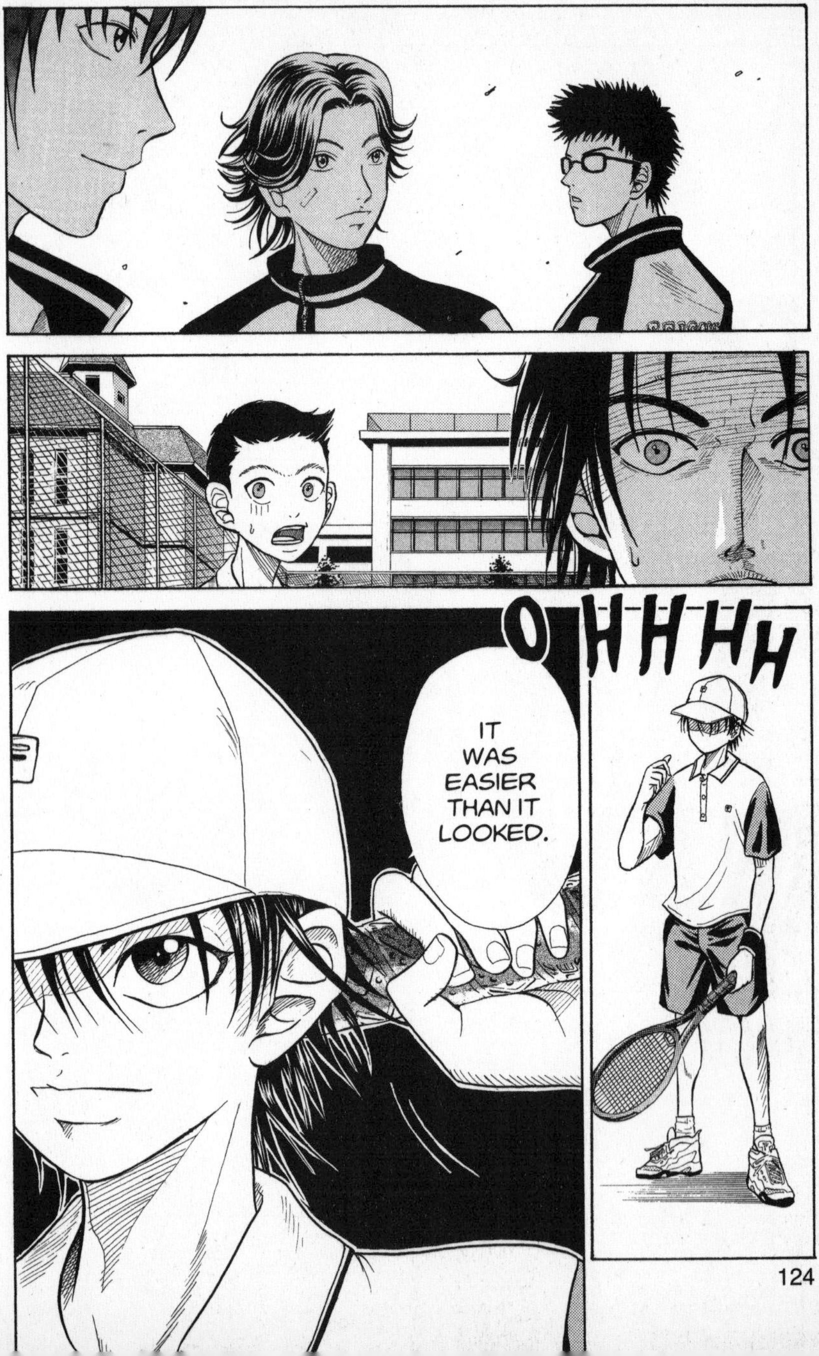
OHHHH
IT WAS EASIER THAN IT LOOKED.

READ THIS WAY

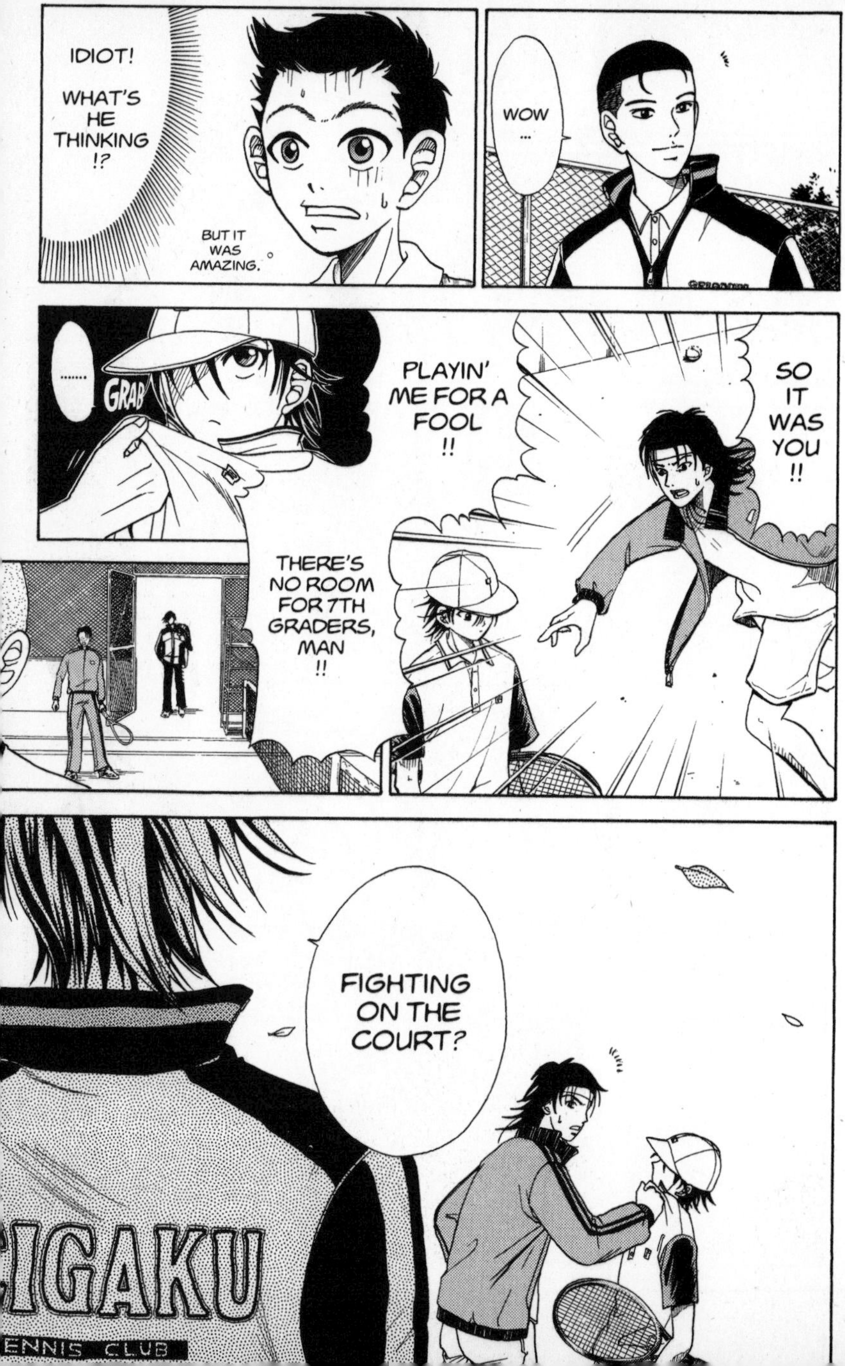
WOW ...
IDIOT!
WHAT'S HE THINKING !?
BUT IT WAS AMAZING.
SO IT WAS YOU !!
PLAYIN' ME FOR A FOOL !!
THERE'S NO ROOM FOR 7TH GRADERS, MAN !!
......
GRAB
FIGHTING ON THE COURT?
IGAKU
ENNIS CLUB

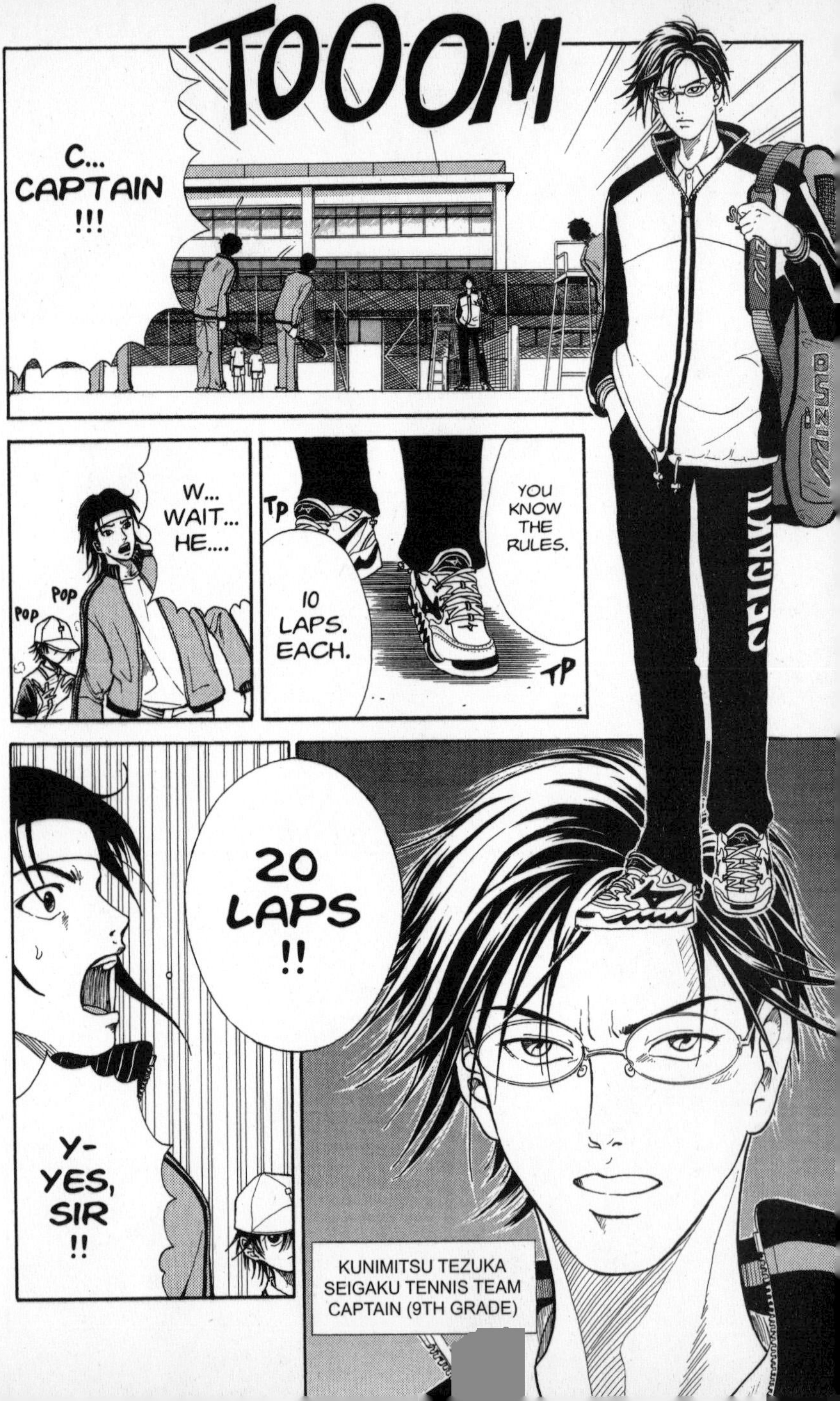
TOOOM
C... CAPTAIN !!!
YOU KNOW THE RULES.
TP
10 LAPS. EACH.
TP
W... WAIT... HE....
POP
POP
KUNIMITSU TEZUKA
SEIGAKU TENNIS TEAM
CAPTAIN (9TH GRADE)
20 LAPS !!
Y- YES, SIR !!

READ THIS WAY

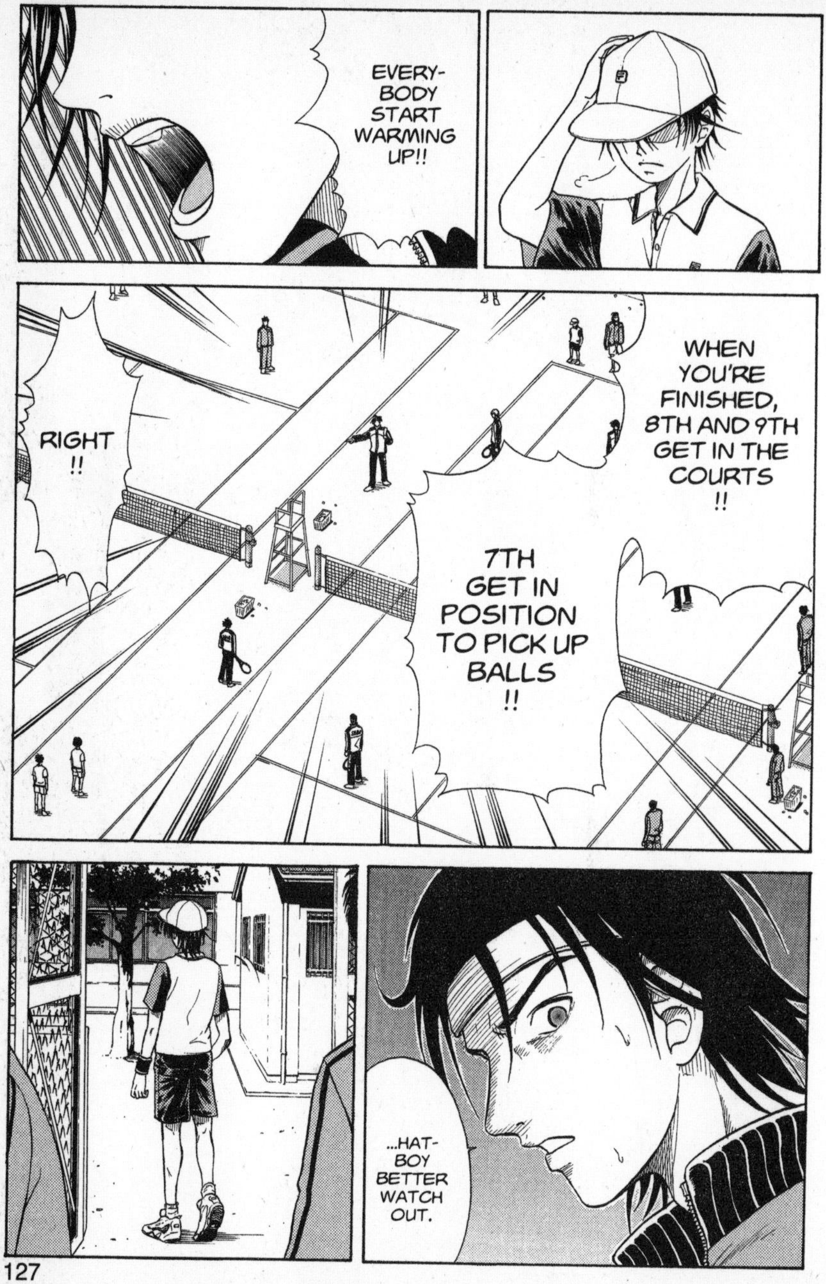
EVERY-BODY START WARMING UP!!
WHEN YOU'RE FINISHED, 8TH AND 9TH GET IN THE COURTS!!
7TH GET IN POSITION TO PICK UP BALLS!!
RIGHT!!
...HAT-BOY BETTER WATCH OUT.

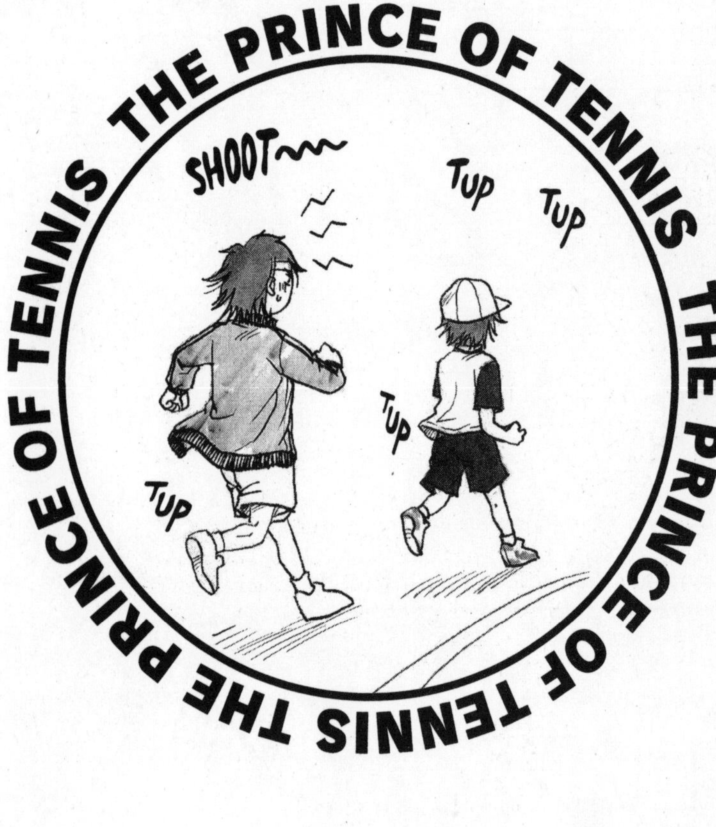
THE PRINCE OF TENNIS THE PRINCE OF TENNIS THE PRINCE OF TENNIS THE PRINCE OF TENNIS
TUP
TUP
SHOOT~~
TUP
TUP

Genius 5
DUST COVERED RACQUET

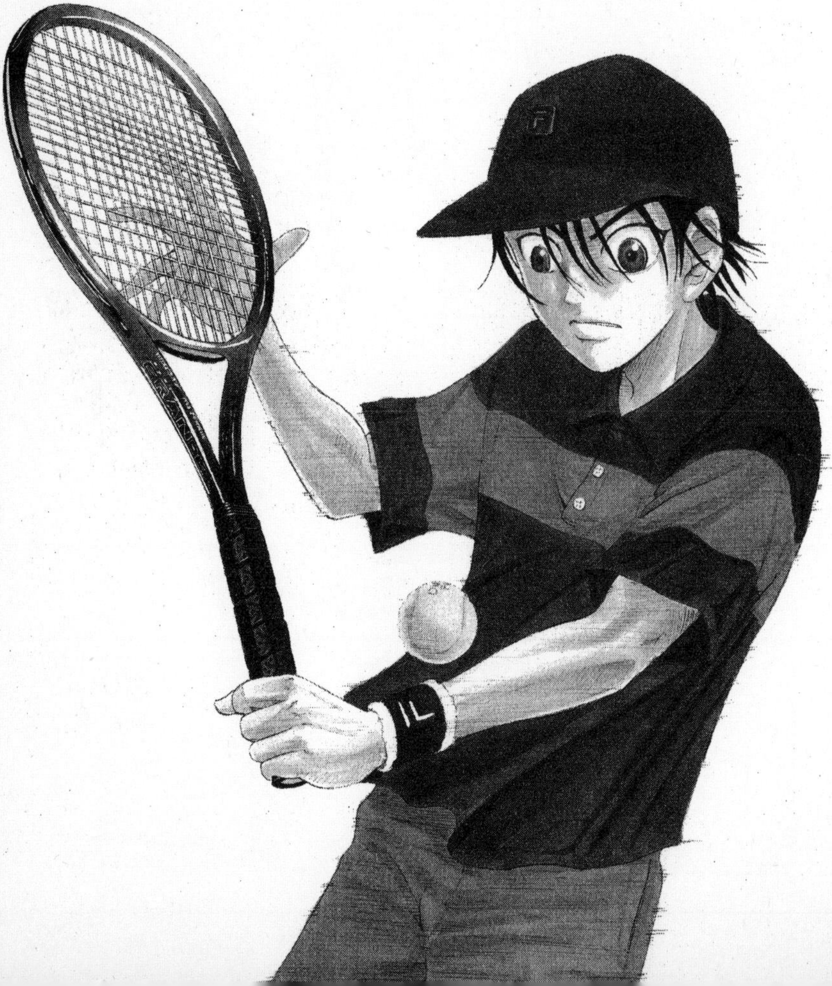

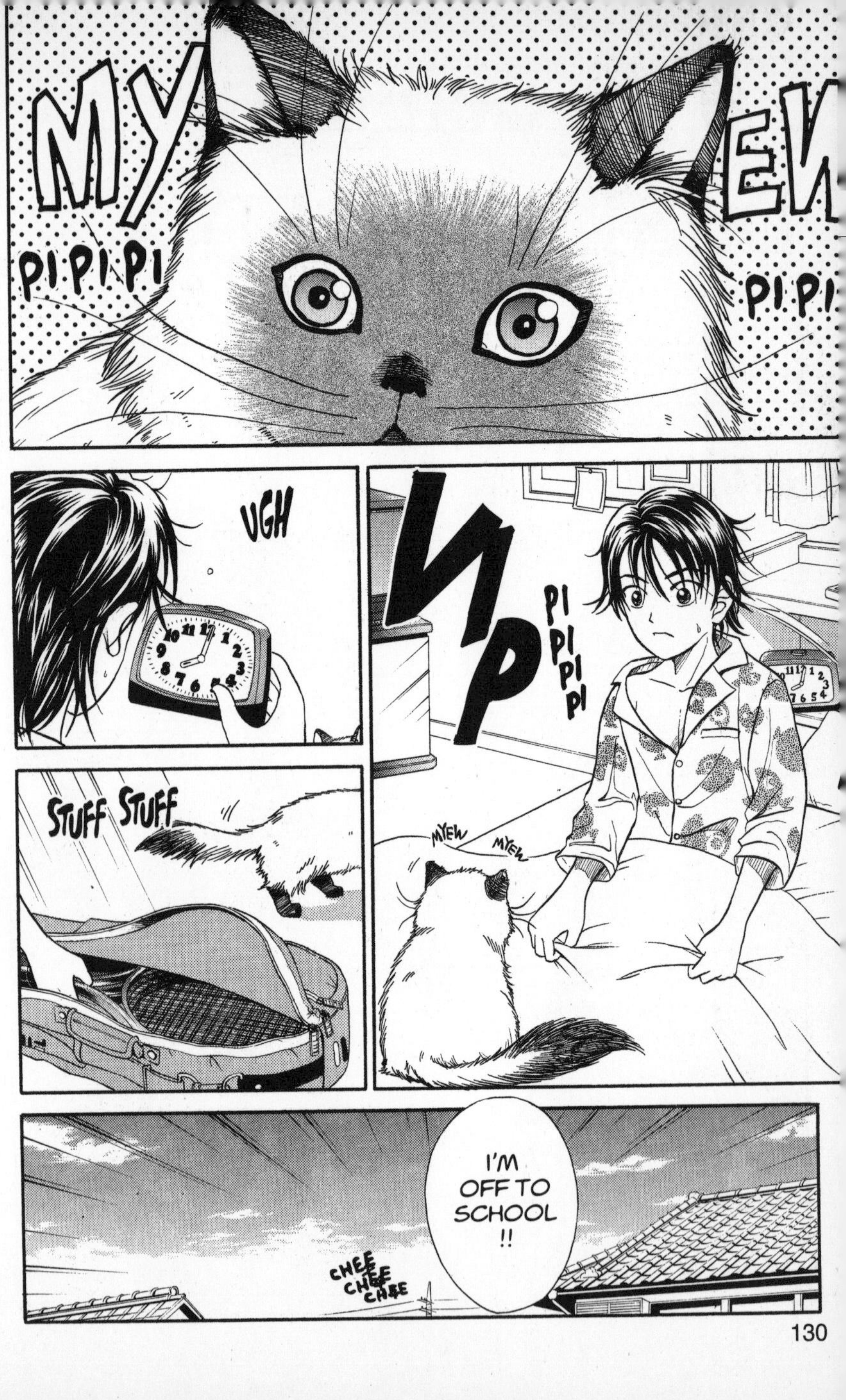
MY EW
PI PI PI
PI PI
UP
PI PI PI PI PI
MYEW MYEW
UGH
STUFF STUFF
I'M OFF TO SCHOOL !!
CHEE CHEE CHEE CHEE

READ THIS WAY

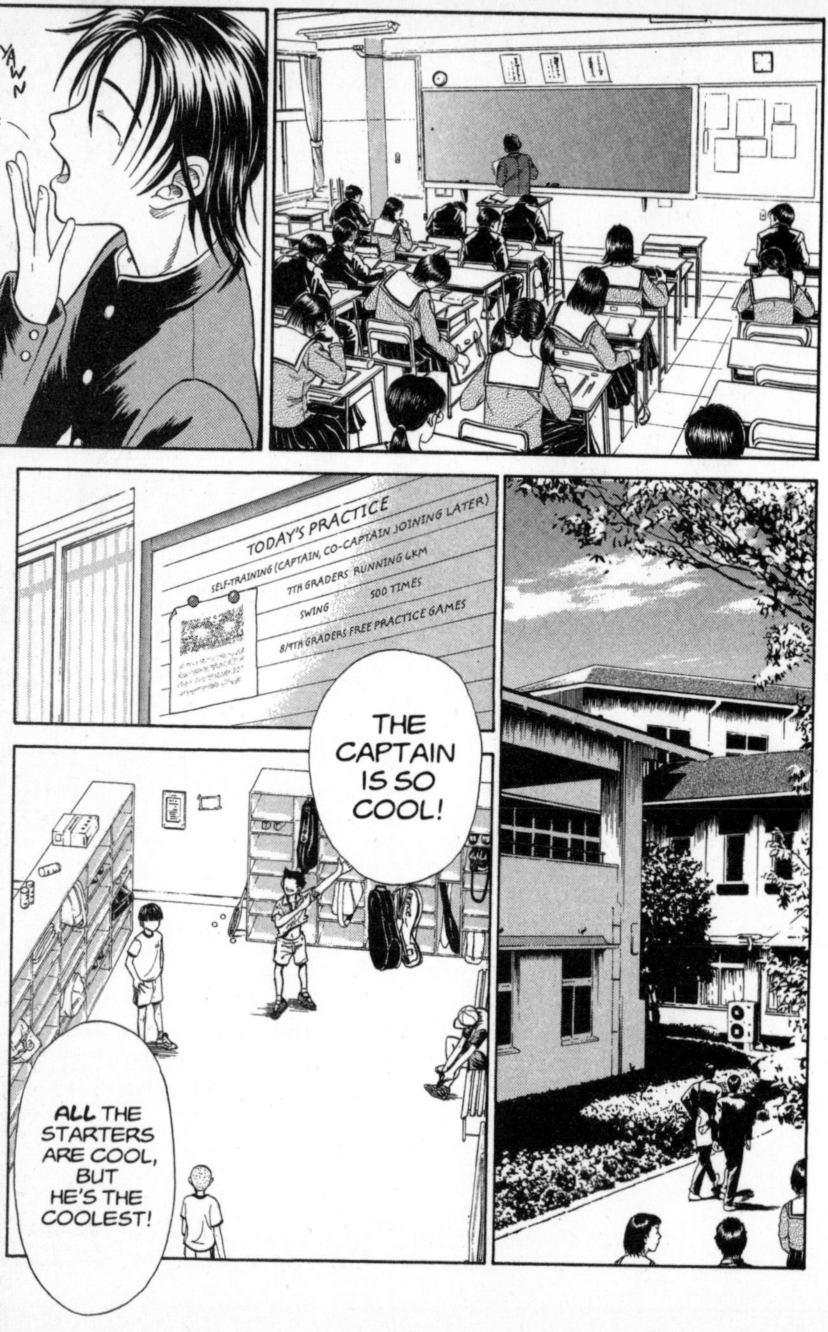
YAWN
TODAY'S PRACTICE
SELF-TRAINING (CAPTAIN, CO-CAPTAIN JOINING LATER)
7TH GRADERS RUNNING 6KM
SWING 500 TIMES
8/9TH GRADERS FREE PRACTICE GAMES
THE CAPTAIN IS SO COOL!
ALL THE STARTERS ARE COOL, BUT HE'S THE COOLEST!

READ THIS WAY

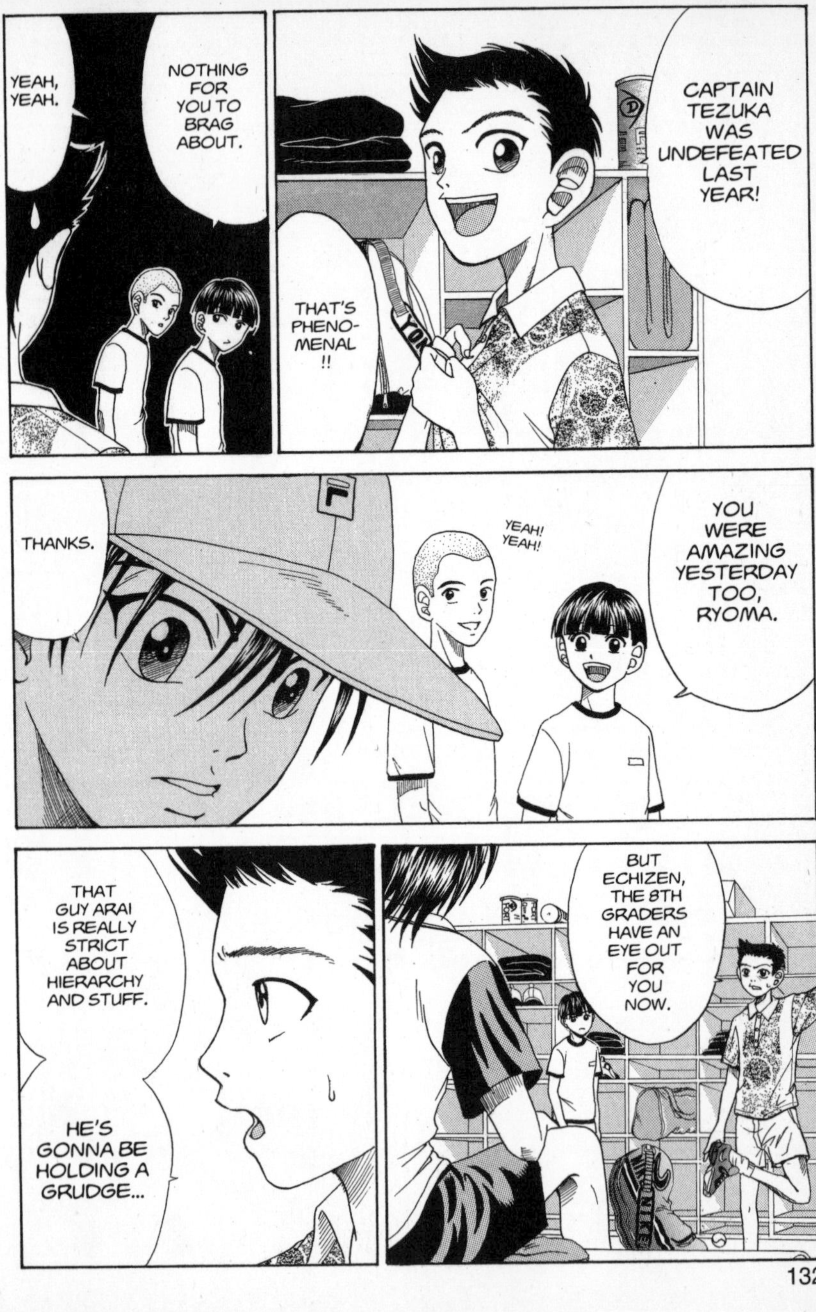
CAPTAIN TEZUKA WAS UNDEFEATED LAST YEAR!
THAT'S PHENOMENAL !!
NOTHING FOR YOU TO BRAG ABOUT.
YEAH, YEAH.
YOU WERE AMAZING YESTERDAY TOO, RYOMA.
YEAH! YEAH!
THANKS.
BUT ECHIZEN, THE 8TH GRADERS HAVE AN EYE OUT FOR YOU NOW.
THAT GUY ARAI IS REALLY STRICT ABOUT HIERARCHY AND STUFF.
HE'S GONNA BE HOLDING A GRUDGE...

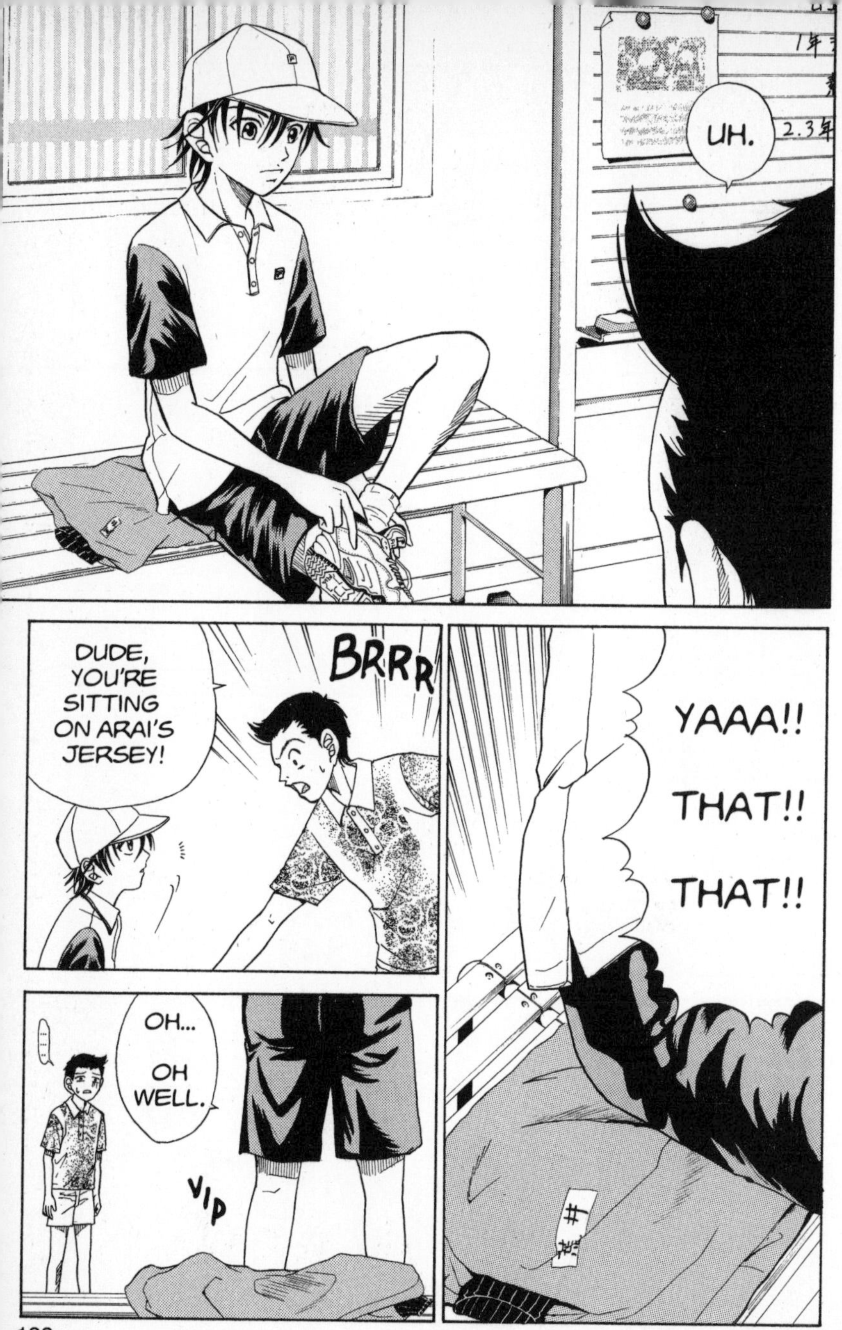
UH.
YAAA!!
THAT!!
THAT!!
DUDE, YOU'RE SITTING ON ARAI'S JERSEY!
BRRRR
...
OH...
OH WELL.
VIP

READ THIS WAY

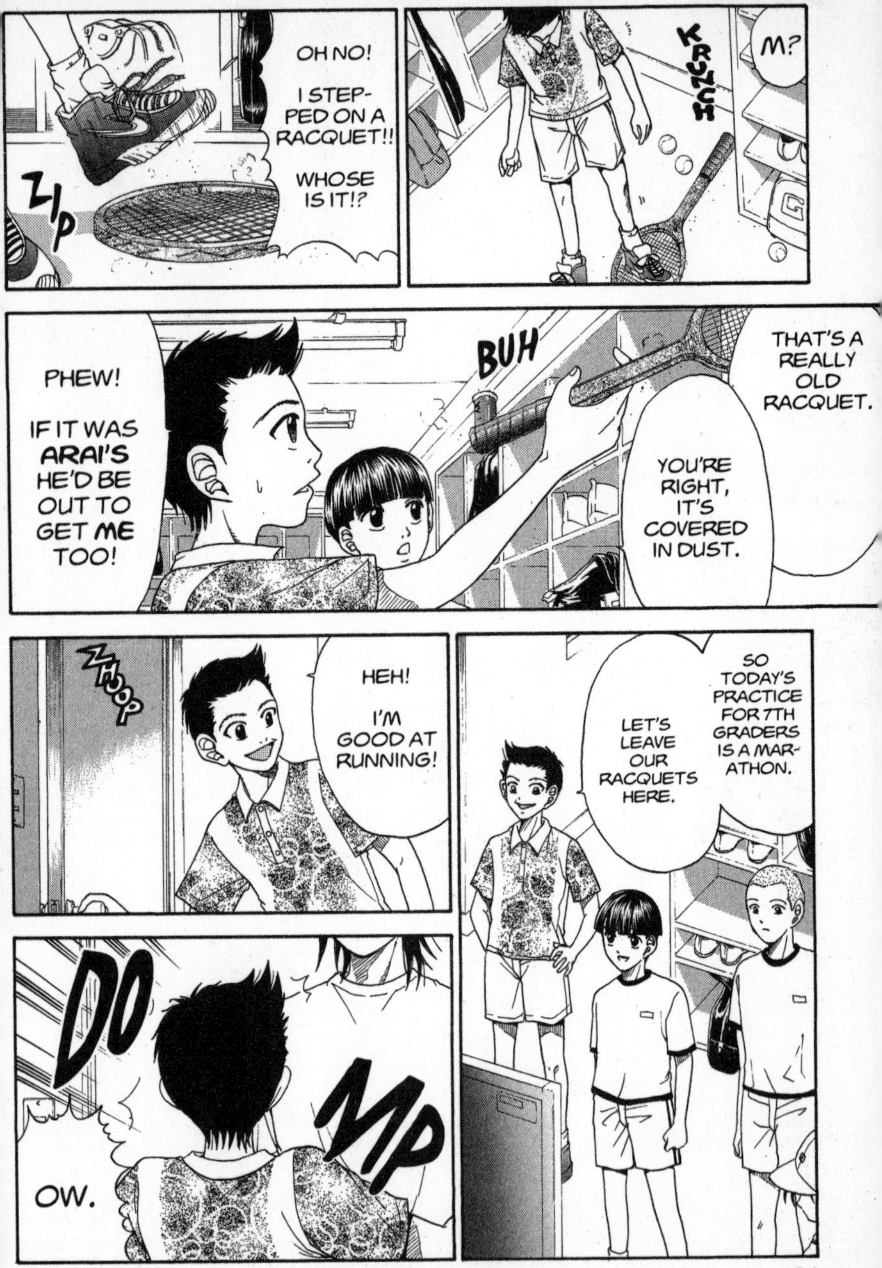

M?
KRUNCH
OH NO!
I STEP-PED ON A RACQUET!!
WHOSE IS IT!?
ZIP
THAT'S A REALLY OLD RACQUET.
BUH
YOU'RE RIGHT, IT'S COVERED IN DUST.
PHEW!
IF IT WAS ARAI'S HE'D BE OUT TO GET ME TOO!
SO TODAY'S PRACTICE FOR 7TH GRADERS IS A MAR-ATHON.
LET'S LEAVE OUR RACQUETS HERE.
HEH!
I'M GOOD AT RUNNING!
ZHOOP
DOMP
OW.

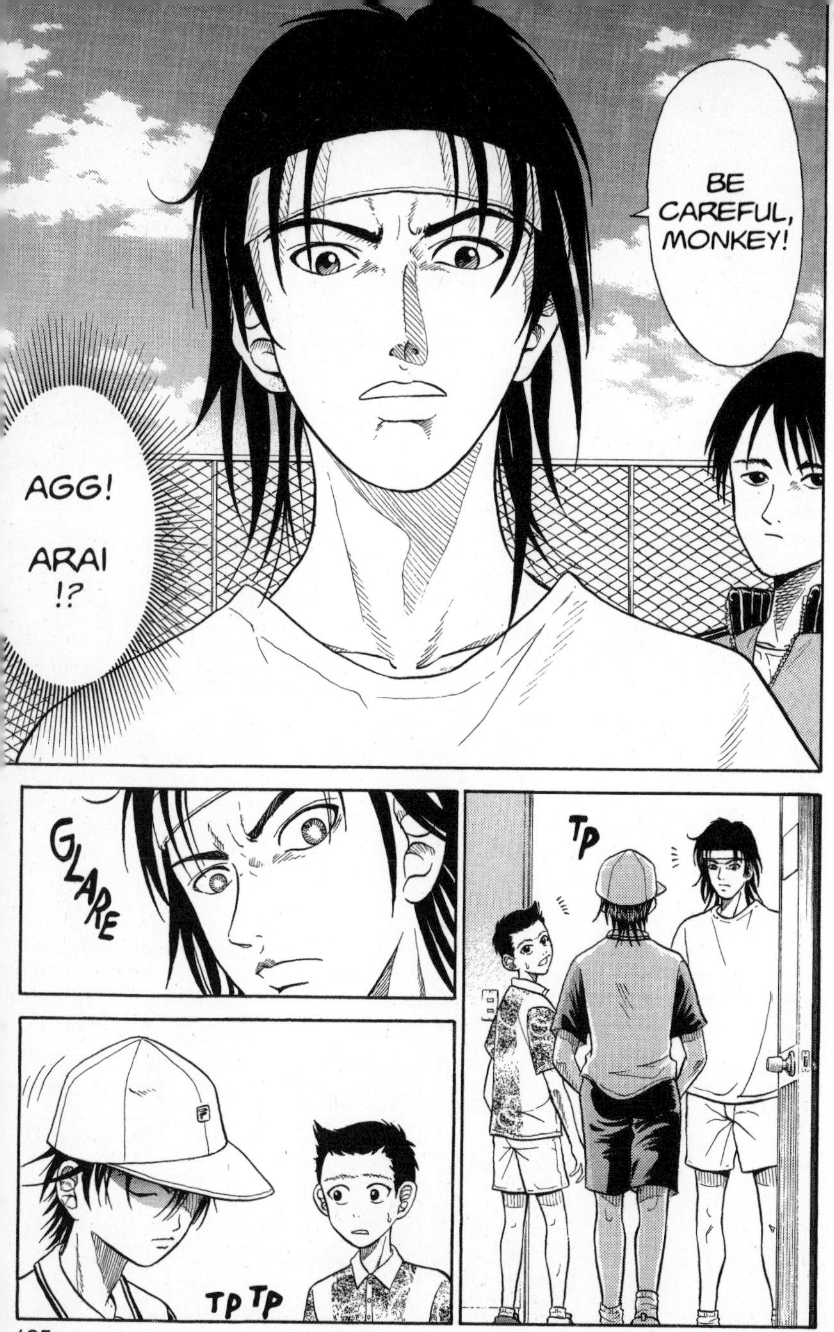
BE CAREFUL, MONKEY!
AGG!
ARAI !?
TP
GLARE
TP TP

HELLO.

TP TP

THAT'S THE KID YOU WERE TALKING ABOUT, RIGHT ARAI?

YEAH.

KH...

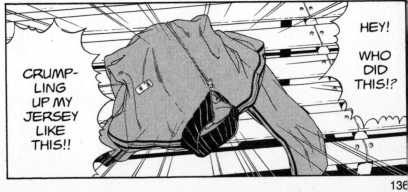

HEY!

WHO DID THIS!?

CRUMPLING UP MY JERSEY LIKE THIS!!

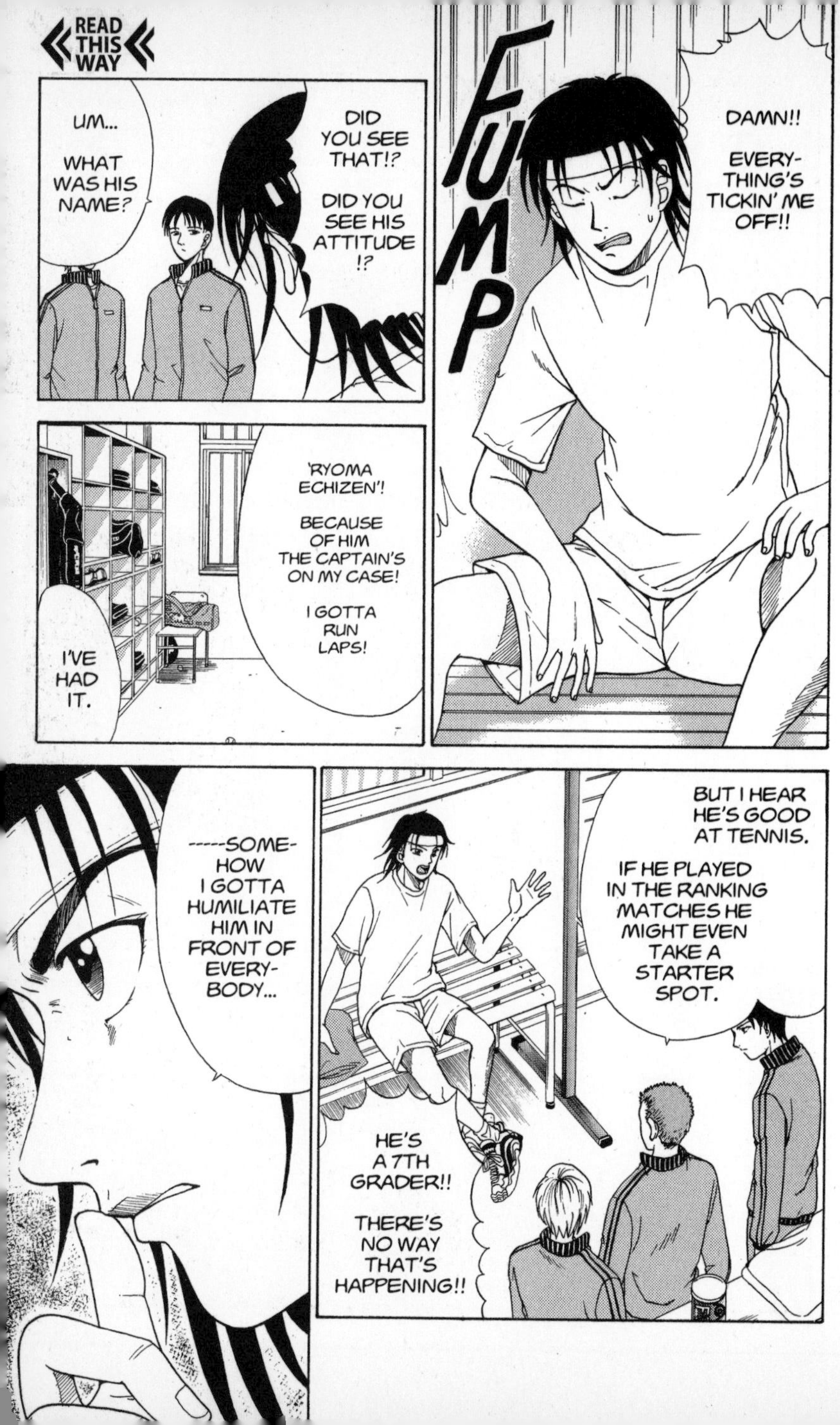
READ THIS WAY
FUMP
DAMN!! EVERY-THING'S TICKIN' ME OFF!!
DID YOU SEE THAT!? DID YOU SEE HIS ATTITUDE !?
UM... WHAT WAS HIS NAME?
'RYOMA ECHIZEN'! BECAUSE OF HIM THE CAPTAIN'S ON MY CASE! I GOTTA RUN LAPS!
I'VE HAD IT.
BUT I HEAR HE'S GOOD AT TENNIS. IF HE PLAYED IN THE RANKING MATCHES HE MIGHT EVEN TAKE A STARTER SPOT.
HE'S A 7TH GRADER!! THERE'S NO WAY THAT'S HAPPENING!!
-----SOME-HOW I GOTTA HUMILIATE HIM IN FRONT OF EVERY-BODY...

READ THIS WAY

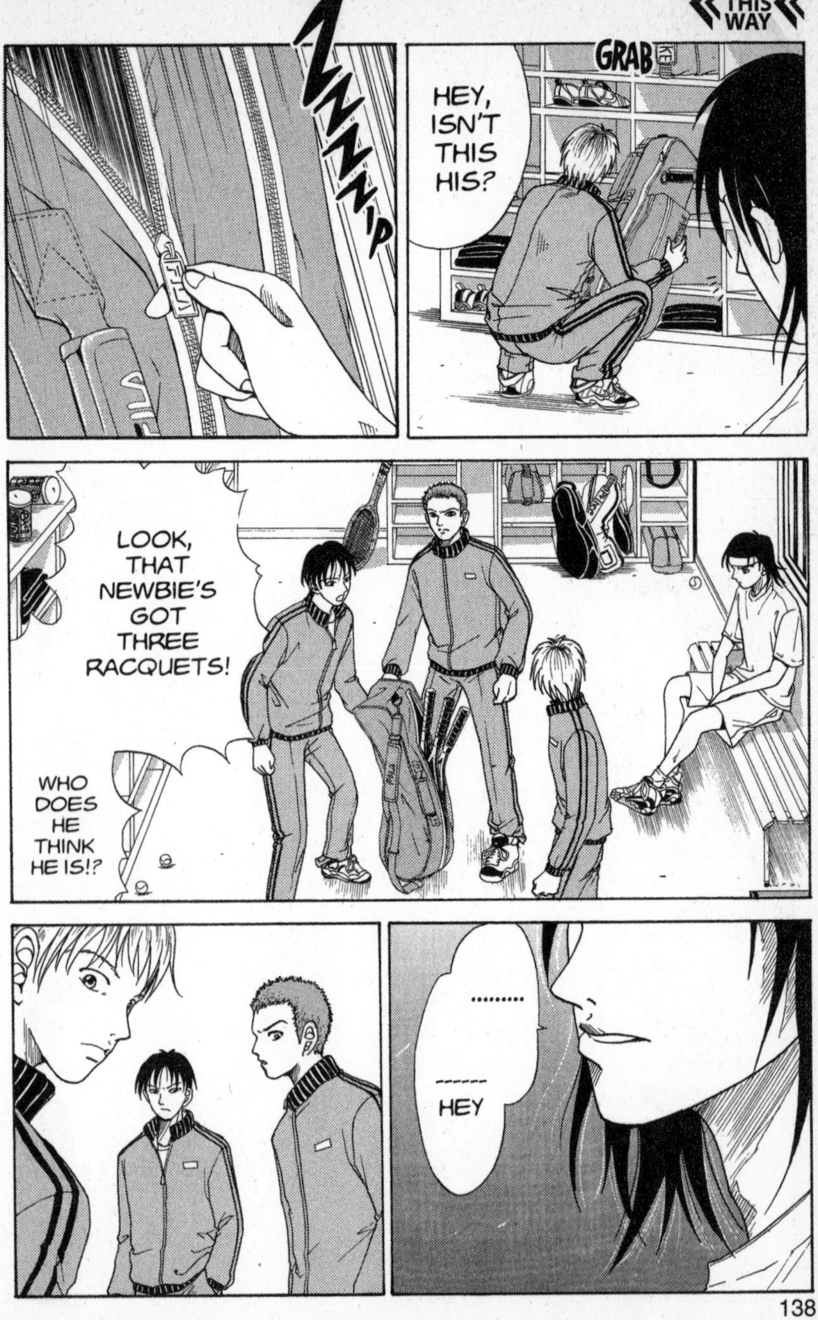
GRAB
HEY, ISN'T THIS HIS?
ZZZZZIP
LOOK, THAT NEWBIE'S GOT THREE RACQUETS!
WHO DOES HE THINK HE IS!?
....
------ HEY

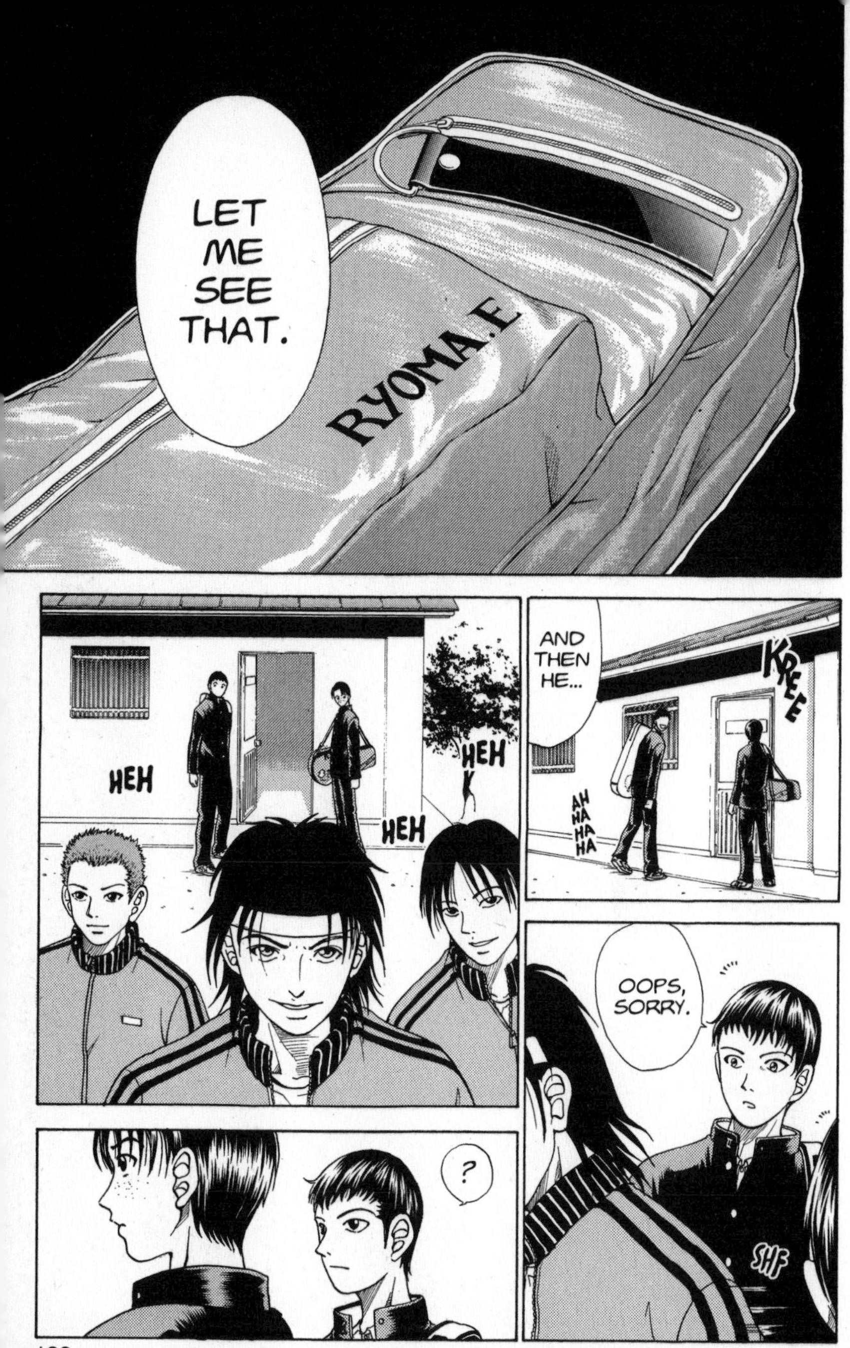
LET ME SEE THAT.
RYOMA.E
AND THEN HE...
KREEE
AH HA HA HA HA
HEH
HEH
HEH
OOPS, SORRY.
SHF
?

READ THIS WAY

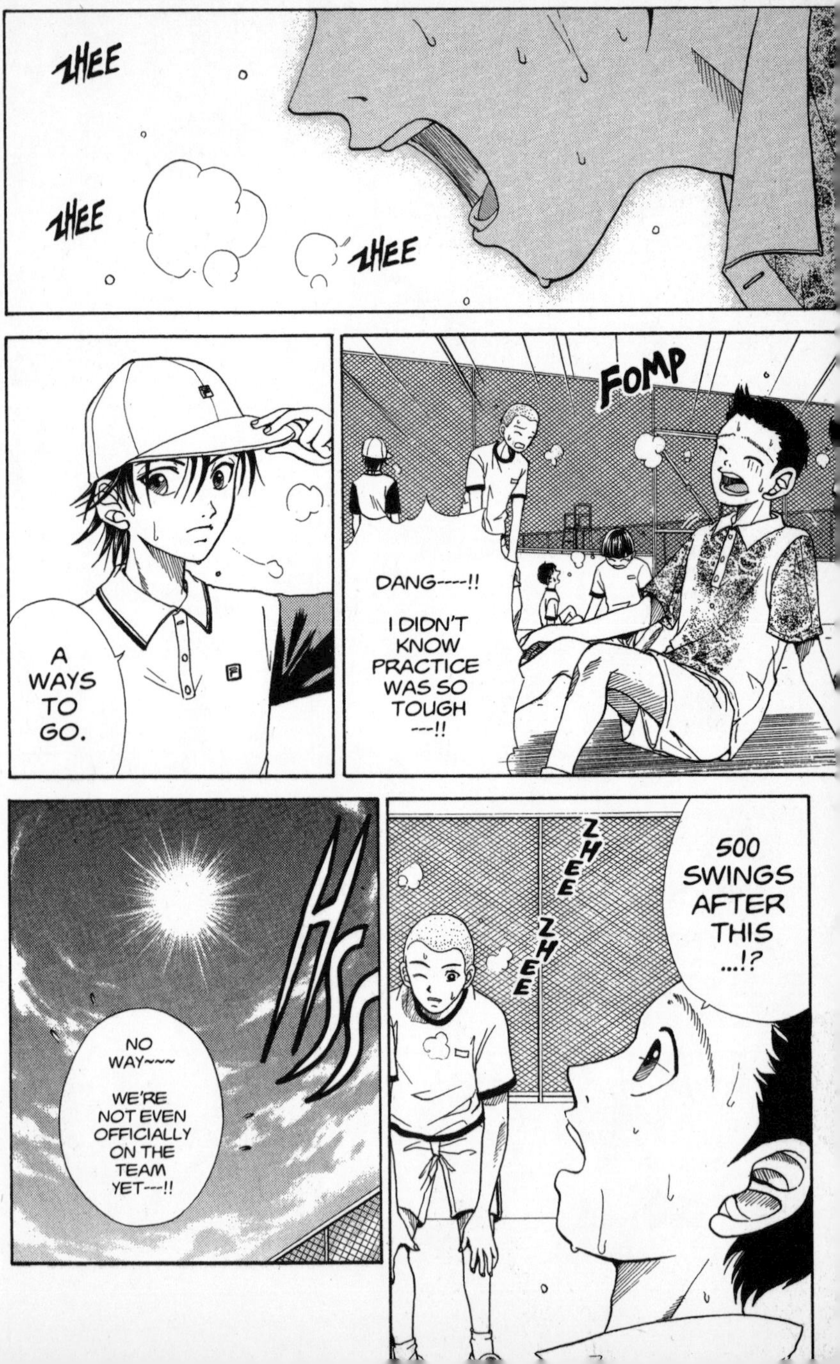
ZHEE
ZHEE
ZHEE
FOMP
DANG----!!
I DIDN'T KNOW PRACTICE WAS SO TOUGH ---!!
A WAYS TO GO.
500 SWINGS AFTER THIS ...!?
ZHEE
ZHEE
HS
NO WAY~~~
WE'RE NOT EVEN OFFICIALLY ON THE TEAM YET---!!

READ THIS WAY

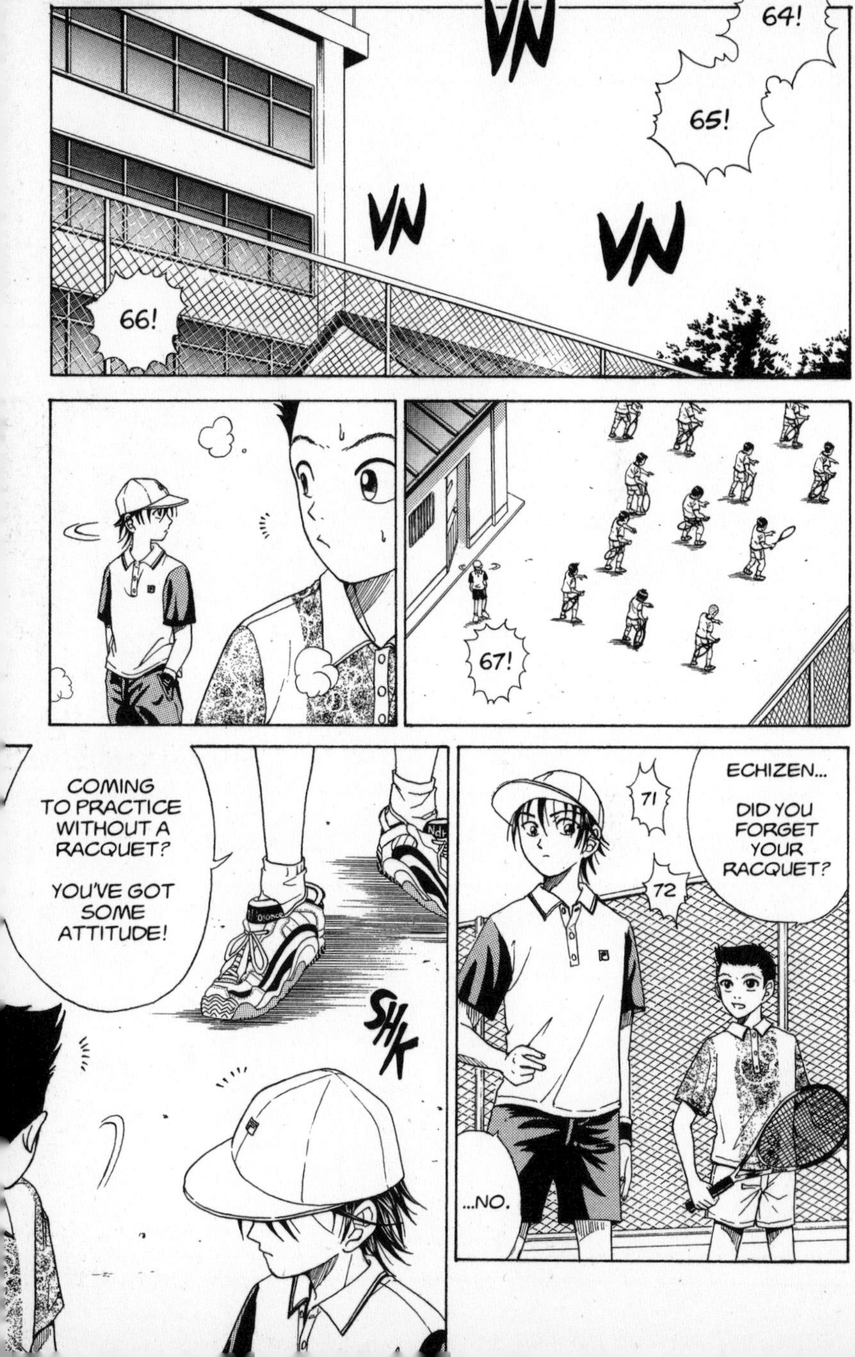

64!
VN
65!
VN
VN
66!
67!
ECHIZEN...
DID YOU FORGET YOUR RACQUET?
71
72
...NO.
COMING TO PRACTICE WITHOUT A RACQUET?
YOU'VE GOT SOME ATTITUDE!
SHK

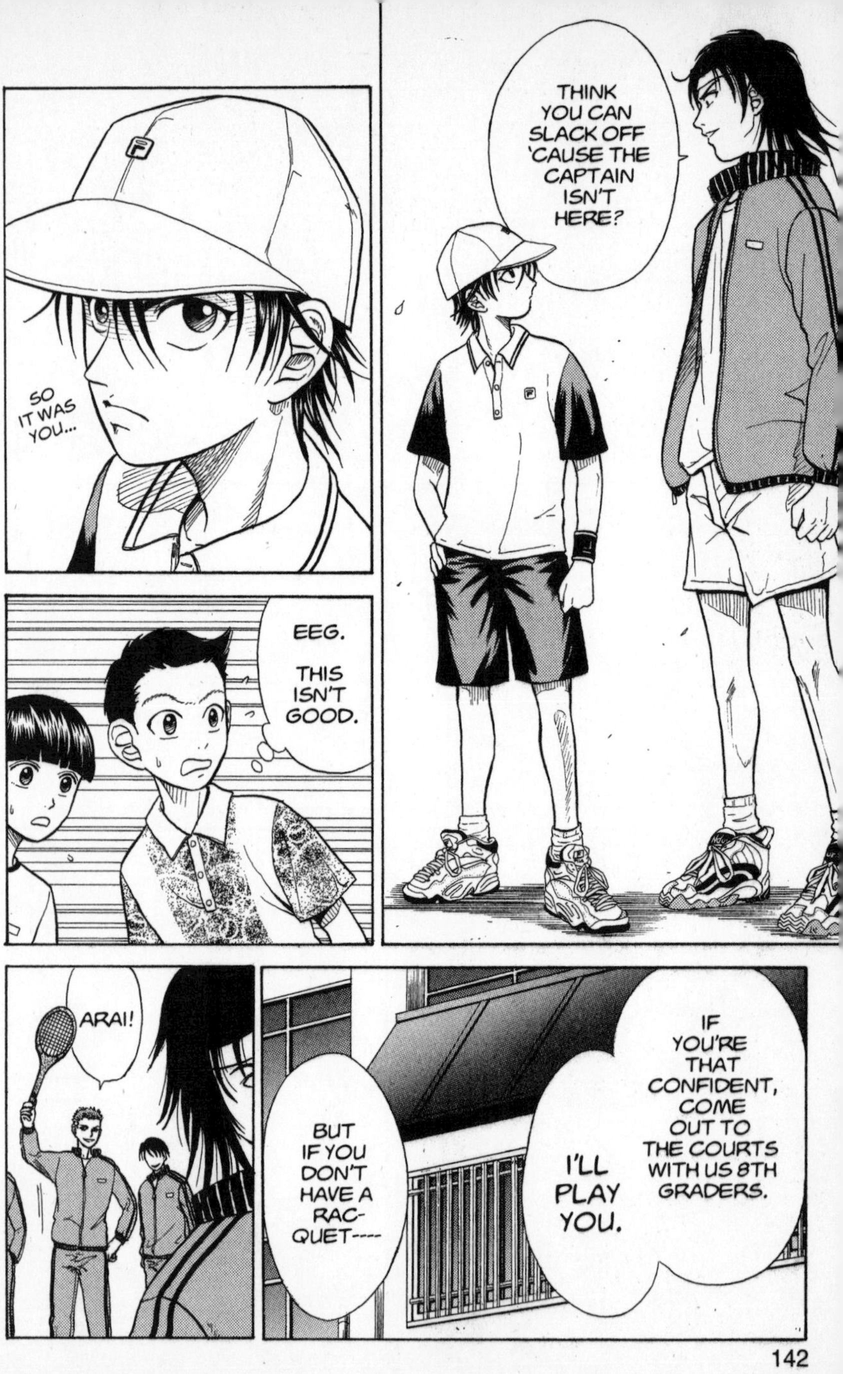
THINK YOU CAN SLACK OFF 'CAUSE THE CAPTAIN ISN'T HERE?
SO IT WAS YOU...
EEG.
THIS ISN'T GOOD.
IF YOU'RE THAT CONFIDENT, COME OUT TO THE COURTS WITH US 8TH GRADERS.
I'LL PLAY YOU.
BUT IF YOU DON'T HAVE A RAC-QUET----
ARAI!

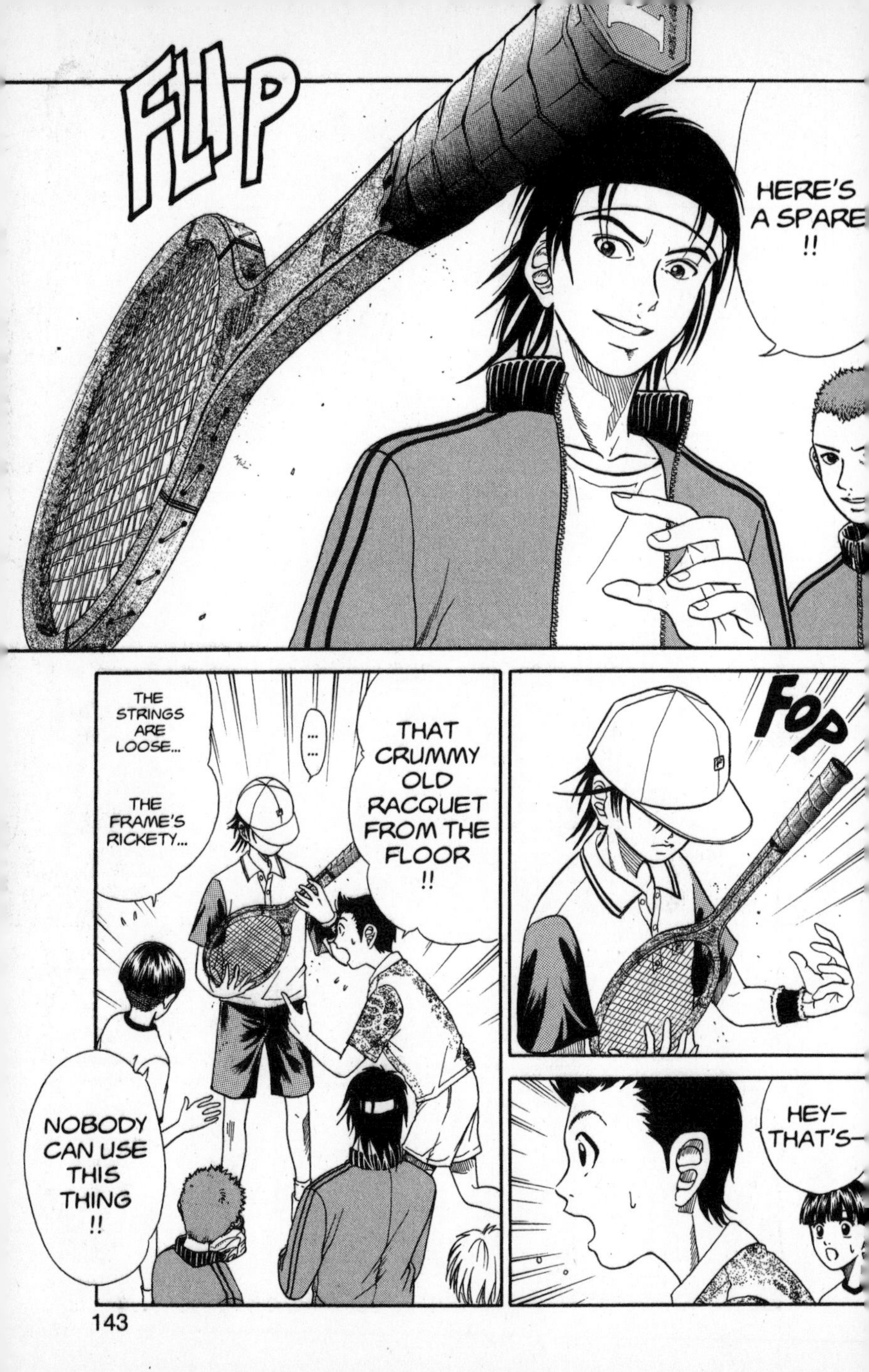
HERE'S A SPARE!!
FLIP
FOP
HEY— THAT'S—
THAT CRUMMY OLD RACQUET FROM THE FLOOR!!
... ...
THE STRINGS ARE LOOSE...
THE FRAME'S RICKETY...
NOBODY CAN USE THIS THING!!

READ THIS WAY

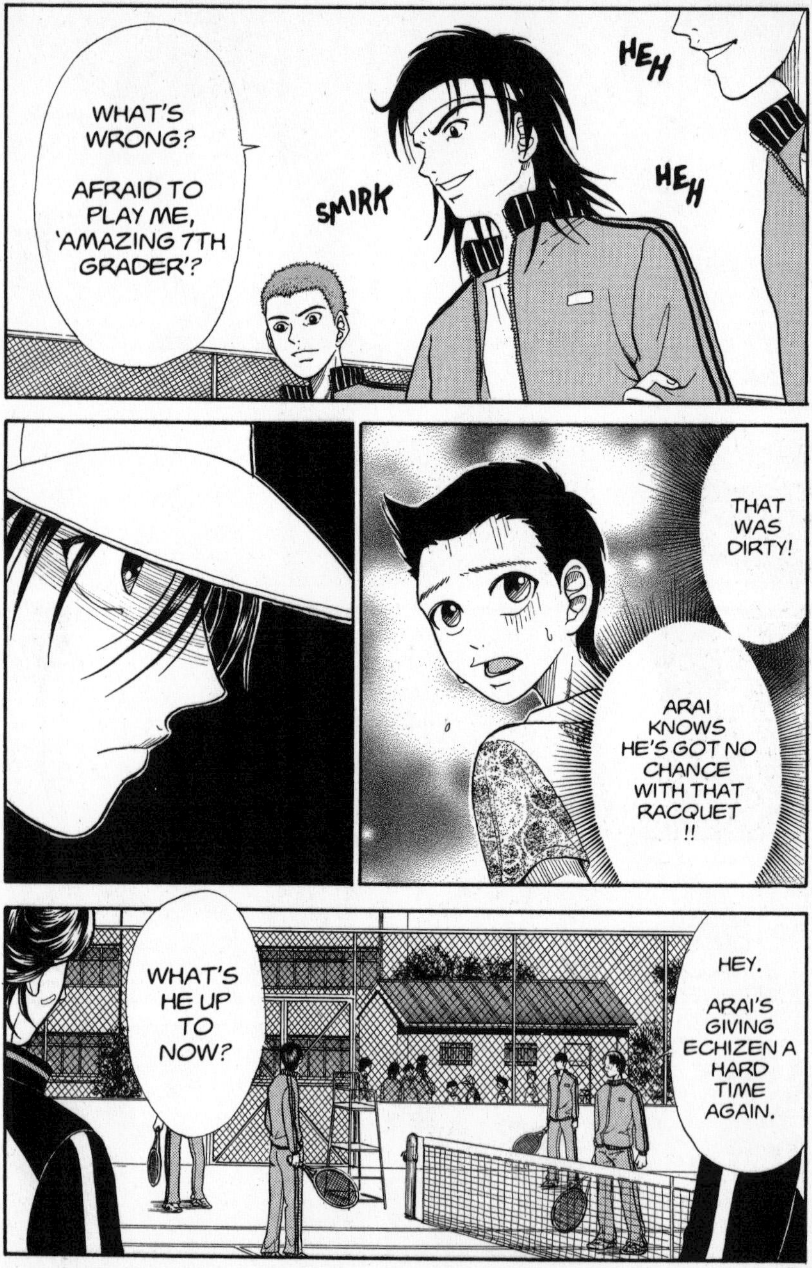

HEH
HEH
WHAT'S WRONG?
AFRAID TO PLAY ME, 'AMAZING 7TH GRADER'?
SMIRK
THAT WAS DIRTY!
ARAI KNOWS HE'S GOT NO CHANCE WITH THAT RACQUET !!
HEY.
ARAI'S GIVING ECHIZEN A HARD TIME AGAIN.
WHAT'S HE UP TO NOW?

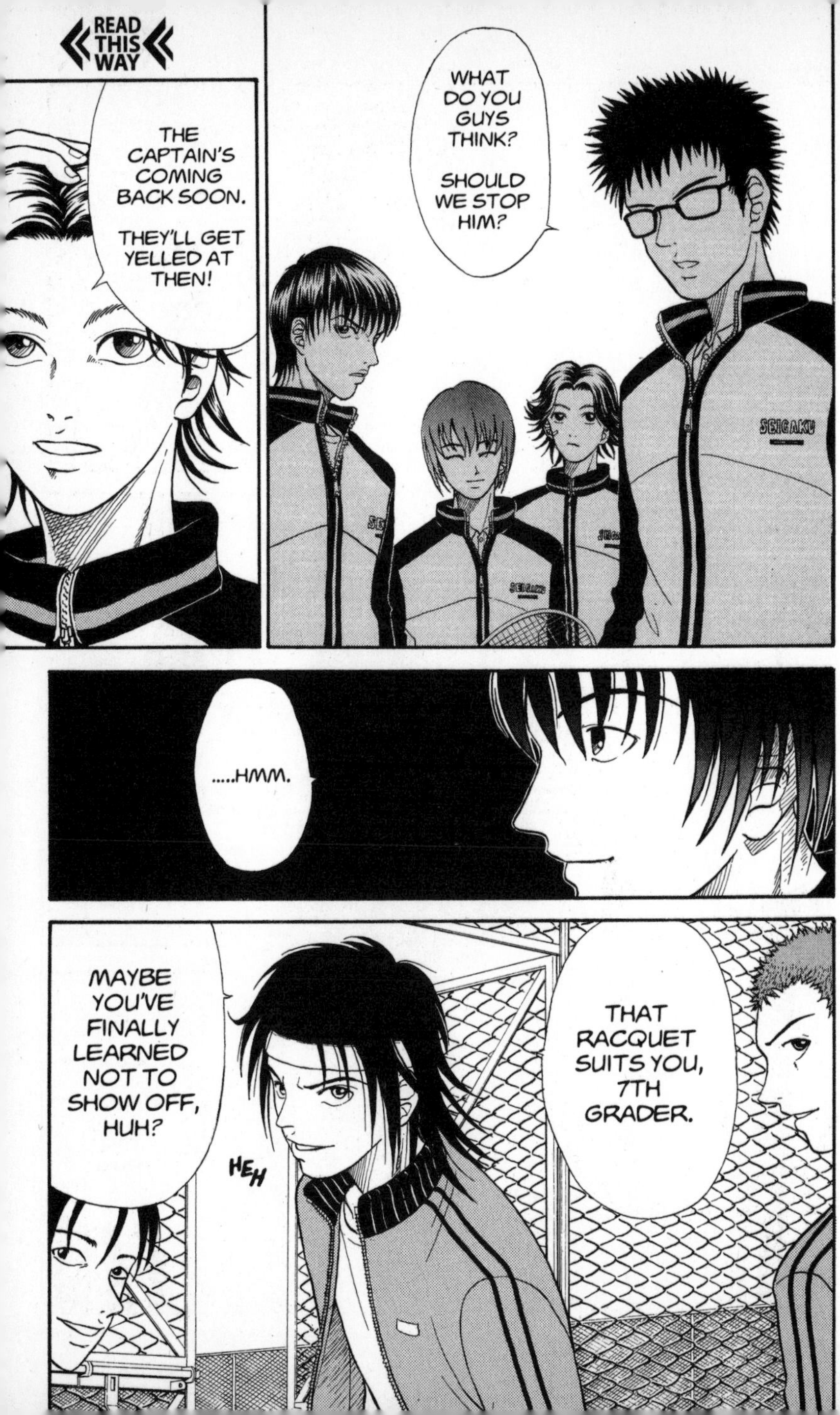
READ THIS WAY
WHAT DO YOU GUYS THINK? SHOULD WE STOP HIM?
THE CAPTAIN'S COMING BACK SOON. THEY'LL GET YELLED AT THEN!
.....HMM.
THAT RACQUET SUITS YOU, 7TH GRADER.
HEH
MAYBE YOU'VE FINALLY LEARNED NOT TO SHOW OFF, HUH?

MAYBE NOW YOUR 3 PRECIOUS RACQUETS'LL TURN UP!

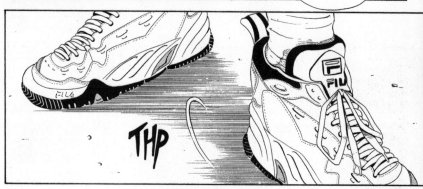

THP

TP

TP TP

H... HEY?

WHERE YOU GOING ECHIZEN ...?

WEAKLINGS ALWAYS HAVE TO RESORT TO PETTY TRICKS.

READ THIS WAY

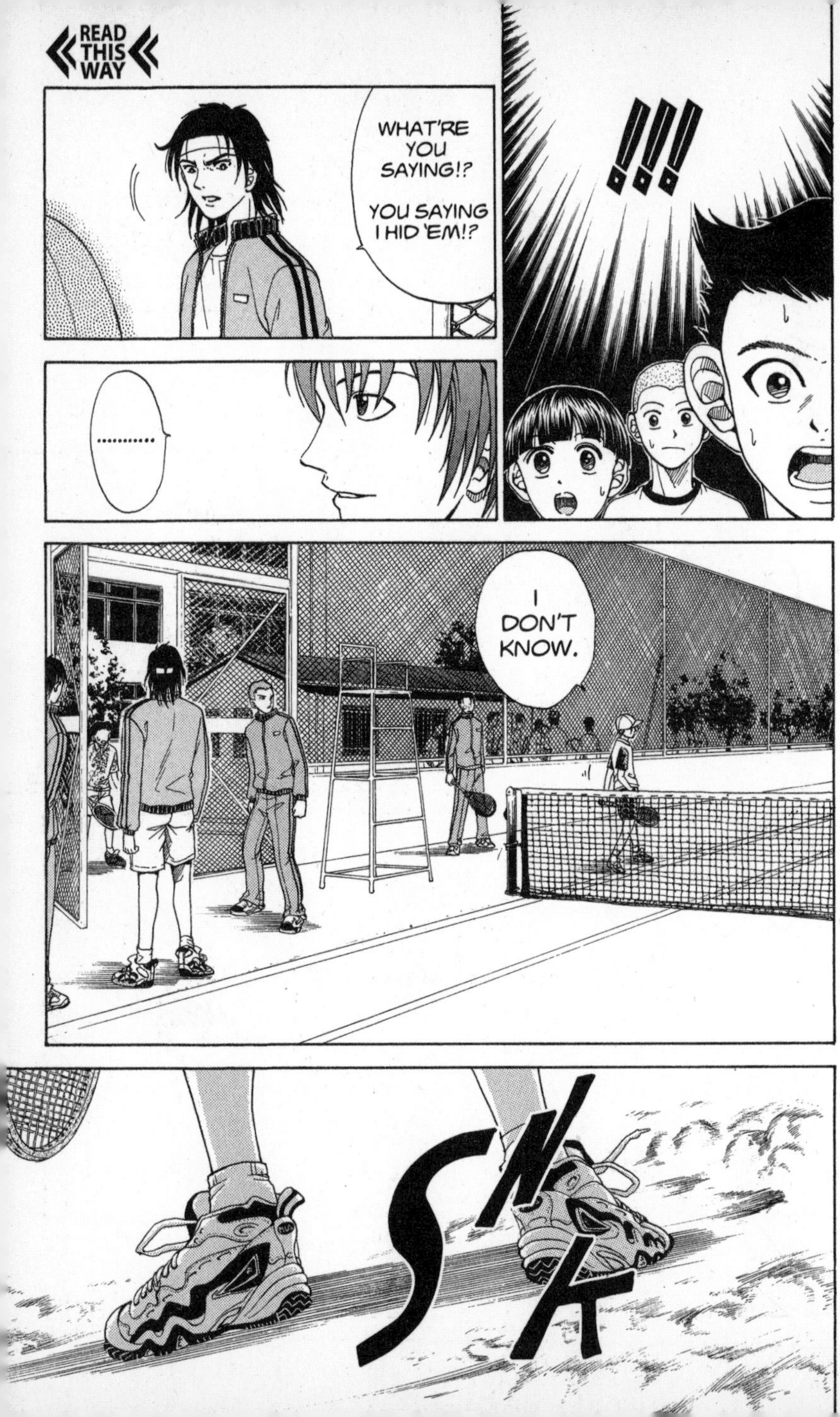
!!!
WHAT'RE YOU SAYING!?
YOU SAYING I HID 'EM!?
....
I DON'T KNOW.
SNK

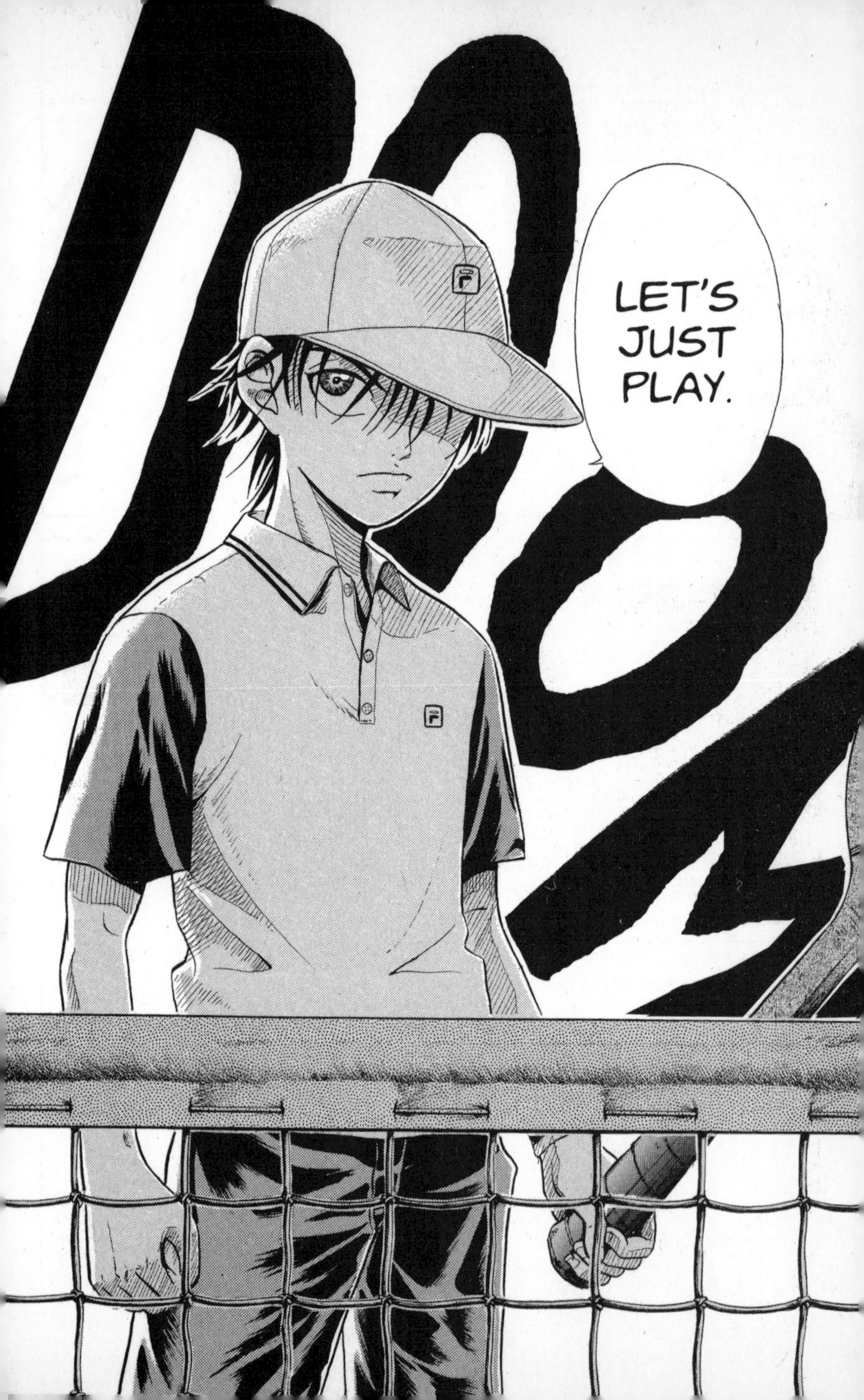
LET'S JUST PLAY.

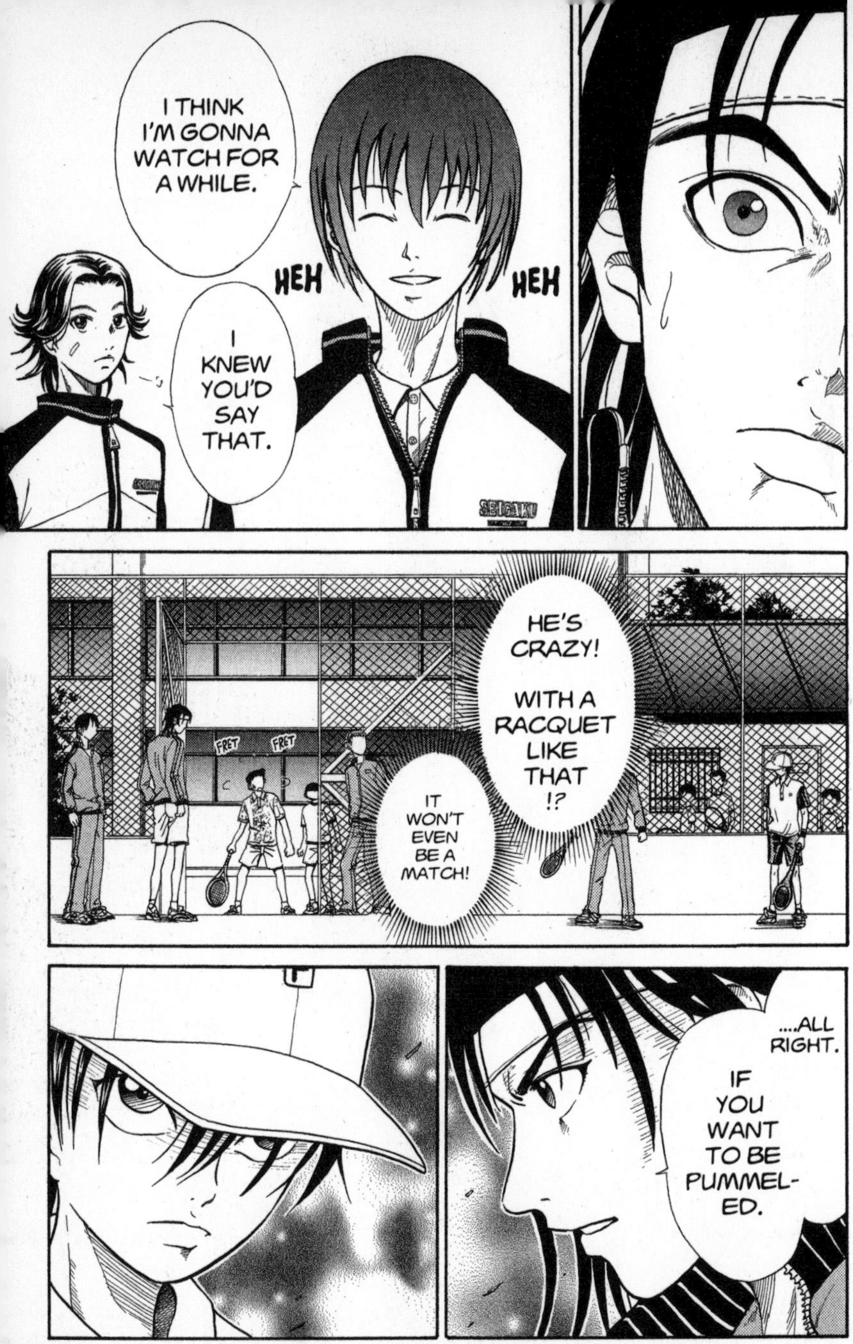
I THINK I'M GONNA WATCH FOR A WHILE.
HEH
HEH
I KNEW YOU'D SAY THAT.
HE'S CRAZY!
WITH A RACQUET LIKE THAT!?
IT WON'T EVEN BE A MATCH!
FRET
FRET
....ALL RIGHT.
IF YOU WANT TO BE PUMMEL-ED.

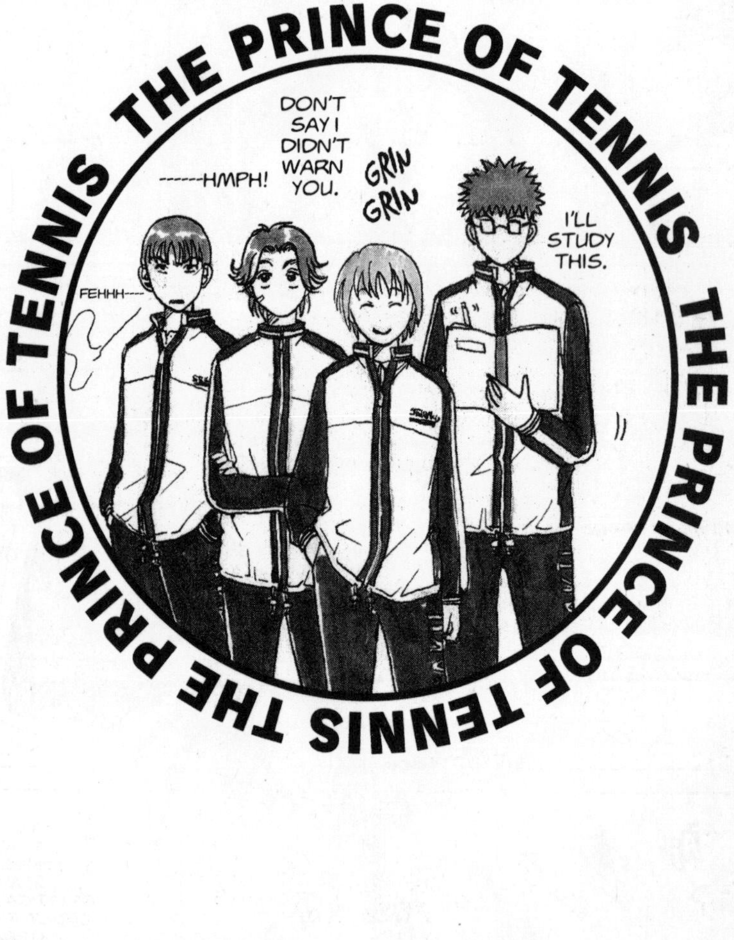
THE PRINCE OF TENNIS THE PRINCE OF TENNIS THE PRINCE OF TENNIS
I'LL STUDY THIS.
GRIN GRIN
DON'T SAY I DIDN'T WARN YOU.
------HMPH!
FEHHH----

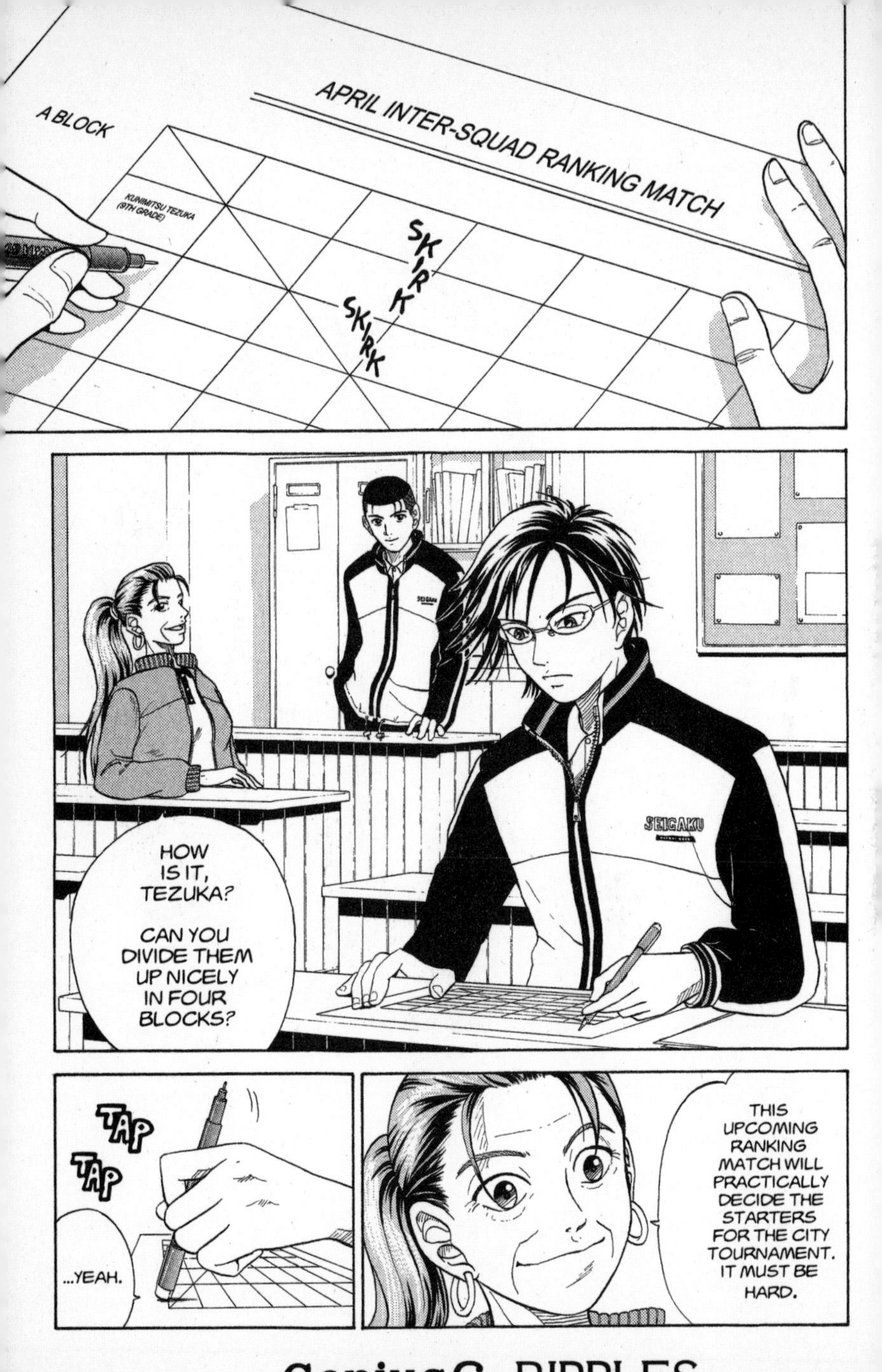
APRIL INTER-SQUAD RANKING MATCH
A BLOCK
KUNIMITSU TEZUKA (9TH GRADE)
SKIRK
SKIRK
HOW IS IT, TEZUKA? CAN YOU DIVIDE THEM UP NICELY IN FOUR BLOCKS?
SEIGAKU
THIS UPCOMING RANKING MATCH WILL PRACTICALLY DECIDE THE STARTERS FOR THE CITY TOURNAMENT. IT MUST BE HARD.
TAP
TAP
...YEAH.

Genius 6 RIPPLES

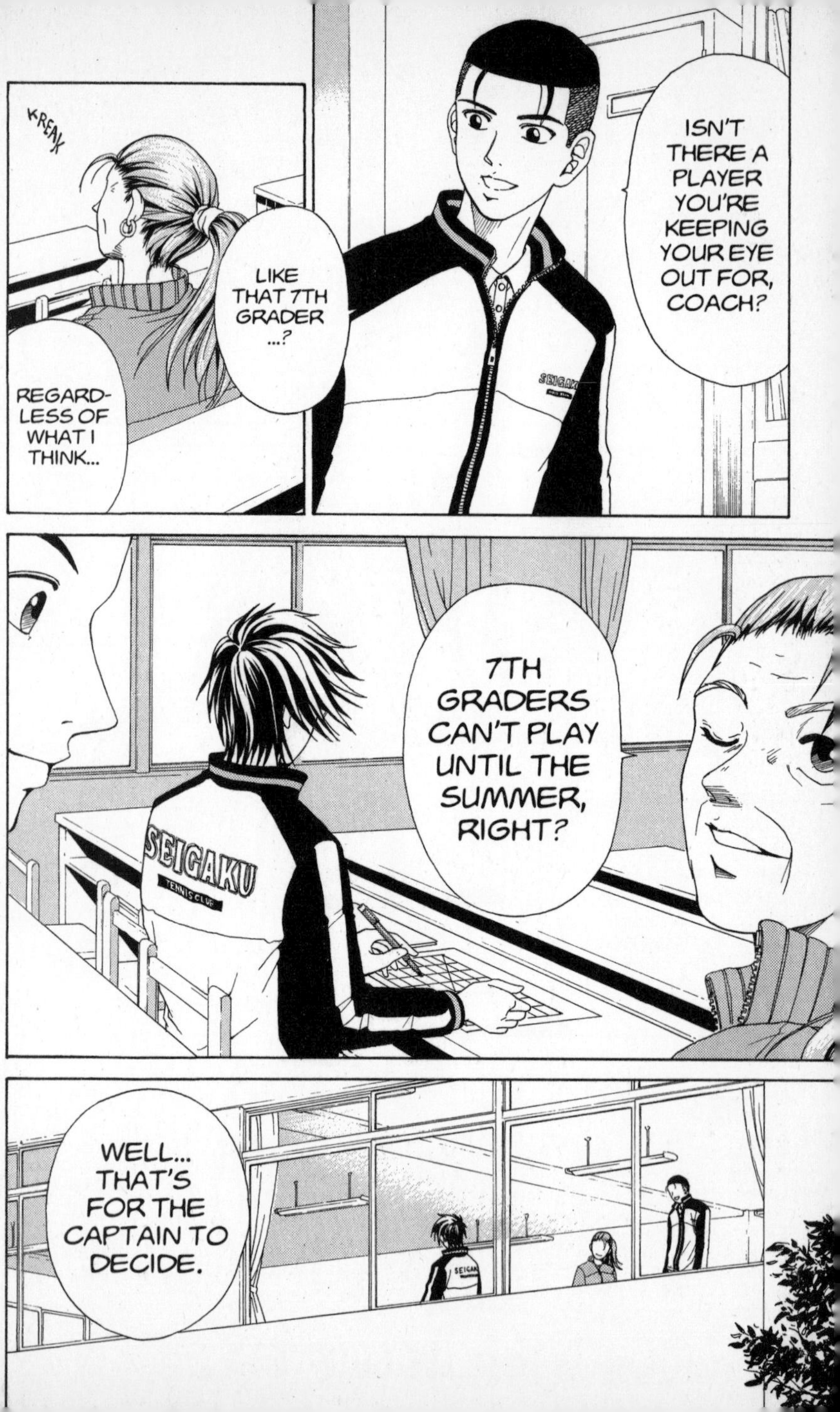
ISN'T THERE A PLAYER YOU'RE KEEPING YOUR EYE OUT FOR, COACH?
LIKE THAT 7TH GRADER ...?
KREAK
REGARDLESS OF WHAT I THINK...
7TH GRADERS CAN'T PLAY UNTIL THE SUMMER, RIGHT?
WELL... THAT'S FOR THE CAPTAIN TO DECIDE.

Genius 6
RIPPLES

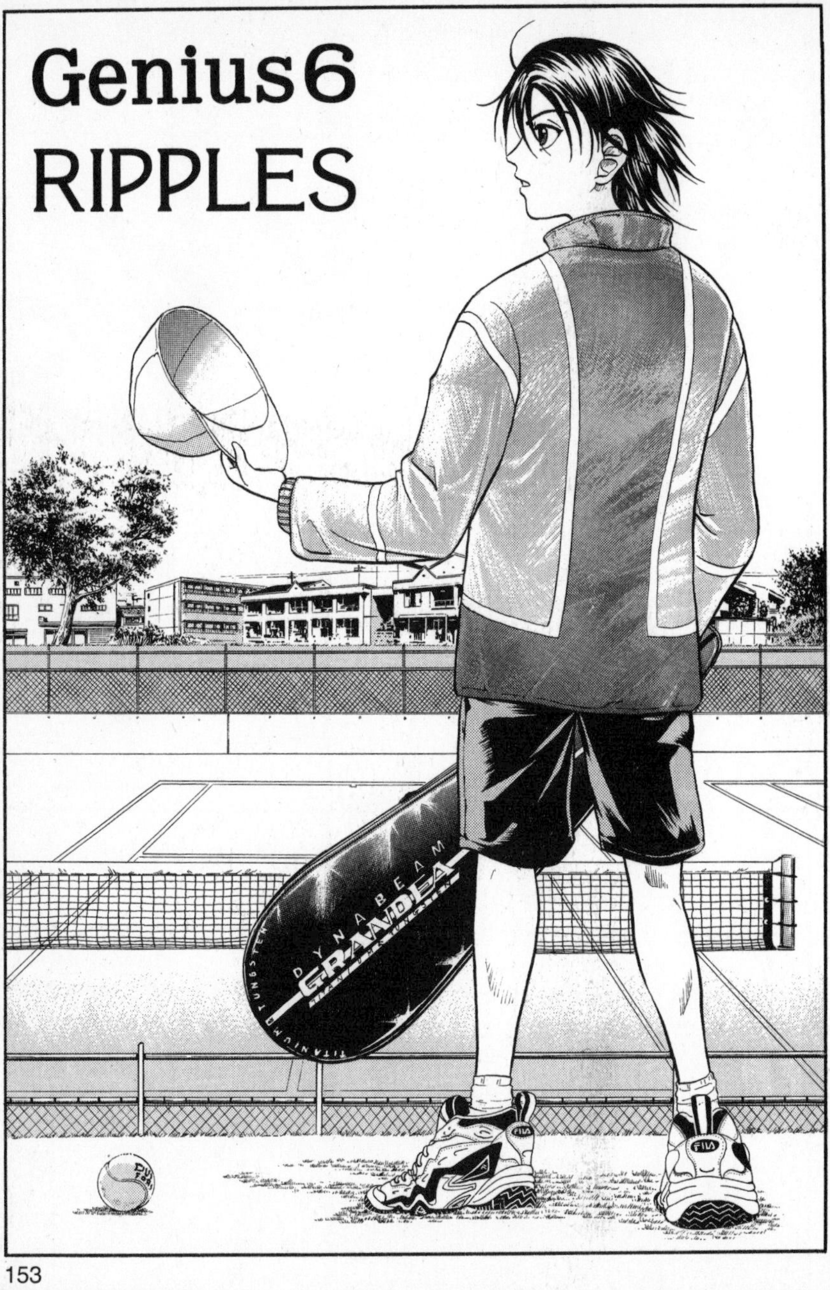
DYNA BEAM
GRANDEA
TITANIUM TUNGSTEN

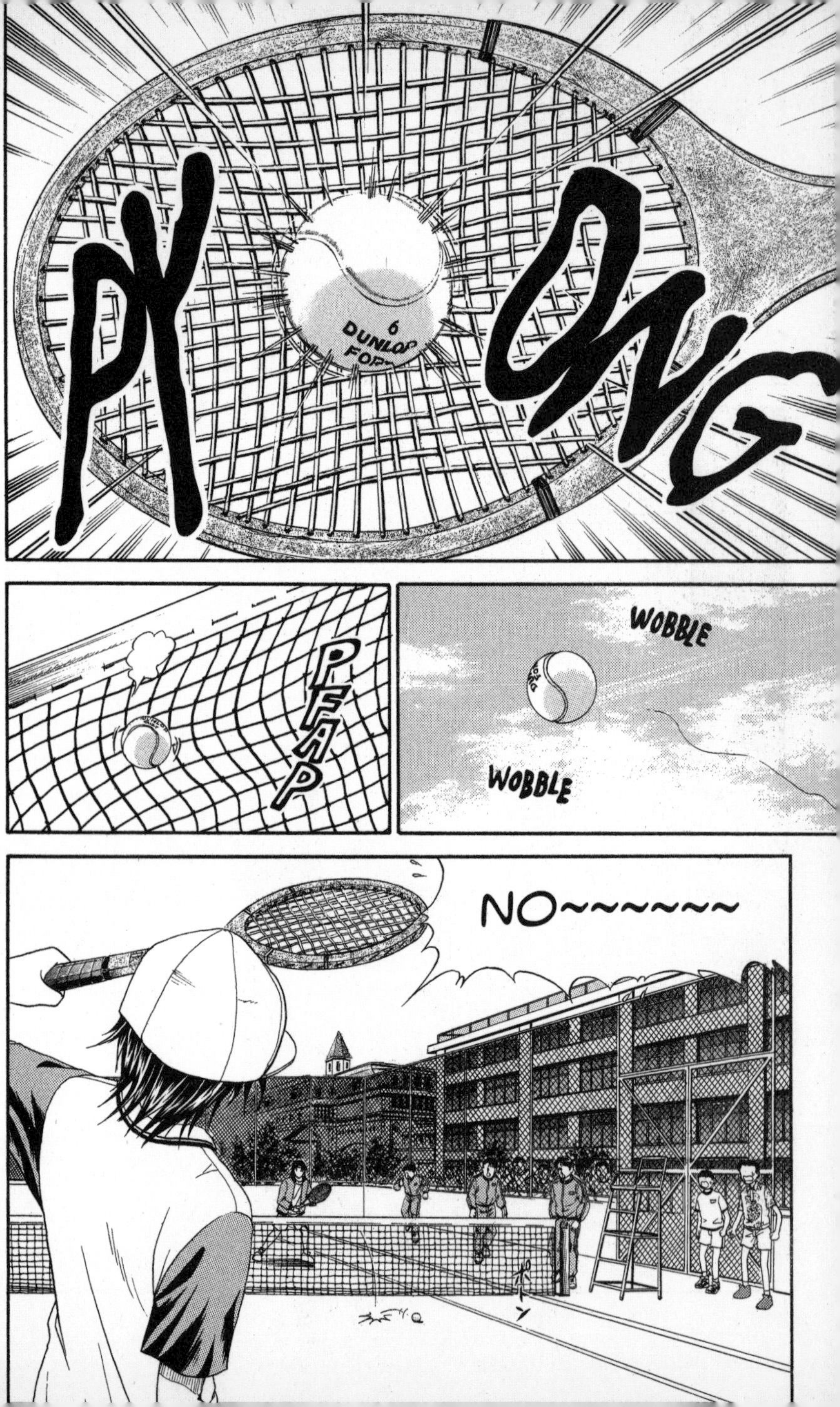
PYONG
6
DUNLOP
WOBBLE
WOBBLE
PFAP
NO~~~~~~~

READ THIS WAY

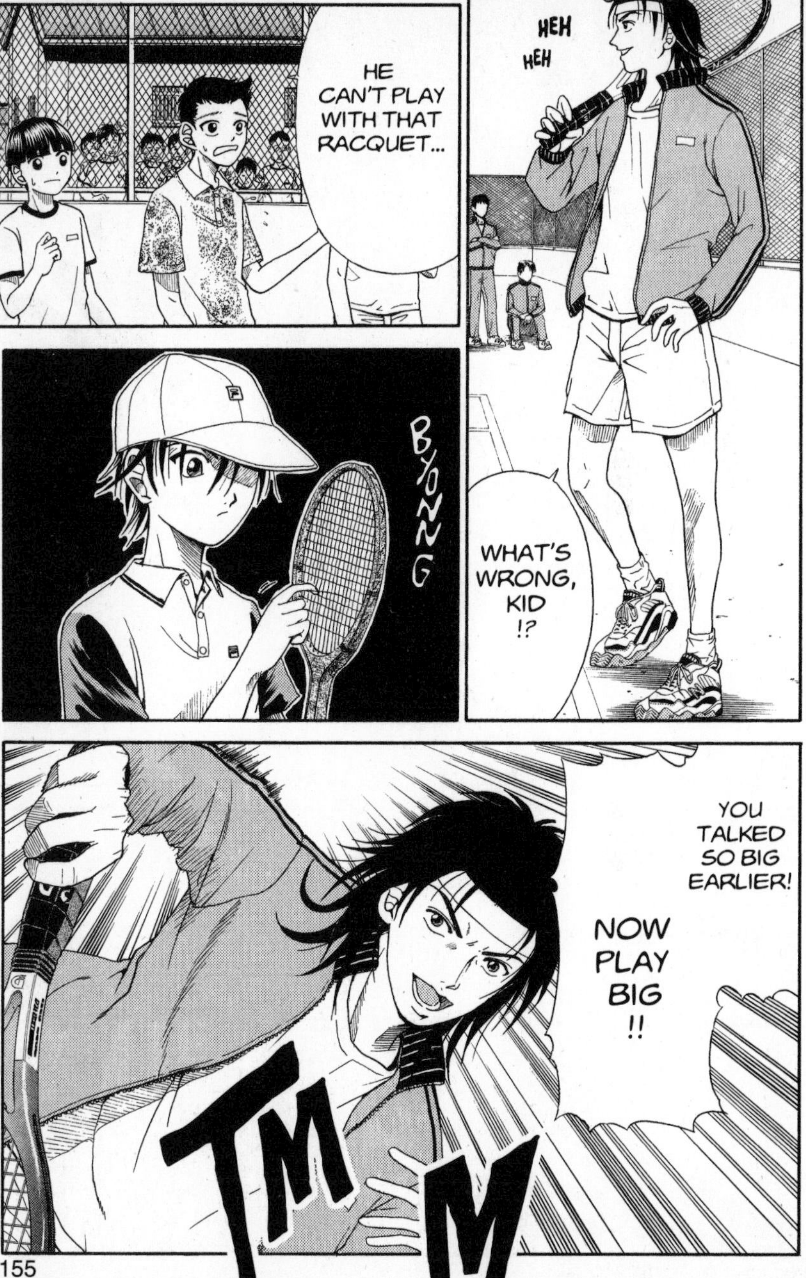
HEH
HEH
WHAT'S WRONG, KID !?
HE CAN'T PLAY WITH THAT RACQUET...
BYONNG
YOU TALKED SO BIG EARLIER!
NOW PLAY BIG !!
TMM

READ THIS WAY

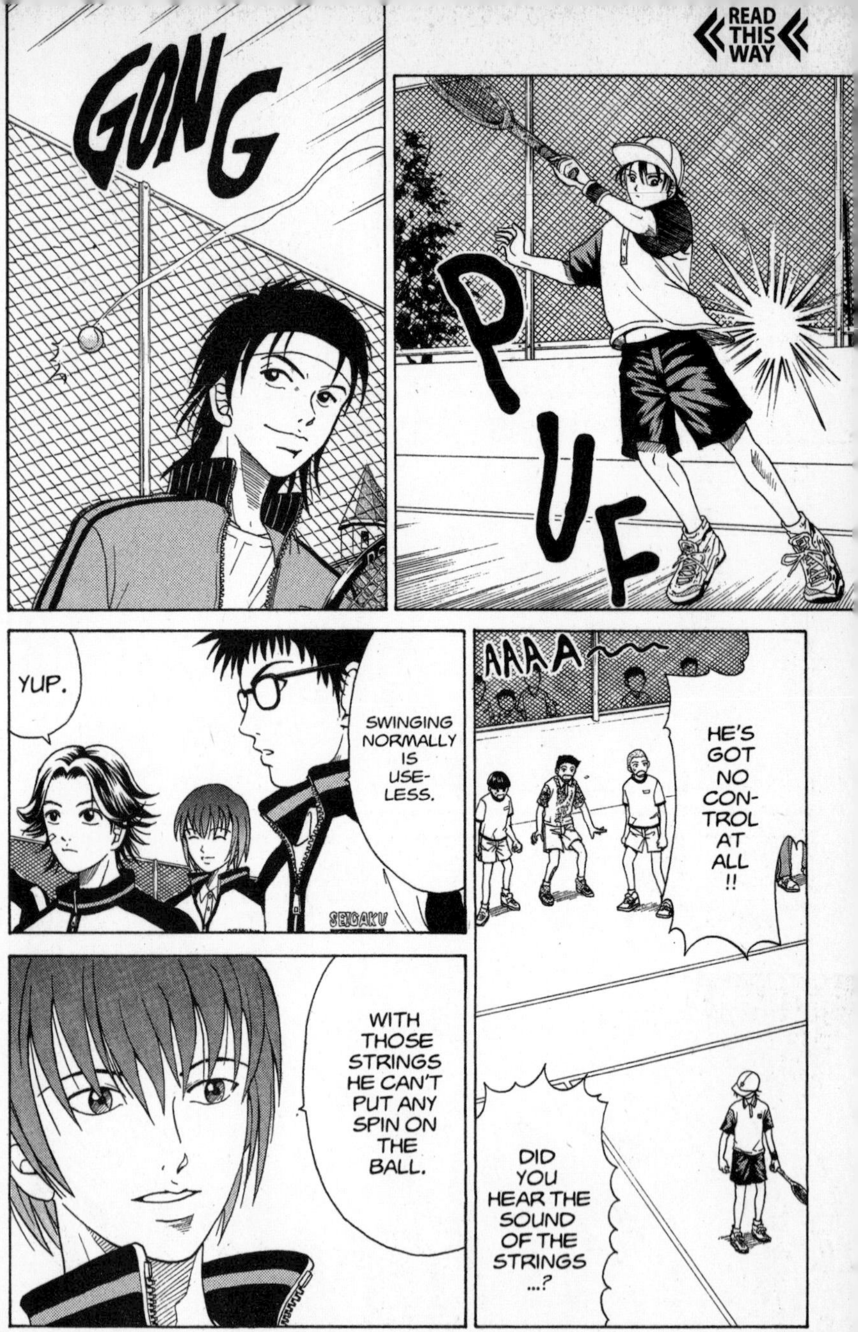
PUF
GONG
AAAA~~
HE'S GOT NO CONTROL AT ALL!!
DID YOU HEAR THE SOUND OF THE STRINGS ...?
SWINGING NORMALLY IS USELESS.
SEIGAKU
YUP.
WITH THOSE STRINGS HE CAN'T PUT ANY SPIN ON THE BALL.

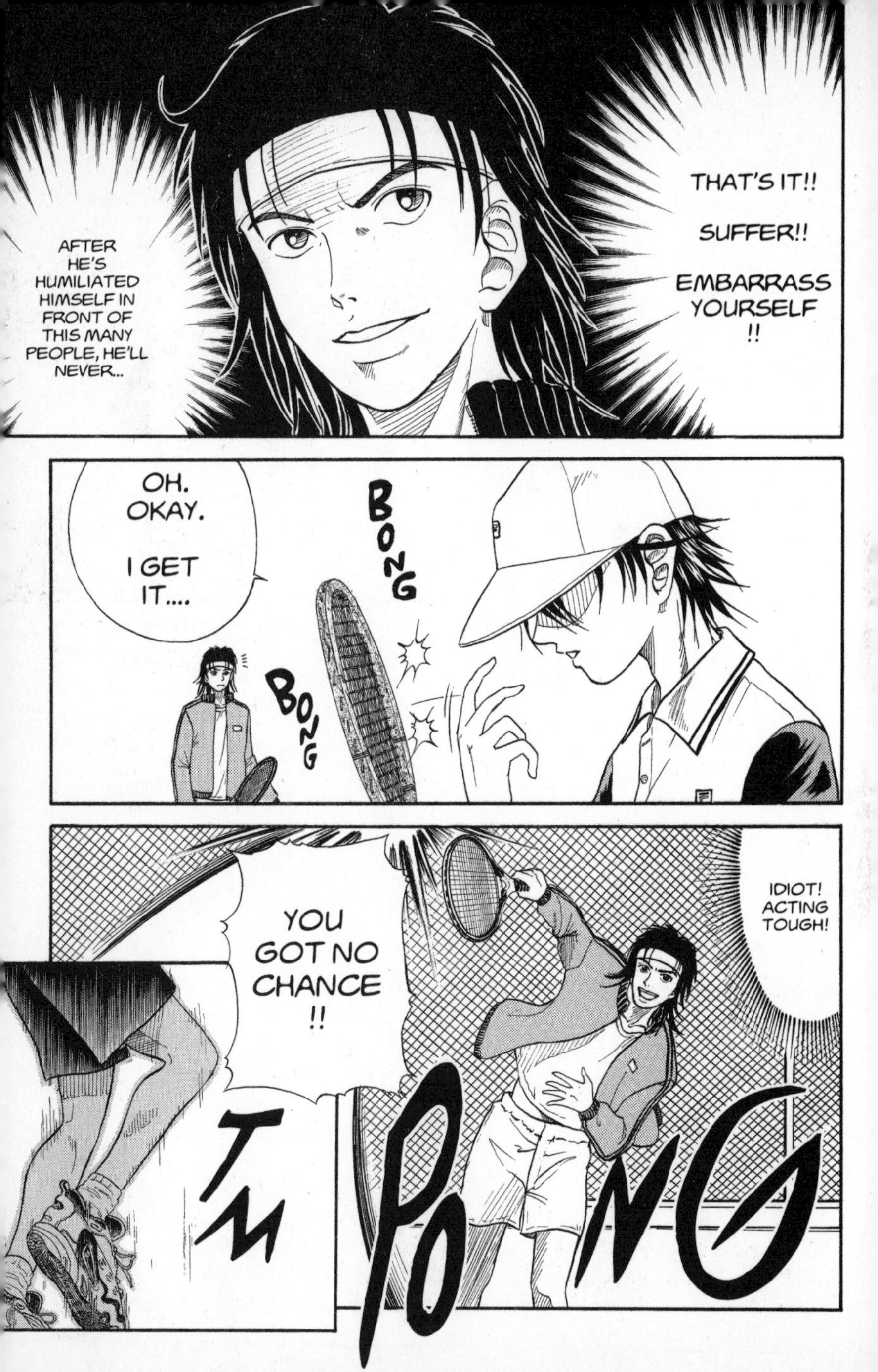
THAT'S IT!!
SUFFER!!
EMBARRASS YOURSELF !!
AFTER HE'S HUMILIATED HIMSELF IN FRONT OF THIS MANY PEOPLE, HE'LL NEVER...
BONG
BONG
OH. OKAY.
I GET IT....
IDIOT! ACTING TOUGH!
YOU GOT NO CHANCE !!
PONG
TM

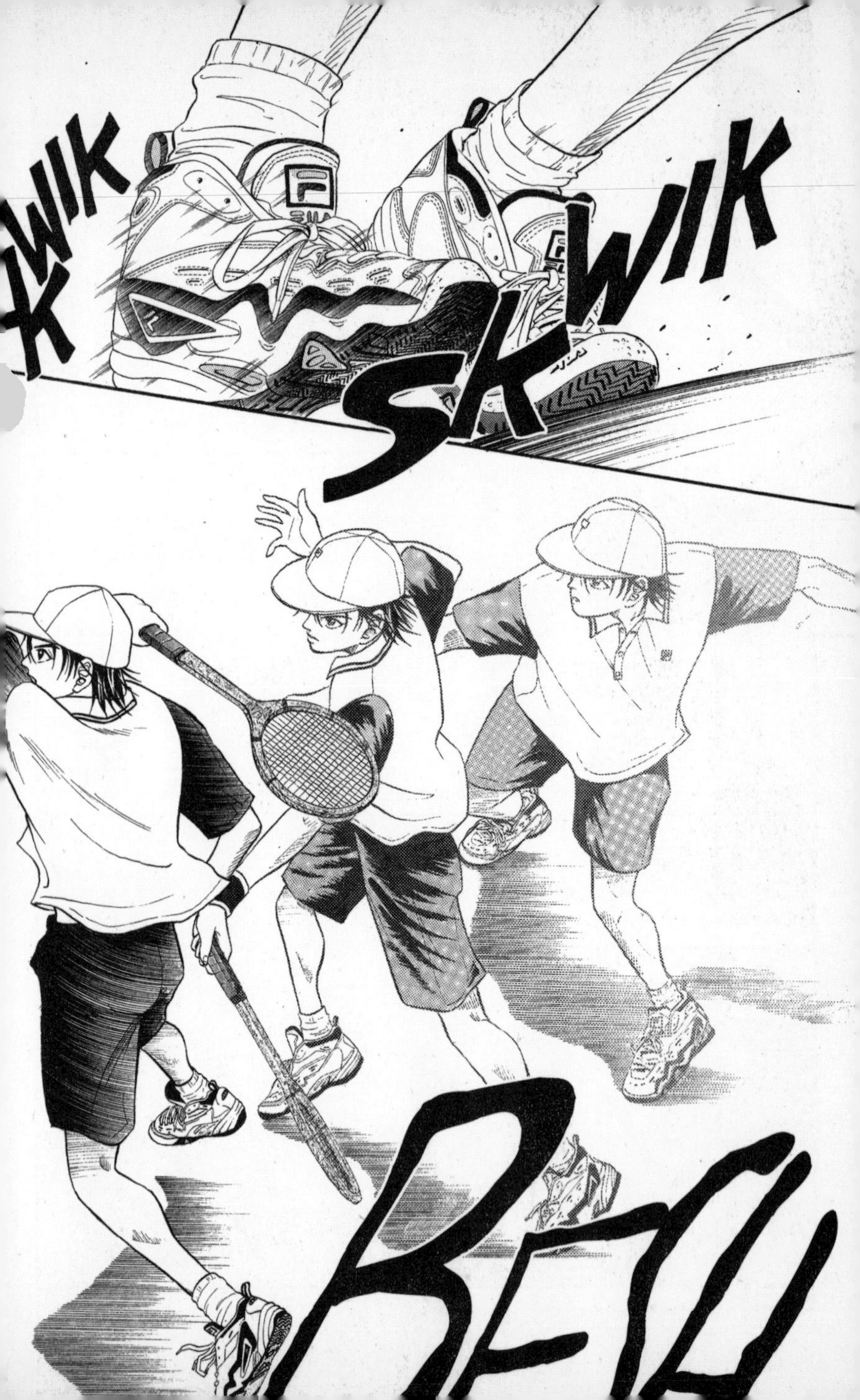
SKWIK
KWIK

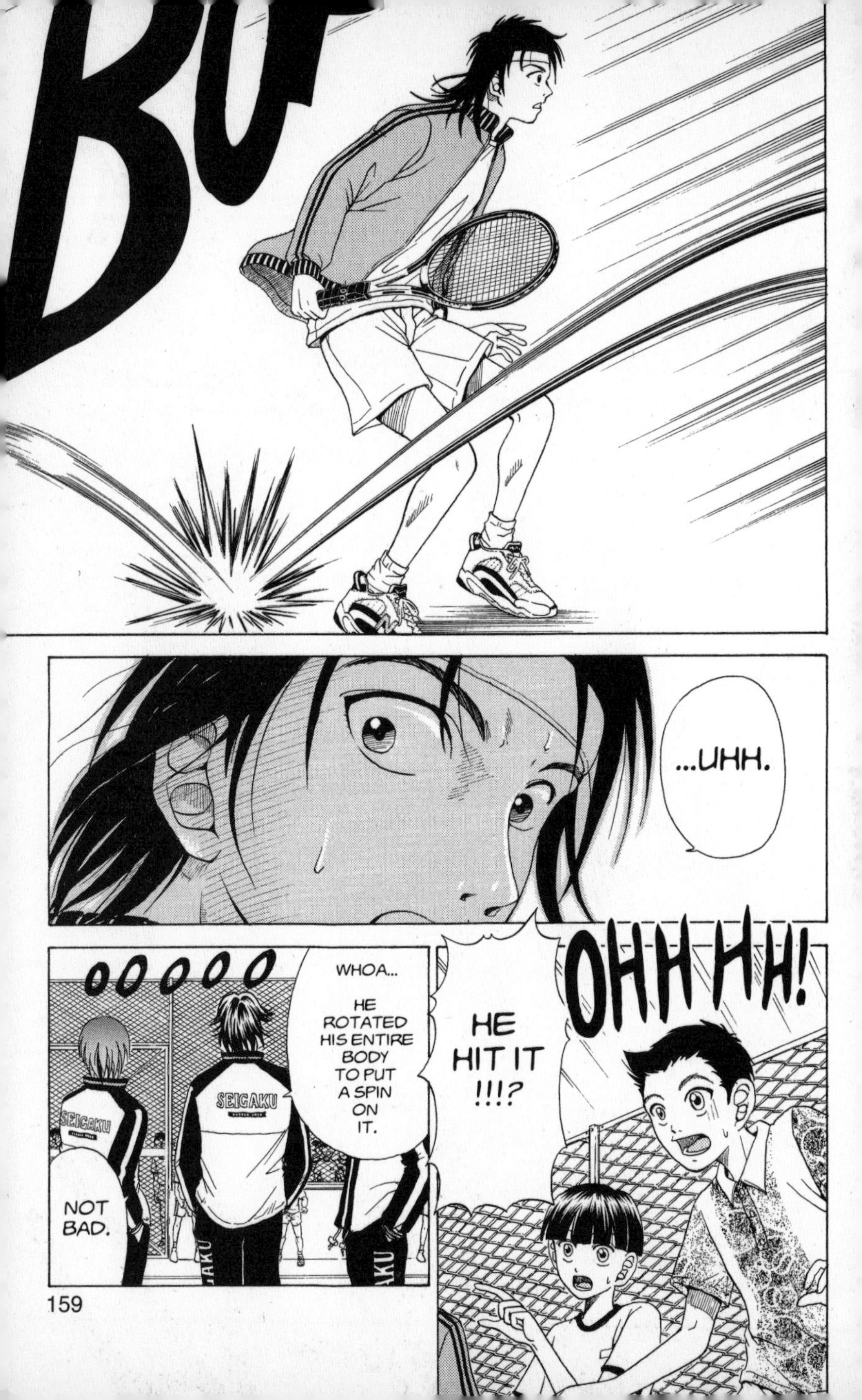
BU
...UHH.
OHH HH!
HE HIT IT !!!?
OOOOO
WHOA... HE ROTATED HIS ENTIRE BODY TO PUT A SPIN ON IT.
NOT BAD.

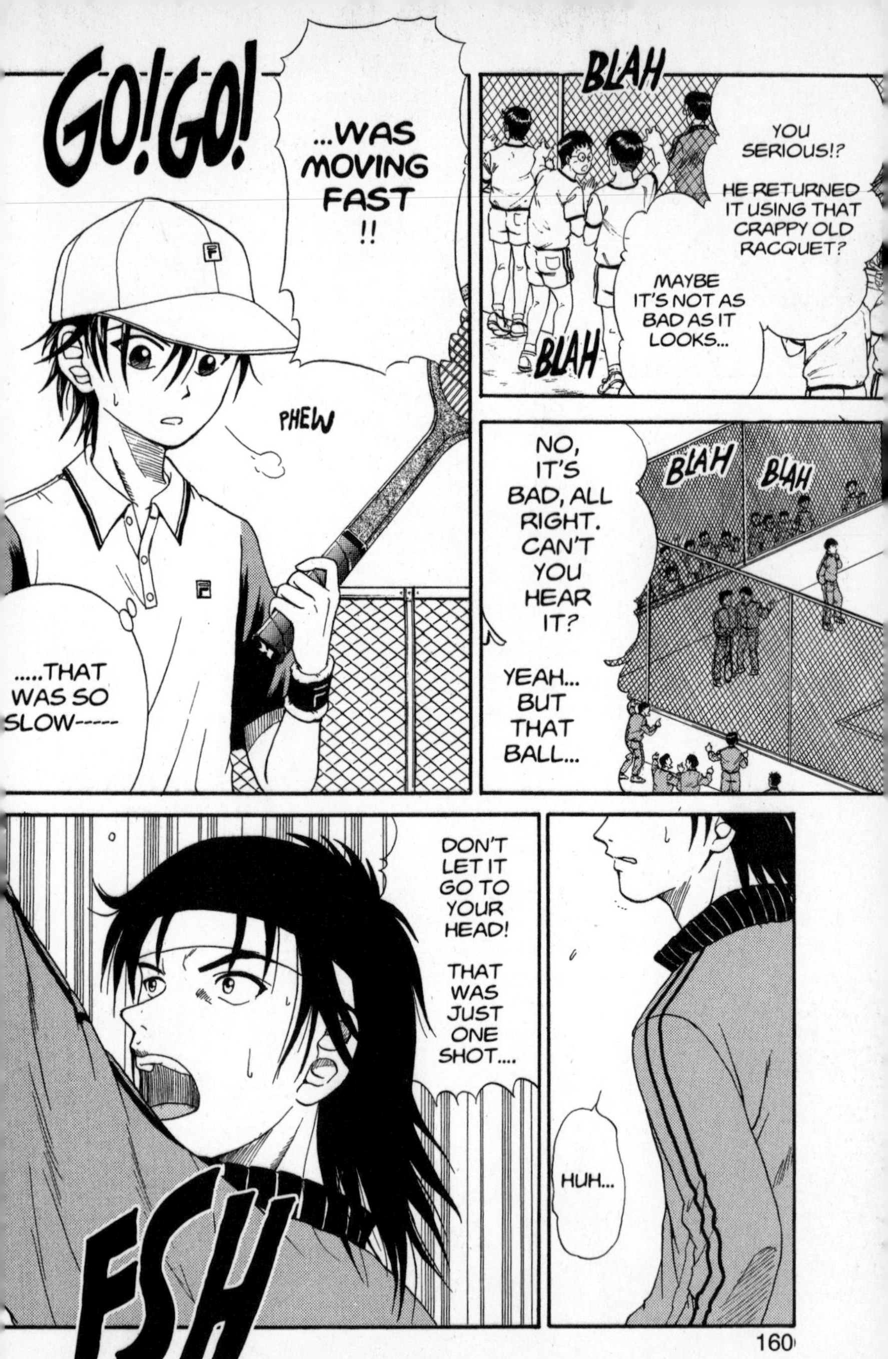
BLAH
YOU SERIOUS!?
HE RETURNED IT USING THAT CRAPPY OLD RACQUET?
MAYBE IT'S NOT AS BAD AS IT LOOKS...
BLAH
NO, IT'S BAD, ALL RIGHT. CAN'T YOU HEAR IT?
YEAH... BUT THAT BALL...
BLAH
BLAH
GO!GO!
...WAS MOVING FAST !!
PHEW
.....THAT WAS SO SLOW-----
HUH...
DON'T LET IT GO TO YOUR HEAD!
THAT WAS JUST ONE SHOT....
FSH

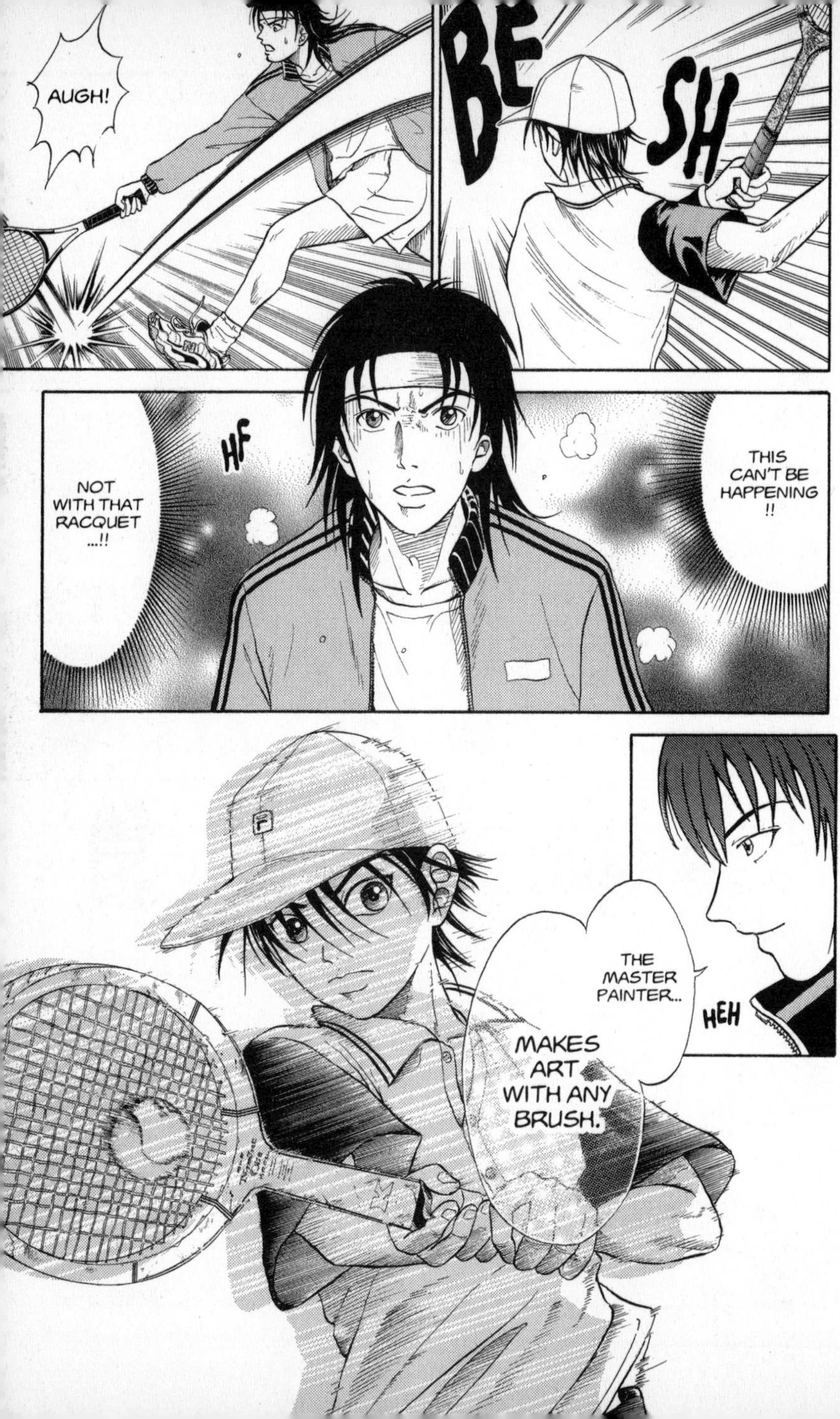
BESH
AUGH!
THIS CAN'T BE HAPPENING !!
HF
NOT WITH THAT RACQUET ...!!
THE MASTER PAINTER...
HEH
MAKES ART WITH ANY BRUSH.

READ THIS WAY

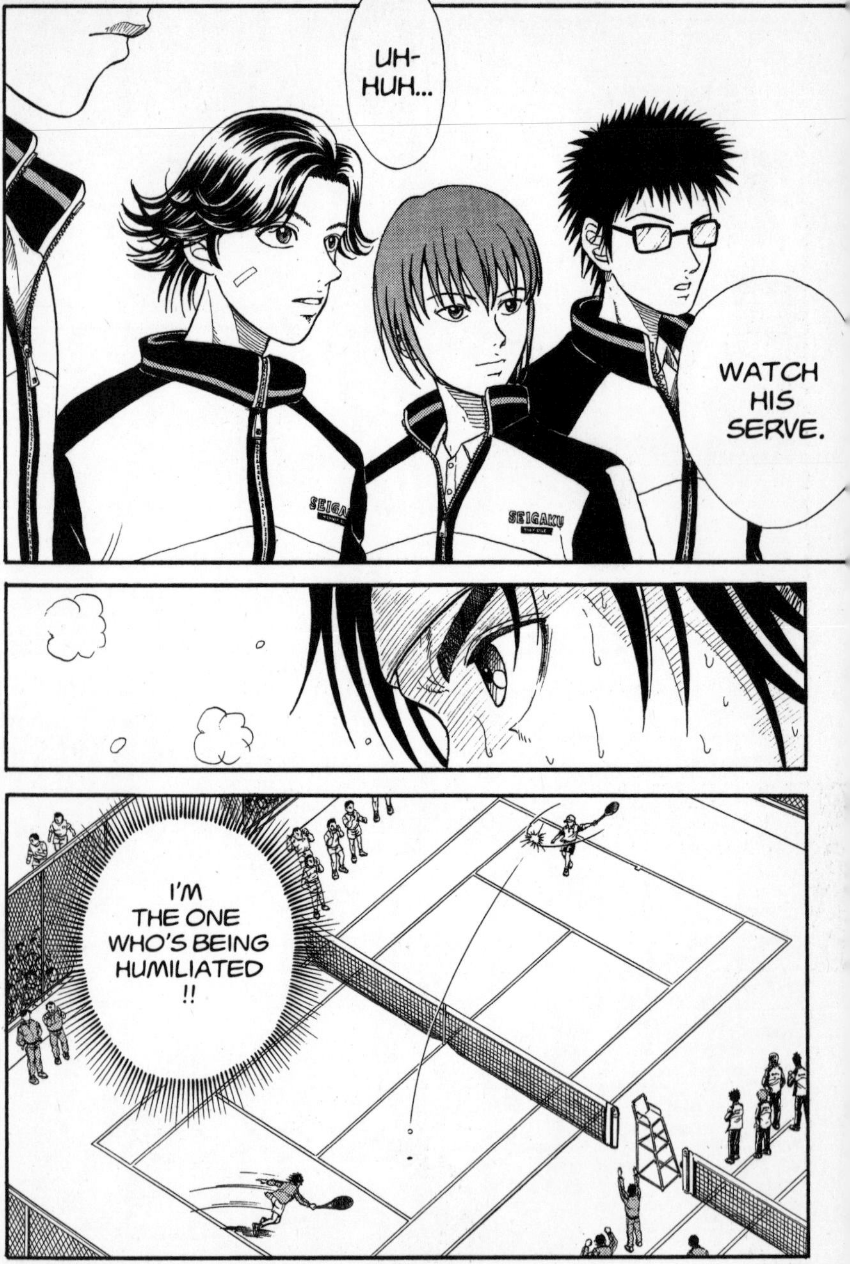
WATCH HIS SERVE.
UH-HUH...
I'M THE ONE WHO'S BEING HUMILIATED !!

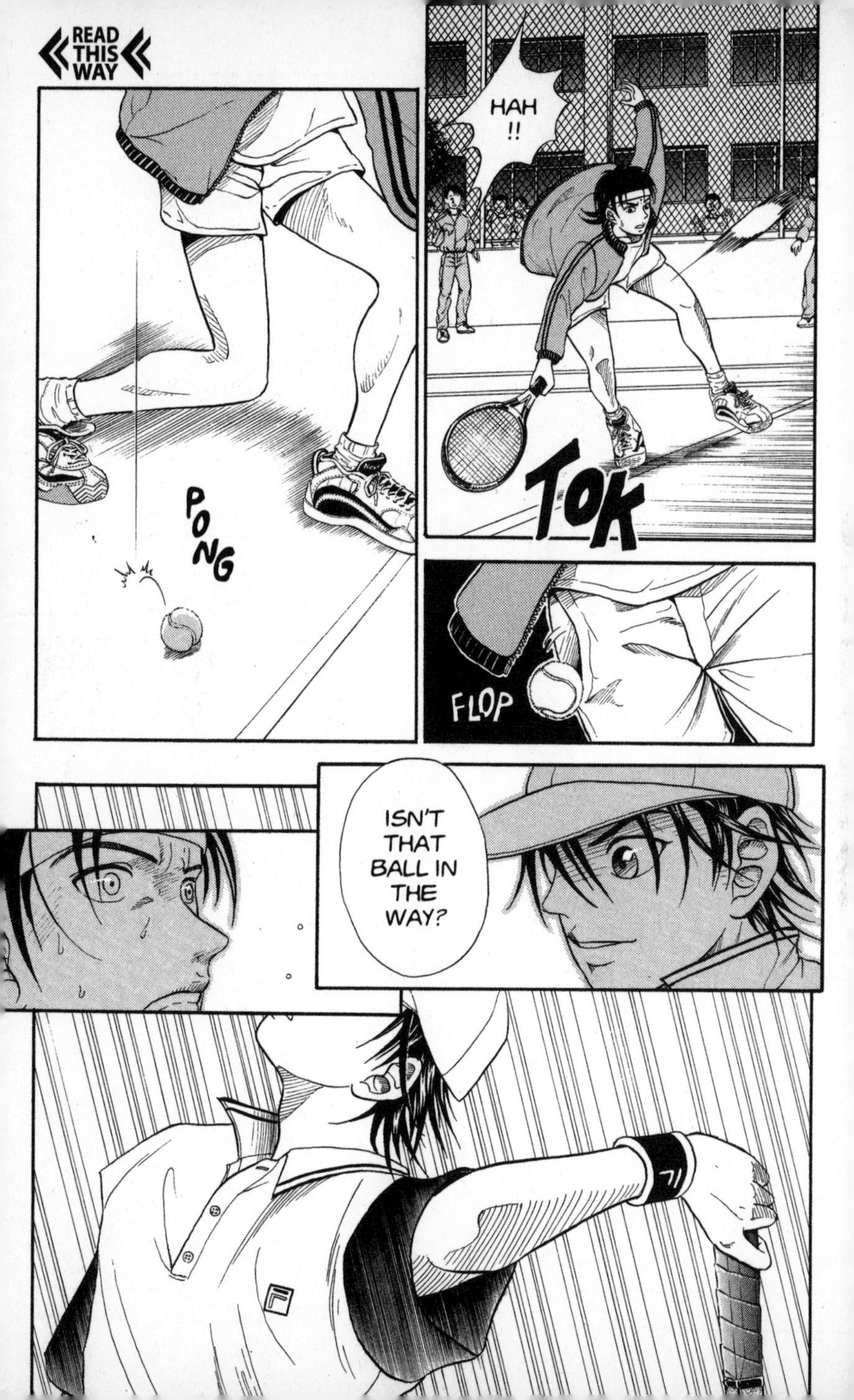
READ THIS WAY
HAH !!
TOK
PONG
FLOP
ISN'T THAT BALL IN THE WAY?

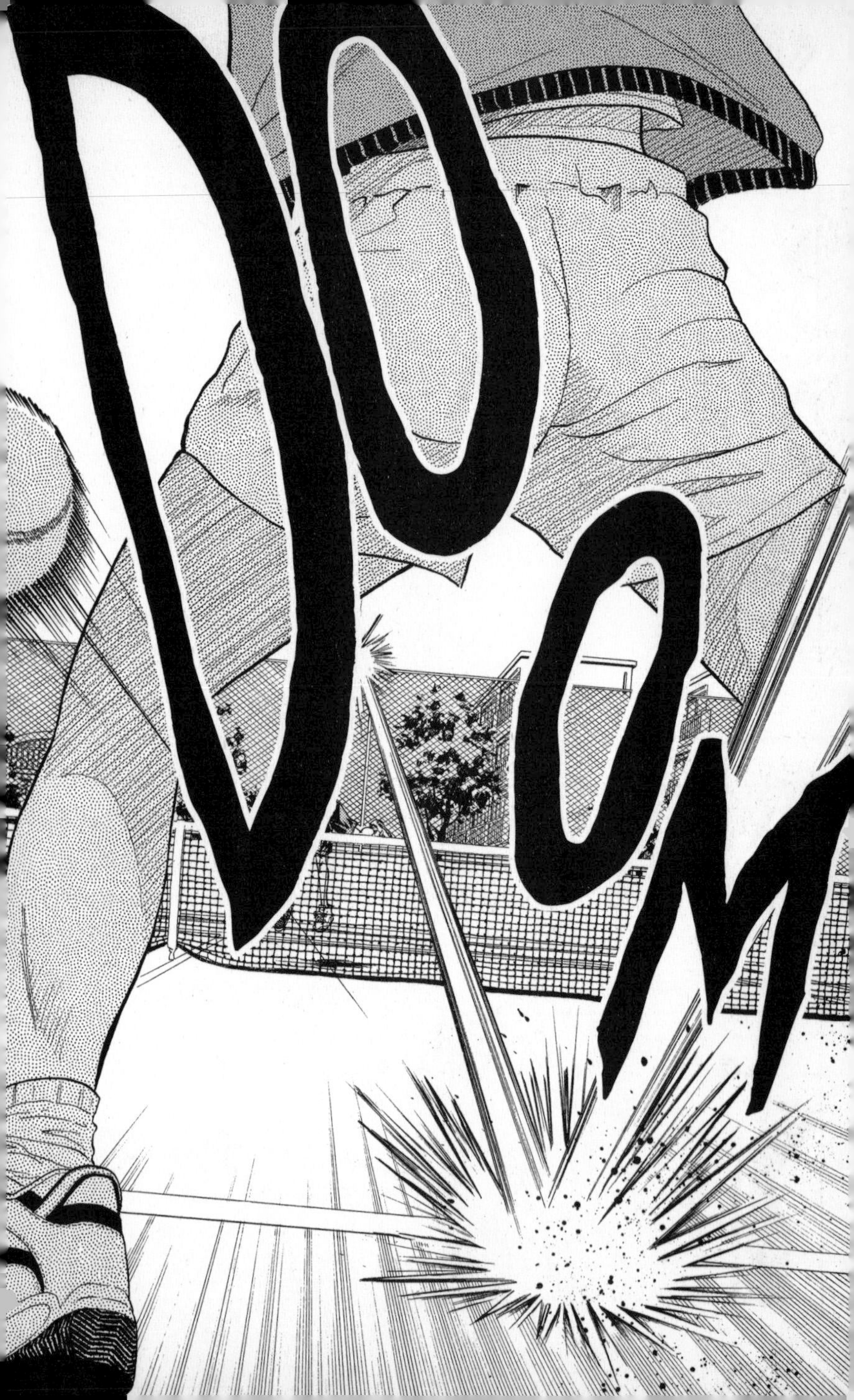
DOOM

READ THIS WAY

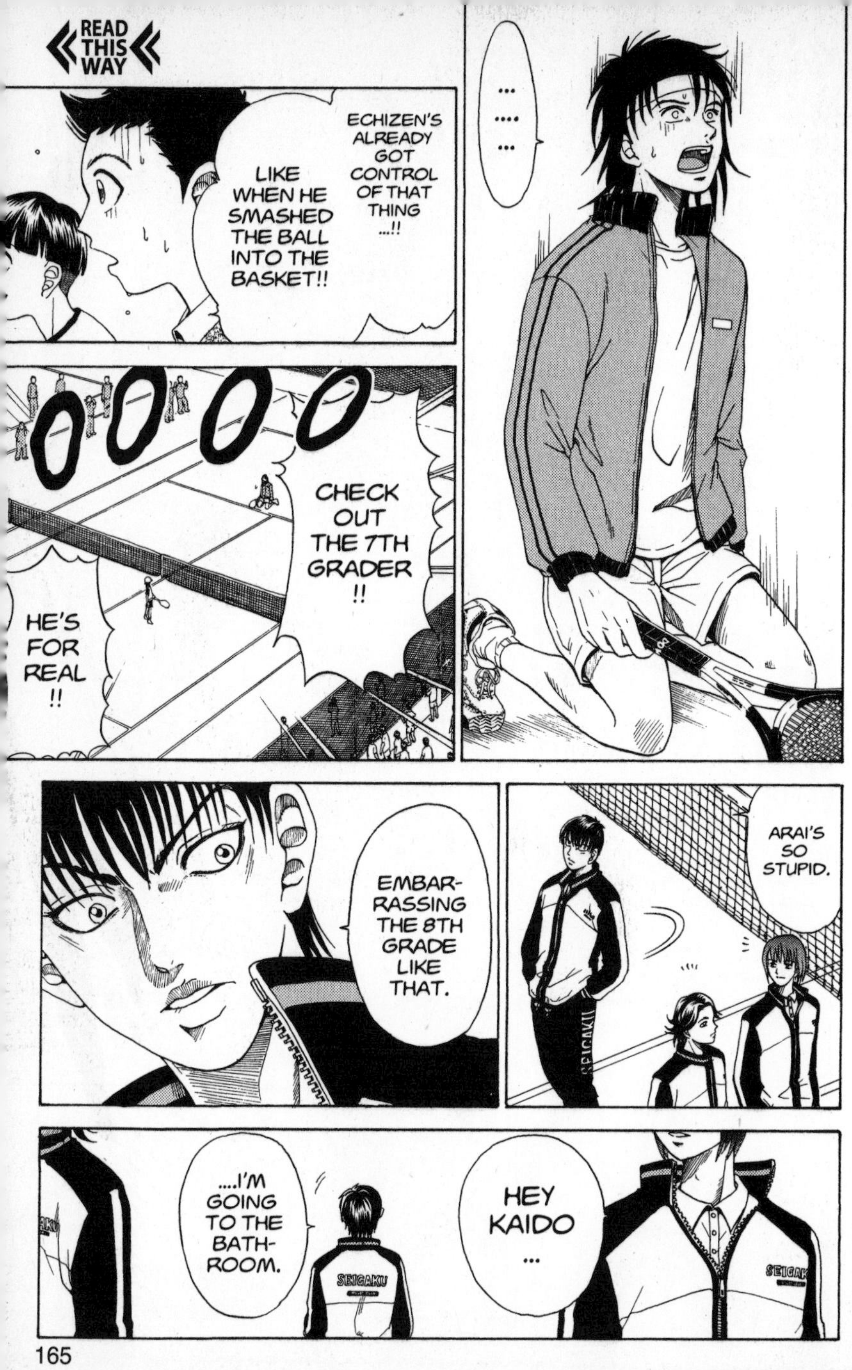

...
....
...
ECHIZEN'S ALREADY GOT CONTROL OF THAT THING ...!!
LIKE WHEN HE SMASHED THE BALL INTO THE BASKET!!
OOOO
CHECK OUT THE 7TH GRADER !!
HE'S FOR REAL !!
ARAI'S SO STUPID.
EMBAR-RASSING THE 8TH GRADE LIKE THAT.
HEY KAIDO ...
....I'M GOING TO THE BATH-ROOM.
SEIGAKU
SEIGAKU

READ THIS WAY

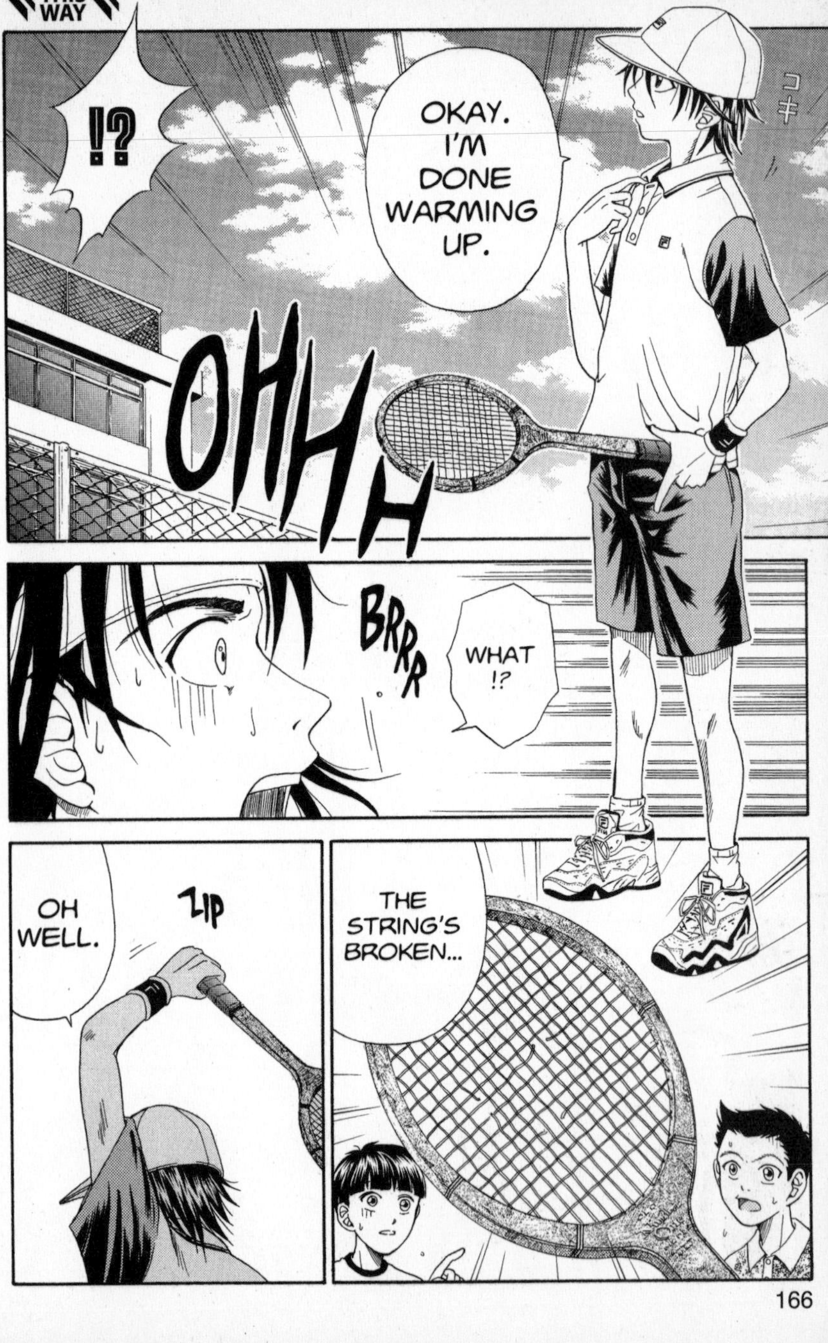
コキ
OKAY. I'M DONE WARMING UP.
!?
OHHH
BRRR
WHAT !?
THE STRING'S BROKEN...
ZIP
OH WELL.

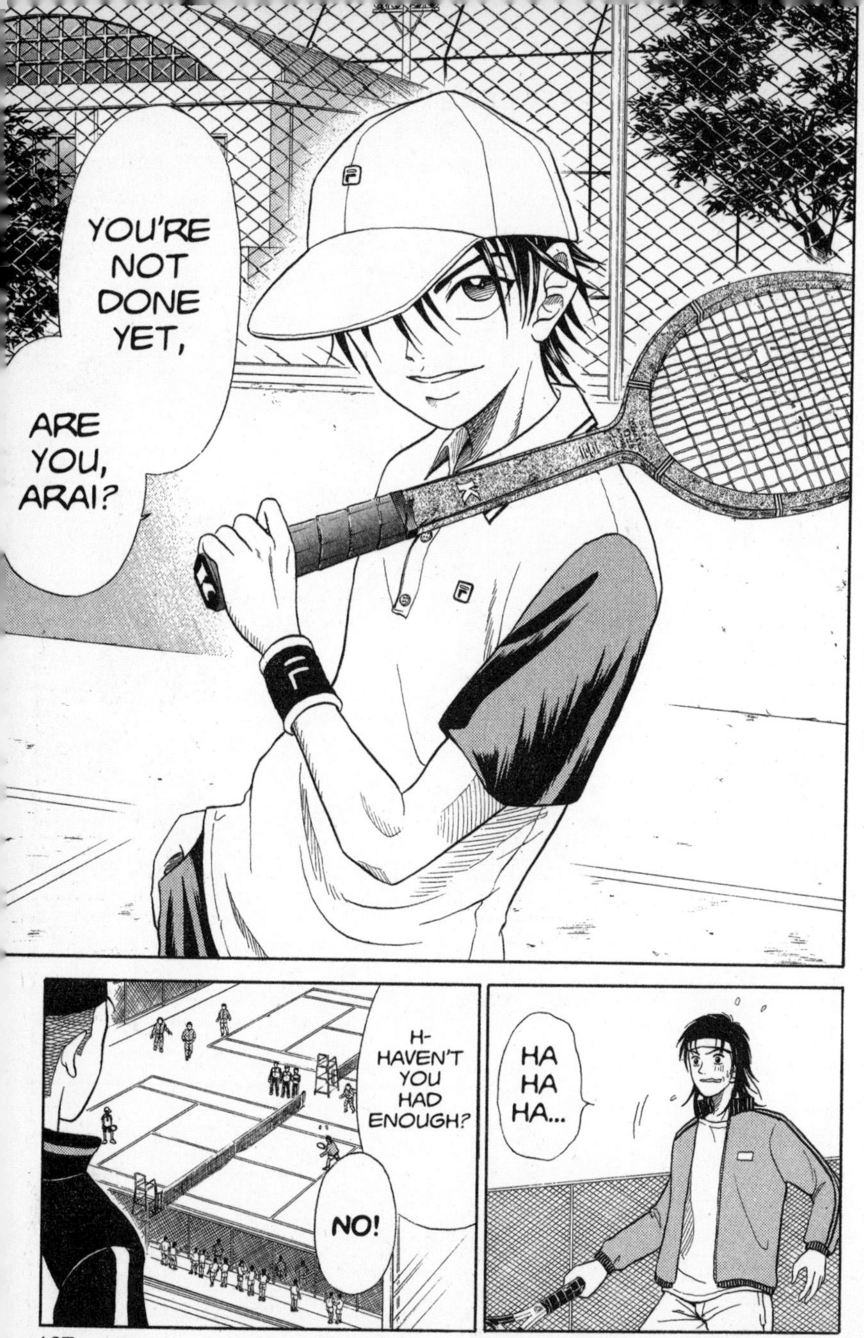
YOU'RE NOT DONE YET,
ARE YOU, ARAI?
HA HA HA...
H-HAVEN'T YOU HAD ENOUGH?
NO!

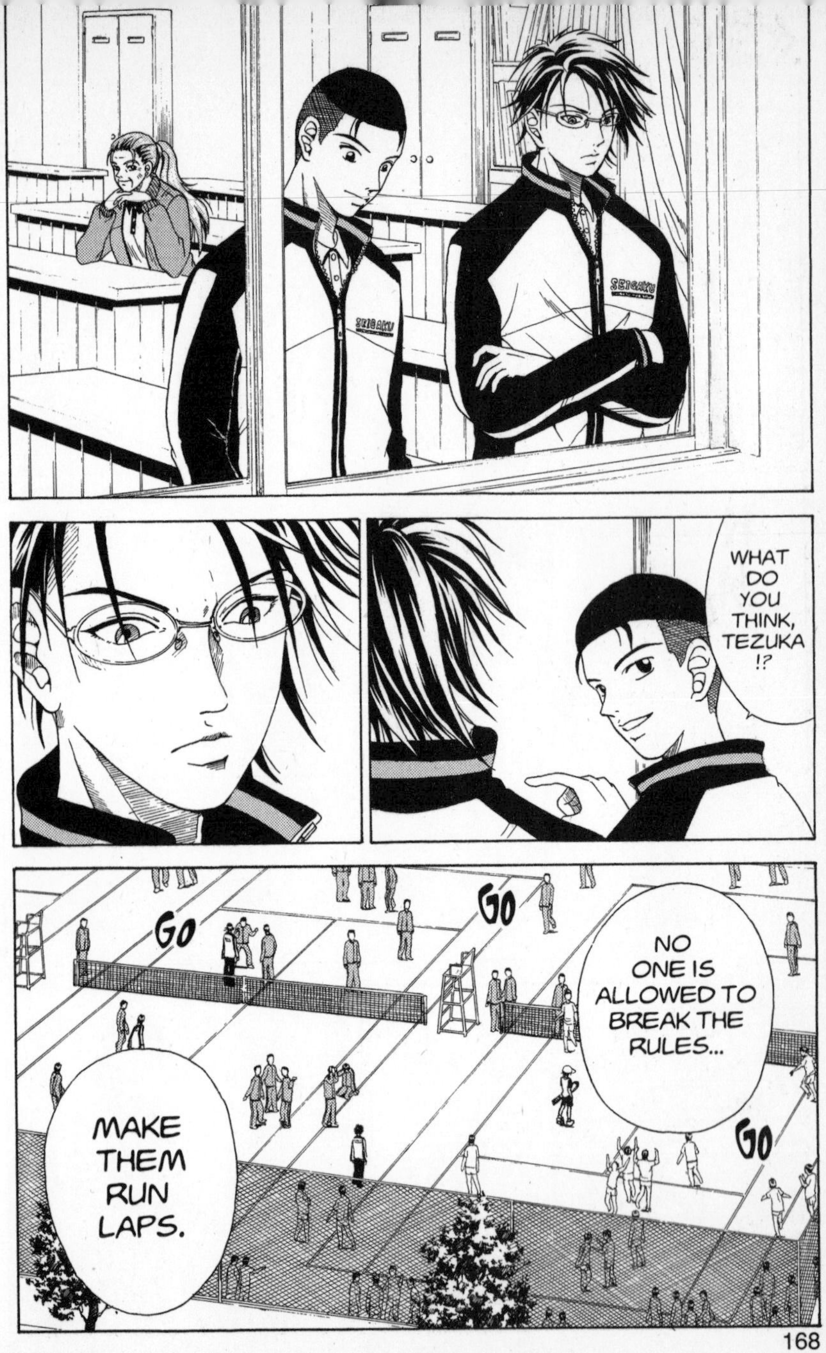
WHAT DO YOU THINK, TEZUKA!?
GO
GO
NO ONE IS ALLOWED TO BREAK THE RULES...
GO
MAKE THEM RUN LAPS.

READ THIS WAY

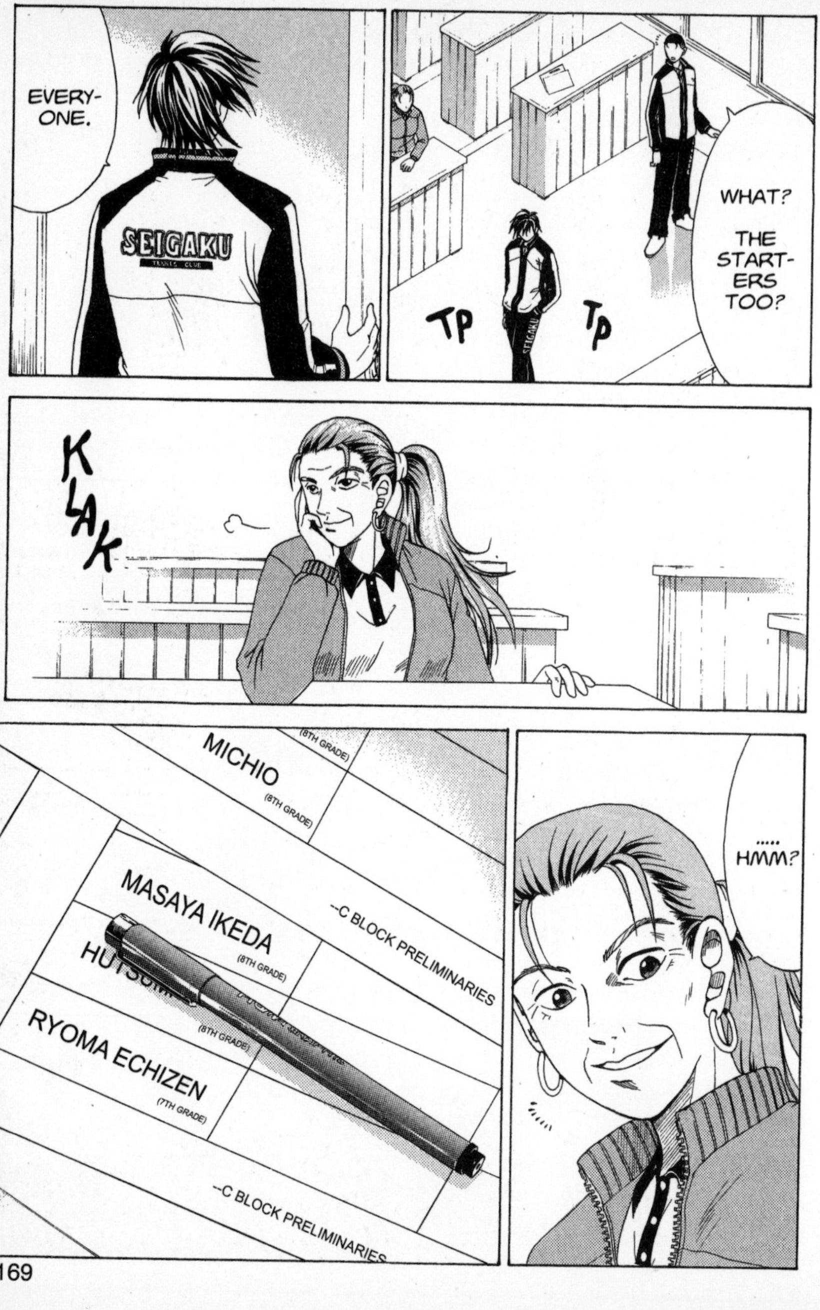
WHAT?
THE STARTERS TOO?
TP
TP
EVERY-ONE.
SEIGAKU
TENNIS CLUB
KLAK
.....
HMM?
(8TH GRADE)
MICHIO
(8TH GRADE)
--C BLOCK PRELIMINARIES
MASAYA IKEDA
(8TH GRADE)
(8TH GRADE)
RYOMA ECHIZEN
(7TH GRADE)
--C BLOCK PRELIMINARIES

PRINCE OF TENNIS VOLUME 1
THANK YOU FOR READING!

- ALL THE CHARACTERS ARE SWEATING IT OUT... BUT WITH A WEEKLY PUBLISHING SCHEDULE, I, THE WRITER, DON'T HAVE TIME TO PLAY TENNIS.
- I LOOK FORWARD TO YOUR LETTERS. 'TOO BUSY TO READ....' NOT A CHANCE!! REALLY FUNNY STORIES, QUESTIONS ABOUT ANYTHING, PASSIONATE LOVE LETTERS TO THE CHARACTERS. LETTERS FROM READERS OF MY PREVIOUS WORK 'COOL,' FROM GIRLS, FROM GUYS, FROM COUPLES, I CAN'T WAIT TO READ THEM. NO MATTER HOW SLEEPY I AM AFTER FINISHING THE SCRIPT, READING FAN LETTERS IS MY JOY AND SOURCE OF ENERGY. I'M NOT LYING!
- I RECEIVED A LOT OF LETTERS WITH QUESTIONS ABOUT THE CHARACTERS AND ABOUT TENNIS. I'D LIKE TO TRY TO ANSWER AS MUCH AS I CAN IN THE NEXT VOLUME.
  KEEP AN EYE OUT FOR RYOMA
  AND PRINCE OF TENNIS!!
  SEE YOU NEXT VOLUME.

テニスの王子様☆
T. Konomi
1999.11.22

WHY DON'T YOU READ THEM AFTER YOU SLEEP?
KLONK
ZZZ
SHUEISHA

READ THIS WAY

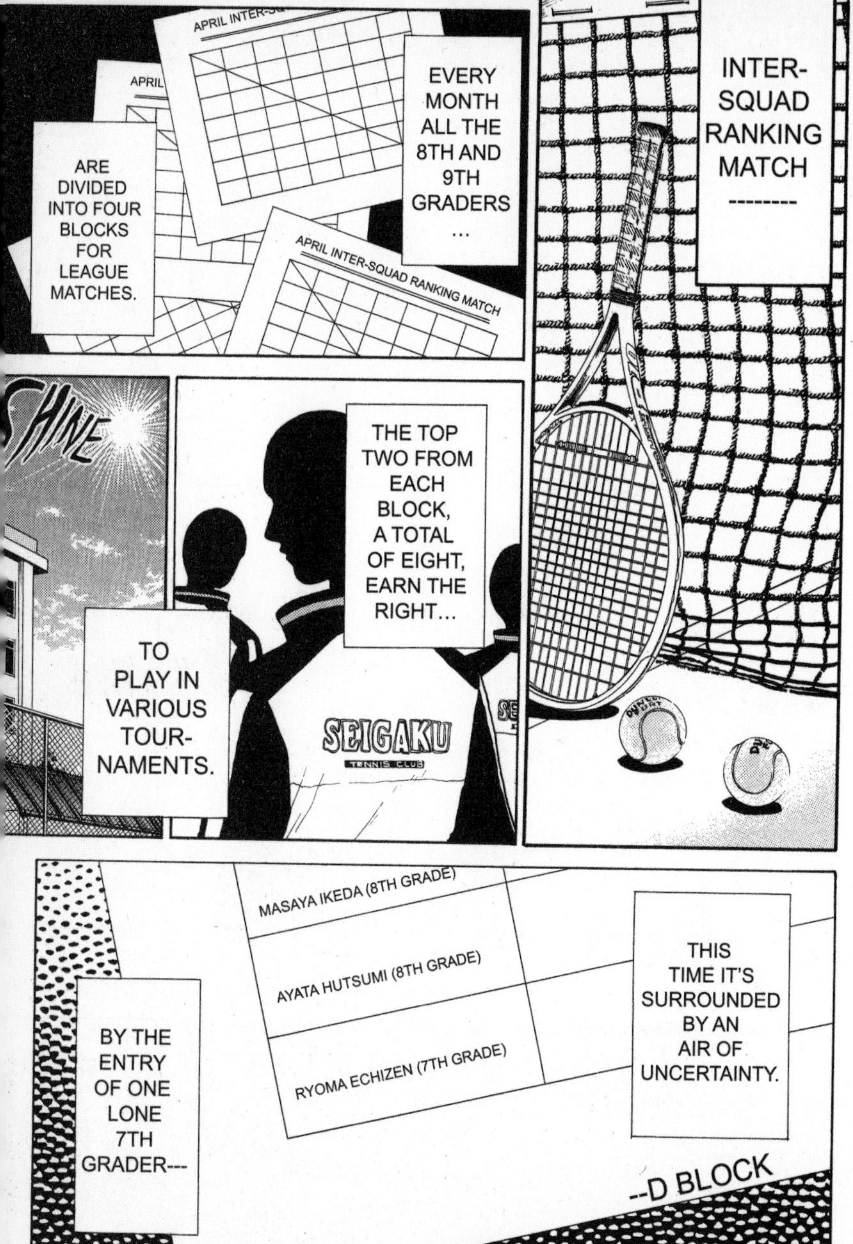
INTER-SQUAD RANKING MATCH --------
EVERY MONTH ALL THE 8TH AND 9TH GRADERS ...
APRIL INTER-SQUAD RANKING MATCH
ARE DIVIDED INTO FOUR BLOCKS FOR LEAGUE MATCHES.
THE TOP TWO FROM EACH BLOCK, A TOTAL OF EIGHT, EARN THE RIGHT...
SEIGAKU
TENNIS CLUB
TO PLAY IN VARIOUS TOUR-NAMENTS.
SHINE
THIS TIME IT'S SURROUNDED BY AN AIR OF UNCERTAINTY.
MASAYA IKEDA (8TH GRADE)
AYATA HUTSUMI (8TH GRADE)
RYOMA ECHIZEN (7TH GRADE)
--D BLOCK
BY THE ENTRY OF ONE LONE 7TH GRADER---

Genius 7 RANKING MATCHES BEGIN!

BATTLE HAS BEGUN!!

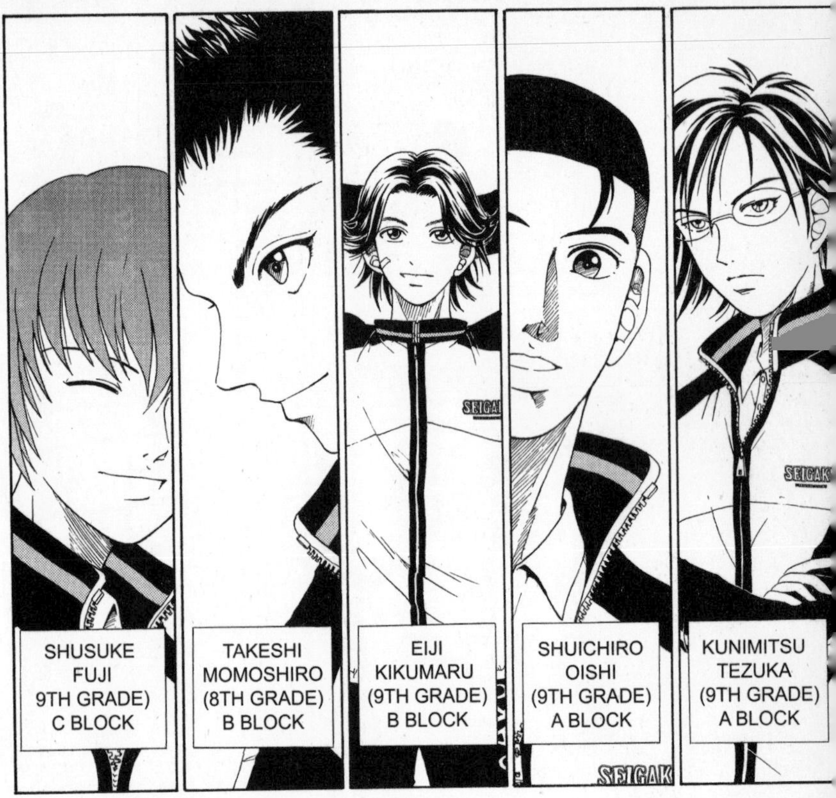

KUNIMITSU TEZUKA (9TH GRADE) A BLOCK
SHUICHIRO OISHI (9TH GRADE) A BLOCK
EIJI KIKUMARU (9TH GRADE) B BLOCK
TAKESHI MOMOSHIRO (8TH GRADE) B BLOCK
SHUSUKE FUJI 9TH GRADE) C BLOCK

Genius 7

THE MATCHES BEGIN!

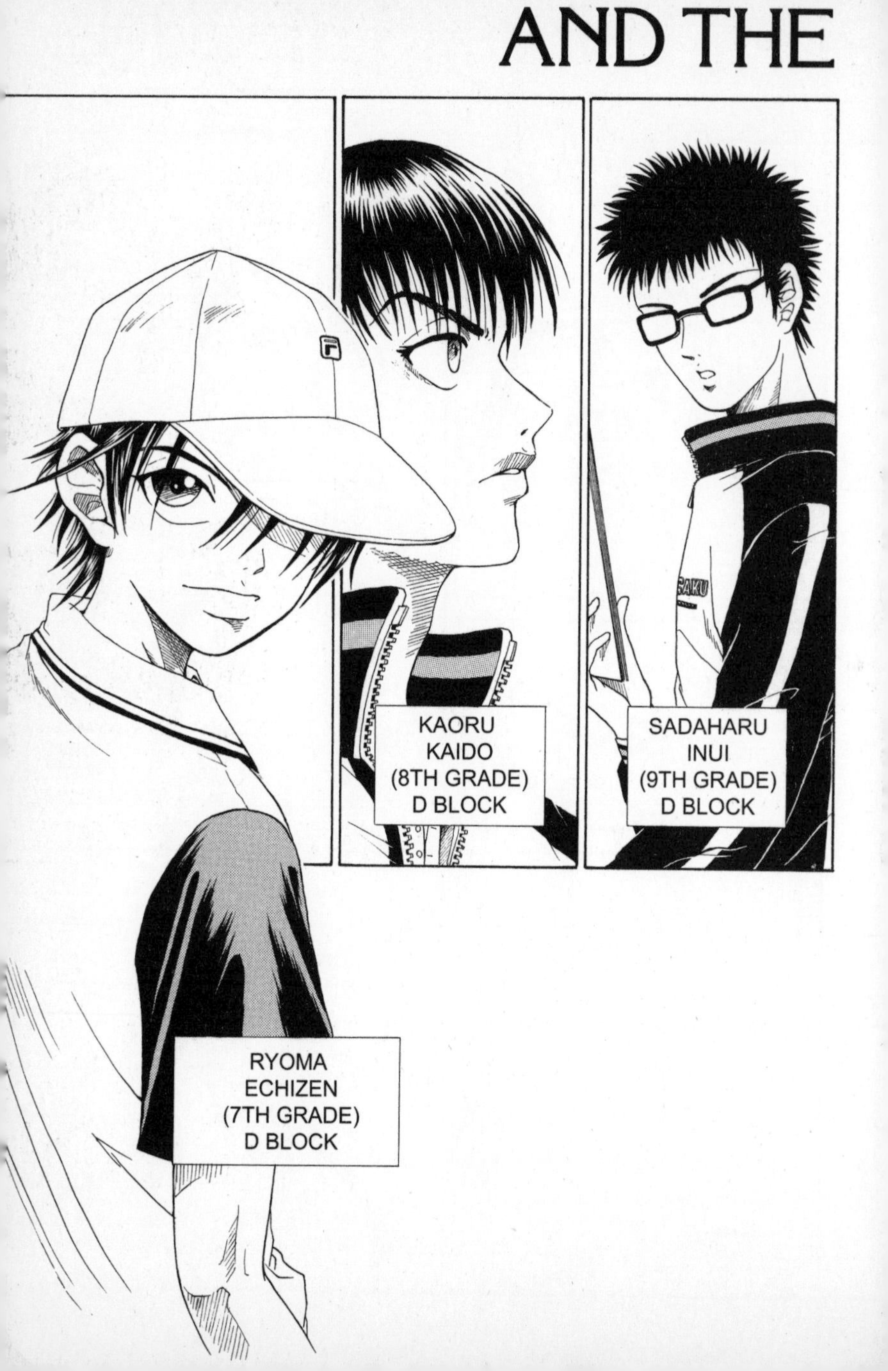
AND THE
SADAHARU INUI (9TH GRADE) D BLOCK
KAORU KAIDO (8TH GRADE) D BLOCK
RYOMA ECHIZEN (7TH GRADE) D BLOCK

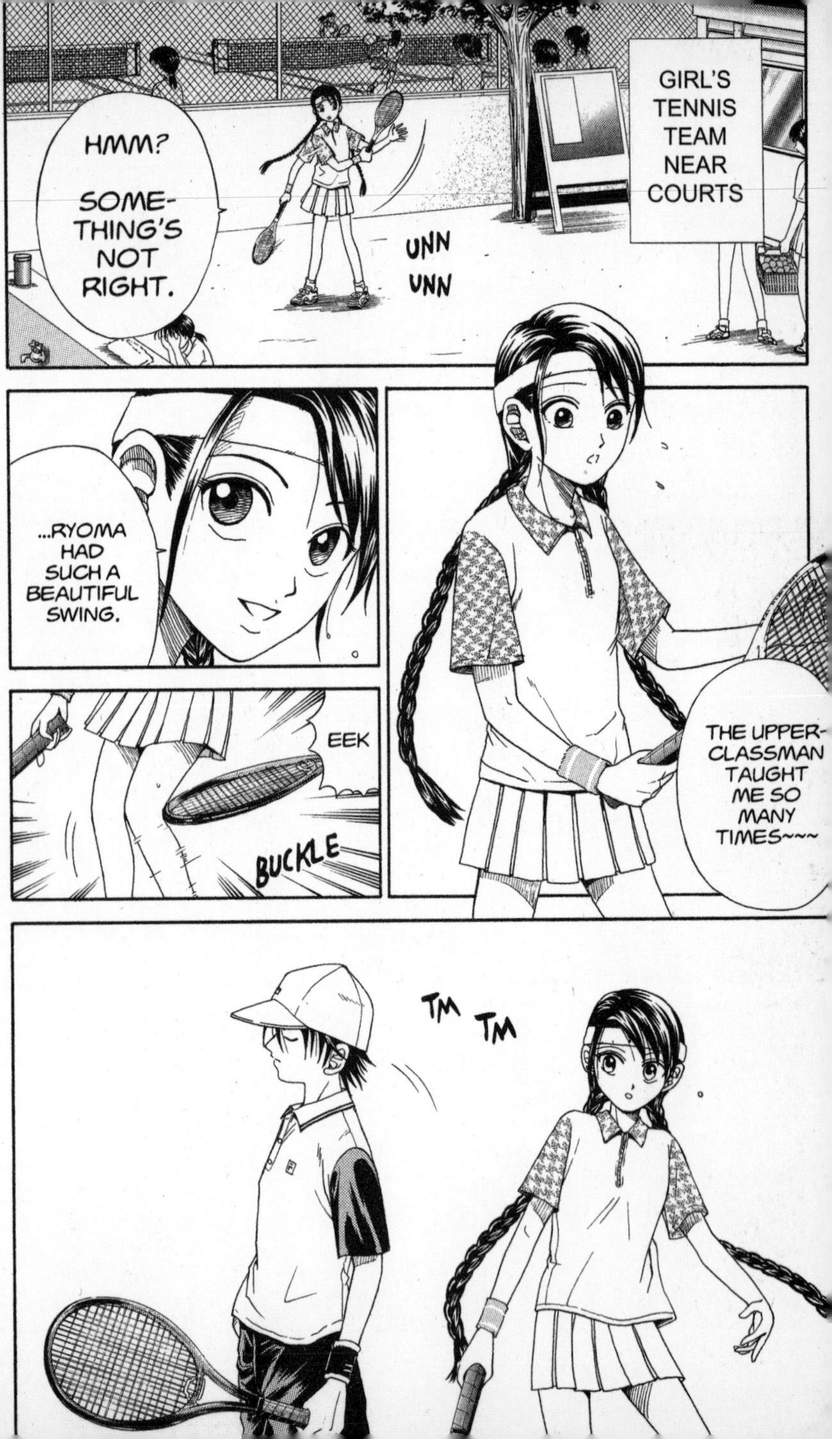
GIRL'S TENNIS TEAM NEAR COURTS
UNN UNN
HMM?
SOME-THING'S NOT RIGHT.
THE UPPER-CLASSMAN TAUGHT ME SO MANY TIMES~~~
...RYOMA HAD SUCH A BEAUTIFUL SWING.
EEK
BUCKLE
TM TM

READ THIS WAY

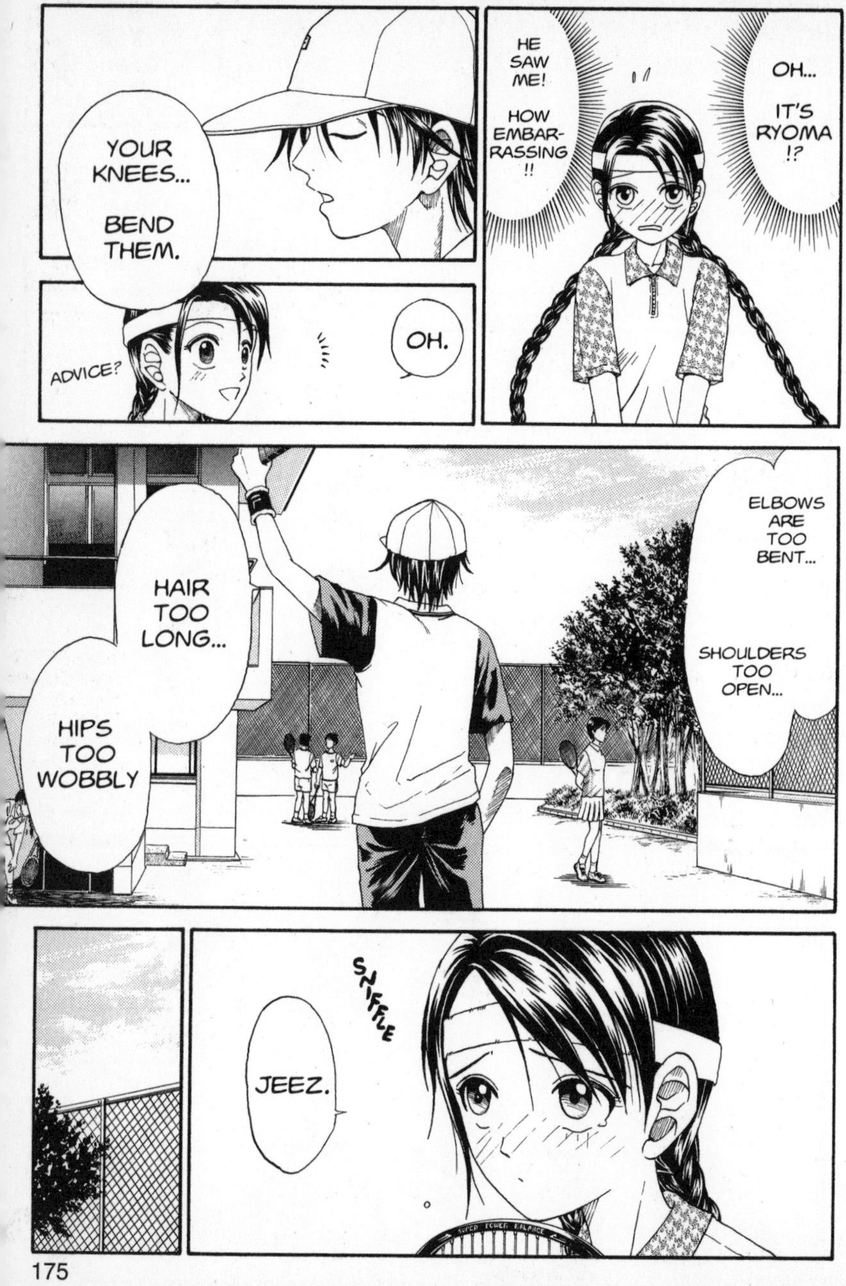
OH... IT'S RYOMA !?
HE SAW ME! HOW EMBARRASSING !!
YOUR KNEES... BEND THEM.
OH.
ADVICE?
ELBOWS ARE TOO BENT...
SHOULDERS TOO OPEN...
HAIR TOO LONG...
HIPS TOO WOBBLY
SNIFFLE
JEEZ.

READ THIS WAY

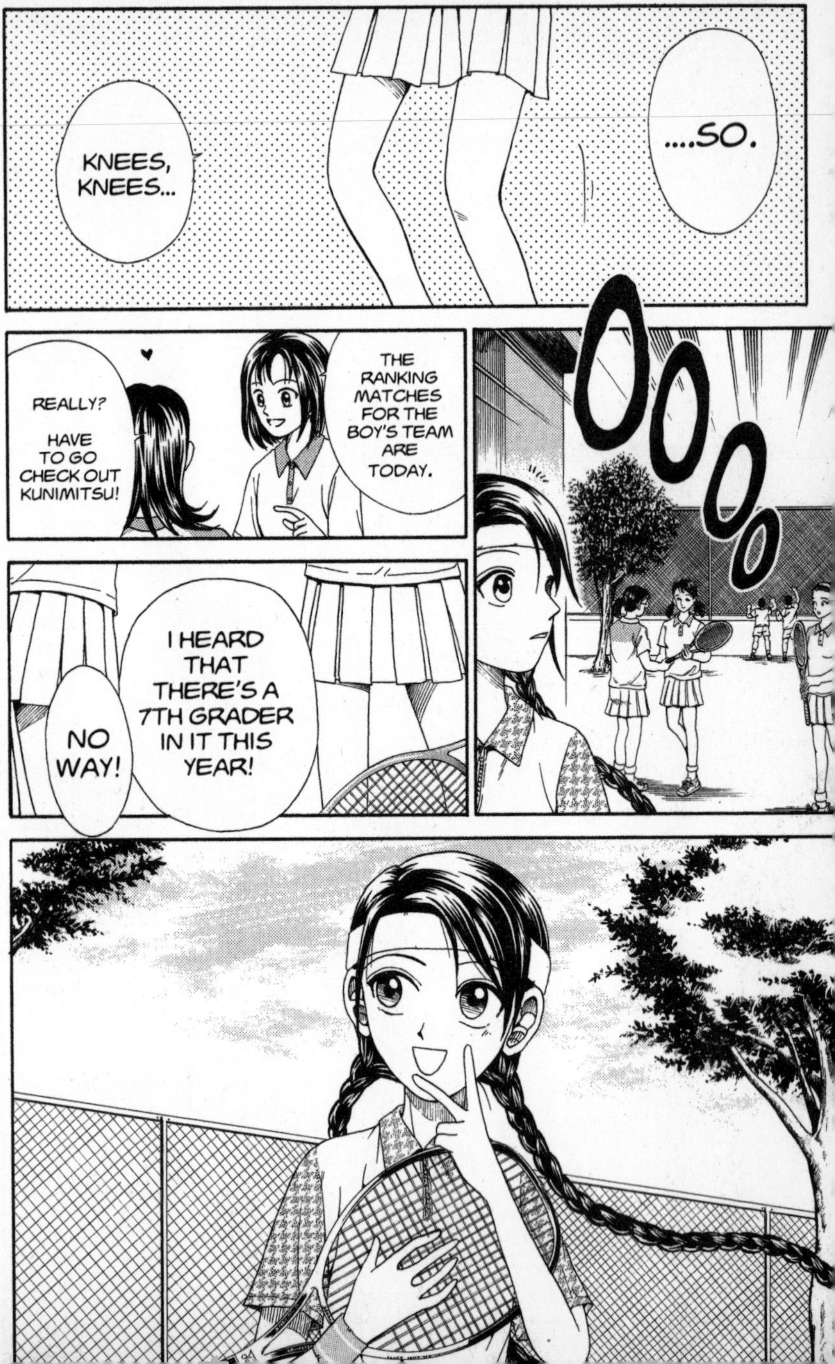
....SO.
KNEES, KNEES...
OOOO
THE RANKING MATCHES FOR THE BOY'S TEAM ARE TODAY.
REALLY? HAVE TO GO CHECK OUT KUNIMITSU!
I HEARD THAT THERE'S A 7TH GRADER IN IT THIS YEAR!
NO WAY!

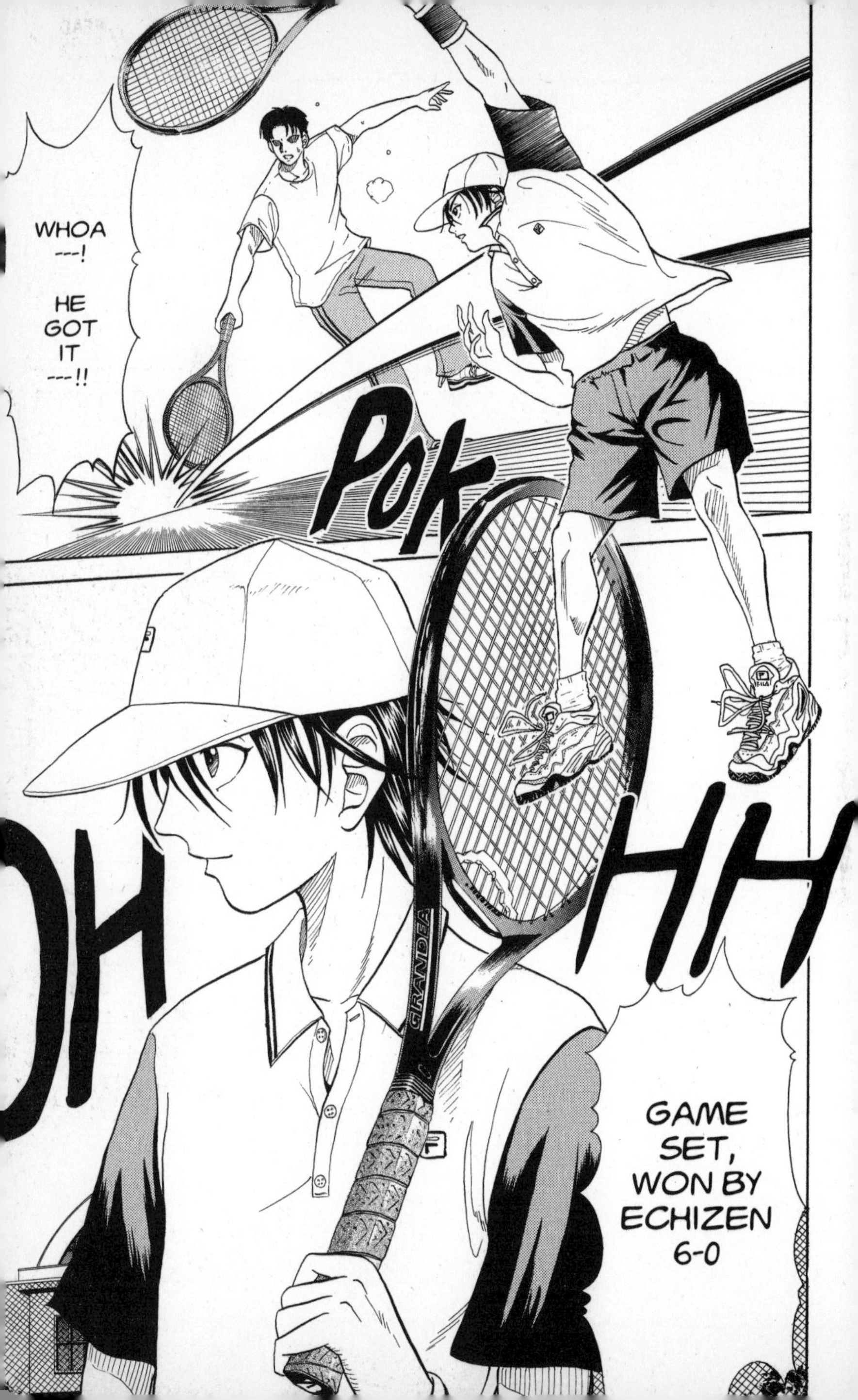
POK
WHOA---!
HE GOT IT---!!
OHHH
GAME SET, WON BY ECHIZEN 6-0

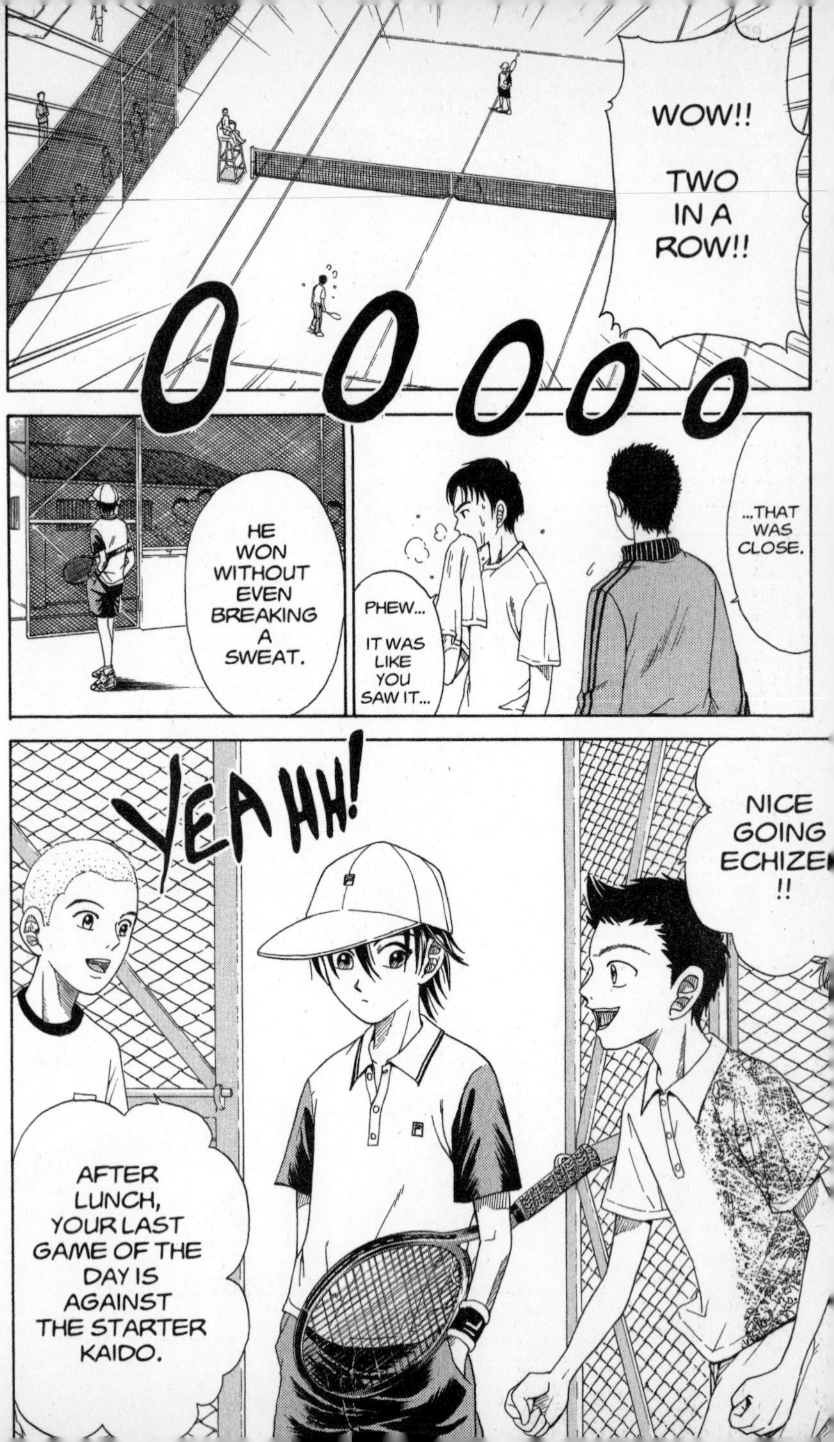
WOW!! TWO IN A ROW!!
OOOOO
...THAT WAS CLOSE.
PHEW... IT WAS LIKE YOU SAW IT...
HE WON WITHOUT EVEN BREAKING A SWEAT.
NICE GOING ECHIZE !!
YEAHH!
AFTER LUNCH, YOUR LAST GAME OF THE DAY IS AGAINST THE STARTER KAIDO.

I'M HUNGRY...

GROWL

YOU COULD NEVER BEAT A 9TH GRADE STARTER,

BUT MAYBE AN 8TH GRADER!

D BLOCK RYOMA ECHIZEN, 6-0.

CAN I GO EAT NOW?

NOT LISTENING TO ME AGAIN.

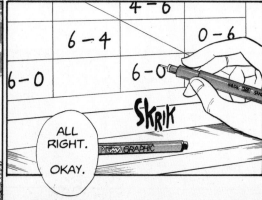

4 - 6

6 - 4

0 - 6

6 - 0

6 - 0

SKRIK

ALL RIGHT.

OKAY.

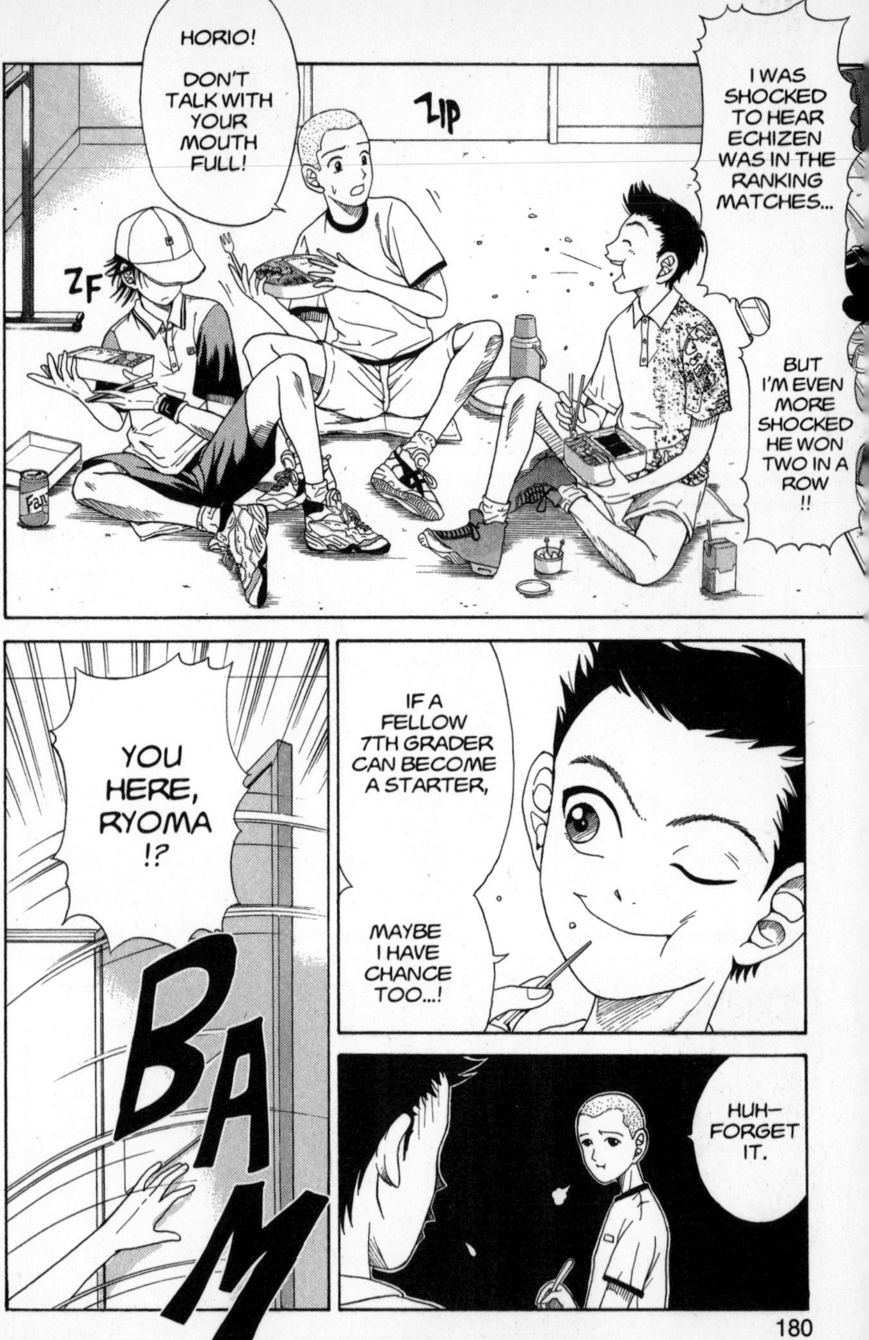
I WAS SHOCKED TO HEAR ECHIZEN WAS IN THE RANKING MATCHES...
BUT I'M EVEN MORE SHOCKED HE WON TWO IN A ROW !!
ZIP
HORIO! DON'T TALK WITH YOUR MOUTH FULL!
ZF
IF A FELLOW 7TH GRADER CAN BECOME A STARTER,
MAYBE I HAVE CHANCE TOO...!
HUH— FORGET IT.
YOU HERE, RYOMA !?
BAM

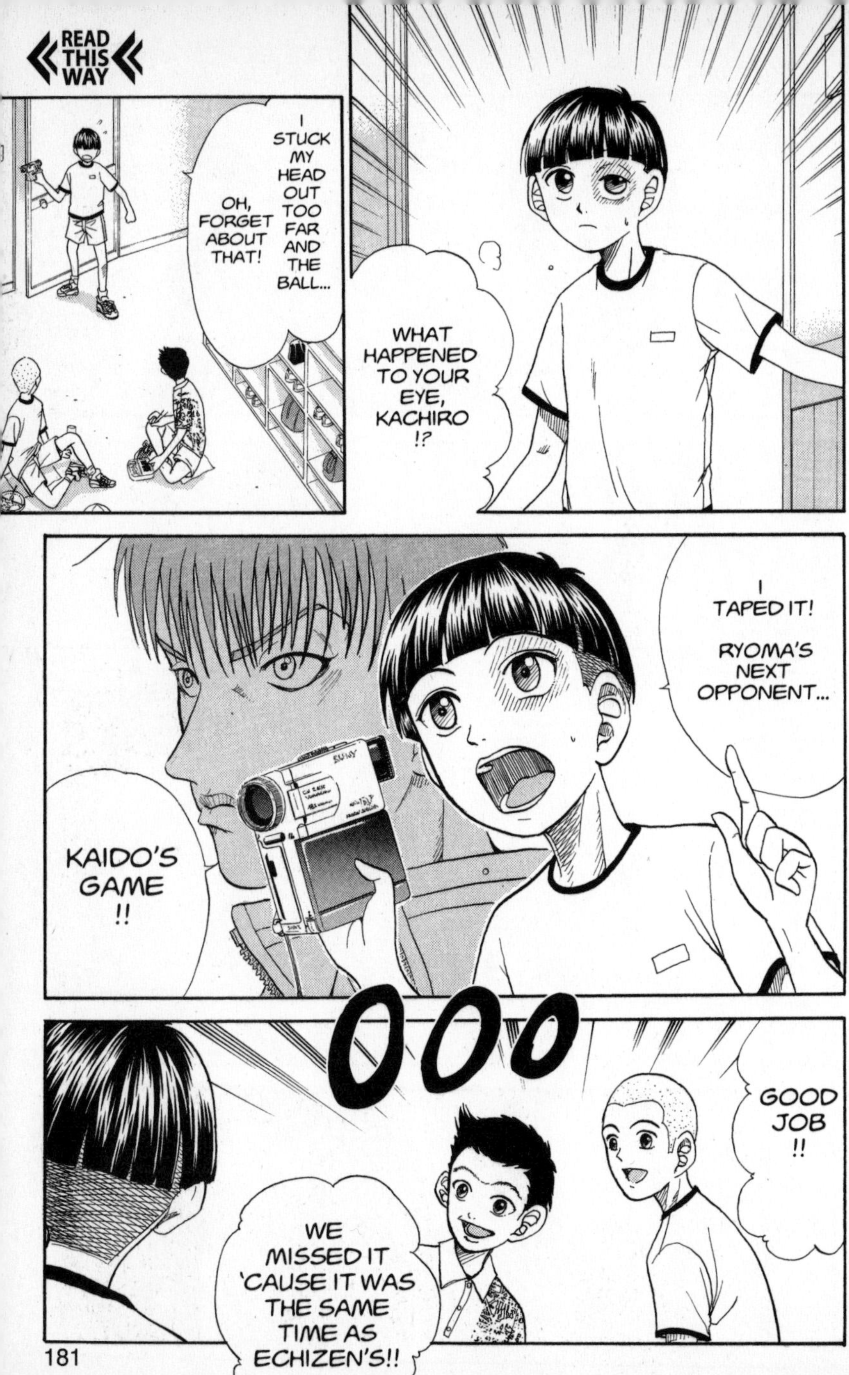
READ THIS WAY
WHAT HAPPENED TO YOUR EYE, KACHIRO!?
I STUCK MY HEAD OUT TOO FAR AND THE BALL...
OH, FORGET ABOUT THAT!
I TAPED IT!
RYOMA'S NEXT OPPONENT...
KAIDO'S GAME!!
OOO
GOOD JOB!!
WE MISSED IT 'CAUSE IT WAS THE SAME TIME AS ECHIZEN'S!!

READ THIS WAY

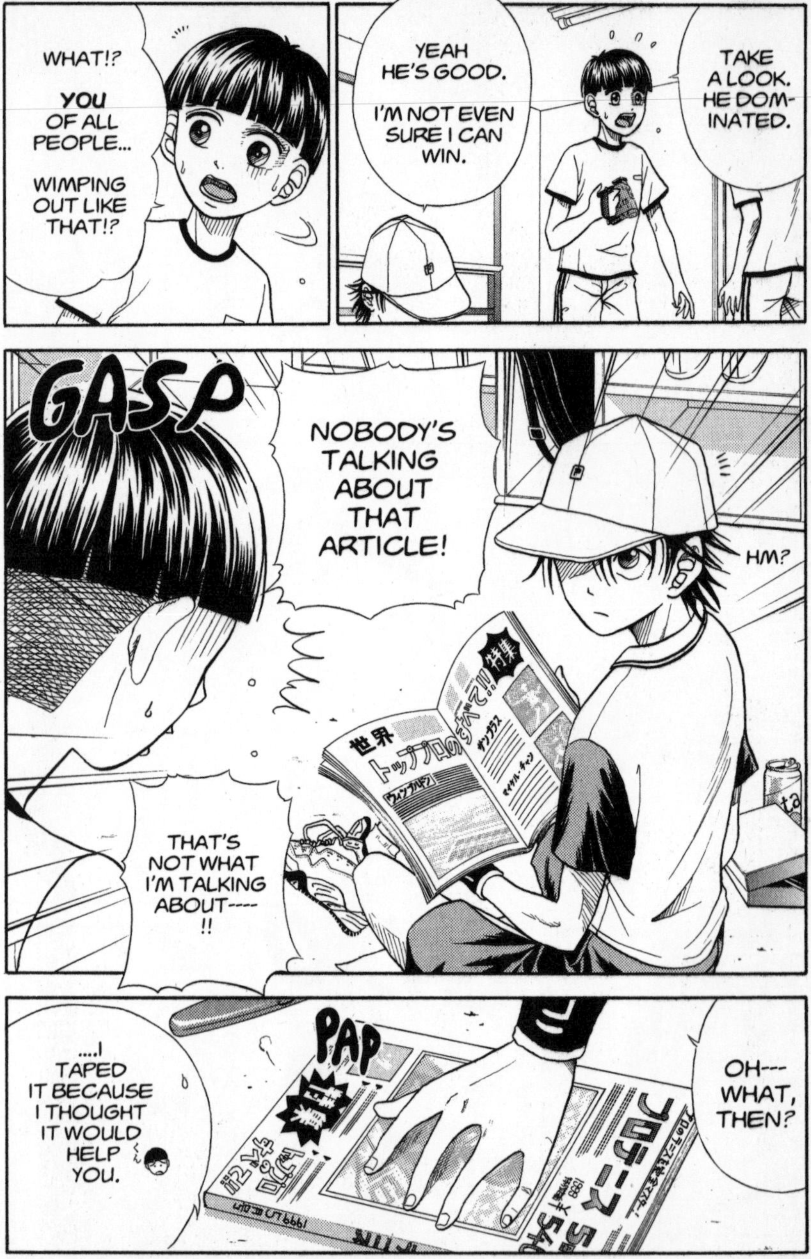
TAKE A LOOK. HE DOMINATED.
YEAH HE'S GOOD. I'M NOT EVEN SURE I CAN WIN.
WHAT!? YOU OF ALL PEOPLE... WIMPING OUT LIKE THAT!?
NOBODY'S TALKING ABOUT THAT ARTICLE!
GASP
HM?
THAT'S NOT WHAT I'M TALKING ABOUT---- !!
OH--- WHAT, THEN?
PAP
....I TAPED IT BECAUSE I THOUGHT IT WOULD HELP YOU.

READ THIS WAY

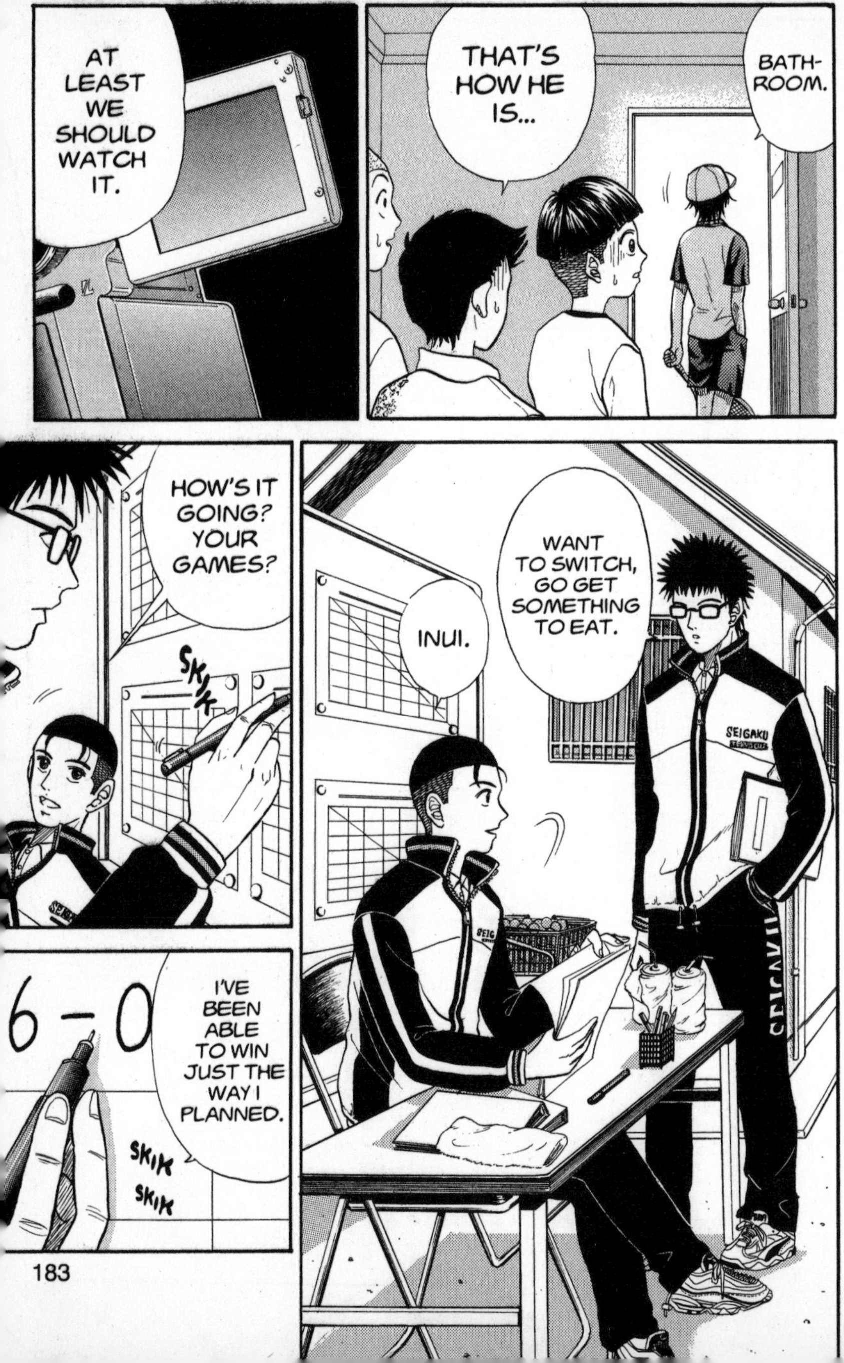

BATH-ROOM.
THAT'S HOW HE IS...
AT LEAST WE SHOULD WATCH IT.
WANT TO SWITCH, GO GET SOMETHING TO EAT.
INUI.
HOW'S IT GOING? YOUR GAMES?
SKIK
6-0
I'VE BEEN ABLE TO WIN JUST THE WAY I PLANNED.
SKIK
SKIK

READ THIS WAY

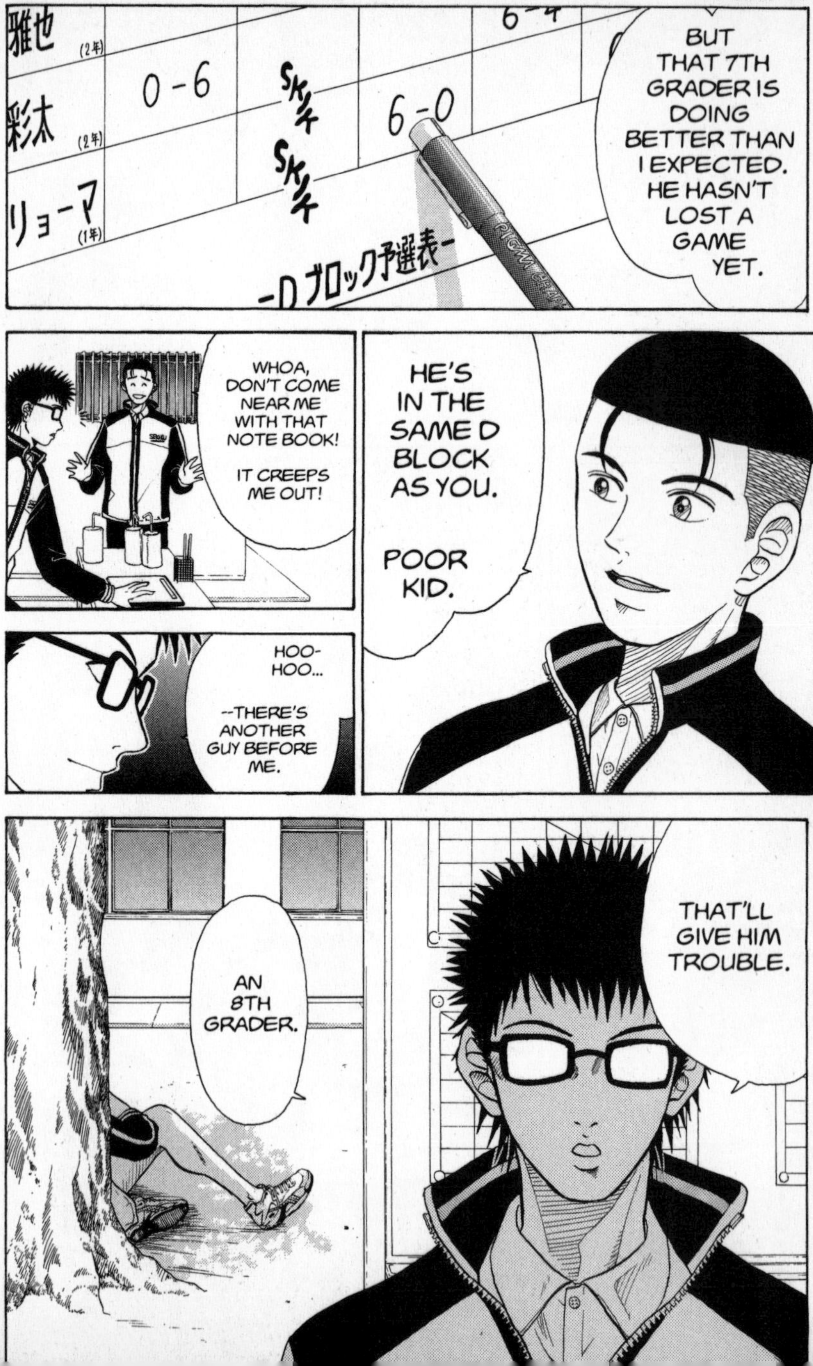
雅也 (2年)
彩太 (2年)
リョーマ (1年)
6-4
0-6
6-0
SKIK
SKIK
−Dブロック予選表−
BUT THAT 7TH GRADER IS DOING BETTER THAN I EXPECTED. HE HASN'T LOST A GAME YET.
HE'S IN THE SAME D BLOCK AS YOU.
POOR KID.
WHOA, DON'T COME NEAR ME WITH THAT NOTE BOOK!
IT CREEPS ME OUT!
HOO-HOO...
--THERE'S ANOTHER GUY BEFORE ME.
THAT'LL GIVE HIM TROUBLE.
AN 8TH GRADER.

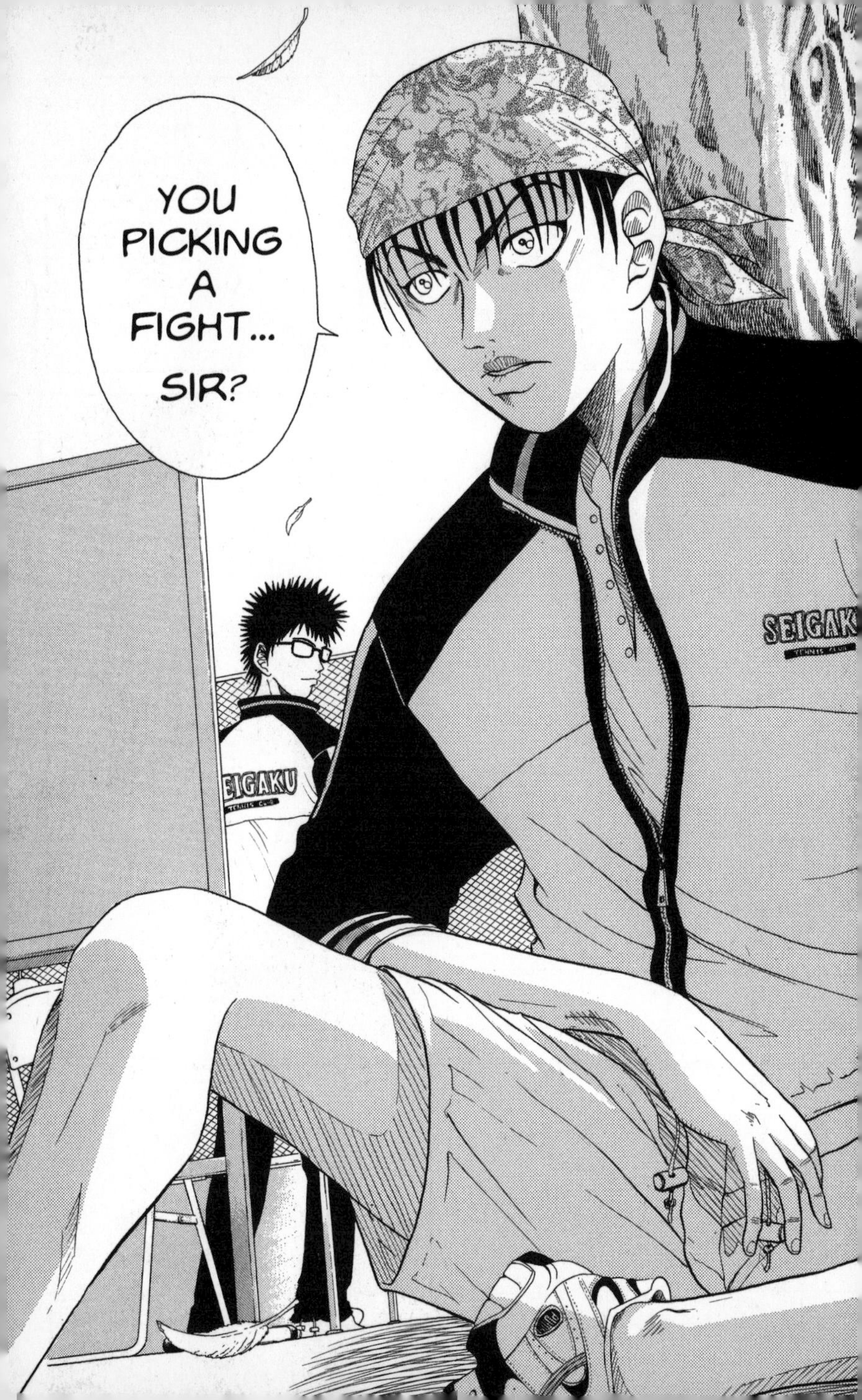
YOU PICKING A FIGHT... SIR?
SEIGAKU
SEIGAKU

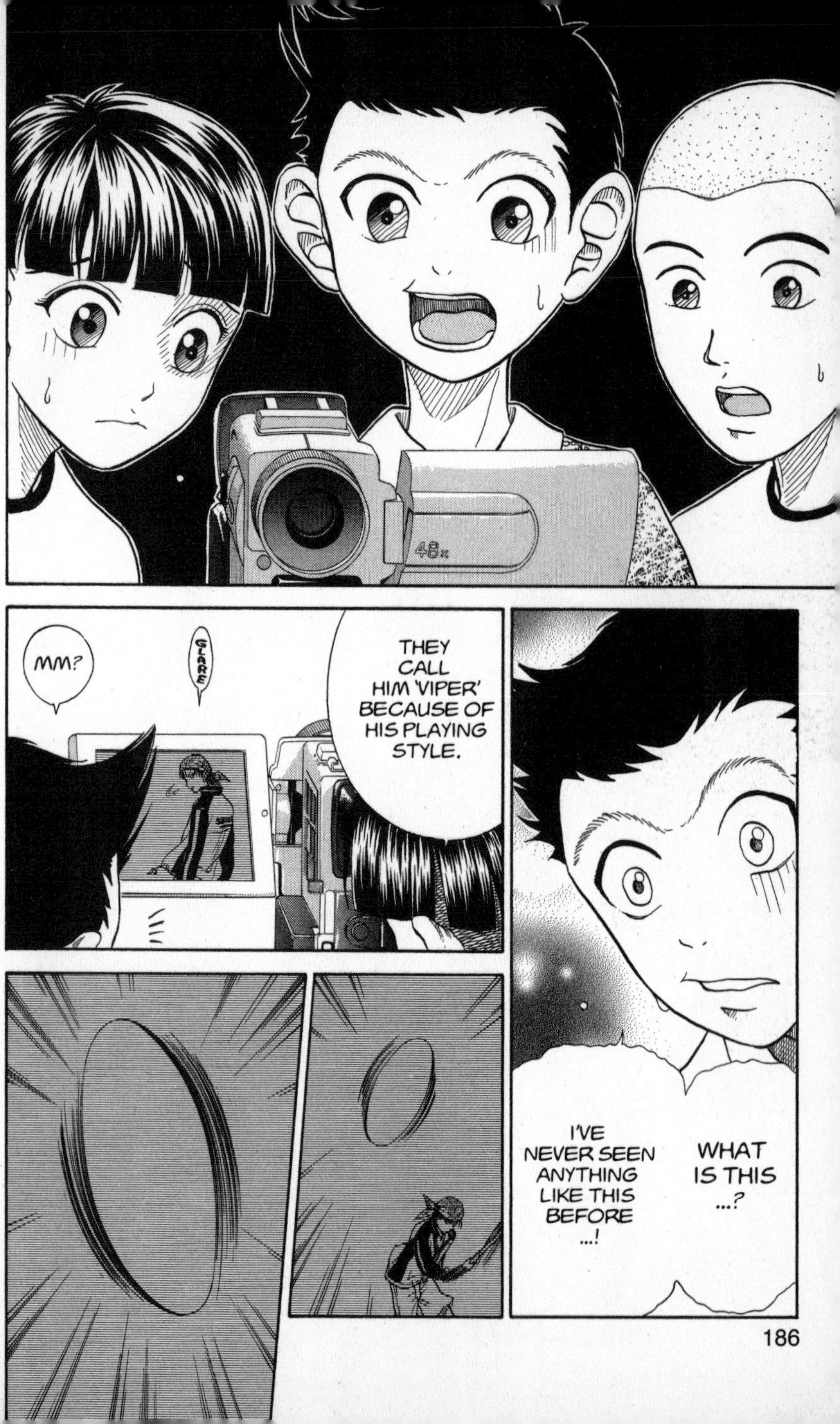
WHAT IS THIS ...?
I'VE NEVER SEEN ANYTHING LIKE THIS BEFORE ...!
THEY CALL HIM 'VIPER' BECAUSE OF HIS PLAYING STYLE.
GLARE
MM?

READ THIS WAY

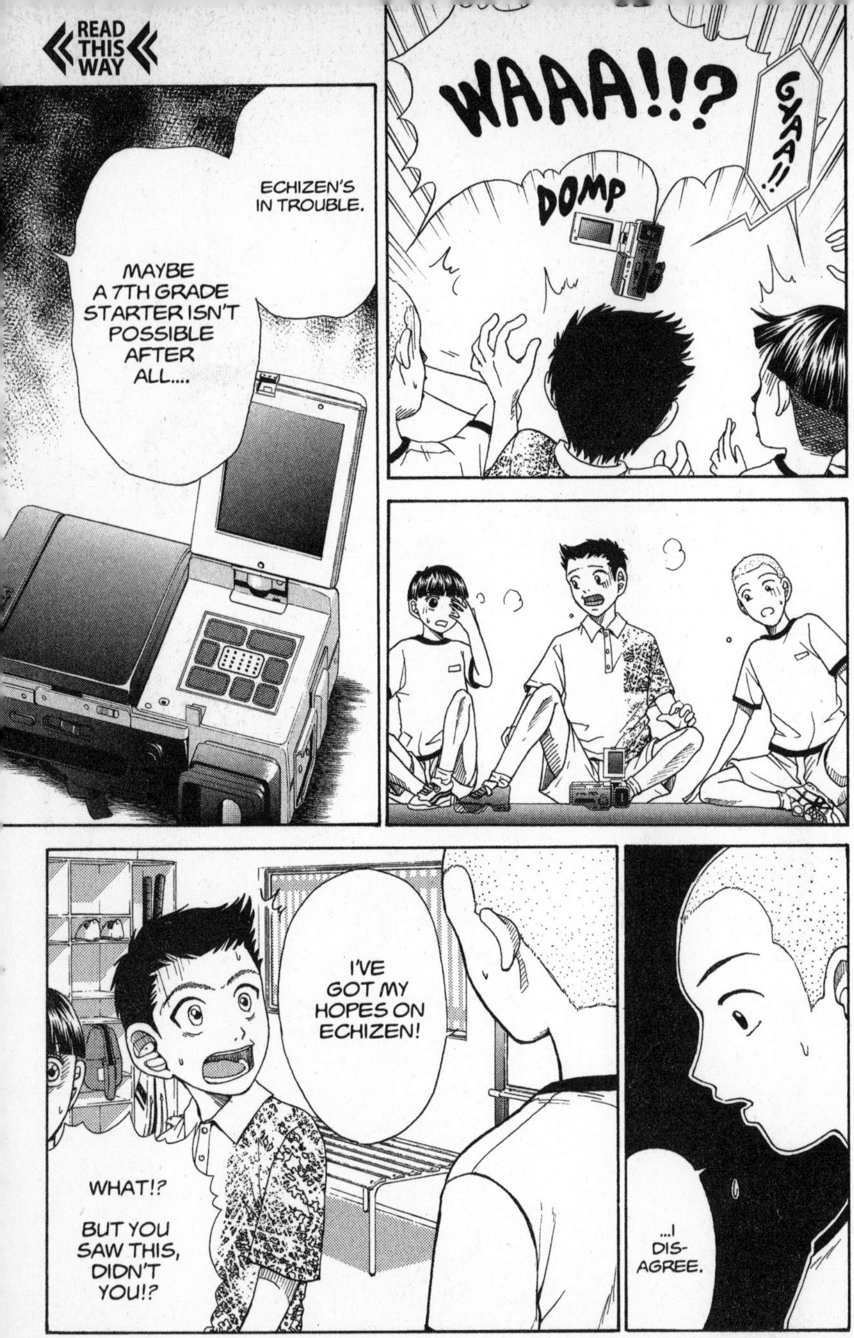
WAAA!!?
GYAAA!!
DOMP
ECHIZEN'S IN TROUBLE.
MAYBE A 7TH GRADE STARTER ISN'T POSSIBLE AFTER ALL....
...I DIS-AGREE.
I'VE GOT MY HOPES ON ECHIZEN!
WHAT!?
BUT YOU SAW THIS, DIDN'T YOU!?

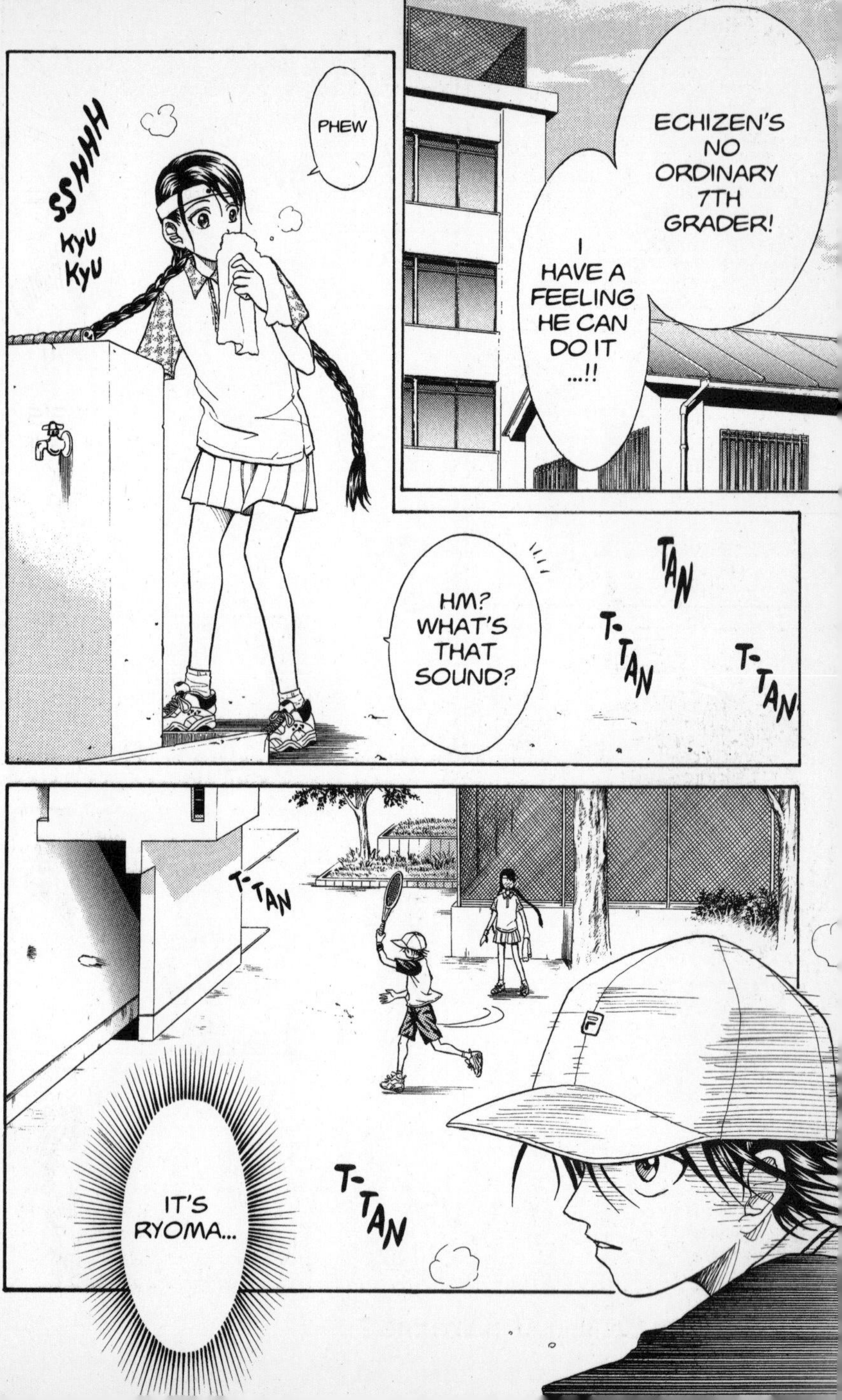
ECHIZEN'S NO ORDINARY 7TH GRADER!
I HAVE A FEELING HE CAN DO IT ...!!
HM? WHAT'S THAT SOUND?
TAN
T-TAN
T-TAN
PHEW
SSHHH
KYU KYU
T-TAN
T-TAN
IT'S RYOMA...

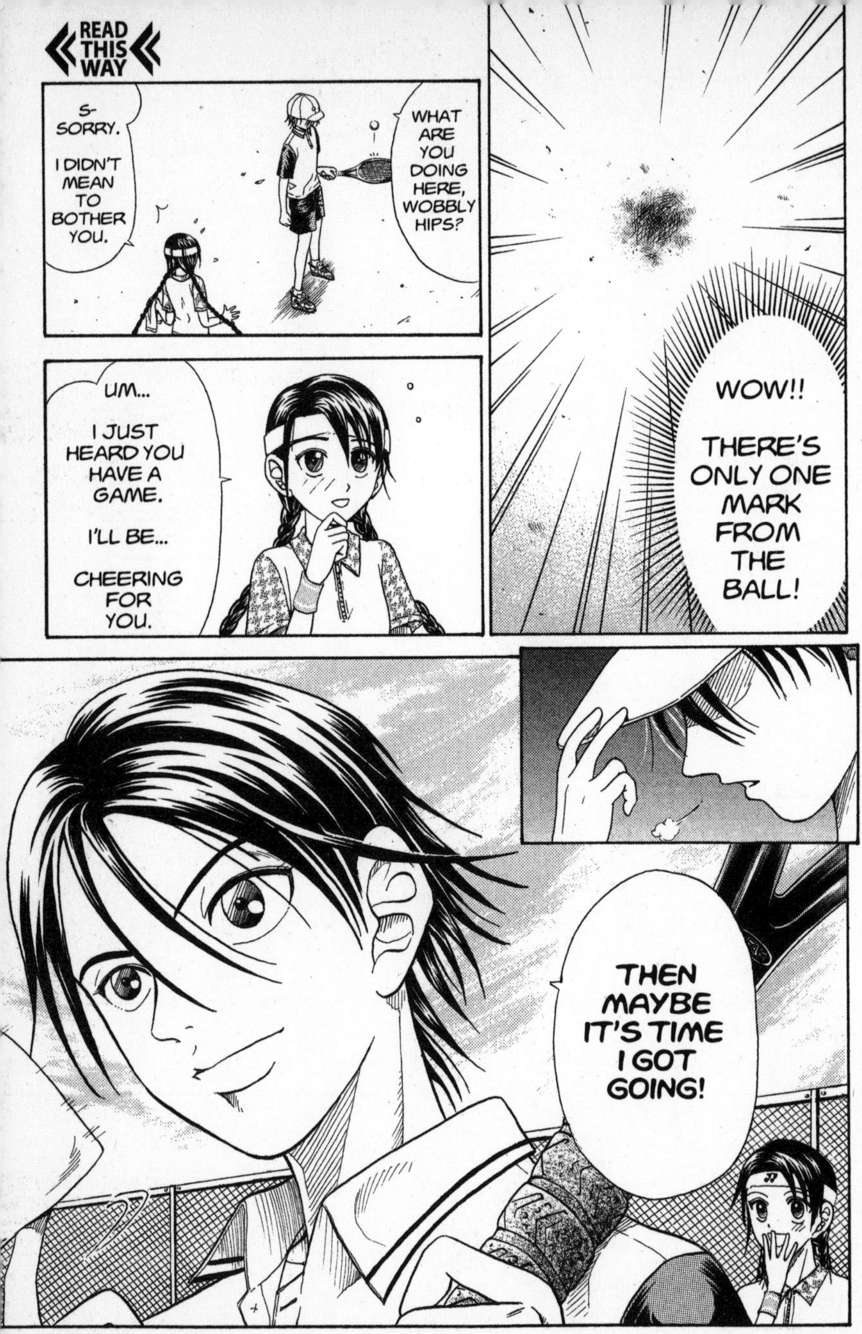
READ THIS WAY
WOW!! THERE'S ONLY ONE MARK FROM THE BALL!
WHAT ARE YOU DOING HERE, WOBBLY HIPS?
S-SORRY. I DIDN'T MEAN TO BOTHER YOU.
UM... I JUST HEARD YOU HAVE A GAME. I'LL BE... CHEERING FOR YOU.
THEN MAYBE IT'S TIME I GOT GOING!

To Be Continued in Volume 2

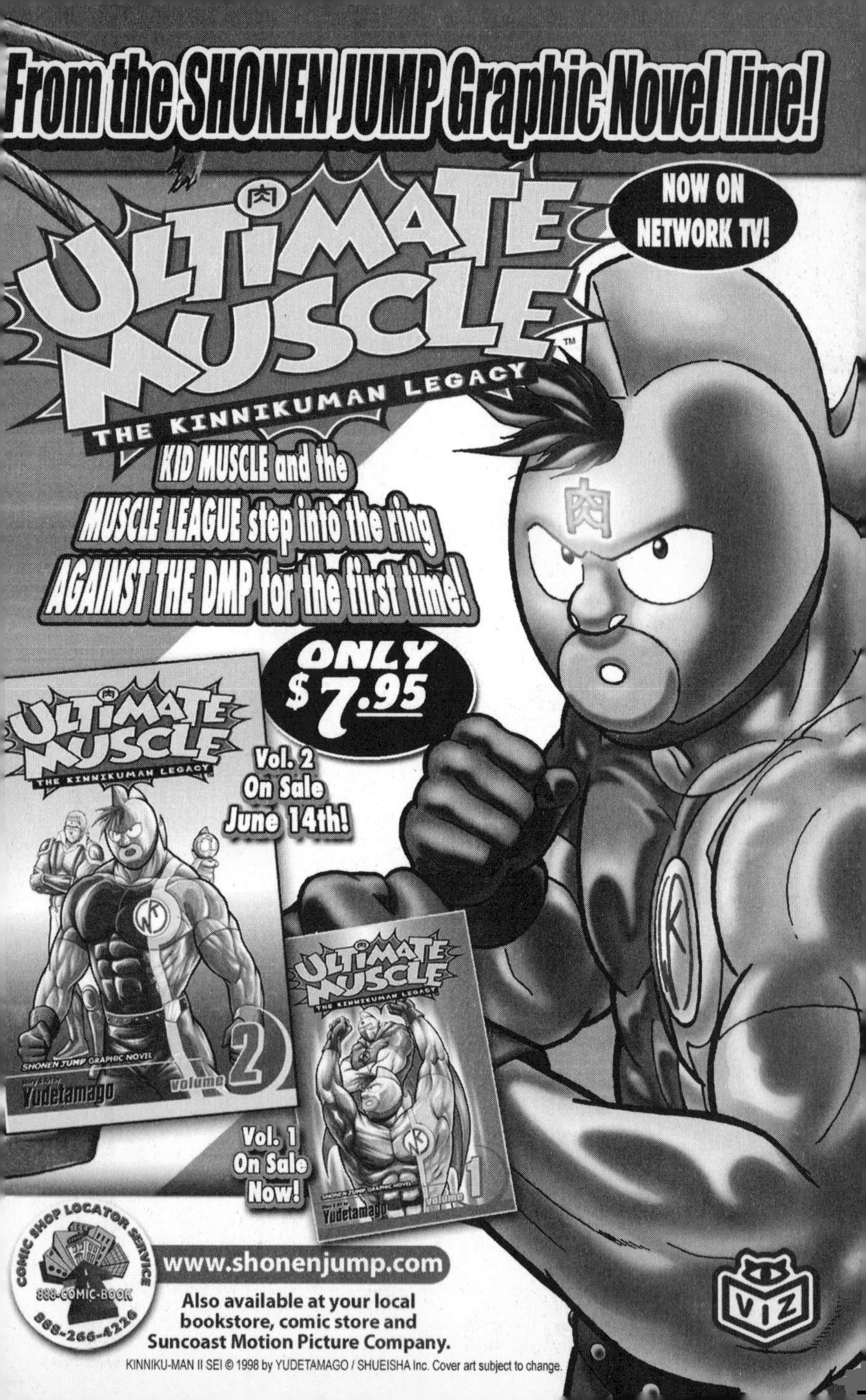
From the SHONEN JUMP Graphic Novel line!
NOW ON NETWORK TV!
ULTIMATE MUSCLE™
THE KINNIKUMAN LEGACY
KID MUSCLE and the MUSCLE LEAGUE step into the ring AGAINST THE DMP for the first time!
ONLY $7.95
Vol. 2 On Sale June 14th!
Vol. 1 On Sale Now!
SHONEN JUMP GRAPHIC NOVEL
Yudetamago
volume 2
volume 1
COMIC SHOP LOCATOR SERVICE
888-COMIC-BOOK
888-266-4226
www.shonenjump.com
Also available at your local bookstore, comic store and Suncoast Motion Picture Company.
KINNIKU-MAN II SEI © 1998 by YUDETAMAGO / SHUEISHA Inc. Cover art subject to change.
VIZ

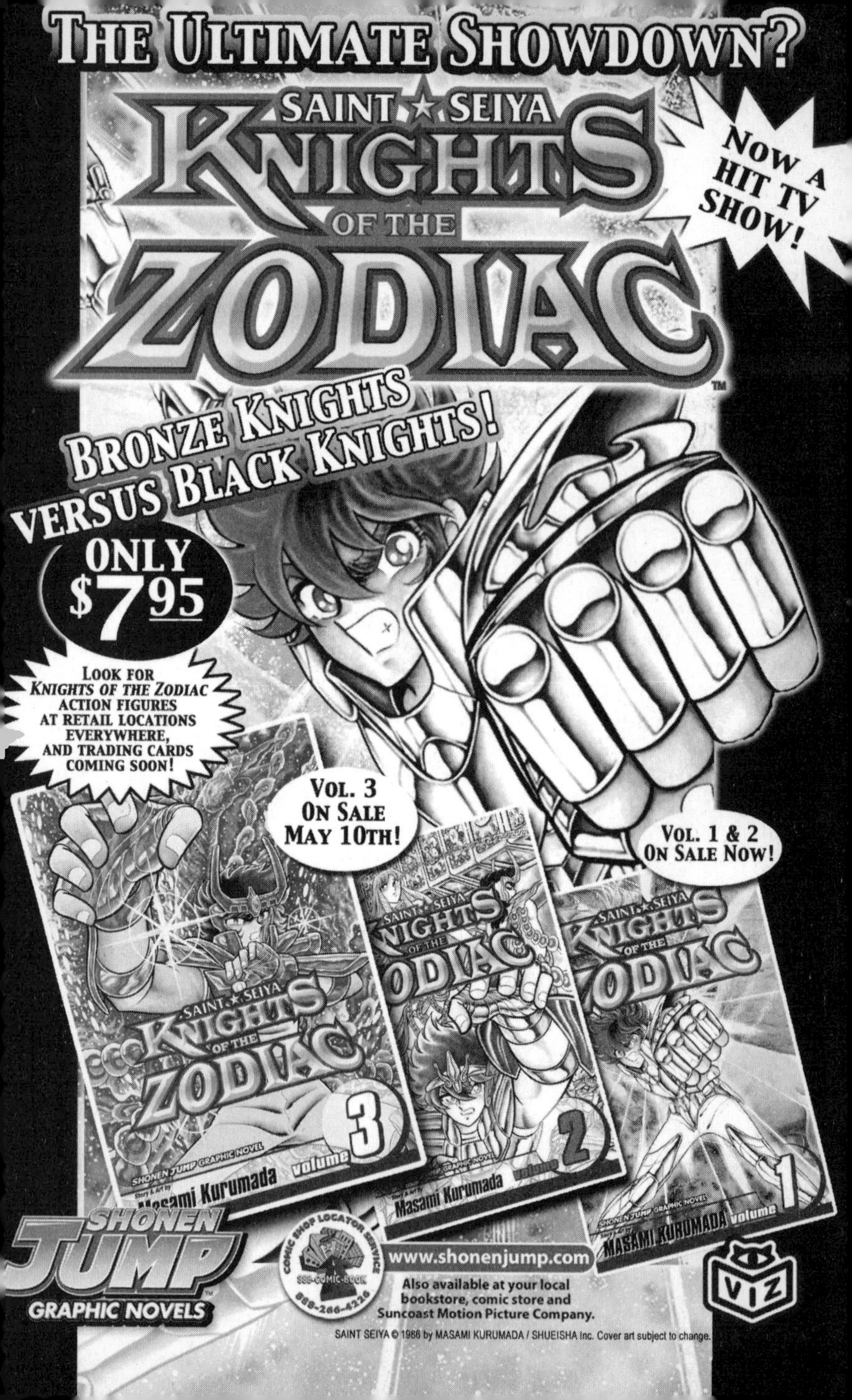
THE ULTIMATE SHOWDOWN?
SAINT ★ SEIYA
KNIGHTS OF THE ZODIAC™
NOW A HIT TV SHOW!
BRONZE KNIGHTS VERSUS BLACK KNIGHTS!
ONLY $7.95
LOOK FOR KNIGHTS OF THE ZODIAC ACTION FIGURES AT RETAIL LOCATIONS EVERYWHERE, AND TRADING CARDS COMING SOON!
VOL. 3 ON SALE MAY 10TH!
VOL. 1 & 2 ON SALE NOW!
SHONEN JUMP GRAPHIC NOVELS
COMIC SHOP LOCATOR SERVICE 888-COMIC-BOOK 888-266-4226
www.shonenjump.com
Also available at your local bookstore, comic store and Suncoast Motion Picture Company.
VIZ
SAINT SEIYA © 1986 by MASAMI KURUMADA / SHUEISHA Inc. Cover art subject to change.